Corporate Survival: The Critical Importance of Sustainability Risk Management

Corporate Survival: The Critical Importance of Sustainability Risk Management

Dan R. Anderson

iUniverse, Inc.
New York Lincoln Shanghai

Corporate Survival: The Critical Importance of Sustainability Risk Management

Copyright © 2005 by Dan R. Anderson

iUniverse books may be ordered through booksellers or by contacting:

iUniverse
2021 Pine Lake Road, Suite 100
Lincoln, NE 68512
www.iuniverse.com
1-800-Authors (1-800-288-4677)

Front cover image by: Stockli, Nelson, Hasler
Laboratory for Atmospheres Goddard Space Flight Center
http://rsd.gsfc.nasa.gov/rsd
NASA Earth Observatory team
http://earthobservatory.nasa.gov/

ISBN-13: 978-0-595-36460-2 (pbk)
ISBN-13: 978-0-595-80892-2 (ebk)
ISBN-10: 0-595-36460-8 (pbk)
ISBN-10: 0-595-80892-1 (ebk)

Printed in the United States of America

This book is dedicated to:

my parents, Phyllis and Milt Anderson;

my daughters, Kristin and Robin;

and my wife, Joan.

Contents

FOREWORD AND ACKNOWLEDGMENTS

I have been teaching and conducting research in the Actuarial Science, Risk Management and Insurance Department at the University of Wisconsin-Madison School of Business since 1970. I am also on the adjunct faculty of the Institute for Environmental Studies. After publication of my first article on loss reserve evaluations, based on the results of my dissertation, I published an article entitled, "What Role Will the Insurance Industry Play in the Fight against Pollution." *CPCU Annals*, March 1972. Since then most of my ensuing research and publications have been related to environmental risk management. Research areas have included insurance and compensation systems for natural disasters, insurance and liability systems for nuclear power plant risks, asbestos and Superfund insurance coverage litigation, environmental insurance markets and products, and incorporating environmental risk management systems into corporate strategic planning. I have also taught the liability risk management course almost every year since I started at the University of Wisconsin. In 2003, I introduced a new course on environmental risk management into our curriculum. As I began to understand the importance of social justice risks, I changed the focus of the course to sustainability risk management. I am also the leader of a faculty group to promote the development of other courses in the environmental strategy, sustainability and corporate social responsibility areas in the School of Business.

I offer this brief introduction to demonstrate that I have been observing and thinking about sustainability risk management issues for virtually my entire career. I believe that I have an extensive perspective from which to offer an analysis of the importance of sustainability risk management and where the field is heading. It is clear to me that sustainability risks will increasingly impact businesses and organizations. Firms that fail to develop systems for managing these risks will do so at their own peril. The good news is that businesses, which do develop sustainability risk management systems, will strengthen their reputation and reap competitive advantages, as well as reducing risk costs and increasing profits. These are the central ideas of my book.

I have attempted in this book to construct my thoughts and arguments on sustainability risk management so that they will be understandable and useful across various disciplines. I would hope that risk managers, insurance officials, business executives, professors, engineers, scientists, politicians, lawyers, members of environmental and social justice organizations, and even the general public could read this book and find it useful in their respective fields and in their lives. For those readers seeking further elaboration on specific areas, I provide considerable documentation and information sources for the various subjects covered in this book.

I would like to thank a number of individuals who have helped me at various stages of the book. Several of my colleagues, both inside and outside of the School of Business, read sections of the book. They include my colleague in risk and insurance, Joan Schmit, Erhard Joeres, Patrick Eagan, Jon Foley, and David Dybdahl. A special thanks goes to Tom Eggert, who in addition to reading a section of the book, also teaches several of the environmental strategy, sustainability and corporate responsibility courses mentioned above. My very good friends, Pat Alea, a management consultant, and Bruce Collick, a MRI systems engineer, BBF, graciously offered advice and suggestions throughout the book planning and development process. Another good friend, Judy Schector, an organizational development consultant, introduced me to Tom Eggert and The Natural Step, both of which have had a crucial influence on my life. For the past several years, I have attended an environmental breakfast seminar organized by Bill Cronon. The seminars were always interesting and I feel that the book is better because of the knowledge I acquired and the discussions we had. Fritz Hasler, an old friend from graduate school days in the 1960s, and his colleagues, took the terrific satellite picture used on the cover. I am most grateful for the funding of my professorship provided by Leslie P. Schultz, retired Chairman, President and CEO of USLICO, and his firm.

Over the years, I have had a number of research assistants who helped me in my research efforts. I feel that at least a part of their efforts, which I have greatly appreciated, are included in this book They include Tom Wander, Joan Schmit, Patricia (Hammes) Heim, John Schaefer, Anne DiBella, Joann (Danz) Paiva, Lisa (Helsing) Bastian, Jaewook Chung, Nilüfer Durak, Zhao Ye, Wenli Wang, and Jianwei Xie. I also want to recognize the students, who took my sustainability risk management course, for their enthusiasm and willingness to explore some different ideas inside the business school. Their papers and discussions in class helped to crystallize my thinking for parts of the book.

I am a faculty advisor to two student organizations in the business school that focus on sustainability issues. Our meetings and the various guest speakers at our meetings provided an enhanced prospective on a variety of issues presented in the book. Both these groups were recently formed by student initiatives. I am particularly grateful to the founders and/or presidents, Bryant Moroder, Kurt Baehmann, Danielle (Davis) Ewalt, Mark Thomsen, Elizabeth Keller, Rebecca Petzel and Grant Wheeler of BASE (Business Action for Sustainable Enterprise); and John Ikeda, Matt Messinger, Sam Adams, Michael Crow, Eric Jordan, Felix Wolfinger and Andrew Freedman of Net Impact.

This book would not have been possible without the support and involvement of my family. The love and support of my parents, Phyllis and Milt Anderson, provided me with a strong foundation, which has bolstered me throughout my entire life. My wife, Joan Nugent, not only gave me her love, support and patience, she also read the entire manuscript and offered numerous suggestions that greatly improved the reading and flow of the text. My daughter, Kristin, who works at Norton Arnold, an environmental consulting firm in Seattle, offered numerous thoughts and observations for the book. My other daughter, Robin, with her creative talents and great enthusiasm, has encouraged me throughout the entire process of writing the book.

I want to thank my publisher, iUniverse, for their many supportive efforts in producing the book. I especially appreciate the dependable and prompt work of Michael Fiedler, Rachel Krupicka, and others at iUniverse, who assisted in the overall development of the book. I want to thank and praise Brenda Jansen for her expert assistance in the manuscript coordination and preparation. While these many individuals offered assistance and input, the views expressed in this book are entirely my own and not those of these individuals or the University of Wisconsin.

INTRODUCTION

Actively participate in your own survival
Tom Wolfe, river guide

Let me explain the titles of the book and the introduction. In the spring of 2003, I went on the trip of a lifetime with my daughters and their significant others. We ventured on a raft trip down the Colorado River through the Grand Canyon. The leader of our group was Tom Wolfe. Given that risk management is my area of expertise at the University of Wisconsin-Madison, I was most impressed with the solid risk management practices that Tom employed in getting our group safely through the Grand Canyon, without impairing the enjoyment of the experience. For instance, hygiene and food serving practices were careful and effective and no one got sick on the trip. Some of the trips up side canyons were moderately difficult, even scary, but we all completed our hikes safely. And we certainly left our campgrounds immaculately clean, leaving only footprints. There were risks associated with the trip, but I felt they were controlled risks.

It was Tom's homey sayings that most captured my attention as they offered terrific risk management advice. Examples included, "Never be in a hurry to hurt yourself," and "Always wear your life jacket when scouting a rapid." But my favorite was "Actively participate in your own survival," which is a clever way of advising that you should take care of yourself, as you are largely responsible for your own well-being and survival.

When I returned home from the trip, I came across a talk given by Chris Pomfret from the marketing department of Birds Eye Foods, a division of Unilever, at a company sponsored Sustainability Conference. She talked about how "sustainability is all about the long-term security of our supply chain." In her wrap up, she exclaimed, "You don't do sustainability for short-term sales, but for survival."

I immediately thought of Tom's advice, "Actively participate in your own survival." While it certainly applies to a raft trip through the Grand Canyon, I was surprised to hear a company executive use the survival terminology in speaking about her company's sustainability strategy. But as I contemplated her remarks, it made perfectly good sense to me, particularly when talking about the issue of sus-

1

tainability. Indeed, sustainability is ultimately about survival as an individual, as a business, as a society, as a global community. If we do not sustain our natural systems, then our survival is at stake as is a company's survival like that of Unilever.

Sustainability Risk Management

This book is about sustainability risk management. If we cannot maintain sustainable water systems, risks will be produced for individuals, farmers, livestock and wildlife that will not have water. If we overload our atmosphere with pollutants and greenhouse gases, we may impair our health and cause devastating climate changes. Corporations may be liable for damages resulting from water depletion or the overloading of the atmosphere. Governments, whose polices and regulations—or lack of them—have allowed this to happen, will also incur risks.

For Unilever, sustainable oceans and waters are critical, as they are the world's largest fish buyer for their products. In the mid 1990s, Unilever and environmentalists shared a common problem—marine fishing stocks were being dangerously over-fished. At first their relationship was adversarial, with Greenpeace running a campaign against Unilever's practices of buying excessively large quantities of fish for their products. Unilever responded by partnering with the World Wide Fund for Nature (WWF) to form the Marine Stewardship Council (MSC). The Council would become the leading independent certifier of fisheries. To obtain a MSC label, fish products must come from well managed fisheries that preserve ecosystems. Unilever plans to have 75 percent of its fish products come from sustainable sources by 2005. Sainsbury's, the large European retailer, whom Unilever supplies, plans to distribute only MSC labeled fish by 2010.[1]

Unilever's actions are a great example of sustainability risk management. Unilever avoided further negative publicity and pressure from Greenpeace. It partnered with an environmental NGO (non-government organization) to set up a certification system, which guaranteed sustainable fisheries on which its products depend. Unilever's financial condition was protected and the environment was improved. All this was accomplished voluntarily without any new government regulations.

The Erin Brockovich case illustrates how not having sustainability risk management systems in place can result in major liabilities. Pacific Gas & Electric (PG&E) Company paid a record $333 million settlement for poisoning the water in the small California town of Hinkley. Damages to the residents included cancer, kidney and liver diseases, serious respiratory problems, and colon diseases like Crohn's. The cancer-causing chemical, Chromium 6, which caused the damages, was purchased from Betz Laboratories to act as a coolant for PG&E's natural gas. PG&E damaged an important ecosystem, groundwater, and their actions lead to numerous deaths and injuries, for which it was found liable. PG&E incurred substantial reputation damage and negative publicity by having the story made into a popular movie, starring Oscar winning Julia Roberts.

Natural systems, which are being depleted, degraded or impaired, produce risks that will adversely impact individuals, businesses and governments. The only way to effectively manage the risks of depleting natural resources in the long run is to develop sustainable systems. Sustainability risk management will always employ insurance and other risk financing tools to help to protect corporations and other potentially liable parties. But for sustainability risk management to succeed, corporations must also alter, change, and adjust risk control systems through innovation and creativity in order to produce sustainable natural systems. Or to paraphrase Tom Wolfe, "Actively participate in managing your own sustainability risks."

Sustainability risk management is part of the overall concept of sustainable development. Sustainable development has been discussed for over 20 years, but its clearest early articulation was captured in the 1987 with the publication of the "Brundtland Report," entitled *Our Common Future*. The report was produced by the World Commission on Environment and Development, chaired by Norwegian Prime Minister Gro Harlem Brundtland, and defined sustainable development as "development that meets the needs of the present world without compromising the ability of the future generations to meet their own needs."

Sustainability risk management is also about social justice issues of fairness and equity. We should not exploit workers or other countries anymore than we should exploit the natural environment. John Elkington, author of *Cannibals with Forks* and Chairman of Sustainability, a leading U.K. consulting firm, introduced the concept of the triple bottom line in 1997. The triple bottom line includes the financial performance of the company, its environmental record, and its social efforts in treating workers, peoples and communities in a fair and equitable manner. Sustainability requires attention to all three legs of the triple bottom line. Just as a stool would tip over if one or two of its legs are removed, risks will be incurred if businesses only pay attention to the financial bottom line.

If we do not develop sustainable systems, we will not survive as a society. But assuming a more optimistic future-that we learn to develop sustainable systems-the process will not occur uniformly over the corporate world. Those firms in the forefront will reap the advantages and avoid or minimize the risk costs by changing these methods of business. Those corporations that lag behind will incur the disadvantages and may be devastated by the risk costs. I am hoping that this book will help corporations and their risk management systems to be at the forefront, and to demonstrate to the laggards the immense risk costs of maintaining their status quo positions.

In the 1990s, risk management strategy has been expanded by the development of enterprise or holistic risk management. Legal and operational/event risks, traditionally handled by risk managers, are being combined with financial (e.g., currency exchange, interest rate, credit), business and political risks to construct an overall risk profile of the firm. My view is that sustainability risks to date have only been dealt with marginally by the risk management community. With this book, I hope to expand the concept of enterprise risk management to more completely incorporate sustainability risk management.

Impediments to Sustainability Thinking

One of the big impediments to sustainability risk management thinking is the negative corporate attitudes that developed in the early days of environmental command and control regulation. After decades of neglect, environmental regulations, like the Clean Air and Water Acts in the early 1970s, were needed to rescue and protect the environment. It was clear that corporate behaviors to clean the air and water would not be voluntarily adopted by businesses. Environmental regulations were often deemed unnecessary and excessive by business. Regulations were typically resisted and seen in a negative light as only adding costs, and not benefits, to a business.

The Superfund system, established by the Comprehensive Environmental Response, Compensation and Liability Act (CERCLA) in 1980, with its strong liability rules of retroactive, strict and joint and several liability, "to make the polluter pay," was particularly upsetting to business. The Superfund system also led to negative thinking in the risk management and insurance industries, as much of the Superfund liabilities were passed on to the insurance industry through old general liability policies.

Gradual Enlightenment

For many years, environmental risk management was seen as consisting of compliance programs to meet regulatory requirements and strategies to mitigate Superfund costs. CEOs and Boards of Directors had little interest in environmental risk management, except to note the costs and their perceived negative effects of the programs. In the last twenty years, an entirely different approach to dealing with environmental conditions has been slowly evolving. Under this approach, environmental risk management is seen as an integral part of overall business and strategic management. Sustainable development and environmentally friendly systems and products are emphasized. It is proactive rather than reactive. The orientation is positive rather than negative. Environmental risk management systems are seen as adding value to products and services, creating a competitive advantage, improving community image and employee morale, reducing costs, and increasing the bottom line.

As more enlightened environmental risk management systems were developing, it became apparent that maintaining profitable businesses with good environmental management systems was not enough to produce long run sustainability. Attention must be brought to various social justice issues, including safe working conditions, fair wages, equity, diversity and human rights. Consideration must be given to a broad array of stakeholders. Social responsibility and ethical behavior must factor into corporate strategy. As noted by Katherine Ellison in writing about Elkington and other sustainability leaders in *Nature Conservancy*, "a company's moral behavior (is) a factor in its very survival."[2] Sustainability risk management must then encompass all three components of the triple bottom line—economic, environmental and social justice.

This new level of sustainability risk management is still in its early stages. For those firms with enlightened systems, more still needs to be done. Many firms have done little if anything to evolve from a negative compliance and liability abatement attitude to a more enlightened sustainability risk management view. The point to be made is that while there has been some progress, huge potential exists for further development and the business opportunities that go along with this development.

Ray Anderson, CEO of Interface, is an excellent example of an executive that is leading the way to sustainability. Stumped by a request to deliver a company speech on his environmental vision, he happened upon Paul Hawken's *The Ecology of Commerce*. Anderson had a veritable epiphany and totally changed the way that Interface had been run. He pledged that by 2020 Interface would be a completely sustainable company producing no dangerous waste, no harmful emissions and using no oil. To date, waste has been reduced 80 percent, water intake 78 percent, emission of greenhouse gases 46 percent, energy consumption 31 percent, and the use of petroleum based material 28 percent. Not only has Interface substantially reduced its sustainability risks, its total savings in the process have been $231 million.[3]

A principal argument to be made in this book is that the adoption of more enlightened sustainability risk management strategies is inevitable. The exposure of business to sustainability risks is increasing rapidly, although many may not realize it. Corporate executives have the choice to be proactive, like Ray Anderson, and begin now to develop or further refine sustainability risk management systems, or wait and be forced into it by liability suits, boycotts, competitive pressures, loss of customers, shareholder actions, reputation damage, regulation and increasing risk costs. The problem of waiting is that a business may not survive its procrastination. In today's fast moving economic world, not recognizing and managing risks appropriately can result in devastating financial, liability, reputation, regulatory and criminal repercussions. Witness the case of Andersen, LLP, once the flagship of accounting firms, virtually disintegrating in the wake of the Enron debacle. Granted Andersen's collapse did not directly involve environmental and social justice liabilities and penalties, but I feel similar risk situations are developing in the sustainability area that potentially could have equally devastating effects.

Avoiding an Andersen like situation in the sustainability area would be an obvious benefit to a business firm. But even if such a serious risk situation does not evolve, the actions taken by the firm to bolster its sustainability risk management systems will still end up saving the firm money and improving its financial situation in the long run. I am arguing that developing such systems is a guaranteed win-win decision for a business, while failing to develop them is a guaranteed lose-lose situation.

A company's reputation and brand value are also enhanced by employing sustainability risk management techniques. An Environics study found that at least two-thirds of 25,000 customers surveyed in the United States, Canada and Western Europe "form impressions based partly on a company's ethics, environmental impact and social responsibility."[4]

The net effect of developing sustainability risk management strategies will be to help produce sustainable environmental and social systems. In addition, it will not only result in the survival of businesses and economic systems, it will result in more prosperous systems.

Common Ground

Traditionally environmentalists and social justice activists have been pitted against businesses. They are seen as being on opposite sides of the fence. How often have you heard that a choice must be made between the environment and jobs? While this antipathy has been somewhat lessening, it still describes the typical tension that often exists today. What I would like to argue is that environmentalists, social activists and businesses can actually get to the same place, although it might be with a somewhat different rationale.

Environmentalists and social activists base their beliefs on ethics and practical considerations. We protect and work to preserve the environment and social values because it is the right thing to do. More importantly, we are all dependent on the environmental ecosystems for our very existence. There are limits to our resources and the ability of natural systems to absorb pollutants and waste. The destruction of ecosystems and living species is wrong and threatens our survival. It is also wrong not to maintain certain standards of fairness and equity among peoples, regions and countries. It is better to err on the cautionary side, rather than to wait for a crisis to take action. Action to lessen pressure on the environment and our social systems should be taken before there are irreversible and uncontrollable consequences. We should decrease environmental and social justice risks not just to help business, but also to save our environment and social systems.

While some business leaders may make decisions based on environmental ethics and sustainability values, most decisions are shaped by business principles. Obviously, businesses need to follow the law and meet regulatory requirements. Beyond that, businesses will typically only take positive environmental or social justice actions if the benefits through increased sales and profits or reduced risk costs exceed the costs of those actions.

The costs of positive actions are quite straightforward and measurable. For instance, they might include the cost of installing a recycling program, the cost of a machine guard, the cost of reducing emissions of a harmful pollutant, or the cost of changing a production system to eliminate a potentially dangerous raw material input. The costs are also in the present period. The measurement of the benefits is not as straightforward. Many benefits need to be estimated or have a value assigned to them and the benefits tend to manifest in the future. More importantly, businesses tend to underestimate the benefits of reducing future sustainability risk costs. Underestimating the benefits leads corporations to be slow in adopting sustainability risk management strategies.

It is easy to explain why traditionally no attention was paid by the corporate world to sustainability risk management systems—the benefits were largely perceived as having zero value. Either the risks were not apparent or general ignorance or indifference led individuals and businesses to believe that there were no discernible benefits. That situation has changed dramatically, so that today the benefits are substantial, although often underestimated. I will show that not only are the benefits for corporations considerable today, but they will continue to increase in the future, particularly in reducing risk costs deriving from liability suits, consumer boycotts, shareholder actions, reputation damage and regulation. A key benefit will be the reduction in environmental damages and more fairness and equity in social systems. So while environmentalists, social activists, and business executives may use a different decision making processes and sets of values, they can end up with the same results, namely the reduction in environmental damages, the preservation of natural capital, and advances in social justice.

The realization of common ground has led to partnerships between corporations and NGOs. Home Depot's partnership with the Forest Stewardship Council (FTC) is a good example. Home Depot is the world's largest home improvement retailer. In the late 1990s, environmental groups organized protests against the company for failing to ensure that the wood it purchased was not coming from endangered forests. To quell the protests, Home Depot became the first home improvement retailer in the U.S. to adopt FSC (Forest Stewardship Council) principles. Home Depot was worried the protests could hurt business and its reputation. FSC wanted trees not being taken from endangered forests. This lead to pressure on timber companies like Boise Cascade, who supplies Home Depot, to change its practice of using trees from old growth forests (see Chapter 3). Home Depot currently is a member of the Certified Forest Products Council, a U.S. based certification organization that works in partnership with FSC, and also a member of the Global Forest and Trade Network.[5] Several other examples of partnerships are presented in Chapter 9.

Who Needs to Read this Book

I am focusing this book on professionals in the risk management and insurance industry. Since risk managers are often not directly connected to the Environmental, Health & Safety (EH&S) area, they may not give sustainability risks the attention that they deserve. But in my opinion, a fundamental responsibility of risk managers is to anticipate all the risks that may adversely impact the firm, not just the ones for which they have primary responsibility in the firm.

Likewise, insurers may not be giving the environmental and social justice risk areas the attention they deserve, because insurers exclude pollution and employment practice risks from standard liability policies. They may feel that their exposure is limited. As the Superfund and asbestos risks have demonstrated, substantially more exposure may exist than originally was anticipated. In addition, as insurers write more environmental and employment practice liability insurance as separate policy coverages, their exposure will increase.

Insurance brokers and risk consultants, like risk managers, are responsible for anticipating all the various risks faced by a firm, including sustainability risks. Brokers need to guard against concentrating on those risk areas that have heavy insurance coverage. Such a strategy may limit the scope of the risks that they identify. Risk management consultants are also not giving sustainability risks enough attention. I saw one elaborate risk consultant's chart, entitled enterprise risk management, which listed 88 different risk areas, but none were titled environmental, social, or sustainability risks.

I hope that the ideas presented in this book would stimulate discussions among my academic colleagues in university programs in risk management and insurance. I welcome their thoughts and comments. I also hope that the concepts and strategies that I have presented will work their way into some of their lectures and research. Risk management and insurance students need to be exposed to sustainability risk management, and sustainability presents a fertile area of research.

Principal purposes of this book are to present a strong, documented case as to why I feel sustainability risks are becoming a critical risk area, and to provide a number of guidelines, examples and sources as to how these risks can be efficiently managed. I thought that by bringing this wealth of information together in this book, it would make it easier and more convenient for various professionals in the risk management and insurance industry to appreciate and to deal with this important risk area. While I highlight and summarize a number of diverse subjects, substantial references are included for those readers desiring further detail and elaboration.

The message and tone of this book is positive. It is more than a doomsday, negative accounting of environmental and social problems, although these problems are certainly documented and discussed. The book shows how environmental and social justice risks can be managed to benefit the corporation, economically, environmentally, and socially. There are costs involved, but as I will argue, the benefits of reducing and managing sustainability risks far exceeds the costs. Risk management professionals can make a substantial contribution to their firms by effectively managing sustainability risks. If these risks are ignored, given the wealth of available information and data, they risk losing their jobs and possibly incurring professional liability.

CEOs and boards of directors would benefit by paying attention to this book. Corporate management has the responsibility for the firm's financial bottom line.

This book is not about telling CEOs and directors how to run their core business. But it is very much about how to manage environmental and social justice risks. Sustainability risk management should be part of overall strategic management. Sustainability risks have the potential to cause debilitating financial losses to the corporation. Besides loss of profits and a declining stock price, directors and officers face the potential of personal liability for the decisions they make in regard to environmental and social justice situations. As will be shown, properly managing sustainability risks can have a number of advantages for improving the financial bottom line including a net reduction in costs, increased profits and a rising stock price. Given that the strategies for accomplishing these standards are available, as exemplified by the number of companies and organizations that are employing sustainability risk management techniques, directors and officers that fail to act will in all likelihood be held accountable for breaching their fiduciary duties.

A fundamental tenet of sustainability risk management strategy is that it is good for business and also good for the environment and society. In most cases, it can be shown that a win-win result is possible. Environmentalists, social justice groups and NGOs may find the concepts and ideas discussed in this book useful in their efforts to lessen the damage and pressure on the environment, workers and societies. This might include developing partnerships with corporate management that have proved quite effective (see Chapter 9).

This book might stimulate ideas regarding litigation. I would anticipate that those firms that are motivated to create positive changes in their sustainability risk management programs will see markedly reduced litigation. For those firms that continue to ignore sustainability risks, particularly given the availability of options and methods presented in this book and other texts, I would suggest that they may become targets for litigation actions. While I am not encouraging unreasonable lawsuits, firms that ignore sustainability risks will find little sympathy if their litigation problems escalate.

Policy makers and regulators may find some of the ideas discussed in this book worth pursuing. The overall framework of the ideas presented in this book is market based. It is a type of voluntary or self-regulation system, rather than government based command and control techniques. Considerable financial incentives exist in the form of reduced risk costs for adopting sustainability risk management strategies, and employing these strategies will improve the firm and also environmental and social conditions.

A Business Case for Sustainability

In this book, I am making a business case for managing sustainability risks. Sustainability risk management can reduce overall costs, increase profits, produce competitive advantage, increase the stock price, and result in greater financial gain for the firm and its shareholders. Ignoring these risks will have the opposite effects and in a worst case situation could imperil the survival of the firm.

Strong moral and ethical arguments can be and should be made for managing sustainability risks. I am emphasizing the business case for managing sustainability risks. While corporations can employ moral and ethical principles to justify their decisions, substantial evidence exists that the business case for managing sustainability risks is compelling.

Reference has been made to the triple bottom line—a business needs to be successful economically, environmentally and socially. If emphasis is only on the economic performance of the firm, then escalating risk costs in the environmental and social justice areas will ultimately cause the financial condition of the firm to deteriorate. But if sustainability risk management strategies are employed to reduce these risk costs, the financial condition will improve and the firm will prosper.

By basing my arguments on the business case for managing risks, it provides strong financial incentives to risk managers, insurers, CEOs and boards of directors for properly managing sustainability risks. In addition, if the business case can be made, then shareholders, environmentalists, social activists, NGOs, lawyers, and regulators are also provided with a strong case for bringing actions against those companies, which refuse to accept that sustainability risks must be addressed and properly managed.

Business Opportunities

In a *Harvard Business Review* article, "Beyond Greening: Strategies for a Sustainable World," Stuart Hart, the S.C. Johnson Professor of Sustainable Global Enterprise at Cornell University, states that "sustainable development will constitute one of the biggest opportunities in the history of commerce."[6] Innovation is the key. New technologies, new design techniques, indeed even new industries will develop in the response to the need to create sustainable systems. The business opportunities are almost limitless. To maintain business growth, within sustainability constraints, is going to require fundamental changes in our business systems. Those involved in the risk management field have the opportunity to respond to these fundamental changes with risk management innovations and solutions. The business world also has the responsibility to employ innovation to create solutions to the many problems and challenges that create these business opportunities. As noted, Paul Hawken, in his book, *The Ecology of Commerce*:

> "Corporations, because they are the dominant institution on the planet, must squarely address the social and environmental problems that afflict humankind."[7]

Structure

Chapter 1 discusses various examples of sustainability risks. Particular emphasis is put on the increasing stresses being put on natural ecosystems like water, oceans and forests. Sections on social justice risks, chemical exposures and biodiversity are also included. It will become increasingly difficult to ignore these risks. It can be expected that individuals, NGOs, governments and the courts will increasingly look to responsible parties to provide compensation for damages done to natural ecosystems and for injuries to individuals.

Chapter 2 examines various developments and trends that are making corporations more vulnerable to expanding liabilities for sustainability risks. Scientific discoveries, new government regulations, new theories of liability, the discovery process, the accumulation of liability exposures, increased transparency, and attorney pressures are all expected to contribute to increasing liabilities for environmental and social justice damages.

Chapter 3 looks at various boycotts of Shell Oil, Boise Cascade, Nike, Starbucks and Citigroup for poor environmental and social justice performance, and corporate reactions to these boycotts. Lessons learned from the Andersen and Merrill Lynch cases are incorporated. The expansion of the boycott tool, along with eco-labeling and the increasing exposure of corporations to reputation damage, are explored.

Chapter 4 examines investor and shareholder actions. The percentage of all funds that are invested according to Socially Responsible Investment (SRI) criteria is over 10 percent and growing. Their performance often tops non-SRI funds. Not being included in a SRI fund can damage the firm's reputation and reduce the demand for the firm's stock. Competitors that are included in SRI funds gain competitive advantage. Stockholder resolutions and other investor actions can bring pressure and embarrassment to boards of directors.

Chapter 5 looks at directors and officers (D&O), who may face the greatest potential liability from environmental and social justice risks. New laws like Sarbanes-Oxley and innovative judicial precedents are combining to magnify D&O risks deriving from the environmental and social justice areas. Public outrage and increased prosecutions for corporate scandals are increasing the risk of criminal convictions, which could spread to sustainability risks.

Chapter 6 examines two major old sustainability risk issues, asbestos and Superfund, and documents their past and continuing impacts on corporations and the insurance industry. While these situations cannot be altered, lessons can be learned for dealing with future sustainability risks.

Chapter 7 analyzes one of the most important new and developing sustainability risks, global warming/climate change. The science of global warming/climate changes is discussed. Anticipated risks and the response of the risk management and insurance sectors are examined. The Kyoto Treaty, developments in the European Union and emissions trading are discussed. As these risks are evolving, there is still time to take appropriate risk management action. Firms that fail to do so may suffer major losses through boycotts, reputation damage, liability suits, and shareholder actions.

Chapter 8 deals with one of the more intriguing new sustainability risk areas-genetically modified crops. The science of GM crops is discussed as are their benefits and risks. Important regulatory developments are examined. Risk management and insurance strategies for dealing with the new GM risks are analyzed.

Chapter 9 covers sustainability risk management strategies and methods, along with numerous examples of companies that are employing these strategies and methods. Major environmental and social justice risks are in their early stages of development. Firms have time to incorporate risk control methods and other risk management strategies to mitigate their exposures. Among strategies discussed are supply chain initiatives, waste reduction, service orientation, Life Cycle Assessment and Design for Environment, design initiatives, partnerships with NGOs, business associations, and United Nations programs. Pressures presented by EU regulations, WEEE, RoHS, and REACH, are examined along with their accompanying opportunities and risks.

Chapter 10 covers sustainability risk financing, including environmental insurance and other risk financing techniques. Several new financing products are available to the risk managers and will be examined, as will the major insurance providers. Corporations are generally uninsured for many of the environmental and social justice exposures discussed in this book. The critical exclusions and restrictions in existing policies are examined. Arguments for enhanced sustainability risk financing are presented.

Chapter 11 offers further business opportunities, summary comments and some final thoughts.

Each of the chapters-indeed many of the chapter sections-could comprise an entire book or series of books. My purpose is to try to give the reader an overall idea of the issues being discussed, as well as to provide documentation, supplementary information, sources, websites, etc., that a reader interested in more depth on the subject could pursue. I anticipate that my main audience will be a busy risk manager, insurance official or corporate executive that does not have the time to examine the hundreds of documents and sources of information that I compiled in researching and writing this text.

More than Survival

I began this introduction telling about our raft trip down the Colorado River through the Grand Canyon. While it was clearly important to survive the trip, the main reasons for going were the incredible experience of being in the Grand Canyon, the excitement of whitewater rafting, and the communion of family and friends. A business operation is analogous to a canyon trip. While it definitely is important for the business to survive, the main reasons for being in business are to produce quality products and services, provide jobs, make profits and contribute to the community. Employing sustainability risk management principles will not only permit the firm to survive, it will contribute to the firm being a profitable, ongoing and sustainable operation.

INTRODUCTION—ENDNOTES

[1] James Allen and James Root, "The New Brand Tax," *Wall Street Journal,* September 7, 2004.

[2] Katherine Ellison, "the bottom line redefined," *Nature Conservancy,* Winter 2002.

[3] Michelle Conlin, "From Plunder to Protector," *Business Week,* July 19, 2004.

[4] James Allen and James Root, "The New Brand Tax," *Wall Street Journal,* September 7, 2004.

[5] www.rainforests.net; Jim Carlton, "Once Targeted by Protesters, Home Depot Plays Green Role," *Wall Street Journal,* August 6, 2004.

[6] Stuart Hart, "Beyond Greening: Strategies for a Sustainable World," *Harvard Business Review,* January-February, 1997.

[7] Paul Hawken, *The Ecology of Commerce—A Declaration of Sustainability,* HarperBusiness, New York, 1993.

1

SUSTAINABILITY RISK ASSESSMENT

○ ○

This contamination has been an unprecedented experiment: We are subjecting whole populations to exposure to chemicals which animal experiments have proven to be extremely poisonous and in many cases cumulative in their effects. These exposures now begin at or before birth and—unless we change our methods—will continue through the lifetime of those now living. No one knows what the results will be because we have no previous experience to guide us.

*—Rachel Carson, author of **Silent Spring***

Millions of children die in Africa who shouldn't die, who it would be very easy to save. The fact that we don't apply the resources to the known cures or to finding better cures is really…the most scandalous issue of our time.

—Bill Gates, CEO, Microsoft

Risk assessment is the first step in the risk management process. The basic idea is to identify and evaluate the seriousness of the risks facing the organization. To the extent that data is available, past loss frequencies and severities are evaluated in order to predict what risks the firm might be expected to face in the future. In order to use risk management funds in the most efficient manner, risks are prioritized so that attention and dollars can be first directed to those risks that present the most serious threats to the financial viability of the firm.

Risk assessment is critical to developing strategies for managing risks. If a risk situation is not identified and assessed, then nothing will be done about it. Risk control and financing tools will not be employed, and any resulting losses may cause serious harm to the unprepared firm.

An important source of information for assessing an organization's risks is to examine losses that have occurred in the past to the organization or related firms in their respective industry. There is an old saying in risk assessment that you hope the unexpected loss happens to your competitor first.

In the sustainability area, some significant past loss situations would include the 1989 Exxon Valdez Oil spill in Prince William Sound, Alaska and the oil spill/leaks from the tanker Prestige, which sank off the Spanish coast in November 2002. Other prominent examples include chemical disasters like the Union Carbide plant leaks of metho-isocyanide gas in Bhopal India in 1984, which resulted in thousands of deaths and tens of thousands of injuries, and the 1976 dioxin spill in Seveso, Italy. Love Canal, in the late 1970s, triggered the enactment of the Superfund program, which resulted in the billions of dollars of liabilities for cleaning up hazardous waste sites being picked up by corporate America, including the insurance industry. Harmful products like asbestos and tobacco, which have resulted in hundreds of thousands of claims from injured workers and customers, are also considered within the realm of sustainability risks.

When losses of this magnitude occur, firms and/or governments typically take action to attempt to mitigate the occurrence and consequences of similar losses in the future. The information that risk managers and regulators glean from past loss events proves most useful is their risk assessment and management strategies.

Risk assessment becomes more complicated when risk situations are developing, but have yet to manifest into actual losses. If losses have not occurred, then risk managers may not include these risks in their assessments, or they may feel pressure from corporate officers not to spend risk management budget dollars on a situation that has yet to result in any losses. Similarly, regulators may feel new requirements are not necessary, or they may incur pressure from affected parties not to develop these requirements, in the absence of defined losses that have actually occurred.

If a risk situation is serious enough, risk managers may include these risks in their assessments, even though no losses have actually developed or no regulations are in effect. Failure to do so may result in financially debilitating consequences for the firm if major losses from these risk areas occur in the future. Such losses may be magnified if the risk condition has been building up over a long period of time. Superfund liabilities are a perfect example. Hazardous wastes were improperly disposed of for over a hundred years, but largely ignored by corporate America and its insurers, because these activities had not resulted in any actual liabilities being incurred. But the enactment of the Superfund program, with its retroactive liability provision, made corporate America and its insurers liable for cleaning up past improperly disposed hazardous wastes (see Chapter 6).

The subject and purpose of this book is to help the corporate world and its insurers from making another Superfund type miscalculation-indeed one that could dwarf Superfund in its resulting losses. Broadly speaking, this developing risk situation derives from the unsustainable practices of corporations and societies worldwide. If appropriate sustainability risk management techniques are not developed and implemented by the business world, catastrophic and inevitable financial consequences will be forthcoming.

The good news in that there is still time to develop and adopt sustainability risk management strategies. In the remainder of this chapter, several sustainability risks emanating from the environmental and social justice areas will be examined. Environmental ecosystems and social justice conditions are not sustainable under current business practices. Inevitably, damages will escalate to the point that accountability will be demanded. The longer these damages are ignored and not included in risk assessment practices, the greater will be the magnitude of resulting financial consequences. Once these unsustainable risk situations are recognized and assessed, then corporations can get along with the business of adopting sustainability risk management practices—they can actively participate in their own survival and become long term profitable enterprises.

Ecosystem Services

Traditionally, ecosystem services have been thought of as unlimited, infinitely renewable and "free." While these services were considered to provide substantial value, e.g., fresh water to drink, air to breathe, there was no concept of damages to these systems, as they were felt to be inexhaustible.

As ecosystems come under stress and it becomes clear that there are limits to the services they provide, the concept arises that damages can be caused to ecosystems. From a risk management standpoint, this concept of incurred damages is critical in that without damages caused by a party's actions or activities, there can be no liability. The point here is that businesses, organizations and individuals have generally not been found liable for damages to ecosystem services. It was felt these systems are so immense and capable of regeneration and recovery, that permanent damages were literally impossible. Once this notion is re-examined, and ecosystem damages are recognized as possible, real and occurring, then an enormous exposure to potential liabilities arises for businesses, organizations or individuals who might be found to be associated with causing these damages.

Value of Ecosystem Services

Ecosystems can be thought of as nature's capital or assets. Examples would include oceans, groundwater, forests, soils, wetlands and the atmosphere. Ecosystem services include services provided by natural systems. Ecosystem services would include the water we drink, the air we breathe, fish provided from the ocean, forest products, medicines from plants, waste treatment, pollination, pollution control, nutrient cycling, recreational opportunities and climate regulation. While values are clearly provided, there was little emphasis on attempting to quantify these values, as these resources were provided without cost and considered to be unlimited.

As it becomes more apparent that ecosystem services are not unlimited and are being compromised, attempts have been made to estimate values for these services. These are difficult tasks, as resources provided by ecosystems are not priced and captured in our commercial markets or valued in measures like gross domestic product. Groups of scientists and economists have employed various estimation techniques to value these services. One noted study was conducted by Robert Costanza, et.al.,[1] in which a group of scientists gathered and examined a large number of studies that estimated the value of a wide variety of ecosystem services. From this assemblage of studies, the authors estimated that the average annual value of world ecosystem services was US $33 trillion, with a range of US $16-54 trillion. These values were roughly double the global gross product for the comparable time period of the study. Table 1-1 shows the main ecosystem service categories and their estimated values.

Table 1-1

Ecosystem Services and Values

Number	Ecosystem service*	Ecosystem functions	Examples	Value ($ Billions)
1	Gas regulation	Regulation of atmospheric chemical composition.	CO_2/O_2 balance, O_3 for UVB protection, and SO_x levels	1,341
2	Climate regulation	Regulation of global temperature, precipitation, and other biologically mediated climatic processes at global or local levels.	Greenhouse gas regulation, DMS production affecting cloud formation.	684
3	Disturbance regulation	Capacitance, damping and integrity of ecosystem response to environmental fluctuations.	Storm protection, flood control, drought recovery and other aspects of habitat response to environmental variability mainly controlled by vegetation structure.	1,779
4	Water regulation	Regulation of hydrological flows.	Provisioning of water for agricultural (such as irrigation) or industrial (such as milling) processes or transportation.	1,115
5	Water supply	Storage and retention of water.	Provisioning of water by watersheds, reservoirs and aquifers.	1,692
6	Erosion control and sediment retention	Retention of soil within an ecosystem.	Prevention of loss of soil by wind, runoff, or other removal processes, storage of stilt in lakes and wetlands.	576
7	Soil formation	Soil formation processes.	Weathering of rock and the accumulation of organic material.	53
8	Nutrient cycling	Storage, internal cycling, processing and acquisition of nutrients.	Nitrogen fixation, N, P and other elemental or nutrient cycles.	17,075
9	Waste treatment	Recovery of mobile nutrients and removal or breakdown of excess or xenic nutrients and compounds	Waste treatment, pollution control, detoxification.	2,277
10	Pollination	Movement of floral gametes.	Provisioning of pollinators for the reproduction of plant populations.	117
11	Biological control	Trophic-dynamic regulations of populations.	Keystone predator control of prey species, reduction of herbivory by top predators.	417
12	Refugia	Habitat for resident and transient populations.	Nurseries, habitat for migratory species, regional habitats for locally harvested species, or overwintering grounds.	124
13	Food production	That portion of gross primary production extractable as food.	Production of fish, game, crops, nuts, fruits by hunting, gathering, subsistence farming or fishing.	1,386
14	Raw materials	That portion of gross primary production extractable as raw materials.	The production of lumber, fuel or fodder.	721
15	Genetic resources	Sources of unique biological materials and products.	Medicine, products for materials science, genes for resistance to plant pathogens and crop pests, ornamental species (pets and horticultural varieties of plants).	79
16	Recreation	Providing opportunities for recreational activities.	Eco-tourism, sport fishing, and other outdoor recreational activities.	815
17	Cultural	Providing opportunities for non-commercial uses.	Aesthetic, artistic, educational, spiritual, and/or scientific values of ecosystems.	3,015
*We include ecosystem 'goods' along with ecosystem services.				33,266

Permission granted from Nature Magazine (http://www.nature.com) and Dr. Robert Costanza at University of Vermont. Costanza, et.al., "The Value of the World's Ecosystem Services and the Natural Capital," Nature, Vol. 387, 15 May,1997, pp. 253-260

The following quote from the study captures the importance and relevance of their efforts:

"As natural capital and ecosystem services become more stressed and more 'scarce' in the future, we can only expect their value to increase. If significant, irreversible thresholds are passed for irreplaceable ecosystem services, their value may quickly jump to infinity. Given the huge uncertainties involved, we may never have a very precise estimate of the value of ecosystem services. Nevertheless, even the crude initial estimate we have been able to assemble is a useful starting point (we stress again that it is only a starting point). It demonstrates the need for much additional research and it also indicates the specific areas that are most in need of additional study. It also highlights the relative importance of ecosystem services and the potential impact on our welfare of continuing to squander them."[2]

The concept of establishing values for ecosystems and the services they provide is being developed by "ecological economists," like Gretchen Daily and Geoffrey Heal. Daily is the Director of Stanford's tropical research program at the Center for Conservation Biology. In her book with co-author Katherine Ellison, *The New Economy of Nature: The Quest to Make Conservation Profitable*, she writes that "Much of Mother Nature's labor has enormous and obvious value, which has failed to win respect in the marketplace until recently."[3] Heal is a professor of public policy and business responsibility at Columbia University and the author of *Nature and the Marketplace: Capturing the Value of Ecosystem Services*. In his book, he argues that there are powerful economic reasons for protecting natural ecosystems. Both Daily and Heal agree that "pricing ecosystem services is an important tool for making decisions about nature and for making the case for conservation."[4]

When liability litigation results, it can be expected that the ideas, studies and concepts of experts like Costanza, Daily and Heal will be used to set values for damages. Alternatively, since many of these estimated values for ecosystems are roughly approximated, damages might be determined by juries, judges and in turn used as estimates of values for ecosystem services. In either case, the concept of ecosystem values and damages and their quantification is real. Whereas in the past, the concepts of such damages and liability were moot, today they are real and can only be expected to develop and expand.

Demand Exceeds Replacement Capacity

The failure to adequately value Nature's ecosystem services has lead to an excess demand for these services. A 2002 study, lead by Mathis Wackeragel, program director for Refining Progress, found that human demand on resources has doubled since 1961 and currently exceeds the Earth's replacement capacity by 20 percent. As noted by Wackernagel, "We are no longer living off nature's interest, but nature's capital. Sustainable economies are not possible if we live beyond the means of nature."[5]

The study, entitled "Tracking the Ecological Overshoot of the Human Economy," was produced by an international team of researchers. The team estimated the ecological footprint of humanity. The study represented the first effort to construct a comprehensive accounting system to estimate the cost borne by nature of human activity.[6]

While ecosystem services are "free," certain responsibilities are required to allow these services to keep flowing in a sustainable manner. If more ecosystem services are used than replaced, then the system becomes unsustainable. For example, if more water is drawn from an aquifer than is replaced, the level of the aquifer will go down. If more fish are caught than are reproduced, then the total fish stock will decrease. Such practices are unsustainable, because at some point, we run out of water or we run out of fish.

In order to gain some appreciation of the increased stresses, pressures and potential damages to some of the world's principal ecosystems, documented evidence of damages will be presented in the next sections. Sustainability risks arising from damages to these environmental ecosystems will also be assessed.

Oceans/Fisheries

A 2003 study was published in *Nature* by Ransom Meyers and Boris Worm, which concludes that in just 50 years, industrial-scale commercial fishing has depleted the oceans' populations of large predatory fishes by 90 percent. These fish include marlin, tuna, swordfish, halibut, grouper and cod. This research is the single most comprehensive study ever conducted of the world's fisheries.[7]

Sophisticated technology like sonar and satellite positioning systems have allowed fleets to hone in on pockets of abundance. As areas were fished out (the authors estimate that it took 10-15 years for fish populations to crash in a particular area), fleets would move farther out to sea. While this practice maintained harvests, eventually it is a self-defeating practice, as the fleets run out of new areas to fish.

This study clearly illustrates points being made in the previous section. Before 1950, less sophisticated fishing techniques restricted fishing harvests so that fish populations were stable, at least on a global basis. While considerable value was produced by these fishing harvests, they were provided as a free product or service by the oceans' ecosystems and any apparent damage to fisheries, with certain exceptions like whaling, was limited. In the last 50 years, fish takes have exceeded the fisheries' regenerative capabilities to the point that world fish populations of predatory fish are only 10 percent of what they were 50 years ago. Even with corrective action, some of the fish populations may never recover. The scarcity of the fish increases the per unit value of this ecosystem service, and damages have clearly been done to these ecosystems. With damages comes the possibility for liability being assessed against various parties; fishermen, fishing fleets, governments, fish processors, food companies and their insurers. Boycotts against restaurants and food companies that sell certain fish types are already occurring.

Another study was released in 2003 by the Pew Oceans Commission. The 18-member commission conducted a three year $5.5 million study, entitled "America's Living Oceans: Charting a Course for Sea Change."[8] The oceans under U.S. jurisdiction cover approximately 4.5 million square miles, an area which exceeds its land mass. The study detailed extensive damages being done to U.S. ocean waters that are caused by over fishing, pollution from river runoffs, runaway development that is replacing coastal wetlands and estuaries, and the introduction of invasive species.

The Commission put forth five priority objectives for the United States:

1. Declare a principled, unified national ocean policy based on protecting ecosystem health and requiring sustainable use of ocean resources.

2. Encourage comprehensive and coordinated governance of ocean resources and uses at scales appropriate to the problems to be solved.

    a. The regional scale of large marine ecosystems is most appropriate for fisheries management and for governance generally.

    b. Coastal development and pollution control is most appropriately addressed at the watershed level.

3. Restructure fishery management institutions and reorient fisheries policy to protect and sustain the ecosystems on which our fisheries depend.

4. Protect important habitat and manage coastal development to minimize habitat damage and water quality impairment.

5. Control sources of pollution, particularly nutrients that are harming marine ecosystems.

To accomplish these objectives, the Commission put forth 26 recommendations for governance for sustainable seas including those listed below:

- Enact a National Ocean Policy Act to protect, maintain, and restore the health, integrity, resilience, and productivity of our oceans.

- Establish regional ocean ecosystem councils to develop and implement enforceable regional ocean governance plans.

- Establish a national system of fully protected marine reserves.

- Establish an independent national oceans agency.

- Establish a permanent federal interagency oceans council.

- Redefine the principal objective of American marine fishery policy to protect marine ecosystems.

- Separate conservation and allocation decisions.

- Regulate the use of fishing gear that is destructive to marine habitats.

- Establish a permanent fishery conservation and management trust fund.

- Develop an action plan to address non-point source pollution and protect water quality on a watershed basis.

- Institute effective mechanisms at all levels of government to manage development and minimize its impact on coastal ecosystems.

- Redirect government programs and subsidies away from harmful coastal development and toward beneficial activities, including restoration.

- Address unabated point sources of pollution, such as concentrated animal feeding operations and cruise ships.

- Strengthen control over toxic pollution.

- Implement a new national marine aquaculture policy based on sound conservation principles and standards.

- Develop and implement a comprehensive national ocean research and monitoring strategy.

- Improve the use of existing scientific information by creating a mechanism or institution that regularly provides independent scientific oversight of ocean and coastal management.

The Commission concluded, "This nation must decide how it will choose to meet the crisis in our oceans. Fundamentally, this is not a decision about us. It is about our children, and actions we must take to bequeath them thriving oceans and healthy coastlines."

The reaction by California Republican Representative Richard Pombo, Chair of the House Resources Committee, illustrates the political difficulties of trying to change current unsustainable ocean practices. He criticized the study as being backed by radical environmentalists who wish to increase federal regulation over fisheries and stated, "The pictures are nice, but this study contributes about as much to fisheries management as a coffee table book about coffee tables."[9]

The study in *Nature* by Meyers and Worm and the Pew Commission study provide extensive documentation for what increasingly is becoming an obvious conclusion. Unless there are changes in current practices, collapsed fishing stocks will not recover and the general state of the oceans, particularly coastal ocean areas, will continue to deteriorate. The Pew Commission made several recommendations listed above, which if enacted, should hopefully reverse some of the damaging trends. On a global basis, at the 2002 World Summit on Sustainable Development in Johannesburg, a declaration signed by most attending countries called for restoring fishing stocks by 2015.

The harvesting practices of the world's fishing industry are clearly not on a sustainable basis. If nothing is done, scientific evidence and trends indicate that many stocks will be totally destroyed. The fishing industry faces drastic reductions in its harvests, potential litigation for damages to fishing stocks, consumer/ NGO boycotts and/or new government regulations to alter its present practices. Liabilities and boycotts could extend up to food companies that use fish in their food products. And of course, liability insurers of any involved parties may have to provide defense costs and indemnification for damages.

Coral reefs are an integral part of ocean ecosystems. Coral reefs are important for fish habitat, beach erosion control, storm protection, economic fishing, and aesthetic tourist values. Some 27 percent of the world's coral reefs have been degraded by 2002, up from 10 percent in 1992. This percentage could climb to 40 percent by 2010 without loss control actions. Warming seas, linked to human induced global warming, stress corals to the point that they expel algae that live within them, leaving the corals white or bleached.[10] In Chapter 7, an Australian research study is discussed, which concludes that the Great Barrier Reef is at risk of losing most of its coral by 2050 and could collapse by 2100 due to global warming. Pollution, mining and the use of explosives and cyanide for fishing also stress coral reefs. The degradation of the world's coral reefs is documented in an extensive report entitled, *Status of Coral Reefs of the World: 2004,* authored by Global Coral Reef Monitoring Network.[11]

Other groups have offered further evidence of the deteriorating condition of the world's oceans. A 2002 study titled, "Health of the Oceans," by the Ocean

Conservancy reports that many species of fish and marine life have been reduced to near extinction. The report cites over fishing as being the most responsible factor, ahead of pollution and other human activities. It states that of the fish stocks that can be assessed, nearly half are depleted or being over fished. Yet, the status of over two-thirds of the fish is unknown.[12] Recreation based activities also produce pressure. For instance, cruise ships produce enormous amounts of wastes. It is estimated that the world's cruise ships discharge 90,000 tons of raw sewage and garbage into the oceans every day.[13]

The National Research Council estimates that every eight months U.S. coastal waters collectively receive 11,000,000 gallons of oil as runoff from urban areas—the equivalent of the Exxon Valdez spill in Alaska. Researchers estimate that 38 dead zones have been identified as being linked to human activities, most along the Gulf and Atlantic coasts. Admiral James Watkins, Chair of the U.S. Commission on Ocean Policy, notes that the most infamous may be the dead zone which forms each spring and summer in the Gulf of Mexico. The Mississippi River flushes pesticide-laden runoff from farmland into the Gulf to form a "dead zone" the size of the state of Massachusetts. The nutrients trigger huge algae blooms, which use up all the water's oxygen when they die and decompose.[14]

In April 2004, the U.S. Commission on Ocean Policy released a 500 page plus preliminary report assessing the nation's coastal waters. The Commission was appointed by President Bush, and the report represents the first review of coastal management in 35 years. In a word, the Commission's Chair, Admiral Watkins stated, "Our oceans and coasts are in serious trouble."[15] The Commission issued several recommendations including:

- Manage coastal waters on an ecosystem—based management, evaluating the health of entire ecosystems.

- Create a National Ocean Council within the White House

- Establish a trust fund, which would draw up to $4 billion from royalties for offshore energy exploration.

- Double federal research spending to $1.3 billion a year.

- Ratify the United Nations Convention on the Law of the Sea (launched in 1982, the convention has been signed by 145 nations, with the U.S. one of the few holdouts).

- Reform current regional fisheries management councils by separating scientific assessments of how much fishing is sustainable from economic and political decisions.

- Reduce nutrient rich runoff pollution, which creates "dead zones" as mentioned above.

The report notes that considerable economic values are associated with healthy ocean waters. Recreation values on an annual basis were estimated at $59.4 billion, commercial fishing at $28 billion, and sport fishing at $20 billion. These values are good examples of the "free" ecosystem services discussed in the previous section. The report also alluded to aesthetic values: "We also love the oceans for their beauty and majesty and for their intrinsic power to relax, rejuvenate and inspire."[16]

The final report of the U.S. Commission on Ocean Policy was put on President Bush's desk in the fall of 2004. In response to the report, President Bush created a new federal panel to coordinate oceanic policy. The head of the panel will be James L. Connaugton, Chair of the White Council on Environmental Quality. It is the responsibility of this panel, along with the Bush Administration and the U.S. Congress, to take action on the Commission's recommendations.[17]

Water

The world's freshwater systems are coming under increasing pressure. Freshwater systems are provided primarily by groundwater/aquifers, and also by lakes and rivers. Several studies have documented a deteriorating situation as regards these systems. According to a UN report *Global Challenge, Global Opportunity,* half of the world's population could face serious water shortages by 2025.[18] Water use worldwide has increased six fold over the 20th Century, twice the rate of population growth. Over one billion people in developing countries do not have access to safe drinking water and 2.5 billion lack adequate sanitation facilities. Contaminated water kills 2.2 million people a year. In rural Asia and Africa, women on average walk about six kilometers (over three miles) for water.

Agricultural use comprises 70 percent of water consumption, with industry use at 20 percent and residential/municipal use at 10 percent. Much of the agricultural food production in the last half of the 20th Century was built on the expansion of irrigation systems. According to the Worldwatch Institute's *State of the World* (2002) report, irrigated areas almost tripled from 100 million hectares in 1950 to 274 million hectares in 1999. Forty percent of the world's food is produced on irrigated fields. Nearly 10 percent of the world's grain harvest is now produced by drawing down on water supplies. In northern China, water tables are falling 1—1.5 meters per year to irrigate corn and wheat crops. Besides China, areas threatened include those in India, North Africa, the Middle East and the United States. More efficient irrigation systems will be needed to reverse these unsustainable trends.[19]

A 2003 United Nations report entitled, *Groundwater and Its Susceptibility to Degradation: A Global Assessment of the Problem and Options for Management,* provides information on the importance of groundwater and numerous examples of groundwater stresses. In introducing the report, United Nations Environment Programme Executive Director, Klaus Toepfer, states:

> "Some two billion people and as much as 40 per cent of agriculture is at least partly reliant on these hidden stores. Groundwater also supplements river flows, springs and wetlands vital for rural and urban communities and wildlife. Indeed most of the world's liquid freshwaters are found not in rivers and lakes, but below ground."[20]

Several examples of groundwater stresses were documented in the report. In the United States, 400 million cubic meters of groundwater in Arizona are removed annually, approximately double the amount being replaced by recharge from rainfall. In Mexico, the number of over exploited aquifers increased from 32 in 1975 to 130 in the 1990s. Half of Spain's 100 aquifers are over-exploited. Some 20 percent of the water in the Ogalla/High Plains Aquifer of the U.S. Midwest has been removed. The aquifer spans the Great Plain states from Texas to South Dakota. While the depletion of the aquifer has been slowed in recent years, it is still going down. Table 1-2 from the Earth Policy Institute's *Outgrowing the Earth: The Food Security Challenges in an Age of Falling Water Tables and Rising Temperatures,* by Lester Brown, gives several more examples of aquifer depletions around the world.

Table 1-2
Underground Water Depletion in Key Countries

Country	Description
Mexico	In Mexico, where a third of all water used comes from underground, aquifers are being depleted throughout the northern arid and semiarid regions. In a country where irrigated land is more than three times as productive as rain-fed land, the loss of irrigation water from aquifer depletion will be costly.
United States	Overpumping is widespread, and the overpumping of the vast Ogallala or High Plains aquifer—essentially a fossil aquifer that extends from southern South Dakota through Nebraska, Kansas, eastern Colorado, Oklahoma, and Texas—is a matter of national concern. In the Southern Great Plains, irrigated area has shrunk by 24 percent since 1980 as wells have gone dry.
Saudi Arabia	When the Saudis turned to their large fossil aquifer for irrigation, wheat production climbed from 140,000 tons in 1980 to 4.1 million tons in 1992. But with rapid depletion of the aquifer, production dropped to 1.6 million tons in 2004. It is only a matter of time until irrigated wheat production ends.
Iran	The overpumping of aquifers is estimated at 5 billion tons per year. When aquifers are depleted, Iran's grain harvest could drop by 5 million tons, or one third of the current harvest.
Yemen	This country of 21 million people is unique in that it has both one of the world's fastest-growing populations and the fastest-falling water tables. The World Bank reports that the water table is falling by 2 meters or more a year in most of Yemen.
Israel	Both the coastal aquifer and the mountain aquifer Israel shares with Palestinians are being depleted. With severe water shortages leading to a ban on irrigated wheat, the continuous tightening of water supplies is likely to further raise tensions in this region.
India	Water tables are falling in most states in India, including the Punjab and Haryana, the leading grain-surplus states. With thousands of irrigation wells going dry each year, India's farmers are finding it increasingly difficult to feed the 18 million people added each year.
China	Water tables are falling throughout northern China, including under the North China Plain. China's harvest of wheat has fallen in recent years as irrigation wells have dried up. From 2002 to 2004, China went from being essentially self-sufficient in wheat to being the world's largest importer.

Source: Lester R. Brown, Earth Policy Institute, *Outgrowing the Earth: The Food Security Challenge in an Age of Falling Water Tables and Rising Temperatures,* New York, W.W. Norton & Co., 2005.

In some areas of the world, droughts are aggravating water shortages as acquirers are not replenished by rain water. In the United States, eleven western states are in the midst of a six year drought. The enormous reservoirs of Lake Powell and Lake Mead are both half empty. Droughts mean dry forests and brush increasing the fire risk. The wildfires in Southern California in October 2003, which claimed 24 lives and destroyed 3,710 houses, was one of the worst wildfires in the nation's history. The drought also made pines more vulnerable to the bark beetle, which then creates more fuel from dead trees. Australia is experiencing its worst drought in a century. Other areas of Austro Asia have also experienced low rainfall, as have wide areas of Africa and China. Lake levels, such as those in the Aral Sea in Russia, Lake Chad in Africa and Lake Chapala in Mexico, have decreased drastically from a combination of overuse for agricultural and commercial needs and inadequate rainfalls.[21]

In short, the hydrological cycle that supplies the aquifers with water is being outstripped by the volume of human demands, pollution of water resources and poor water management. Aquifers have limits—they have a finite capacity. If the water levels of aquifers are decreasing, despite recharging, then they will go dry if current practices are not altered. Even before they go dry, the increased concentrations of minerals at low levels can make the water undrinkable. To avoid this inevitable result, current practices must be changed to allow aquifers to recover, or at a minimum, to stabilize. For aquifers to remain viable for the long run, sustainable use of groundwater must be incorporated. The interested reader might look at *Water Follies* by Robert Glennon for an excellent examination of groundwater pumping and the problems this has created in the United States.

The author does not pretend that adjustments in current practices are easy. But certainly these adjustments will be less burdensome and drastic than those adjustments that would need to be made after the aquifer runs dry. Knowledgeable individuals agree that at this point in time the situation of declining groundwater levels can be reversed. The technology and the processes exist—it is the political difficulties of making regulatory changes that is hampering the solutions.

A report issued in summer 2003 by the U.S. Interior Department's Bureau of Reclamation entitled, "Water 2025: Preventing Crises and Conflict in the West," provides guidelines for local and regional planning for water use in the West.[22] Unless well thought out strategies and plans are implemented to handle water crises when the supplies fall, or in some places even when levels are normal, the potential for future conflicts over water use is very high.

Similar to the problem of declining fish stocks, solutions exist, but vested interests impair implementation. As with declining fish stocks, lack of action will almost certainly trigger liability suits and crisis-driven government solutions. The agricultural industry and industries in general may see their operations disrupted and production levels slowed or even halted, and they may incur potentially enormous liability claims, boycotts, and expensive changes required by crisis-driven government regulations. A report by the UN Environment Programme Finance Initiative and the Stockholm International Water Institute entitled, *Risks of Water Scarcity: A Business Case for Financial Institutions,* examines the considerable risks of water shortages to investors and financial institutions.[23] Incorporating appropriate sustainability risk management techniques will allow various business sectors and governments to mitigate these costs and develop sustainable methods to maintain freshwater supplies into the future.

Deforestation

Deforestation resulted in a decline of 2.4 percent of the world's forested area in the decade of the 1990s. The highest rates were in Africa, at over seven percent per decade, and in Latin America at somewhat under five percent per decade. In Europe and North America, natural forests have actually expanded since 1990. Almost all of the deforestation is taking place in tropical regions, which contain slightly less than half of the world's forests. Most of the deforestation is due to the expansion of agriculture.

The capacity of forests to provide goods and services is decreasing. Forests provide a variety of economic services in addition to forest products, including water and soil conservation, flood control, climate change mitigation and protection of biodiversity. Trees regulate the flow of water between soils and the atmosphere; their roots hold soils in place, preventing erosion; and their branches, bark, leaves, and soils provide habitat to the largest collection of biodiversity of any ecosystem on the planet. Nearly 30 per cent of the world's major watersheds have lost three-quarters or more of their original forest cover, reducing water quality and increasing the risk of floods. Forests harbor about two-thirds of known terrestrial species, many forest-dwelling large mammals, and half of the large primates. Nine percent of all known tree species are at some risk of extinction. Deforestation means lost lives and livelihoods. In 1998 alone, forest clearing was blamed for contributing to a landslide in India that killed 238 people, and for worsening flooding in China that killed 3,000 and caused $20 billion in damage.

There are more than 1.7 billion people in 40 nations, with critically low levels of forest cover, who rely on forests for fuel wood, timber, and other goods and services. Of the 500 million people living in and around tropical forests, 150 million are members of indigenous groups that depend on forests and forest resources to sustain their way of life.[24]

The situation playing out in the Amazon rainforest illustrates the difficulties and conflicts involved in maintaining a sustainable forest strategy. The Amazon basin is larger than all of Europe and extends over nine South American countries. The Amazon rainforest accounts for more than half of what remains of the word's tropical forests, and is estimated to contain up to 30 percent of the earth's biodiversity. For years, struggles have existed between conservation groups who want to maintain the rainforest and businesses, farmers and settlers who desire to cut the trees for logging and to burn the trees to make room for grazing cattle and raising crops-principally soybeans.

At the Earth Summit in Rio de Janeiro in 1992, a series of accords were signed aimed at protecting ecosystems, including forests. Brazil, as host of the Summit, signed these accords. Yet, within three years of the Summit, the annual deforestation rate in the Amazon had doubled to over 11,000 square miles, an area the size of Maryland. For the next few years, pressures were eased through government action and NGO campaigns, so that by the beginning of the millennium, the rate had been reduced to 6,000 square miles a year, an area the size of Connecticut. One of the main government tools that Brazil used was the creation of the world's largest tropical national park and the demarcation of lands of indigenous tribes. This latter action resulted in more than 385,000 square miles or 12 percent of Brazil's territory, an area the size of France and England combined, being transferred to Indian control. Setting aside these lands for parks and indigenous peoples sets up enforcement systems particularly among the Indian tribes who have become aggressive defenders of the rainforest under their control. Another enforcement technique that has decreased the deforestation rate is the use of satellite images to monitor various regions. In some states with a particularly high deforestation rate, like Mato Grasso, the rate of deforestation was cut by more than one half.

Through August 2002, satellite images showed that the annual deforestation rate had again increased—this time to around 10,000 square miles, an area the size of New Jersey. The 12 month period ending August 2003 showed only a light moderation at 9,169 square miles, the size of Massachusetts. Regrettably, data for 2004 indicated deforestation rates exceeding 10,000 square miles, the second highest annual rate after 1995. Greenpeace warns that at these rates the rainforest could be completely wiped out in 80 years. Scientists say that about 20 percent of the Amazon rainforest has already been consumed.

While environmentalists were initially encouraged by the election of Luiz Inacio Lulu da Silva to the Presidency in January 2003, they quickly became dismayed when President da Silva unveiled a four year $66 billion infrastructure development plan, "Brazil for Everyone." Principal components of the plan include two natural gas pipelines through part of the Amazon rain forest, and the further paving of highway BR-163, which connects Cuiaba, the capitol of Mato Grasso, in the southern part of the rainforest, with Santarem on the Amazon River. From here the Atlantic Ocean can be reached. The improvement of this highway, which runs through the heart of the rainforest, will facilitate the movement of agricultural products from the south to the Amazon River and the Atlantic Ocean and on to international markets. Highways and roads through the rainforest are particularly damaging to the rainforest. It is estimated that about 80 percent of the deforestation in the Amazon occurs in a 31 mile corridor on either side of the highways and roads. When roads become paved, the rate of deforestation accelerates.

The increasing importance of soybean production in Brazil creates further political and commercial pressure to cut down more of the rainforest. In the words of President da Silva, "This region can't be treated like it was something from another world, untouchable, in which the people don't have the right to the benefits." One of the key benefits derives from the growing of soybeans. Developments in world agricultural markets have allowed Brazil to become a major exporter of soybeans. Economic expansion and the growth of the middle class in China have greatly increased their demand for soybeans. As recently as ten years ago, China was a net exporter of soybeans, but today China is the world's biggest importer of soybeans and soy products. Brazil, as the second largest exporter behind only the United States, has seen the demand for soybean production skyrocket. The Brazilian government's recent decision to allow GM soybeans will only accelerate this trend. In states like Mato Grosso that has savannas in the south but rainforests in the north, which comprise a major portion of the southern Amazon basin, there is great pressure to turn more of the rainforest into agricultural lands for soybean production. Mato Grasso, which means dense jungle, already is a major soybean producer. Indeed, the new governor of Mato Grasso, Blairo Maggi, and his family are one of the country's leading producers, transporters, and exporters of soybeans. The Brazilian press refers to him as the Soybean King.[25]

We again find a similar situation as with declining fish stocks and groundwater levels, namely that annual net losses of forest are unsustainable. Current practices will result in the disappearance of forest ecosystems. There are solutions but they require political cooperation. Without changes in current practices, the logging, timber and agricultural industries and businesses that use and sell forest products will be subject to potential liability claims, consumer/NGO boycotts, shareholder actions and crisis government solutions. As rainforests like the Amazon continue to diminish, pressures can be expected to rise. The costs of all these actions can be avoided by adopting sustainable forestry practices as a critical risk management technique.

Desertification

Desertification is an environmental trend related to the two previous problem areas, water shortages and deforestation. The United Nations Convention to Combat Desertification announced, in summer 2004, that sizeable portions of the world were becoming deserts every year. The pace has accelerated from 624 square miles per year in the 1970s to 1,374 square miles per year at the end of the century. By 2025, two-thirds of arable land in Africa may disappear, along with one third in Asia and one-fifth in South America. Up to one-third of the Earth's surface is at risk.

Deforestation, overtaxed water supplies, increasing population, weak conservation techniques and global warming are all given as causes. Struggling populations on the edges of deserts, like the Gobi desert in China and the Saharan desert in Africa, are particularly vulnerable. In an effort just to survive, trees are cut for firewood, grasslands are over-grazed, fields are over-farmed, and water becomes more scarce.[26]

Biodiversity

One of the more disturbing aspects of unsustainable economic development and globalization is the extinction of species and the resulting loss of biodiversity. Biodiversity risks are complex and not that well understood. Species have developed over millions of years and are connected to the environment for good evolutionary reasons. When they become extinct, their ecological role or purpose in the inter-connected environment is lost. If the extinct species was a primary food source for another species, then that species may become endangered and even extinct. Or if the extinct species is a predator of another species, then that species may grow uncontrolled. The loss of a keystone predator like tigers, sharks, polar bears or wolves can have severe adverse impacts on ecosystem diversity and balance. In general, loss of biodiversity reduces the ability of all life forms to adapt to a changing environment.

It is doubtful that many firms would face liabilities for the extinction of a species. Making the proximate cause connection and establishing damages to affected parties would be difficult if not impossible. If legislation is passed, like the Endangered Species Act in the United States, loss of business or fines may result, such as those associated with the timber industry and the effects of their operations on the habitat of the spotted owl. Negative publicity and even boycotts could result if a business' activities were shown to be associated with harming endangered species or the habitats of unique species. There are of course huge ethical issues raised when humans, as the dominant world species, cause the extinction of other species, because we all share the same planet and resources.

Since many of the above sections demonstrate the adverse effects of economic development on the natural world, I thought it would be useful to briefly look at some studies on extinct or endangered species to get some idea of the magnitude of the problem. While specific risk costs may not accrue to individual businesses, protection of biodiversity, if for no other reasons than ethical concerns, is an important part of sustainability risk management.

A 2002 report by the United Nations Environment Programme (UNEP) entitled, "The Global Environmental Outlook-3 (Geo-3)," predicts a bleak outlook for the natural world in general and species extinction in particular. A brief summary of the report at the ECES website notes that the:

> "UN report by 1,100 scientists warns that 70 percent of the natural world will be destroyed over the next 30 years due to over-population, deforestation, pollution, global warming, spread of non-native species, and other human impacts, causing the mass extinction of species and the collapse of human society in many countries."[27]

Over the next 30 years, the report estimates that the mass extinction crisis will wipe out 24 percent or 1,130 of the world's mammals, including Siberian tigers, black rhinoceroses, Asian elephants, cheetahs and mountain gorillas, the Philippine eagle, and the Amur leopard. Some 12 percent or 1,183 of the world's birds and 5,611 plants are also expected to become extinct. Using estimates from the World Conservation Union, 30 percent of fish, 25 percent of reptiles and 20 percent of amphibians are also at risk of extinction. In total there are 11,046 endangered species of plants and animals that have been identified. While some may still live in a zoo or conservancy, none would survive in the wild. Habitat destruction and the introduction of alien species are the primary causes of the threatened extinctions. The authors of the report point out that these are conservative estimates and actual numbers will likely be higher, given for instance, that only four percent of the known plant species have been properly evaluated.[28]

A 2004 study in Britain of decreasing numbers of butterflies (13 percent decrease) provides evidence that extinction rates are also accelerating in the insect world.[29] Another contributing factor is global warming. A 2004 study published in *Nature* predicted that if present warming trends continue, 15 to 37 percent of the 1,103 different species they studied will become extinct by 2050.[30] A study of amphibians, published in *Science* in fall 2004, found that 122 species have disappeared since 1980 and another 1,900 (32 percent) are in danger of becoming extinct.[31]

If action is not taken, this will represent the sixth great wave of extinction. The last occurred about 65 million years ago with the extinction of the dinosaurs. The first wave of great extinctions took place about 440 million years ago, which eliminated some 75 percent of the Earth's animals. The potential sixth great wave of extinction is unique in that it would result from the activities of a single species-humans-rather than from catastrophic environmental changes. Over the past 500 years, human activities are known to have caused 816 species extinctions, although the true number is estimated to be far higher. Of the 128 documented species of extinct birds, 103 are known to have become extinct since 1800. The pace of extinction has also increased. Noted biodiversity expert, E.O. Wilson, states that "The extinction rate is now at crisis proportions, perhaps a hundred to a thousand times higher than before humanity came along."[32]

In discussing the possibility of reversing the mass extinction predicted by the UN report, Jeff McNeely, chief scientist at the International Union for Conservation of Nature (IUCN) in Geneva, stated:

> "It could go either way. It could be a golden age of nature conservation, or it could be a disaster scenario. If we assume a doomsday scenario then we're going to live in a greatly oversimplified world. Most of the remaining species are going to be widely dispersed and cosmopolitan. We will have lost many of the large mammals and birds, and life in general, will be more homogeneous, with a smaller capacity to adapt to changing environment."[33]

If the species loss is linked to the environmental damage caused by identifiable industries, public reaction may result in large costs to these enterprises.

Synthetic Chemicals

The explosion in the production of synthetic chemicals began during the World War II period. As science produced new discoveries and techniques, synthetic chemicals were used in a wide variety of products and processes. Packaging, clothes, furniture, television sets, computers, toys, recreational equipment, automobiles, appliances, cookware, electrical transformers, lubricants, paints, and pesticides are but a few examples. Many of these products made our lives easier and more convenient in our work, home and leisure activities.

Some 80,000 plus synthetic chemicals are now on the world market. A thousand new substances are introduced each year. The U.S. production of synthetic chemicals in the early 1990s was 1,600 pounds per capita. An average television is made of 4,360 chemicals. Yet only around 3,000 or 3-4 percent of total chemicals in use have been studied for their effects on living systems. Those studied in depth include the compounds of DDT, PCBs, and dioxin, which are now banned in many countries in the world.[34]

Given the production and use of synthetic chemicals worldwide, it would be expected that most peoples are exposed to these chemicals. It is still surprising that virtually all individuals, if tested, will find some 250 chemical contaminants in their body fat regardless of where they live in the world. A striking example is PCBs, which were used in hundreds if not thousands of products and are found everywhere—in soil, air, water, mud of lakes, rivers, estuaries, the ocean, fish, birds and other animals, including humans.[35]

It is not only the ubiquity of chemicals, but also their persistence that produce risks. Many chemical compounds do not easily break down. Indeed, it is often their stability, like the use of PCBs in electrical transformers, that made them so initially attractive. But PCBs can persist for decades, some types even for centuries. Once chemicals contaminants get into the air, water, soil, or in your body, they will stay for a long time.

The fact that chemicals are in the breast milk of virtually all the world's women guarantees that these chemicals will be passed along to their offspring. Various studies of breast milk contamination have found that babies take in the highest doses of contaminants that they will experience in their entire lives. These levels will be 10-40 times greater than the daily exposure of an adult. In just six months of breastfeeding, an average baby in the U.S. and Europe gets the maximum recommended lifetime dose of dioxin, and five times the allowable daily level of PCBs set by international health standards for a 150 pound adult.[36]

Studies have reported disturbing findings of increasing diseases in children. While direct causal links with chemicals have not been established, the evidence strongly suggests an association with environmental contaminants. For instance, the childhood cancer rate in Canada increased 28 percent from 12.5 cases per 100,000 children under 15 in 1970 to 15.5 cases in 2000. Other studies have documented similar results in the United States and Germany. In the United States, the childhood cancer rates increased 26 percent between 1973 and 1999. But in the United States some childhood cancer rates were much higher. Acute lymphocytic leukemia rose 62 percent, brain cancer rose 50 percent, and bone cancers rose 40 percent. In addition, former rare conditions in children are increasing. These include autism, learning disabilities, allergies, and attention deficit disorders.[37]

A U.S. EPA 2003 report, *America's Children and the Environment,* found that U.S. children are getting asthma at more than double the rate of two decades ago. The percentage of children with asthma went from 3.6 percent in 1980 to 7.5 percent in 1995 to 8.7 percent in 2001, a total of 6,300,000 children. This report also found that 5,000,000 U.S. women, or 8 percent of those in the childbearing ages of 16-49, had at least 5.8 parts per billion of mercury in their blood as of 2000. EPA has found that children born to women with blood concentrations above 5.8 parts per billion are at risk of adverse health effects, including reduced developmental IQ and problems with motor skills such as eye-hand coordination. The report noted that mercury is a persistent pollutant, with the three major sources for mercury emissions being coal fired power plants, municipal waste incinerators, and medical waste incinerators. The report also documented that the number of U.S. children with elevated levels of lead in their bodies was 300,000 in 2000.[38]

A study published in September 2004 in the *New England Journal of Medicine* found that air pollution in Southern California can stunt the development of lung growth in children. A group of 1759 school children were tested over 8 years from fourth grade to high school graduation. After 30 years of air pollution regulations, air pollution persists and still results in harm. Underpowered lungs lead to a permanent reduction in the ability to breathe, which can lead to a lifetime of health problems, even premature death. This is the most comprehensive study ever conducted on children's exposure to dirty air.[39]

High profile examples provide further evidence. A high incidence of leukemia among children in the city of Woburn, Massachusetts was associated with well water being contaminated by trichloroethylene, a solvent used to strip grease from metals. Their plight became the subject of a book by Jonathan Harr, *A Civil*

Action, which was also made into a movie. Another high profile case was the 1986 nuclear disaster at the Chernobyl power station. The incidence of thyroid cancer in children who lived near the site is up to 100 times higher than normal.[40]

Yet possibly more insidious is the subtle ways in which children absorb chemicals. Dr. Sandra Steingraber, author of *Living Downstream,* points out that children can be exposed to higher amounts of any given toxin in the environment because of their fast metabolisms. Children drink 2-5 times more water than adults and consume three to four times more food relative to their body weight than adults. Fetus are particularly vulnerable because their brains are 50 percent fat by weight and chemicals often concentrate in fatty tissue. In addition, the placenta does not block or protect the fetus from absorbing chemicals.[41]

For the interested reader, a book by Professor Colleen Moore of the University of Wisconsin-Madison entitled, *Silent Scourge: Children, Pollution and Why Scientists Disagree,* is recommended. Professor Moore's book examines the impacts on children of six common pollutants, lead, mercury, PCBs, pesticides, noise and radioactive and chemical wastes. For each pollutant, she reviews the scientific evidence presented in various studies.

For those individuals and societies that are not in direct proximity to the production and use of synthetic chemicals, the combination of wind, ocean currents, and the ingestion of animals at the top of the food chain guarantees their exposure. These risks are tragically demonstrated by the plight of the people living on Broughton Island.

Broughton Island lies off Baffin Island, west of Greenland, more than 1,600 miles from the industrial cities of southern Ontario and 2,400 miles from the industrial centers of Europe. The peoples of Broughton Island have a steady diet of wild fish and game including seals, polar bears, caribou and whales. Through wind and water currents, and migrating fish and birds, the Artic has become a principal final depository of volatile persistent chemicals, manufactured and used thousands of miles away. These chemicals become concentrated, up to millions of times, as they move up the food chain to the fish and game consumed by the Broughton Islanders. Researchers have found that babies take in seven times more PCBs than the typical infant in southern Canada or the United States. Overall, people on Broughton Island have the highest levels of PCBs found in any human population with the exception of those people in an area contaminated by an industrial accident.[42]

The emphasis on illnesses caused by synthetic chemicals has focused on those chemicals that are carcinogenic or cancer causing, such as dioxin, DDT and PCBs. The *Report on Carcinogens* by the U.S. Department of Health and Human

Services lists 58 substances that are known to be human carcinogens and 188 substances as reasonably anticipated to be human carcinogens.[43] Until recently, much of the medical and epidemiological research has focused on chemicals suspected of being carcinogenic. More recently, there has been an increasing concern with chemicals acting as endocrine disruptors. In their book, *Our Stolen Future*, Theo Colborn, Dianne Dumanoski and John Peterson Myers offer a comprehensive examination of the threats of chemicals in disrupting the endocrine system.

The endocrine system produces a series of hormones that regulate the body's vital internal processes and guide critical phases of prenatal development. If the right hormones do not get to a developing fetus at the appropriate time, principal areas of development can be disrupted with disturbing results. Various studies have shown that these results can include low sperm counts, infertility, genital deformations, neurological disorders, developmental and reproductive problems, weakened immune system, and hormonally triggered human cancers, such as breast and prostate cancer.

These problems can result from exposure to low doses of chemicals, as was shown by a study of the effects lawn care pesticides on mice at the University of Wisconsin.[44] Most of the cancer epidemiology research has looked at larger dosage exposure, following "the dose makes the poison" dictum, and assumed some minimal exposure level was safe. Extrapolating low dose responses from high dose testing has been called into question by a study published in *Environmental Health Perspectives* by Wade Welshons, et. al. Other studies have shown that timing is critical. If the fetus is exposed to only a small dose of a chemical at a critical time in the fetus's development, it may be devastating, but at another time it may have no effect.[45]

Readers are recommended to examine *Our Stolen Future* for themselves, but a summation of the authors' conclusions is included here:

> "In our view, the evidence clearly indicates that these chemicals are already affecting some humans as well as many species of wildlife, but at the moment the magnitude and seriousness of this problem are still unknown. Numerous studies, however, show that astoundingly small quantities of these hormonally active compounds can wreak all manner of biological havoc, particularly in those exposed in the womb. During this creative and vulnerable time, the chemical messages carried by hormones trigger key events essential for normal development, ranging from the sexual differentiation of males to the orderly migration of nerve cells necessary for the construction of a well-functioning brain. By scrambling these hormone messages, synthetic chemicals can undermine a baby's development with consequences that will last a lifetime. Wildlife studies vividly demonstrate that these chemicals have the power to derail

sexual development, creating intersex individuals that are neither male nor female. They can sabotage fertility, erode intelligence, undermine the immune system, and alter behavior."[46]

It is clear that a myriad of adverse effects associated with synthetic chemicals have been documented or are in the process of being documented. The increasing liability risks to chemical companies is obvious. For instance, in August 2003 Monsanto and Solutia (a company spun off from Monsanto) agreed to a $700 million settlement paid to 20,000 Anniston, Alabama residents from damages resulting from PCB contamination. Insurers will pay $160 million of the damages with the companies paying the rest. The $700 million is on top of a previous $100 million already awarded by the jury in the case.[47] DuPont recently agreed to a $340 million settlement for contaminating drinking water supplies in Ohio and West Virginia with the chemical perfluo-rooctanoic acid (PFOA). This chemical has been used for years in the production of Teflon.[48] Two chemicals, perchlorate and methyl tertiary-butyl ether (MTBE), have recently received considerable attention for liability risks associated with groundwater contamination. Perchlorate is the main ingredient in solid rocket fuel used by the Pentagon and defense contractors. MTBE is an additive that oil companies added to gasoline.[49]

Liabilities of course can spread beyond manufacturers to users of chemicals. For example, the EPA has ordered General Electric spend up to $500 million to dredge toxic PCBs from the bottom sediment of the Hudson River. General Electric, which used PCBs in the manufacture of electric capacitors at its Hudson Falls and Fort Edward factories, had been permitted by New York State to dump the PCBs in the Hudson for three decades. In 1976, PCBs were banned by the U.S. Congress and the Hudson River site was declared a Superfund site in the mid 1980s. The Hudson River operation, involving dredging up an estimated 100,000 pounds of PCBs in hotspots of the total 1,000,000 pounds deposited, is the most ambitious river cleanup in U.S. history.[50] Currently the cleanup is on hold, as GE is challenging the constitutionality of parts of CERCLA (Superfund).[51] A similar situation is playing out in my home state of Wisconsin. At issue is the cleanup of PCBs deposited by paper companies into the Fox River. The potential financial costs could be in the same range as the GE—Hudson River case.

The above examples are large, dramatic cases involving substantial amounts of chemical contamination, huge corporations and hundreds of millions of dollars in damages. Based on existing and ongoing research, it seems likely that these cases may be just the tip of the iceberg. Considering how ubiquitous chemicals are in the manufacturing of hundreds of thousands of products, and their persistence in landfills, waterways, the atmosphere and living beings, the potential for liability suits is enormous:

In one of her last speeches before she died in 1964, Rachel Carson warned that:

> "This contamination has been an unprecedented experiment: We are subjecting whole populations to exposure to chemicals which animal experiments have proven to be extremely poisonous and in many cases cumulative in their effects. These exposures now begin at or before birth and—unless we change our methods—will continue through the lifetime of those now living. No one knows what the results will be because we have no previous experience to guide us."[52]

To paraphrase her from a risk management perspective—"We are involved in an unprecedented environmental liability risk experiment. No one knows what the financial impact will be because litigation is just beginning."

Possibly even more appropriate for this book is a warning concerning survival from the authors of *Our Stolen Future*:

> "Because hormone-disrupting chemicals act broadly and insidiously to sabotage fertility and development, they can jeopardize the survival of entire species—perhaps in the long run, even humans. This might be hard to imagine in a world facing soaring human numbers, but the sperm count studies suggest environmental contaminants are already having an impact on the human population as a whole, not just on individuals. In their assault on development, these chemicals have the power to erode human potential. In their assault on reproduction, they not only undermine the health and happiness of individuals suffering from infertility, they attack a fragile biological system that over billions of years of evolution has allowed life to miraculously recreate life."[53]

Social Justice Risks

Social justice refers to concepts of fairness and equity in dealing with workers, local communities and peoples in other countries. In this book, I am using social justice as an umbrella term to refer to various areas and issues. These include corporate social responsibility (CSR), social, environmental and ethical (SEE), social capital, human capital, ethics, human rights, diversity, gender equity, working conditions and compensation for workers, anti-discrimination policies, and privacy protection. Sustainability strategies for dealing with social justice risks comprise the third leg in the triple bottom line. Businesses have always been interested in economic performance, or the financial bottom line. Serious involvement by business in the environmental area has evolved over the last two-three decades, and social justice risks are the most recent area that has gained the attention of management.

Businesses face a myriad of risks in the social justice arena. Being the last to receive attention means that risk management programs for dealing with social justice risks are generally the least developed. Many companies still do not feel that businesses should pay any heed to this area, following the dictum of Milton Friedman that "the social responsibility of business is to make profits". The main business objective should be to maximize the value to shareholders. It was traditionally felt that only the government was responsible for dealing with social fairness and equity concerns through programs like progressive taxation, welfare, Social Security and national health insurance.

Today, businesses must deal with social justice risks that subject them to liability suits, boycotts, and shareholder actions with resulting damage to their reputations and brand values. In 1996, Texaco agreed to pay out $176 million to settle a race-discrimination suit. More recently, Wal-Mart, the world's largest company on the basis of revenues, is currently involved in the largest class action gender discrimination suit ever filed, because of its alleged poor treatment, compensation and promotion of its women workers. In June of 2004, a federal judge in California gave the green light to a class action on the behalf of 1.6 million women who have worked at Wal-Mart since December 1998. This could result in a liability judgment or settlement in the billions of dollars and substantial damage to Wal-Mart's reputation and future revenues.[54] Within a few days of each other in July 2004, Morgan Stanley settled for $54,000,000 and Boeing settled for up to $72,500,000 in discrimination suits brought by their female employees, again involving compensation and promotion discrepancies.[55] Other large past gender discrimination settlements include State Farm in 1992 for $157,000,000 and Voice of America for $508,000,000.[56]

Merrill Lynch has worked since 1996 to resolve gender discrimination cases by over 900 women. Some 95 percent of the cases have been settled at a cost of more than $100 million. In August 2004, a federal district judge dealt a blow to Merrill's efforts to control the remainder of the unresolved cases by ruling that plaintiffs can consider a finding in a previous case that the firm engaged in "a pattern and practice of discrimination" against women who worked in its brokerage operations.[57] In April 2005, UBS, Europe's largest bank, was ordered by a federal jury in New York to pay $29 million to Laura Zubulake for sex discrimination.[58]

Recent rule changes in the European Union are expected to produce a substantial increase in gender discrimination suits. Britain, which incorporated some of the rule changes before the EU rule goes into effect in October 2005, has experienced a substantial increase in gender discrimination actions.[59]

Injuries to workers are one of the more common social justice risks. Workers compensation laws obligate employers to pay for their employees injuries by providing compensation for lost wages and medical expenses. If corporations do not provide a safe working environment, their workers compensation costs can be high. Companies or industries can also incur risks beyond workers compensation. For instance, a report released in 2005 by the Human Rights Watch (HRW) harshly criticized the meat packing industry. The report entitled, "Blood, Sweat and Fear: Workers' Rights in U.S. Meat and Poultry Plants," marked the first time HRW has criticized a single industry in the United States. The report concludes that the worker conditions are so bad that they violate basic human rights. Three companies are highlighted: Tyson Foods for poultry, Smithfield Foods for pork, and Nebraska Beef. The report illustrates that corporations can incur substantial negative publicity and reputation damage, in addition to high workers compensation costs, for providing unsafe working conditions.[60]

Globalization has had a substantial impact on bringing awareness to social inequities. No longer can a company say that it received raw materials from an overseas supplier or finished products from an overseas contractor, without consideration given to how these suppliers or contractors are treating their workers. As the Nike situation demonstrates (see Chapter 3), considerable business and reputation damage can result by not knowing this information. Claims being brought under the Alien Tort Claims Act are producing additional risks for U.S. companies from activities in foreign countries (see Chapter 5 and 10).

The World Health Organization (WHO) warns that urban areas in Asia are growing so fast that economies, services and infrastructures cannot cope. Increases are expected in disease, crime, violence, environmental degradation, pollution, poverty, and unhealthy lifestyles. World-wide urban areas are gaining around 67 million people a year, and by 2030, 60 percent of the projected world population of 8.3 million people will live in cities.[61] These pressures all increase social justice risks for global corporations.

The country of Bangladesh, with a population of 130 million people, squeezed into an area the size of Wisconsin, with people living on a dollar a day, is almost an urbanized city-country onto itself. The people of Bangladesh are suffering the twin afflictions of arsenic-contaminated water and the Asian Brown Cloud. Some 35 million are drinking arsenic-contaminated water, most likely due to natural processes, taken from tube wells. Mistakes in the original testing of the well water and poor information systems to warn the people are resulting in what the World Health Organization calls the "largest mass poisoning of a population in history.[62] The Asian Brown Cloud is a blanket of pollution and particles, primarily from biomass (wood and dung used in household stoves) burning and industrial emissions(coal burning plants), that spreads across Afghanistan, Pakistan, India, and Sri Lanka, as well as Bangladesh. The cloud disrupts weather patterns, damages crops and results in premature deaths from respiratory diseases.[63] The low lying land in Bangladesh is also particularly susceptible to rising sea levels produced by global warming.

Equity across generations is an important social justice goal and essential component of sustainable development. Today's generation should satisfy its needs, but not at the expense of using more than its fair share of natures resources. Leaving our children with our debts and imperiling their ability to take advantage of the world's ecosystem services is fundamentally unfair and unjust.

Business cannot be expected to solve all social inequities. Governments must also be involved, but unlike a few years ago, corporations must help to solve these inequities, particularly ones that are directly connected to their respective businesses. Some sobering statistics from a United Nations report demonstrate why both businesses and governments will need to employ all their energies to deal with the world's social inequities.

1. The world's population is 6.2 billion people. Around 20 percent or 1.2 billion live on less than $1 a day. Half the world's population exists on less than $2 a day.

2. More than two thirds of the world's population, or 4.4 billion people, live in developing countries. Of this group, nearly 60 percent lack basic sanitation, almost a third do not have access to clean water, one quarter lack adequate housing, 20 percent do not have access to modern health services, and 20 percent of the children do not attend school through grade five. Developing countries also tend to have the highest population growth, which compounds these problems.

3. Unclean water and associated poor sanitation kill over 12 million people each year.

4. Indoor air pollution-soot from the burning of wood, dung, crop residues, and coal for cooking and heating are estimated to kill more than 2.2 million each year.

5.   The world's richest countries, with 20 percent of the global population, account for 86 percent of total private consumption, whereas the poorest 20 percent of the world's people account for just 1.3 percent of total private consumption.

6.   A child born today in an industrialized country will add more to consumption and pollution over his or her lifetime than 30 to 50 children born in the developing countries.[64]

A survey by the *Wall Street Journal* of Nobel prize winners in economics asked them to list the World's greatest economic challenge. Several mentioned poverty and disease in poorer countries. As noted by Laurence Klein of the University of Pennsylvania, "The reduction of poverty and disease in a peaceful political environment is the challenge of our lifetime."[65] Bill Gates, CEO of Microsoft, the world's richest person, has been actively involved through his foundation in attempting to alleviate world poverty and disease. He has been particularly upset by the lack of resources committed to Africa by the rich countries. Gates states:

> "Millions of children die in Africa who shouldn't die, who it would be very easy to save. The fact that we don't apply the resources to the known cures or to finding better cures is really...the most scandalous issue of our time."[66]

While not at the same level, similar inequities exist in the United States. For instance, the gap between the rich and poor more than doubled from 1979 to 2000, according to data from the Congressional Budget Office. The data shows that the richest one percent of Americans in 2000 had more money to spend after taxes than the total of the bottom 40 percent. In 1979, the richest one percent had just under half of the total after-tax income of the bottom 40 percent of Americans. The gap in 2000 is the largest between the rich and poor for any year since 1979, the year the budget office began this data, according to the Center for Budget and Policy Priorities.[67] Economists Thomas Piketty and Emmanuel Saez, using IRS data, calculated that the share of income going to the top one percent in 2002 was 14.7 percent, nearly double the amount in the 1970s. This is the highest percentage for the top one percent since the 1920s.[68]

Since the Bush Administration's tax cuts were enacted in 2001, several recent studies show corporations and the wealthy paying a smaller share of the total tax burden.[69] An August, 2004 study by the nonpartisan Congressional Budget Office found that one-third of the tax cut benefits went to the top one percent in income, who earn an average of $1.2 million annually. Their share of the total tax burden fell from 21.9 percent to 20.1 percent. For the middle incomes around $75,600, their tax burden jumped from 18.7 percent to 19.5 percent of all taxes paid.[70]

Differences also exist between the pay for men and women, and the compensation between top executives and ordinary workers. The median pay for all women in 2002 was $30,203, or 76.6 percent of the median compensation of $39,429 for men.[71] This disparity holds for female executives as well as lower level workers. A *Business Week* study documented the differences between men and women in salary and other compensation. A survey was taken of 1,500 alums from the top 30 business schools, who received their MBAs in 1992. A decade later the average salary of women executives was $117,000 or 70 percent of the average salary of $168,000 for the male alums. In the 'other compensation' category, women on the average received $84,000 or only 31 percent of the men's other compensation of $273,000.[72] A study released in 2005, by the Census Bureau, showed that women with bachelor's degrees averaged $38,000 in 2003, or only 60 percent of the $63,000 earned by men with bachelors' degrees.[73]

The gap between the compensation of the top executives and ordinary workers has also increased. A generation ago, the average pay of CEOs at major companies was only 40 times that of an average worker. Today it is 500 times as much.[74] A 2000 study by Towers Perrin showed that CEOs at large U.S. corporations earned 531 times what their hourly employees did on average.[75]

While arguments were made, during the soaring stock markets in the 1990s, that executives were worth this much, the precipitous drop in the markets dampened these arguments. In addition, a basic fairness issue is raised when the disparities between top level executives and workers become so large. The fairness issue becomes especially troublesome when workers are laid off or when executives continue to make high levels of compensation, even when their companies are performing poorly.

To maximize the value to shareholders today requires that management pay attention to all three segments of the triple bottom line: financial performance, environmental performance and social justice performance. Stakeholders including customers, employees, suppliers, NGOs, charities and local communities, must be engaged and treated fairly in ways that engender respect, dignity, trust and honesty. Failure to do so will result in social justice risk costs that will reduce financial performance below the maximum potential values for shareholders.

Shifting Balance of Values

Clearly, we are not considering the equalization of compensation for all the world's peoples or all workers and managers in the United States. But a balance exists that suggests a more reasonable distribution of compensation, consumption and use of natural resources. Ten to 20 years ago, only a small minority of businesses felt that such equity adjustments were within their realm or responsibility. Today, a critical mass of companies support the concept that social justice issues are within the realm of corporate responsibility. Litigation mentioned above and pressure from NGOs and other organizations have produced incentives for managing social justice risks.

More fundamentally, a shift in values has occurred. Many consultants and business leaders have talked or written about this shift. One of the most profound thinkers is John Elkington, founder and chairman of Europe's top sustainability consulting firm. A quote from his book, *Cannibals with Forks,* eloquently captures this shift in values:

> "The nature of the problem, I believe, is that we are seeing a profound values shift in countries around the world. For the most part, this is not something that is being regulated: instead, it is happening as a natural outgrowth of people's evolving awareness and concern. And a key dimension of this shift is the way in which what would have been seen as "soft" values (such as concern for future generations) are now coming in alongside-and sometimes even overriding-traditional "hard" values (such as the paramount importance of the financial bottom line)."[76]

Time to Act

As I was completing this chapter in the spring of 2005, the *Millennium Ecosystem Assessment Synthesis* was released. This report was carried out by over 2,000 professions from around the world under the auspices of the United Nations. The governing board is comprised of international institutions, governments, businesses, NGOs and indigenous peoples. The Millennium Assessment confirms the studies and information presented in this chapter. The four main findings are:

- Over the past 50 years, humans have changed ecosystems more rapidly and extensively than in any comparable period of time in human history, largely to meet rapidly growing demands for food, fresh water, timber, fiber and fuel. This has resulted in a substantial and largely irreversible loss in the diversity of life on Earth.

- The changes that have been made to ecosystems have contributed to substantial net gains in human well-being and economic development, but these gains have been achieved at growing costs in the form of the degradation of many ecosystem services, increased risks of nonlinear changes, and the exacerbation of poverty for some groups of people. These problems, unless addressed, will substantially diminish the benefits that future generations obtain from ecosystems.

- The degradation of ecosystem services could grow significantly worse during the first half of this century and is a barrier to achieving the Millennium Development Goals.

- The challenge of reversing the degradation of ecosystems while meeting increasing demands for their services can be partially met under some scenarios that the MA has considered but these involve significant changes in policies, institutions and practices, that are not currently under way. Many options exist to conserve or enhance specific ecosystem services in ways that reduce negative trade-offs or that provide positive synergies with other ecosystem services.[77]

This chapter was not meant to merely portray dooms day scenarios, but hopefully it has provided ample evidence of the seriousness of the risks we face. We are on an unsustainable path regarding the consumption of ecosystem services, extinction of species, exposure to harmful substances, and social inequities. The good news is that we have time and we can successfully manage these escalating sustainability risks. But the time to act is now.

I do not mean to imply that nothing is being done. Some businesses are serving as role models in developing sound sustainability risk management strategies to respond to these increasing risks. Examples of these businesses and their methods are discussed throughout this book. Given what I see as the inevitability of the need to respond, prudent management suggests that resources be allotted today to begin to strengthen sustainability risk management programs. I anticipate a raft of advantages to acting now and significant costs to delaying action. Participating in your own survival requires developing sustainability risk management programs today. In this book, I am focusing on business firms surviving and prospering by managing and controlling their increasing sustainability risks. But of course, we are ultimately concerned with the survival of ecosystems and social systems, on which we all depend to live.

CHAPTER 1—ENDNOTES

[1] Robert Constanza, et.al., "The Value of the World's Ecosystem Services and the Natural Capital," *Nature*, Vol. 387, 15 May, 1997.

[2] Ibid.

[3] Jim Morrison, "How Much is Clean Water Worth?," *National Wildlife*, February/March, 2005.

[4] Ibid.

[5] Gary Polakovic, "Humans are Using up Nature," *Los Angeles Times* reported in *Capital Times*, June 26, 2002.

[6] Mathis Wackernagel, et.al., "Tracking the Ecological Overshoot of the Human Economy," *Proceedings of the National Academy of Sciences*, Vol. 99, No. 14, July 9, 2002.

[7] Ransom Meyers and Boris Worm, "Rapid Worldwide Depletion of Predatory Fish Communities," *Nature*, Vol. 423, 15 May 2003.

[8] Pew Oceans Commission, "America's Living Oceans: Charting a Course for Sea Change," May, 2003.

[9] Jim Carlton, "Drastic U.S. Actions Are Urged To Save Coasts From Overfishing," *Wall Street Journal*, June 5, 2003.

[10] Worldwatch Institute, *State of the World 2002*; Global Coral Reef Monitoring Network (GCRMN).

[11] Global Coral Reef Monitoring Network, *Status of Coral Reefs of the World*, Townsville, Queensland Australia: Australian Institute of Marine Science, 2004.

[12] Ocean Conservancy, *Health of the Oceans Report*, 2002.

[13] Worldwatch Institute, *State of the World 2002*.

[14] Peter N. Spotts and Kenneth R. Weiss, "Study Delves Into Troubled Waters; America's Treatment of its Oceans Under Scrutiny," *Population Press,* Summer 2003.

[15] Felicity Barringer, "Federal Oceans Commission Finds Decline Along Coast," *New York Times,* April 21, 2004.

[16] Parts of this section based on following sources: U.S. Commission on Ocean Policy, *Preliminary Reports,* April 2004; Felicity Barringer, "Federal Oceans Commission Finds Decline Along Coasts," *New York Times,* April 21, 2004; "Bottom-of-the-Sea Treaty," *Wall Street Journal,* March 29, 2004; Kenneth R. Weiss, *L.A. Times,* "Oceans are hurting, panel says," *Capital Times,* April 21, 2004.

[17] Cornelia Dean, "Bush Forms Panel to Coordinate Ocean Policy," *New York Times,* December 18, 2004.

[18] United Nations, *Global Challenge, Global Opportunity,* 2002.

[19] Worldwatch Institute, *State of the World 2002.*

[20] B.L. Morris, et.al., *Groundwater and Its Susceptibility to Degradation: A Global Assessment of the Problem and Options for Management,* United Nations Environment Program, 2003.

[21] Information for parts of this section from Michael Janofsky, "In the Dry Dry West, A Search for a Solution," *New York Times,* June 2, 2003; www.fire.ca.gov/php/fire_er_siege.php; John Shaw, "Ruinous Drought in Australia Called the Worst in 100 Years," *New York Times,* November 24, 2002; Jim Carlton, "A Lake Shrinks, Threatening Mexican Region," *Wall Street Journal,* September 3, 2003.

[22] U.S. Interior Department's Bureau of Reclamation, "Water 2025: Preventing Crises and Conflict in the West," 2003.

[23] UNEP Financial Initiative and Stockholm International Water Institute," *Risks of Water Scarcity: A Business Case for Financial Institutions,* Stockholm: Swedish International Development Agency, 2004; Roz Bulleid, "Investors

Warned of Potential Water Resource Risks," *Environmental Finance,* September 2004.

[24] Data and information from Worldwatch Institute, *State of the World 2002*; United Nations, *Global Challenge—Global Opportunity,* 2002.

[25] Information for this section taken from Larry Rohter, "Amazon Forest Is Still Burning, Despite Pledges," *New York Times,* August 23, 2002; Tony Smith, "Rain Forest Is Losing Ground Faster in Amazon, Photos Show," *New York Times,* June 28, 2003; Larry Rohter, "Relentless Foe of the Amazon Jungle: Soybeans," *New York Times,* September 17, 2003; Matt Moffett, "Brazil's President Sees New Growth In The Rain Forest," *New York Times,* October 16, 2003; "Destruction of Brazil's Rain Forest Seems to Slow," *New York Times,* April 8, 2004; "Amazon destruction in 2004 2nd worst ever," *Capital Times,* May 19, 2005.

[26] United Nations Convention to Combat Desertification reported in Chris Hawley, Associated Press, "A Third of Earth's Land at Risk of Becoming Desert," *Capital Times,* June 16, 2004.

[27] www.eces.org

[28] United Nations Environment Programme, "The Global Environmental Outlook—3 (GEO-3)," 2002.

[29] J.A. Thomas, et.al., "Comparative Losses of British Butterflies, Birds, and Plants and the Global Extinction Crises," *Science,* Vol. 303, 19 March 2004.

[30] C.D. Thomas, et. al., "Extinction Risk from Climate Change," *Nature,* 427, January 8, 2004; see Chapter 7 for further discussion of this study.

[31] Simon N. Stuart, et.al., "Status and Trends of Amphibian Declines and Extinctions Worldwide," *Science,* Vol. 306, December 3, 2004.

[32] www.eces.org

[33] UN report summarized at www.eces.org

[34] Theo Colborn, Dianne Dumanoski and John Peter Myers, *Out Stolen Future,* New York: Plume Penquin, 1997; William McDonough and Michael Braungart, *Cradle to Cradle,* New York: North Point Press, 2002.

[35] Theo Colborn, Dianne Dumanoski and John Peter Myers, *Out Stolen Future,* New York: Plume Penquin, 1997.

[36] Ibid.

[37] "Canaries in the Cancer Wards," *Toronto Globe & Mail,* February 22, 2003.

[38] EPA, *America's Children and the Environment,* US Environmental Protection Agency, 2003.

[39] Miguel Bustillo, Los Angeles Times, in "Smog to blame for lifetime lung damage," printed in *The Capital Times,* September 9, 2004; Gauderman, W. James, et. al., "The Effect of Air Pollution on Lung Development from 10 to 18 Years of Age," *The New England Journal of Medicine,* Volume 351, No. 11, September 9, 2004.

[40] "Canaries in the Cancer Wards," *Toronto Globe & Mail,* February 22, 2003.

[41] Ibid.

[42] Theo Colborn, Dianne Dumanoski and John Peter Myers, *Out Stolen Future,* New York: Plume Penquin, 1997.

[43] U.S. Department of HHS, *Report on Carcinogens,* 11th edition, 2005.

[44] Maria Fernanda Cavieres, James Jaeger and Warren Porter, "Developmental Toxicity of a Commercial Herbicide Mixture in Mice: I. Effects on Embryo Implantation and Litter Size," *Environmental Health Perspectives,* Vol. 110, No. 11, November 2002.

[45] Wade V. Welshons, et.al., "Large Effects from Small Exposures, I. Mechanisms for Endocrine-Disrupting Chemicals with Estrongenic Activity," *Environmental Health Perspectives,* Vol. 111, No. 8, June 2003.

[46] Theo Colborn, Dianne Dumanoski and John Peter Myers, *Out Stolen Future,* New York: Plume Penquin, 1997.

[47] "$700 Million Settlement in Alabama PCB Lawsuit," *New York Times,* August 21, 2003.

[48] Jared Wade, "Easy Being Green," *Risk Management,* July 2005; Thaddeus Herrick, "EPA says Teflon Chemical May Pose Health Risk," *Wall Street Journal,* January 13, 2005.

[49] Liane Jackson, "Factory Site Faces Tidal Wave of Toxic Tort Complaints," *Corporate Legal Times,* Vol. 13, No. 141, August 2003; Alexei Barrionuevo, "Oil Companies Lose Effort to End Suits Over Contaminated Water," *New York Times,* April 21, 2005.

[50] Kirk Johnson, "G.E. Facing Order To Remove Toxins From Hudson River," *New York Times,* December 6, 2000.

[51] "GE Challenge to Superfund Can Move Forward," *Business & Legal Reports,* March 17, 2004.

[52] Theo Colborn, Dianne Dumanoski and John Peter Myers, *Out Stolen Future,* New York: Plume Penquin, 1997.

[53] Ibid.

[54] Ann Zimmerman, "Judge Certifies Wal-Mart Suit As Class Action," *Wall Street Journal,* June 23, 2004

[55] Kate Kelly and Colleen DeBaise, "Morgan Stanley Settles Bias Suit for $54 Million," *Wall Street Journal,* July 13, 2004; J. Lynn Lunsford, "To Settle Sex-Bias Suit, Boeing Agrees to Pay Up to $72.5 million," *Wall Street Journal,* July 19, 2004.

[56] Advisen Insight for Insurance Professionals, August 20, 2004.

[57] Patrick McGeehan, "Court Makes Merrill's Past Part of Sex Bias Arbitration," *New York Times,* August 4, 2004

[58] Eduardo Porter, "USB Ordered to Pay $29 million in Sex Bias Lawsuit," *New York Times,* April 7, 2005.

[59] Kerry Capell, Laura Cohn, Rachel Tiplady, and Jack Ewing, "Sex-Bias Suits: The Fight Gets Ugly," *Business Week*, September 6, 2004.

[60] Steven Greenhouse, "Rights Group Condemns Meatpackers On Job Safe," *New York Times,* January 26, 2005.

[61] Associated Press, "WHO Warns on Asian City Pollution," *Wall Street Journal,* October 15, 2003.

[62] Barry Bearak, "'The Largest Mass Poisoning' of people in History," *International Herald Tribune,* July 15, 2002.

[63] United Nations Environmental Program, "The Asian Brown Cloud: Climate and Other Environmental Impacts," 2002.

[64] United Nations Population Fund, 2001

[65] David Wessel & Marcus Walker, "Good News for the Globe," *Wall Street Journal,* September 3, 2004.

[66] Paul Haven, "Gates: African Poverty's 'scandalous'," *Associated Press,* in *Capital Times,* January 27, 2005.

[67] Lynnley Browning, "U.S. Income Gap Widening, Study Says," *The New York Times*, September 25, 2003.

[68] Steven Rattner, "The Rich Get (Much) Richer," *Business Week*, August 8, 2005.

[69] Edmund L. Andrews, "Big Gap Found in Taxation of Wages and Investments," *New York Times,* May 8, 2004; Justin Lahart, "Corporate Tax Burden Shows Sharp Decline," *Wall Street Journal,* April 13, 2004; John McKinnon, "Many Companies Avoided Taxes Even as Profits Soared in Boom," *Wall Street Journal,* April 6, 2004.

[70] Edmund L. Andrews, "Report Finds Tax Cuts Heavily Favor the Wealthy," *New York Times,* August 13, 2004; Jonathan Weisman, *Washington Post,* "Bush cuts shift more taxes to middle class, report finds," *Capital Times,* August 13, 2004.

[71] U.S. Census Bureau, *Income in the United States,* 2002.

[72] Jennifer Merritt, "What's An MBA Really Worth?" *Business Week,* September 22, 2003.

[73] "Data Show Gaps in Women's Income," *Wall Street Journal,* March 28, 2005.

[74] Paul Krugman, "The Outrage Constraint", *New York Times,* August 23, 2002.

[75] Gretchen Morgenson, "Explaining (or Not) Why the Boss Is Paid So Much," *New York Times,* January 25, 2004.

[76] John Elkington, *Cannibals with Forks,* Gabriola Island BC, Canada: New Society Publishers, 1998.

[77] *Millennium Ecosystem Assessment Synthesis Report,* 2005, www.millennium assessment.org.

2

EXPANDING LIABILITIES FOR SUSTAINABILITY RISKS

o o o o o o o o o o o o o o o o o o o o o o o o o o o o o

No matter how successful some companies may be in devising "stealth" strategies to mask what they are doing, or intend to do, most businesses will increasingly operate in a high-visibility environment. International business will find that the Internet will enormously increase the geographical reach and magnifying (and distorting) power of the goldfish bowl.

*—John Elkington, author of **Cannibals with Forks***

The biggest emerging risk for insurance groups world-wide is the proliferation of the U.S. tort system or elements of it.

—Raj Singh, Chief Risk Officer, Allianz

All firms are subject to a variety of liabilities. These derive from such sources as operating automobiles, ownership of land and property, employment and treatment of workers, manufacturing products, providing professional services, as well as conducting activities that may result in environmental damages. To date, the most dollar liabilities from sustainability risks have originated from the Superfund program and asbestos liabilities (see Chapter 6). Some non-Superfund third party environmental suits have resulted in liabilities. These suits have been relatively moderate to date with a few exceptions (see examples in Chapter 1), but that can be expected to change dramatically in the future. Several developments in the social justice area are also putting litigation pressure on corporations.

These developments, which portend increased environmental and social justice liabilities, are the subject of this chapter.

Traditional Basis for Environmental Liabilities

Outside of Superfund, most environmental liability cases to date have been brought under the common law torts of trespass and nuisance. In short, a tort is a "common law civil wrong for which a court will provide a remedy."[1] Trespass is interference with the possession of property. In environmental situations, contamination, which has migrated to an adjacent property, would be an example of trespass. Nuisance involves an unreasonable or unwarranted use of one's own property that causes a material injury, annoyance or discomfort to the public. Noise or odors emitting from a person's or company's property are common examples of environmental litigation based on nuisance. Nuisance cases can also involve dust, smoke, water pollutants and hazardous substances.

The line between nuisance and trespass is often difficult to delineate. The distinction is captured in the statement from Prosser and Keeton that "trespass is an invasion of the plaintiff's interest in the exclusive possession of his (her) land, while nuisance is an interference with his (her) use and enjoyment of it."[2] Trespass to land is the most common basis on which environmental liability suits have been brought. Under both trespass and nuisance, it is not necessary to prove that the defendant was negligent. The conditions for a trespass or nuisance claim need to be established and connected to the harm done to the plaintiff.

Due to the burden of determining liability based on negligence, trespass and nuisance have been preferred in environmental cases. I feel that liability based on negligence for sustainability risks will become much more common and will require increased attention by risk managers in the future.

Liability Based on Negligence

Typically the general source of most liabilities are those based on the tort of negligence. Four steps are needed to establish liability based on negligence. These four steps are:

1. A duty exists to act in a reasonable and prudent manner.

2. A breach of this duty, i.e., failure to act in a reasonable and prudent manner.

3. Injuries and/or damages are sustained by another party.

4. The breach of duty, i.e., failure to act in a reasonable and prudent manner, is the proximate cause of the injuries/damages.

When these four steps are established, then an individual or business can be held liable and obligated to pay for another's party's injuries/damages.

It is important to note that an individual or business can be negligent without being liable. Steps one and two above-the existence of a duty and the breach of that duty-would constitute negligence. For instance, a person may drive recklessly, which is a negligent act, but if no one is injured, then no liability or responsibility will exist. The negligent act must be connected through proximate cause with the injuries/damages.

In the environmental and social justice areas, a number of developments have the potential to greatly expand liability based on negligence. The standards for negligence are increasing, the concepts for injuries/damages are expanding, and methods for connecting negligence with injuries/damages through proximate cause are improving. Each of these elements of expanding liability will be discussed below.

Increasing Negligence Standards

When establishing the bar for determining negligence, the behavior of a potential negligent party is typically compared to the behavior of other comparable parties. A party is held to be negligent, if his/her behavior is held to not be reasonable and prudent, based on the behavior or standard of care set by other comparable parties. For instance, in determining medical malpractice, a doctor's actions generally are measured against those of doctors in the same area of specialization.

For sustainability risks, a company's record, performance or actions generally would be compared to those of other similar companies to determine negligence. But what would be the measures of reasonable and prudent behavior? In recent years a number of standards to measure environmental and social justice performance have evolved. One of the more prominent is ISO 14000.

ISO 14000, issued by the Geneva, Switzerland based International Organization for Standardization, is a "series of management system standards, covering such areas as process documentation, training, life-cycle assessment procedures and management reporting, and accountability for environmental performance."[3] It is designed to bring "environmental management into the realm of strategic decision making," and requires "top management commitment to environmental management."[4] Section 14001 creates the specific standards for environmental management systems. ISO 14001 certification is particularly important in Europe and Japan, where it is often seen as a necessary requirement for business transactions.[5] (See Chapter 9)

A closely related set of environmental requirements/standards is set forth by the European Union in the Eco-Management Audit Scheme (EMAS). The main difference between EMAS and ISO 14001 is EMAS has additional and more stringent requirements, including the requirement that the certification statement itself, as well as specific information verifying continual performance improvement, be made public[6]

Let us assume a firm has been involved in a situation that resulted in environmental damages. In addition, the company is not ISO 14001 or EMAS certified. In arriving at a finding of negligence, courts or juries may hold that the company did not meet the reasonable and prudent standard because it was not ISO 14001 or EMAS certified. This would be particularly true if competitors within the firm's industry did have such certification.

Standards set by voluntary environmental business organizations could also be used in determining negligence. For instance, the Coalition for Environmentally Responsible Economies (CERES) is a nonprofit organization established in the U.S. in 1989, which sets forth a set of 10 environmental principles for member organizations (see Chapter 9). The titles of the 10 CERES principles are included below:

1. Protection of the Biosphere
2. Sustainable Use of Natural Resources
3. Reduction and Disposal of Wastes
4. Energy Conservation
5. Risk Reduction

6. Safe Products and Services
7. Environmental Restoration
8. Informing the Public
9. Management Commitment
10. Audits and Reports

Using the same scenario above, the 10 CERES principles could be used as standards in determining reasonable and prudent behavior. If a firm was not a member of CERES, or it was determined that its actions fell below the standard of care set forth by CERES principles, its actions may be found to be negligent.

In the social justice area, certification programs also exist. For instance, Social Accountability (SA) 8000 is a system for measuring corporate social accountability. It is a global and verifiable standard used by over 30 industries, which combines management systems of the ISO with conventions of the International Labor Organization. Its principal purpose is to make the workplace more humane. Account Ability (AA) 1000 is another program that defines best practice in social and ethical auditing, accounting and reporting. Actions brought against corporations for social justice risks may use standards as set forth in SA 8000 or AA 1000 to establish negligence (see Chapter 9).

Efforts of competitors in the firm's industry may also be used as a measure of reasonable and prudent actions. For instance, in the paper industry, many companies have removed elemental chlorine in their paper bleaching process. Chlorine can cause injuries to workers and damage to the environment. A paper firm involved in liability litigation, which had not removed chlorine, may be determined to not have acted in a reasonable and prudent manner.

A flame retardant, polybrominated diphenyl ether (PBDE), is causing concern today because studies document that it is showing up in women's breast milk. Rather than wait for more testing, Swedish furniture maker, IKEA, and computer makers, Apple Computer and Hewlett-Packard, have stopped using PBDE. If problems develop, competitors in the furniture and computer industries, who continued to use PBDE, may be held to these companies' standard of care in determining negligence.[7]

Product manufacturers need to pay attention to systems such as Design for Environment (DFE) and Life Cycle Assessment (LCA), or ideas discussed by William McDonough and Michael Braungart in their ground breaking book, *Cradle To Cradle* (see Chapter 9). These systems and ideas emphasize examining the entire product cycle from raw materials through disposal in an effort to design products that minimize environmental damages, as well as worker and customer injuries. Again, a manufacturer involved in product liability litigation, which had not incorporated such systems into its product development, may face a greater chance of being found negligent.

Another test for the reasonable and prudent standard to determine negligence is the foreseeability test. Basically, this test states that if a company could have reasonably foreseen that its actions or activities would result in injuries/damages, then its actions/activities will be held to be negligent. Today hundreds, even thousands, of NGOs are bringing campaigns against corporations. A frequent reason for these campaigns is that NGOs are claiming that the actions of corporations are damaging or have the potential for damaging the environment or workers or communities. For instance, many groups are pointing out the potential damages of genetically modified foods and crops (see Chapter 8). If future damages occur, it will be difficult for a company to claim that they could not have foreseen the damages, as NGOs had been warning them about such damages for years.

The standards of care in determining negligence for sustainability risks are rising. Sound corporate strategy calls for companies to develop or improve their sustainability risk management systems. Certification program standards, voluntary sustainability business organizations, warnings by NGOs and higher government standards all are combining to raise the bar on what constitutes reasonable and prudent actions.

To date, rising negligence standards have yet to result in a documented high volume of sustainability litigation. But corporations which ignore these trends do so at their own peril. A fundamental tenet of sound risk management is to anticipate liability trends before they materialize into liability claims. Taking a proactive approach will reduce or eliminate the probability of these increasing negligence standards resulting in sustainability litigation.

Expanded Scope of Injuries/Damages

Injuries/damages can be categorized as specific, general or punitive. Specific injuries/damages include such items as medical expenses, loss of wages and property damages. The dollar amounts assigned to these injuries/damages are objective, measurable, and often determined by a specific bill or estimate. They are sometimes referred to as economic losses.

General injuries/damages include pain and suffering, emotional distress and loss of consortium. The dollar amounts assigned to these injuries/damages are non-measurable and subjective. These are sometimes referred to as non-economic losses. The expanding scope of both specific and general damages have the potential to increase sustainability liabilities.

In the environmental area, a good example of a specific environmental damage would be natural resource damages. Superfund and the Oil Pollution Act (OPA) define natural resources broadly to include "land, fish, wildlife, biota, air, water, ground water, drinking water supplies, and other such resources." Natural resource damages are for "injury to, destruction of, or loss of natural resources, including the reasonable costs of a damage assessment." The measure of damages is the "cost of restoring injured resources to their baseline condition, compensation for the interim loss of injured resources pending recovery, and the reasonable cost of a damage assessment."[8] Most natural resource damage cases are brought through Superfund and the OPA, but actions can also be brought by states and Native American tribes, as well as private citizens through common law actions.[9]

Another type of specific environmental damage are damages to ecosystem services. Ecosystem services would include the maintenance of a livable atmosphere, gas regulation through the oxygen—carbon dioxide exchange, forest products, marine life, flood control, nutrient boasting systems like nitrogen fixation, greenhouse gas regulation, freshwater systems, erosion control, waste processing, recreation, tourism, and aesthetic/spiritual experiences. While we might have to construct an infrastructure, like drilling a well to bring up water from an aquifer, water provided by groundwater ecosystems is essentially provided without cost.

Given the pressures we are putting on ecosystems, which is discussed in Chapter 1, these estimated values can be expected to increase as shortages develop. At some point, litigation by plaintiffs, adversely affected by loss of ecosystem services, against responsible parties for damaging these ecosystems, could explode. If only a fraction of the value of ecosystem services enters the liability system as damages, the costs could be enormous. Companies, which have done little or nothing to improve their environmental management systems and to mitigate damages to ecosystems, will be particularly vulnerable to liability suits.

Damages are also capable of expansion. Traditionally, general damages had to be associated with a specific injury/damage, like the pain and suffering accompanying a broken arm or loss of consortium resulting from the death of a spouse. Fear of an anticipated future injury/damage did not qualify for general damages. But that situation has changed, as a recent case before the U.S. Supreme Court illustrates.

The case involved asbestos injuries. The question that was brought before the U.S. Supreme Court dealt with whether employees with non-cancerous asbestos related diseases can sue for fear of developing cancer, such as mesothelioma. The court held 5-4 for the right to sue for fear of developing cancer. The breakdown of the judges was unusual. The five judges, Ginsburg, Scalia, Souter, Stevens, and Thomas voted in the majority and four judges Breyer, Kennedy, O'Connor, Rehnquist voted in the minority. This line up and result were unpredictable. It demonstrates that sustainability related liabilities may be expanded by surprising Supreme Court decisions—in this case it involved altering the scope of injuries.[10]

Punitive damages are assessed in a small minority of cases, where the behavior of the party causing the injuries is reckless, egregious, reprehensible, without regard of public health and safety, willful or wanton. Courts sometimes refer to the gross negligence of the defendant. The assessment of punitive damages acts as a punishment in the form of additional monies that must be paid by the defendant. Punitive damages are also meant to change behavior or act as a deterrent to acting in a similar manner in the future.

One of the most famous environmental cases involving punitive damages is the Exxon Valdez case. Following the incredible oil spill damage done to Prince

William Sound by the breakup of the Exxon Valdez on a reef in 1989, a jury, in 1994, awarded 32,000 plaintiffs $5 billion in punitive damages. The plaintiffs consisted of fishermen, communities, businesses and landowners. Exxon had already paid $300 million in specific damages, $2.2 billion in cleanup costs and $1 billion in settlements with the state and federal governments.

Exxon (now ExxonMobil) appealed the case and in 2001, a three judge panel of the United States Court of Appeals for the Ninth Circuit ruled the $5 billion punitive damage award was excessive and returned it to federal district judge Russell Holland. Holland reduced the award to $4 billion and it was again appealed. In August 2003, the United States Court of Appeals for the Ninth Circuit ruled that $4 billion was still excessive. Guidelines from U.S. Supreme Court cases suggest an amount in the range of 1:1 to 1:10, for the ratio of specific damages to punitive damages. Given $300 million in specific damages, this would suggest a punitive damage award in the range of $300 million to $3 billion. Using an alternative calculation for specific damages, ExxonMobil has argued that $25 million would be appropriate. Judge Russell Holland, in January 2004, set punitive damages at $4.5 billion, which ExxonMobil appealed.[11] The case is still being played out. Whatever the final outcome, ExxonMobil has sustained substantial reputation damage.

Expanding Proximate Cause Links

The most difficult issue in establishing environmental liabilities is linking the negligent act with the incurred injuries/damages, that is, determining proximate cause. Without the proximate cause link, liability cannot be established. A corporation may discharge a harmful substance into a water system. Someone may get sick from drinking the contaminated water, but determining that it was the specific corporation and the discharge of the harmful substance that caused the sickness is difficult, many times impossible. The corporation is not held liable for its negligent acts as liability cannot be established due to the lack of the proximate cause link. These injuries or costs are externalized to injured parties and society rather than being assessed against the corporation.

Changes in science may make the determination of the proximate cause link less burdensome. DNA testing has provided a vehicle for marking or determining cause and effects. For instance, a food poisoning death in Ohio from E. Coli contaminated meat was matched with a E. Coli bacteria strain found 1,300 miles away at a Con Agra/Swift Plant in Greeley, Colorado.[12] While the deceased's family may have been able to establish that the death resulted from eating the meat, without DNA testing, it would have been difficult to impossible to determine that the contaminated meat came from a specific plant over 1000 miles away.

A group of researchers at Western Michigan University have developed a new technique, "gene expression signatures." Using this technique, the researchers are mapping how toxic chemicals can impact animal genes. Working with tadpoles exposed to PCBs, they can document genetic changes not only in stressed tadpoles, but more importantly they can predict whether tadpoles that seem healthy are likely to become sick and die. With these techniques, scientists or lawyers could eventually determine whether animals and even human beings that are near pollutant outlets, like an industrial plant, have suffered injuries, even before the injuries became apparent.[13] Given that a 2004 National Cancer Institute report found that at least 80 percent of all cancer cases are linked to the environment,[14] studies like the one at Western Michigan University may help to establish proximate cause links between pollutants and injuries.

Injured parties may be able to prove that their injuries were caused by exposure to a particular harmful substance, but it is often difficult to link the production or manufacture of the substance to a specific company. Traditionally, this linking to a specific party was required to establish liability. An important court case, *Sindell v. Abbott Labs, 1980,* in California, relieved this burden with the establishment of the market share doctrine. This case involved the pharmaceutical drug, DES (diethyl-stilbestrol), which was taken by pregnant women to prevent miscarriage. The drug was found to have the terrible side effect of producing vaginal cancer in the female offspring of the mother. This cancer typically did not develop until the daughters were around 25-30 years old. Because of the extended time period, it was extremely difficult to determine which specific pharmaceutical company produced the DES. Because of the difficulty of this burden and the seriousness of the injuries, the court apportioned the liability to all those companies making DES by examining their respective market shares of the drug when it was sold. This doctrine could be applied to any industry where a number of companies compete for and produce the same product.

The DES case illustrates another proximate cause application. The cancer, which the female children developed from their mothers taking DES, was a rare vaginal cancer, clear cell cancer of the vagina. When this rare cancer was observed in multiple cases by a group of doctors in the Boston area, they discovered that seven of the eight young women treated for this rare vaginal cancer had mothers who had taken DES during the first three months of pregnancy.[15] When rare cancers are associated with a particular substance, there is a strong presumption of proximate cause, even if the precise cause and effect process cannot be medically proven. Another example is mesothelioma, a rare cancer of the lining of the abdomen and lungs, which was discovered to be associated with exposure to asbestos (see Chapter 6).

Germany's Environmental Liability Act provides for a "presumption of proximate cause," as stated in the Act:

> "Where, with regard to the circumstances of the individual case, an installation is inherently capable of causing the respective damage, it shall be presumed that the damage has been caused by that installation."[16]

Here a causal link can be established if the link between an event and injury is qualified as logical. Scientific or technical proof is not required. Under the Act, "presumption of proximate cause," cannot be applied if the company's special operational duties have been complied with, and there has been no breakdown of these operations.

Strict Liability

If strict liability can be applied, the burden of establishing liability is lessened. Under strict liability, negligence does not have to be determined in order to establish liability. It only needs to be shown that a particular situation, circumstance, or condition exists along with the injury. Strict liability applies to several sustainability risk exposures. For instance, strict liability is applied to the responsibility of employers to compensate employees under workers compensation laws. If it is determined that an employee was injured in the course of employment, that is, when he/she was at work, then the employer is responsible for compensating the worker for his/her injuries, like medical expense and wage loss. This responsibility holds whether or not the employer's negligence was involved.

Strict liability also applies to product liability. First put forth in *Greenman vs. Yuba Power Products, 1962,* in California, strict liability does not require that the manufacturer negligently produced the product. It need only be shown that the product was defective to the point of making the product unreasonably dangerous, the danger was not open and obvious, and the defect was the cause of the injury. Strict liability in product liability litigation gives the injured parties greater leverage to pursue their claims against manufacturers.

A general case where strict liability applies, and can be used extensively in environmental cases, is situations involving dangerous or ultra hazardous activities or substances. A common example is contractors, who use dynamite in their construction business, will be held strictly liable for damages resulting from dynamiting operations regardless of how careful they might have been. Proposed EU directives have discussed strict liability being applied to all "extremely hazardous" activities.[17] Applying dangerous or hazardous activities to the environmental area, if a spill or release of a dangerous substance caused substantial injuries/damages, strict liability could definitely apply. An example would be the metho-iso cyanide gas spill at the Union Carbide plant in Bhopal, India, which resulted in thousands of deaths and tens of thousands of injuries.

In Chapter 1, reference was made to the Report on Carcinogens, which lists 246 harmful substances that are known to be human carcinogens or are reasonably anticipated to be human carcinogens. Corporations dealing with these harmful substances could be considered to be involved in a dangerous activity and subject to strict liability. Similarly, corporations working with toxic elements like lead and mercury may be subjected to strict liability. In 2002, over 500 chemicals were included in the Toxic Release Investory (TRI), and again mishandling of these chemicals, which results in injuries, could be subject to strict liability.

Writing in *Environmental Law Handbook,* Sullivan and Steinway state that "Strict Liability takes on a huge role in the burgeoning environmental law field. In fact, the U.S. Environmental Protection Agency itself states 'Most of the statutes, which the EPA administers, are strict liability,' illustrating its widespread use."[18] Most notable is the Comprehensive Environmental Response, Compensation and Liability Act (CERCLA), or Superfund, which is discussed in Chapter 6. For the 700 plus "hazardous substances" that Superfund regulates, strict liability applies to any actions brought by the EPA. EU directives call for the "polluter pays" approach in environmental liability situations, which is essentially strict liability.[19] This wide use in statutory environmental law may facilitate the spread of strict liability to common law litigation.

New Theories of Liability

A new legal theory may be developed by a creative legal team. If accepted by the courts, it can change, often dramatically, a company's or industry's liability exposures. Strict liability and the market share doctrine both discussed above are cases in point. Given the changing dynamics of the world's environmental and social justice conditions, the potential for new types of liability suits seems enormous.

Take for instance global warming risks, which to date have only involved property exposures, but rarely deal with liability issues. Establishing that the actions of a specific company was the proximate cause of global warming, which in turn causes injuries and damages to another party, would clearly be difficult. Making the proximate cause connection with an entire industry or a country as the negligent party may be a less difficult task. The Friends of the Earth International (FoEI) has studied the feasibility of bringing a lawsuit aimed at recouping financial damages caused by global warming.[20] Fossil fuel companies and industrialized countries like the United States, which have rejected the Kyoto Treaty, would be likely targets.

FoEI has previously commissioned a study entitled, "Gathering Storm: The Human Cost of Climate Change," which focuses on injuries and damages.[21] The United Nations estimates the costs of global warming as reaching more than $300 billion a year, so the potential damages are substantial. Other environmental groups including Greenpeace, the World Wildlife Fund, the National Resources Defense Council, U.S. Friends of the Earth and Climate Justice are also exploring litigation strategies.[22] A 2001 paper, "Suing the United States for Global Warming Omissions," by Widener University Law Professor Andrew Strauss, discusses numerous possible litigation strategies.[23]

Island nations such as Kiribati, Tuvalu and the Maldives, are particularly vulnerable to rising sea levels associated with global warming. All have experienced severe flooding caused by storms and high tides in recent years. The Prime Minister of Tuvalu, Koloa Talake, announced that Tuvalu, along with Kiribati and the Maldives, are planning to sue certain western nations and corporations for damages and loss of life and property.[24]

Julian Salt of the UK's Loss Prevention Council Centre for Risk Sciences believes that the potential liability exposure is real and substantial and will impact the insurance industry. He states:

> "I think the islands in the Pacific are going to sue the oil companies and governments for the damage inflicted on them. This is what could collapse the insurance industry. Insurers will end up with a massive bill to pay."[25]

Salt sees two sources of losses for insurers. The first involves liability claims against policyholders charged with contributing to global warming. The second exposure results from investments that insurers have in certain industries, such as energy companies and auto manufacturers.[26]

Another global warming related litigation strategy is demonstrated by the attorney generals of eight states and New York City suing five large coal burning utilities for carbon dioxide emissions. The states are California, Connecticut,

Iowa, New Jersey, New York, Rhode Island, Vermont and Wisconsin. The five utilities are American Electric Power (AEP), Cinergy, the Southern Company, the Tennessee Valley Authority (TVA) and Xcel Energy. These five utilities operate 174 power plants in 20 states and account for about 25 percent of the utility industry's carbon dioxide emissions and 10 percent of the U.S. total emissions. This litigation represents the first state legal action taken directly against companies that discharge carbon dioxide. The suit is based on the common law doctrine of public nuisance, which "provides a right of action to curb air and water pollution emanating from sources in other states."[27] Global climate change risks are discussed in more detail in Chapter 7.

Another novel liability action involves criticisms being brought against the fast food industry for serving unhealthy food. Two heavy teenage girls brought a suit against McDonalds, in late 2002, for damages related to their obesity. It was the first lawsuit of its type to reach a courtroom.[28] In January 2003, Judge Robert Sweet dismissed the lawsuit. His grounds were basically that the girls age, 19 and 14, should have known better, adding, "liability based on over consumption is doomed if the consequences of such over consumption are common knowledge."[29] But Judge Sweet left open the possibility of an amended complaint that McDonald's deceives its customers—even suggesting an example that few McDonald's customers are aware that Chicken McNuggets contain twice the fat of a hamburger.

Even though this case and its appeal were dismissed, the growing obesity problem in the United States and the increasing number of pre-diabetic cases and adult-onset, or Type 2, diabetes in young children suggest such suits may continue to develop. The damages in terms of being over weight, particularly in young children, are apparent and increasing. The question is who, if anyone, is negligent? Even if these cases are not successful, the publicity is negative and reputation damage is incurred. The actions by McDonald's to improve the menu, as well as those by the Kraft (Altria) food company, Frito-Lay (PepsiCo), and Coca-Cola to make nutritional and/or marketing changes in their products, is an indication of the seriousness of the situation. As stated by Margo Wootan, director of nutrition policy at the Center for Science in the Public Interest:

> "The food industry is very worried about being blamed for obesity. And they should be. Obesity is the fastest rising health problem. It's doubled in adults and children and tripled in teenagers over the past 20 years."[30]

New requirements from the U.S. Food and Drug Administration will require labels to include grams of trans fats. Saturated fats labeling has been in place since the early 1990s. In general, pressure will be brought on advertising practices to include more nutritional information, particularly for foods aimed at young people. Pushed by federal regulators and studies such as the 2003 study on underage drinking by the National Academy of Sciences, liquor companies are attempting to reduce their advertising aimed at under aged drinkers.[31]

Negligent marketing claims against the food and liquor industries could be brought following the pattern of litigation brought against the gun manufactures. In this litigation, individuals and cities incurring injuries and damages, because of criminals using guns, sued the gun manufactures on the basis of negligent marketing and distribution. The plaintiffs contend that gun manufacturers knowingly manufactured and sold guns in numbers far greater than would be expected if used only for legal purposes. These guns often wound up in criminal hands, causing injuries to individuals and police officers. While gun litigation has had mixed success, it represents the first time that liability claims have been brought for negligent marketing and distribution practices. Similar claims could be brought against the food and liquor industries based on negligent marketing, product development and advertising.

The general point of above cases is that the creation, expansion and application of new liability theories create serious risk exposures, where none existed before. Historically, corporations have not been held accountable for environmental damages or inadequacies in their treatment of workers or communities. But if liability and boycott pressure can be brought against a fast food company for making its customers fat, what extent of pressure might be brought against companies accused of destroying ecosystems, harming children or treating workers inhumanely? I foresee that companies, which are involved with activities or products that are harmful to customers, workers or the environment, will increasingly be held accountable.

Accumulation of Liability Exposures

Sustainability risks are often characterized by an accumulation of liability exposures. Liability exposures can build up over an extended period of time, before they are actualized and result in liability claims dollars being paid out. The asbestos, Superfund, and tobacco liability areas are all characterized by an accumulation of exposures. When a company or industry begins to incur claims that actually result in monetary payouts, they are faced with a huge inventory of potential claims, which can cause financial havoc over subsequent years. Even if companies or industries make changes to eliminate the continuing build up of future liability exposures, there is nothing they can do about the past exposure accumulation. The same would be true of companies that have repeatedly discriminated against women in their compensation and promotion practices.

Insurers face the same financial exposure, as the claims are passed on to them to be paid under various liability policies. As with their policyholders, insurers cannot do anything to control the claims resulting from past exposures. While insurers can and have changed their policies from occurrence to claims-made, or have put in coverage restrictions or exclusions, this only affects claims deriving from present and future exposures. They cannot change old policies-they must live with the coverage terms provided.

Why would a company continue to build up liability exposures in the first place? One reason is that they may not be aware that its products or activities are causing harm. Another reason is that they do not anticipate being held financially responsible for these building exposures. Another rationale is that they have been successful at fending off liability claims. If liabilities are established by a new law, companies may feel their past acts will be protected under a grandfather provision. Finally, present management may look at these situations as not being their problem, and pass them on to future managements and shareholders. While liabilities may be avoided over the short run, such practices are inconsistent with sound sustainability risk management strategies. Without proper action, these liabilities ultimately will manifest themselves in debilitating financial losses for corporate management and shareholders, and possibly their insurers.

Legal Complexes Need New Cases

The buildup of large legal complexes of lawyers to represent plaintiffs in mass toxic torts complicates the liability accumulation risks. As their work is completed in the asbestos, Superfund and tobacco areas, these legal complexes look for new defendants to sue. Defendants with large accumulations of potential liabilities are a particularly attractive target. The recent increase in silicosis suits provides a telling example.

Silicosis suits have increased dramatically in the last couple years. U.S. Silica, a large supplier of industrial sand, had nearly 15,300 new claims against it in the first half of 2003. This compares to 5,200 new claims for all of 2002 and 1,400 in 2001. One large insurer is handling 30,000 cases in 2003, up from 2,500 a year earlier.[32] Many of the law suits are being brought by lawyers who specialized in asbestos litigation. Indeed, many lawyers are filing two claims for a single individual, one for asbestos and one for silica. Susan Warren, of the *Wall Street Journal,* reports that:

> "Asbestos attorneys are using the same legal machinery to generate silicosis claims, relying on a huge network of chest X-ray screeners, medical experts and local labor unions involved in asbestos litigation."[33]

Silica, or highly purified quartz, is a mineral found in abundance on coastal beaches and sand. It is used to make glass, fiberglass, paints and ceramics, and also in foundry casting. Companies that mine and process sand and industries that use sand, like the construction industry, are among the common defendants. Silica or quartz dust, if inhaled, can produce a chronic lung disease called silicosis, the most common injury claimed in litigation. Some scientists have linked silica exposure to cancer, although few cancer cases have been filed.

Previously discussed risk situations, such as water contamination from perchlorate, a rocket fuel, MTBE, a gasoline additive, PFOA, a chemical used for making Teflon, and breast milk contamination from PBDE, a flame retardant, would seem to be attractive areas for legal complexes to expand their litigation operations. Corporations or industries, which exhibit large accumulation of liability exposures, provide tempting targets. Scientific studies, documenting injuries from a particular contaminant, provide more evidence to augment the success rate of the lawyers bringing litigation, and the legal complexes become like a perpetual motion machine.

Catalytic Event

What often happens in the liability area is that some event significantly changes the probability that the company will actually have to pay for accumulating liabilities. In the asbestos litigation, it was the research by Dr. Irving Selikoff of Mt. Sinai Hospital in New York City, in the 1960s, that first publicly provided scientific data linking asbestos to workers' injuries. It took a few years before the first successful suit for these injuries was accomplished in the 1973 *Borel vs. Fiberboard Paper Products Corporation* decision, but once that happen it opened the floodgate holding back claims of injured parties. These claims are still pouring in today some 30 years later, and being assessed against companies that dealt with asbestos and their insurers (see Chapter 6).

In Superfund, it was the passage of a federal law making companies retroactively liable for the cleanup hazardous wastes. Before its passage in 1980, companies were for the most part legally disposing of hazardous wastes as basically there were no rules. Undoubtedly, they felt that if a law passed it would grandfather them in for past acts, but this did not happen. They were held to be retroactively liable, which triggered a huge inventory of Superfund sites requiring cleanup, with the costs being paid by "potentially responsible parties." Like asbestos, these claims are still being paid today by companies and their insurers (see Chapter 6).

With tobacco liabilities, it was inside company documents that plaintiffs were finally able to obtain through the discovery process. Historically, tobacco companies had been able to protect damaging internal documents through the lawyer-client privilege of work product confidentiality. Combined with the assumption of risk defense, they have been able to successfully defeat liability suits for decades. But when District Court Judge Kenneth Fitzpatrick in a Minnesota courtroom ruled that various documents were not protected by work product privileges, the tobacco companies were forced to turn over 39,000 internal documents to the plaintiffs, after appeals to the Minnesota and U.S. Supreme Courts.[34] Included with these documents were internal evidence that management had deliberately manipulated nicotine levels in cigarettes to make them more additive, which of course makes more loyal or hooked customers. They were also shown to have known about certain dangers associated with smoking, about which they had lied in public. Finally, armed with the knowledge that the sooner young people are hooked on smoking, the more difficult it is to break the addiction, tobacco companies aimed sophisticated advertising campaigns at children. The leverage provided by the damning information in these internal documents would eventually lead to a settlement in litigation brought by a number of states for Medicaid and other state related health care costs, which resulted in the tobacco industry paying out $246 billion dollars to the states over a 25 year period.

Today, situations certainly exist in which potential environmental or social justice liability risks are accumulating. While some companies are actively dealing with these risk situations, many are using the same rationale that asbestos producers, hazardous waste disposers, and tobacco companies used in the past to delay dealing with these accumulating exposures. But these strategies break down once the exposures manifest themselves. Only a proactive sustainability risk management program can prevent and control these accumulating liabilities from causing major financial damages to the effected companies/industries.

Discovery

The discovery process allows the plaintiff access to internal documents of the defendant that relate to the litigation. Often this process produces evidence from the defendant's files that helps the cause of the plaintiffs. Discovery is a powerful legal tool that plaintiffs can use to increase their success in liability litigation. The importance of the documents in the tobacco litigation was mentioned above. Discovery of documents in the files of asbestos defendants, indicating that they had evidence of the harmful effects of asbestos even before the Selikoff studies, helped injured asbestos plaintiffs establish liability of the asbestos companies.[35] In Superfund related litigation, internal documents have been used to prove that companies disposed of hazardous waste at Superfund designated sites. In the discrimination suit against Boeing noted in Chapter 1, discovery of internal documents showed that Boeing had conducted studies for years showing women were unpaid.[36] And the power of the discovery process in the tobacco litigation was mentioned in the previous section.

The tobacco legislation illustrates another trend that is improving effectiveness of the discovery tool. The documents provided at discovery were posted on a website, which means they could be more conveniently accessed for other tobacco litigations. Furthermore, the development of scanners means that documents can be searched electronically for critical information or evidence rather than requiring a person(s) to physically examine the documents. Scanners become particularly important when a defendant may try to overload plaintiffs' attorneys with volumes of records.

The potential of discovery increasing the success rate of plaintiffs has received a boost with the advent of email. Like hard copy documents, emails are subject to discovery. Computer forensic experts can even recover emails that have been deleted.[37] A noted non-environmental case involved action brought against Merrill Lynch. Its analysts were pushing certain stocks to the public, while at the same time indicating in internal emails to their colleagues that these stocks were terrible buys. Their apparent motive was that they did not want to lose the investment banking business of the companies, whose stock they were pushing publicly, but trashing privately. When these emails were discovered, Merrill Lunch had little choice but to settle with the aggrieved parties. Obviously, this episode did considerable damage to Merrill Lynch's reputation.

Another case involved litigation brought against Bayer for injuries associated with their anti-cholesterol drug, Baycol. The discovery of internal emails indicated that 18 months before Baycol was pulled from the market, company officials were worried about injury and death reports from patients taking Baycol. While Bayer won the first case to go to trial, they face 8,400 more suits that have been filed against them.[38]

The Brown Shoe Company illustrates the dangers of postponing action of discovery requests. A Brown Shoe plant leaked a chemical, dichloroethene, which spread to a neighborhood in Denver. The neighborhood claimed property damages and worries of injuries from the chemical, which is listed as a possible human carcinogen by the U.S. Environmental Protection Agency. On the eve of the trial in April, 2003, the judge in the case, Herbert L. Stein III learned from documents, recently disclosed by Brown Shoe, that some workers had told investigators for Brown Shoe lawyers as far back as 1998 that waste chemicals were intentionally dumped on the ground. This discovery contradicted Brown Shoe's denial going into trial that they intentionally disposed of the wastes. The trial was postponed, punitive damages are being considered, and the Judge was visibly upset:

> "I have to tell you that when I read this, there was more than one expletive deleted that came out of my mouth. I can't describe this information as anything less than explosive."[39]

The information revolution has greatly increased the odds that companies, which attempt to hide or cover up some sort of dangerous operation or product, will be found out through the discovery process. When this happens, reputation damage is considerable. Such actions can lead to punitive damages and criminal prosecution. Finally, the firm's liability insurance coverage may be compromised as policies typically require that injuries and damages covered by the policy be "neither expected nor intended from the standpoint of the insured."

It is clear today that many of the activities of business are damaging the environment. In all likelihood, information on the extent of the damage is best known by company officials and may be documented in some fashion in their internal records. Similarly, management may be familiar with, and have records of, mistreatment or underpayment of certain employee groups. Companies, which do not take appropriate sustainability risk management actions to mitigate the harm, may find themselves in a vulnerable situation if and when liability action, armed with the discovery tool, is brought against them.

Increased Transparency

In addition to discovery, the regulatory and public pressure for corporations to become more transparent will make it difficult to obscure negative activities. The best example of more transparency is the increasing use of corporate reports in the environmental and social justice areas. The scope of these reports focused initially in the environmental area. Reports on social justice issues and corporate social responsibility followed or were added to environmental issues, and more recently corporations are producing full blown sustainability reports. While many of the reports are included the firms' existing financial reports, the trend increasingly is favoring a separate stand alone sustainability report.

KPMG initiated a tri-annual series of international surveys of sustainability reporting in 1993. Its report, *The KPMG International Survey of Corporate Sustainability Reporting 2002,* covers environmental, social and sustainability reports from a survey of almost 2000 companies, including the top 250 companies of the Global Fortune 500 companies and the top 100 companies in 19 countries.[40] Corporate sustainability reporting for the Global Fortune 250 increased to a 45 percent participation rate in 2001, up from 35 percent in 1999. Because of high environmental impact, certain industries have a 100 percent participation rate, including mining, forestry, chemicals and synthetics, and transportation. Other industries, with high participation rates, include pharmaceuticals at 86 percent, electronics and computers at 84 percent and the auto industry at 73 percent. Japan has the highest percentage of participating companies at 72 percent. Other high participation rate countries include the United States, Germany, France and the UK. Countries with the lowest reporting rates are Greece, Hungary, Slovenia and South Africa. Besides the KPMG report, another excellent source for sustainability and related reports is the Corporation Register.[41]

A problem across all the reports is the lack of internationally accepted standards and verification. The KPMG Survey found that 25 percent of the reports are verified and 65 percent of these verifications are done by major accounting firms. The efforts of the Global Reporting Initiative (GRI), discussed in Chapter 9, is calling for standardization of reporting guidelines and verification.

Mandatory reporting requirements in some countries are also helping to augment sustainability reporting. For instance, French companies listed on the stock exchange are required to report on their environmental and social performance. The Canadian Securities Commission requires public companies to report financial and operational effects of environmental protection requirements.

Besides printed publications, sustainability reports are typically available on a company's website. Therefore, information is readily accessible for anyone wishing to use it. Environmental and social justice information, which used to be unavailable or difficult to obtain, now only requires a computer and internet connection anywhere in the world. Ready availability increases sustainability risks. This information could be scanned to check for liability, boycott and shareholder action targets.

Other stakeholders can also use environmental, social justice and sustainability reports. A study by the U.S. Investor Responsibility Research Center (IRRC) suggests that environmental reports:

> "Have risen quickly to become a trusted source of information for advocacy groups, institutional investors, investment managers, news media, environmental regulators, and other stakeholders."[42]

A company may be able to temporarily postpone such actions by not putting out a report. But that raises the suspicion that the company may have something to hide. As more corporations provide reports, the pressure grows for those holding back. If competitors produce reports, the pressure increases even more. I think it best that corporations assume the inevitability of operating more openly. As John Elkington concludes in *Cannibals with Forks*:

> "First, no matter how successful some companies may be in devising "stealth" strategies to mask what they are doing, or intend to do, most businesses will increasingly operate in a high-visibility environment. International business will find that the Internet will enormously increase the geographical reach and magnifying (and distorting) power of the goldfish bowl.
>
> Second, voluntary reporting by a relatively small number of companies will help fuel demands for much higher levels of corporate disclosure. The focus will expand from environmental performance to progress against a range of triple bottom line indicators. Some countries will decide that the only way to achieve this is via mandatory reporting requirements."[43]

From a sustainability risk management viewpoint, I like Judy Larkin's, author of *Strategic Reputation Risk Management*, advice: "Work as though everything you say and do is public."[44] Or a favorite saying of mine that I use in class is: "If you do not want to read in the newspapers, about what you are doing, quit doing it."

Erosion of Attorney-Client Privilege

The emergence of large scale corporate scandals, white collar crimes, and questionable tax shelter schemes has given rise to calls for loosening attorney-client privilege. While not directly the result of environmental or social justice crimes, the easing of privilege protection could be employed in future criminal or civil cases involving sustainability risks.

Under the Sarbanes-Oxley Act, the SEC is required to set minimum standards of professional conduct for corporate lawyers. In rules that became effective August 5, 2003, corporate lawyers are required to "report up the ladder to top executives and to the board of directors if necessary if they find evidence of a material violation of securities laws." Furthermore, the SEC is considering a requirement that lawyers, who are unsuccessful in getting the corporation to change, resign publicly—a process known as "noisy withdrawal."

The Justice Department is requesting more waivers of attorney-client privilege in their investigations by sharing information on potential fraudulent violations. The department hinted that it would go easier on corporations in the investigation if they waived privilege. In the Justice Department case brought against Frank Quattrone of CSFB for obstruction of justice charges, David Brodsky CSFB chief counsel, and Kevin McCarthy, director of U.S. litigation, both waived privilege and testified in the case against Mr. Quattrone.

The IRS is considering a lawsuit against Jenkens & Gilchrist, a Dallas law firm offering legal advice on tax shelters. The law firm has denied the IRS's request to give up the names of clients who invested in questionable tax shelters. Jenkens & Gilchrist has indicated it would fight the IRS in court.

The Boeing discrimination case, mentioned in Chapter 1, involved an improper use of the attorney-client privilege. For over 10 years, Boeing investigated whether female employees were paid less than men. The finding of several studies said yes. For several years, Boeing had successfully hidden these studies from plaintiffs' lawyers, as well as requests from *Business Week* attorneys, under attorney-client privilege. After considerable investigation, Judge Marsha J. Pechman, in May 2004, ordered Boeing to hand over these studies, citing "An evolving awareness, as more facts came to light, of how Boeing had inappropriately tried to shield (the documents) from discovery."[45]

At the August 2003 meeting of the American Bar Association, new guidelines were passed, which allowed, but did not require, lawyers to break a client's confidence if they believe it necessary to prevent fraud or crime that would cause financial harm. The ABA's modification of its guidelines actually brought it into line with the state guidelines in 42 states.[46]

Regulatory Arena

Regulatory changes can have a major influence on sustainability exposures in the liability area. The enormous impact of the Superfund law on corporate America and the insurance industry, when the act called for retroactive liability for the cleanup of hazardous waste sites, was mentioned above. It is not so much the regulatory climate, in which corporations operate, but the changes that can cause surprises and disruptions.

For instance, a great deal of concern is being created by global warming/climate change issues and the responses of world governments to the Kyoto Treaty (see Chapter 7). The United States has not ratified the treaty and appears very unlikely that it will, at least while George Bush is President. This raises substantial concerns for U.S. corporations as they procurement make plans for new plants and equipment. If they assume they will not be subject to the requirements of the Kyoto treaty, and then a future administration and Congress ratify the treaty, considerable expense could be incurred in making the necessary changes in plant and equipment procurement strategies. Had the United States ratified the treaty, they would not have to worry about the risks that a change in administrations might have on their business strategies. In some cases, shareholders are bringing pressure for companies to make appropriate changes, assuming that the Kyoto Treaty will eventually be ratified in the United States, to avoid the risk of making hurried changes and expensive alterations in the future (see section on shareholder actions in Chapter 4).

A regulatory change in the other direction, namely de-regulation, can also cause risks. The United States has been in a deregulatory trend now for several years. This trend is extending under the Bush Administration particularly in the environmental area. Many laws are being eased or weakly enforced, and there is an emphasis on voluntary actions of corporate America to protect the environment. With less government regulation, parties opposed to environmental actions of corporations will have to rely more on litigation to change the behavior of business. Thus more environmental liability actions can be expected to fill the void created by the government's retrenchment in the regulatory area.

Governments can call for studies or data collections, which could provide information useful in litigation actions. For instance, a federal government commissioned study, "The State of the Nation's Ecosystems: Measuring the Lands,

Waters, and Living Resources of United States," concluded that "there is a fundamental lack of available data from which sound environmental policy can be
derived." The study was conducted by the H. Heinz III Center for Science, Economics and the Environment and published in 2002. It recommends that information should be collected on the nation's oceans, forests, farmlands, fresh
waters, grasslands, and shrub lands, and urban and suburban areas. It recommends that critical measures be taken to maintain concentrations of elements
needed for life like nitrogen, phosphorous, carbon, and oxygen. The study also
calls for reducing harmful contaminants in various designated areas, and
increased funding for federal agencies and NGOs that are involved with ecosystem issues. The study, headed by William Clark, Professor of International Science, Public Policy, and Human Development at Harvard, collected ideas and
developed recommendations from a panel of 150 experts from academic, business, environmental organizations and the government.[47] An even more ambi-
tious project for data production is the Millennium Ecosystem Assessment,
which was discussed in Chapter 1.[48]

Another major international effort, called Global Earth Observation System of
Systems (GEOSS), will integrate the world's civilian satellites, weather-monitor-
ing networks and similar earth observation systems. The global accord establishing GEOSS was signed by representatives of 61 countries and 38 international
organizations on February 16, 2005, the same day the Kyoto Protocol went into
effect. The main idea is to share and coordinate information from space, land and
sea. Primary applications include improved crop forecasting, climate monitoring
and natural disaster warnings.[49]

As more data on the state of ecosystems is collected and analyzed, the areas
with the most severe problems will be apparent. Causal factors associated with
severe problem areas may also come forth. These causal factors may involve corporate activities. The extent and cause of ecological damages are critical factors in
established accountability and liability. As government financed and other studies
provide more information on the state of ecosystems, their findings can increasingly be used in liability litigation.

Increasing Global Litigation

Recent changes in Europe's generous welfare and benefits programs is prompting
suits by workers, particularly for unemployment claims. Their efforts are being
assisted by recent legal changes in the U.K., Spain, Sweden and Norway in suits
that are similar to U.S. class actions. These efforts are also bolstered by the U.K.'s

decision in 2000 to permit lawyers to charge "conditional" or contingent fees. Some French lawyers are also charging contingent type "success fees." Traditionally, only the United States legal system utilized a contingent fee system, in which lawyers are compensated by a percentage of the award (typically 33 percent), rather than on a fee or hourly basis. A *Wall Street Journal* article noted that insurance executives say "it is the worst thing that could happen to the industry." Allianz's chief risk officer, Raj Singh states:

> "The biggest emerging risk for insurance groups world-wide is the proliferation of the U.S. tort system or elements of it."[50]

The United States is considered to be the most litigious country in the world. Several examples have been reported of increasing litigation in other countries. Many involve environmental or social justice issues. The case of the EU was mentioned in the above section. Rising environmental litigation are also being reported in Japan[51] and Latin America.[52]

China, with its explosive business growth and its potential to become the world's leading economy, is raising the most concern. China is experiencing more litigation brought by workers for injury and compensation claims. The number of labor related arbitration claims and lawsuits increased from 94,000 cases in 1998 to 184,000 cases in 2002.[53] The number of lawsuits in other areas, like defective products and wrongful injury, are rapidly increasing.[54]

At a recent meeting I attended of the International Insurance Society in Hong Kong, concerns were expressed about rising litigation. Reporting on the meeting, *Reactions IIS Reporter* stated:

> "China is a big worry for international insurers. A number of recent legal and regulatory changes appear to be changing attitudes towards liability among the country's newly—affluent middle classes."[55]

Two examples involving sustainability risks were given in the *Reporter*. In one, the People's Intermediate Court, one of the country's highest courts, ruled that 580,000 workers suffering from silicosis could sue their employers, even after collecting workers compensation benefits. In another case, 65 workers sued a battery manufacturer, claiming they were poisoned in the course of their work.[56]

In my opinion, it would be shortsighted for corporate management to assume that the world will not follow the U.S. litigation system. As noted by Swiss Re in a treatise on liability trends, "In the areas where development is most dynamic,

there is no mistaking the American influence with its indelible mark on legislation and the economy."[57] It would also be shortsighted to assume that tort
reform efforts will significantly impede liability litigation, particularly for environmental and social justice risks. I feel there will be little legal, societal or legislative sympathy for those corporations who do not make active efforts to respond
to damaging environmental activities and unfair treatment of workers and communities.

Expanding Liabilities are Inevitable

The developments discussed in this chapter provide convincing documentation
that liabilities for sustainability risks will increase in the future. The good news is
that corporations still have time to incorporate sustainability risk management
strategies to eliminate or mitigate these risks. Companies can decide to take the
lead, to be the standard setters, against which the negligent actions of other firms
will be measured. The reduction in risk costs and the competitive advantages
gained offer overwhelming incentives for taking action now.

With the exception of those firms impacted by Superfund, asbestos and
tobacco liabilities, the actual financial losses to date from sustainability liabilities
have not been that great. This will change as the legal, scientific, regulatory, and
competitive pressures grind forward. I am again struck by the momentum of
forces that will inevitably cause an explosion of new sustainability related liabilities.

CHAPTER 2—ENDNOTES

[1] Thomas F.P. Sullivan, Editor, *Environmental Law Handbook,* Rockville, Maryland: Government Institute, 2001.

[2] Prosser and Keeton on the Law of Torts 622—5th ed., *Environmental Law Handbook,* 1984.

[3] Paul R. Kleindorfer, "Market-Based Environmental Audits and Environmental Risks: Implementing ISO 14000," *The Geneva Papers on Risk and Insurance,* No. 83, April 1997.

[4] Robert A. Woellner, "Management Environmental Risk: The ISO 14001 Business Advantagement," *Proceedings of Environmental Risk Management Seminar,* Nashville: Willis Corroon, January 28-29, 1997.

[5] International Organization for Standardization, *ISO 14001—Environmental Management Systems,* 1st Edition, Geneva, Switzerland: ISO, 1996.

[6] Paul R. Kleindorfer, "Market-Based Environmental Audits and Environmental Risks: Implementing ISO 14000," *The Geneva Papers on Risk and Insurance,* No. 83, April 1997.

[7] Thaddeus Herrick, "As Flame Retardant Builds Up in Humans, Debate Over a Ban," *Wall Street Journal,* October 8, 2003.

[8] www.epa.gov/superfund/programs/nrd/primer.htm.

[9] In addition to the EPA website an excellent source is Preston, Thorgrimson, Shilder, Gates & Ellis, *Natural Resource Damages,* Rockville, Maryland: Government Institute, 1993.

[10] *Norfold & Western Railway Co. vs. Freeman Ayers et al.,* U.S. Supreme Court; No. 01-963. Decided March 10, 2003.

[11] Thaddeus Herrick, "Judge Tells Exxon to Pay $4.5 Billion," *Wall Street Journal,* January 29, 2004; "Time for Exxon to Pay," *New York Times,* January 30, 2004.

[12] Leila Abboud," DNA Matching Helps Track Tainted Meat", *Wall Street Journal,* Jan 21, 2003.

[13] Jim Carlton, "Studying Pollution's Impact on the Genetic Level," *Wall Street Journal,* July 31, 2001.

[14] Sharon Guynup, "Living Clean: Fighting a Silent Killer," *National Wildlife,* Oct/Nov 2004.

[15] Theo Colburn, Dianne Dumanoski, and John Peterson Myers, *Our Stolen Future,* New York: Plumel Penguin, 1997.

[16] Swiss Re, *Liability and liability insurance: Yesterday-today-tomorrow,* Zurich: Swiss Reinsurance Company, 2001.

[17] Ibid.

[18] Thomas F.P. Sullivan and Daniel M. Steinway, "Fundamentals of Environmental Law," *Environmental Law Handbook,* Thomas F.P. Sullivan, Editor, Rockville, Maryland: Government Institute, 2001.

[19] Swiss Re, *Liability and liability insurance: Yesterday-today-tomorrow,* Zurich: Swiss Reinsurance Company, 2001.

[20] B. Hansen, "Friends of the Earth Considers Legal Action to Curb Global Warming," *Environment News Service,* September 15, 2000.

[21] O. Cowell and J. Caras, *Gathering Storm: The Human Cost of Climate Change,* Amsterdam, The Netherlands: Friends of the Earth, September 2000.

[22] K.Q. Seelye, "Global Warming May Bring New Variety of Class Action," *The New York Times,* September 6, 2001.

[23] Andrew Strauss, "Suing the United States for Global Warming Omissions," Red Conference, London, July 10, 2001.

[24] Kim Moore, "Turning up the Heat," *Reactions,* July 2002.

. [25] Ibid.

[26] Ibid.

[27] Andrew C. Revkin, "New York City and 8 States Plan to Sue Power Plants," *New York Times,* July 21, 2004; "A Novel Tactic on Warming," *New York Times,* July 28, 2004.

[28] Marc Santora, "2 Girls Suing McDonald's Over Obesity, *New York Times,* Nov. 21, 2002.

[29] Kevin Helliker and Shirley Leung, "Judge Dismisses Obesity Suit By 2 Girls Against McDonald's," *Wall Street Journal,* January 28, 2003.

[30] David Barboza, "Kraft Plans to Rethink Some Products to Fight Obesity," *New York Times,* July 2, 2003.

[31] Richard J. Bonnie and Mary O'Connell, "Reducing Underage Drinking: A Collective Responsibility," Washington DC, *National Academies Press,* February 1, 2004.

[32] Jonathan D. Glater, "Suits on Silica Being Compared To Asbestos Cases," *New York Times,* September 6, 2003.

[33] Susan Warren, "Silicosis Suits Rise Like Dust," *Wall Street Journal,* September 4, 2003.

[34] *State of Minnesota and Blue Cross and Blue Shield of Minnesota vs. Philip Morris, R.J. Reynolds, et.al.,* 606 N.W. 2nd 676: 2000 Minn. App. Lexis 168.

[35] Paul Brodeur, *Outrageous Misconduct,* New York: Pantheon, 1985.

[36] J. Lynn Lunsford, "To Settle Sex-Bias Suit, Boeing Agrees to Pay up to $72.5 Million," *Wall Street Journal,* July 19, 2004.

[37] Ellen Byron, "Computer Forensics Sleuths Help Find Fraud," *Wall Street Journal,* March 18, 2003.

[38] Melody Petersen, "Bayer Cleared of Liability In a Lawsuit Over a Drug," *New York Times*, March 19, 2003.

[39] Scott Kilman, "'Explosive' Disclosure Raises Stakes in Brown Shoe Lawsuit," *Wall Street Journal*, May 8, 2003.

[40] *The KPMG International Survey of Corporate Sustainability Reporting 2002*, KPMG, 2002.

[41] www.corporateregister.com.

[42] John Elkington, *Cannibals with Forks*, Gabriola Island BC, Canada: New Society Publishers, 1998.

[43] Ibid.

[44] Judy Larkin, *Strategic Reputation Risk Management*, New York: Palgrave Mac-Millan, 2003.

[45] Stanley Holmes and Mike France, "Coverup at Boeing?" *BusinessWeek*, June 28, 2004.

[46] parts of this section from Judith Burns, "Attorney Face a Paradox in the SEC's Conduct Rules," *Wall Street Journal*, August 19, 2003; Lorraine Woellert, "How Much Can You Still Tell Your Attorney?" *Business Week*, September 1, 2003; Kara Scannel and Randall Smith, "Lawyer Details Bids To Avert Destruction of CSFB Documentation," *Wall Street Journal*, October 3, 2003.

[47] www.heinzcenter.org.

[48] www.millenniumassessment.org.

[49] Daniel Michaels, "Global Accord Set for Approval Will Unify Earth-Watching Data," *Wall Street Journal*, February 16, 2005.

[50] Charles Fleming, "Europe Learns Litigious Ways," *Wall Street Journal*, February 24, 2004.

[51] Howard W. French, "Japanese Winning Cleanup Battles, *New York Times,* July 2, 2003.

[52] Roberto Ceniceros, "Pollution Risk Awareness Growing in Latin America," *Business Insurance,* December 11, 2000.

[53] Peter Wonacott, "Poisoned at Plant, Mr. Wu Became A Labor Crusader," *Wall Street Journal,* July 21, 2003.

[54] Elizabeth Rosenthal, "Chinese Test New Weapon From West: Lawsuits," *New York Times,* June 16, 2001.

[55] "Liability Crisis Feared in HK and China," *Reactions IIS Reporter,* July 10, 2005.

[56] Ibid.

[57] Swiss Re, *Liability and liability insurance: Yesterday-today-tomorrow,* Zurich: Swiss Reinsurance Company, 2001.

3

REPUTATION/BOYCOTT SUSTAINABILITY RISKS

o o o o o o o o o o o o o o o o o o o o o o o o o o o o o o o o o o

Targeting brands was like discovering gun powder for environmentalists.

—member of Greenpeace

What Nike did is important, it blows open the whole notion that other companies are putting forward that they can't make such disclosures. Disclosure is important because it allows us to talk to people in these overseas communities—religious leaders, human rights leaders—who are then able to go and examine and verify working conditions.

—Eric Brakken, organizer for United Students against Sweatshops

Reputation/boycott risks may be the greatest sustainability risk faced by most firms. When there is damage to a firm's reputation, it adversely impacts future revenues and future profits, which are at the heart of the firm's raison d'être. Firms often underestimate reputation risk. When a firm's reputation is damaged, it is often very difficult to repair. Reputation damage includes a loss of trust in the business. Its credibility is brought into question. Repair typically is costly and takes a long time and in many cases can never be done. The consequences of reputation damage, namely decreased sales and profits, are not insurable. In risk management terminology, financing for reputation risks is totally retained or self-insured. Damage to a firm's reputation can be swift and sometimes devastating.

Reputation damage usually is a boost to your competitors creating a competitive advantage over your firm.

A boycott can often lead to reputation damages to a firm. The boycott risk has been around for decades, but it has caused particular problems for business in the sustainability area. A sustainability boycott risk typically is triggered by a firm's undesirable actions in the environmental or social justice areas. The boycott campaign is often lead and coordinated by an NGO or similar group. The boycott risk always adversely affects the firm's reputation, again striking at its sales and continuing profits.

Companies with strong brands are particularly vulnerable. Figure 3-1 shows the top 10 company brands and the brand value as a percentage of their market capitalization. Companies with strong brands not only have the most to lose, they are also the most likely to be the target of a boycott. A study by Environics showed that two thirds of 25,000 consumers in the United States, Canada and Western Europe form impressions of a company based partly on its ethics, environmental impact and social responsibility—all critical sustainability concerns.[1] Focusing boycotts on sustainability concerns can alter customers' impressions of a company and their willingness to buy from a company. Targeting well known brands increases the leverage of NGO boycotts or as one Greenpeace member put it, "[targeting brands] was like discovering gun powder for environmentalists."[2]

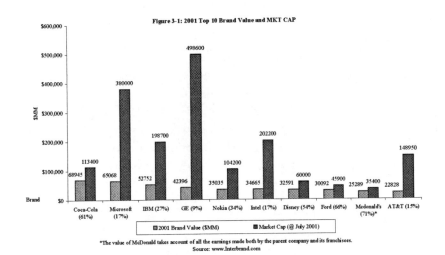

Figure 3-1: 2001 Top 10 Brand Value and MKT CAP

*The value of McDonald takes account of all the earnings made both by the parent company and its franchisees.
Source: www.Interbrand.com

A company which responds positively to a sustainability boycott to its products or activities not only mitigates this risk, but it can also improve its image on a local, national and even an international stage. A more forward looking sustainability risk management strategy would involve adopting sustainability strategies for producing products and conducting activities before a potential boycott commences. Such strategies would include increased transparency, increased stakeholder input and developing partnerships with NGOs. Damage to a company's image and reputation and brand is avoided. Revenues may improve as they offer an alternative to competing firms, particularly if other competitors are the subject of a boycott.

To get an idea of the extent and nature of reputation/boycott risks, several examples will be discussed and documented below. The purpose is to demonstrate that this is not an insignificant sustainability risk. It can have serious ramifications for a company. Examples were chosen to demonstrate a positive response by the affected companies, and provide guidelines for firms in similar situations. In risk management, it is always wise to observe other competitors or related business, for risk problems they may be facing. By observing others troubles, a business can often respond with preemptive risk management strategies.

Shell Oil—Brent Spar

The Brent Spar incident illustrates how dramatically and quickly modern communication systems can allow a consumer boycott to cause a major world corporation to reverse its stance in a sustainability situation. The Brent Spar was an offshore oil platform in the North Sea that was owned by Shell Oil. After two decades of use it was scheduled for disposal in 1995.

A team of Shell Oil scientists and engineers performed an assessment regarding the best available environmental and economic option for disposal. The assessment recommended that the least environmental damage would be produced by disposal of the oil platform in a deep ocean trench. The option of on land disposal was felt to produce greater environmental risks. Of course, the environmental damage in a deep water trench would conveniently not be visible nor measurable—it could only be estimated in the assessment. Not surprisingly, the deep ocean disposal was much less expensive than the on land dismantling and disposal. In Shell's considerable analysis, the best scientific and business solution was deep ocean disposal of Brent Spar.

Greenpeace did not agree with this analysis and followed the Brent Spar out to sea. Rather than using their follow and blocking approach, employed to disrupt whaling operations, Greenpeace decided to transport volunteers onto the deck of the Brent Spar using a helicopter. Then Greenpeace employed modern video cameras and high-tech satellite-based broadcasting gear to establish on-line links with major European wire services. Within hours of being installed on the Brent Spar, virtually every main European broadcast organization was covering head-line images of the confrontation on their main newscasts.

Greenpeace coupled these broadcasts with a consumer campaign to boycott Shell retail products. The boycott was particularly effective in Germany. Within one week, Shell's retail sales in Germany and other European countries had fallen by 30 percent, resulting in hundreds of millions of dollars in lost sales. An emergency meeting of the Shell board reversed the deep ocean disposal of the Brent Spar in favor of on shore disposal.[3]

The Brent Spar incident illustrates some important points about sustainability boycott risks. One, even if a well reasoned and well meaning internal scientific assessment arrives at a particular environmental decision, consumers and the general public may not necessarily agree with the decision. Consumers seem to be reacting to a more basic or fundamental environmental value or logic—you would not just drive your car into a lake to get rid of it—you would take it to a proper disposal facility. Even if scientific analysis showed deep ocean disposal to cause minimal environmental damage, a more basic and logical value system may find that there is something fundamentally wrong with just sinking the Brent Spar in the middle of the ocean.

The second point is that environmental groups like Greenpeace, which have access to modern communication systems like satellite links and the Internet, can transfer news and information to large numbers of viewers/receivers on an instantaneous basis at very little cost. In the past, the towing and disposal of the Brent Spar may very well have gone unnoticed. Even if it had been followed out to sea, several days may have passed before the story could be reported. Finally, the boycott risk can produce some serious risk costs for business. In this case, Shell lost hundreds of millions of dollars in sales in the short time span of a week. These risk costs were not insurable and the negative publicity damaged Shell's environmental reputation.

To their credit, the combination of the Brett Spar incident and pressure brought against Shell for its association with a repressive dictatorship in Nigeria provided a catalyst for Shell. Today, along with BP, they are recognized as the two principal sustainability leaders in the petroleum industry. Shell and BP stand in stark contrast to ExxonMobil. While Shell and BP are leaders in the development of clean renewable energy alternatives, ExxonMobil has made no recognizable efforts according to Greenpeace. ExxonMobil has been a leader in arguing against the link between the burning of fossil fuels and global warming, and in lobbying for development in the Artic National Wildlife Refuge (ANWR). ExxonMobil was the target of Greenpeace's "Don't Buy ExxonMobil" and "Stop Esso" campaigns, and in July 2005 a nationwide boycott by a coalition of environmental organizations was launched against ExxonMobil. Shell and BP accept the global warming science and BP has left Artic Power, the industry lobbying group for ANWR, and has also dropped plans to develop the Liberty oil field in the Artic Ocean.[4]

Boise Cascade—Old Growth Trees

Old growth trees vividly represent a finite resource. In thousands of years, trees planted today eventually would be considered old growth, but for the present and near term generations, there is a limited number. Over 95 percent of old growth trees have already been logged in the United States. On a global basis, around 80 percent have been logged. Many are protected in state and federal parks and forests. For the remaining old growth forests on private and public (where logging is permitted) lands, boycotts have been forcibly used to promote their preservation.

The reversal of Boise Cascade Corporation's policy of cutting old growth trees is a case in point. A full page ad ran in the *New York Times* on September 7, 2001, calling for Boise Cascade to end the cutting of old growth forests. The ad was sponsored by the Rainforest Action Network (RAN) and signed by several notable entertainers, legislators and other environmental groups. The ad mentioned that "400 companies have sworn off the trade of old growth wood products." The ad criticized Boise Cascade for "refusing to embrace modern social values" and for being "out of touch with the vast majority of Americans who believe that old growth trees belong in a forest." The ad also accused Boise Cascade of leading an anti-environmental campaign by contesting RAN's use of civil disobedience, pressuring RAN's founders, and petitioning the IRS to revoke RAN's tax status.

Less than seven months later, the *New York Times* ran a story titled, "Timber Company Reduces Cutting of Old-Growth Trees: Move by Boise Follows Growing Pressure."[5] The article reported that several businesses like Kinko's, L.L. Bean, Patagonia and universities like Notre Dame, had ended their contracts and stopped buying paper from Boise Cascade. The loss of revenues and the bad publicity led Boise Cascade to cease cutting old growth trees "in some undisturbed forests on public and private lands."[6]

Boise Cascade tried to play down the influence of boycott pressure by claiming that old growth wood constituted of less than one percent of its total supply.

Of course, this means that Boise Cascade had incurred all these unnecessary boycott risk costs for less than one percent of its total supply. Pressure continued as Boise Cascade's policy was not total—it would still cut old trees in disturbed areas on private lands. Such a policy would now only constitute a fraction of one percent of its total supply.

In September 2003, Boise Cascade announced it would end purchases of wood from endangered forests, including those in Chile, Indonesia and Canada. The announcement said it would stop cutting timber from virgin forests in the U.S. in 2004. Boise Cascade also said it would start pressuring its suppliers to follow its lead by giving preference to those suppliers whose products come from forests independently certified as being under healthy management. The broad scale of Boise Cascade's policy made it the first leading North American timber manufacturer to adopt such a strategy.[7]

A considerable amount of the pressure to change came from Boise Cascade's customers. The loss of Kinko's business has been noted above. Before boycotting Boise Cascade, the Rainforest Action Network (RAN) and other NGOs had successfully pressured the two leading home improvement chains, Home Depot and Lowe's, to cease using wood originating from environmentally sensitive forests. These firms now give preference to suppliers providing wood from forests certified by the Forest Stewardship Council (FSC) as being under healthy management.[8] Two more big chains, Wickes Lumber and Home Base, followed the examples of Home Depot and Lowe's. At this point in a boycott campaign, firms down the line feel the dual pressure of NGOs and competitors.[9]

In a related development, Forest Ethics, another forest protection NGO, persuaded Staples to triple the recycled content of its paper products in fall of 2002. Forest Ethics was joined in its protects by two student NGOs, Sierra Student Coalition and Ecopledge.[10] In August 2003, Staples, KB Homes and Hayward Lumber, Inc. joined environmental groups in opposing the Bush administration's proposal to allow roads to be built in Alaska's Tongass National Forest.[11]

The Boise Cascade case illustrates a number of important sustainability risk management lessons. One, the boycott risk is real, can result in substantial costs, and can cause a company to change its strategic policy. Two, while companies like Boise Cascade can make decisions based solely on financial factors, they should not assume that everyone, including their customers, act in the same way. Most people who have walked in an old growth forest realize that the values, spirituality and wonder of these old trees can far exceed their monetary value. There is a sense that those experiences should be preserved for future generations. Three, by resisting and being forced into a policy reversal, and then not making this reversal complete until later, Boise Cascade's reputation was still being adversely impacted. How different it might have been had Boise Cascade some time ago interacted with stakeholders, like NGOs and its customers, and worked out a voluntary, non-pressured response to cease cutting old growth trees, and made the policy switch complete, i.e., pledge to cease cutting any old growth trees. I think it is clear that Boise Cascade's future sustainability image would be much improved had they followed this approach. They eventually arrived at the same position—cessation of cutting of old growth trees—but their protracted course resulted in reputation and financial damages along the way.

Nike—Sweat Shops

Nike's failure to manage its supplier subcontractors lead to a boycott based on social justice values. Nike is one of the world's most successful sporting wear and goods companies with 2005 (fiscal year as of May 31, 2005) annual sales over $13 billion and profits exceeding $1 billion. Among endorsers of its products are two of the world's most famous athletes ever, Michael Jordan and Tiger Woods. Nike does not own any factories—all its goods are manufactured by subcontractors. These subcontractors are spread across over hundreds of factories in nearly 40 countries employing hundreds of thousands of workers. They are concentrated in China, Indonesia, Vietnam and Thailand, where roughly 90 percent of Nike shoes are manufactured.[12] Subcontracting and globalizing its manufacturing process decreased Nike's control and created substantial boycott and reputation risks. While Nike's business model called for not directly manufacturing its own products, monitoring of subcontractors and suppliers is still required to mitigate sustainability risks.

Beginning in the 1990s, Nike was heavily criticized for producing its goods, particularly athletic shoes, in sweatshop conditions. These conditions included child labor, exposure to dangerous chemicals, work weeks up to 80 hours, sexual harassment, and verbal abuse. United Students Against Sweatshops was a driving force in putting pressure on Nike. Jonah Perretti made a seemingly innocuous email request to personalize his shoes with the word "sweatshop." Nike's denial was followed by a second request from Peretti to send him "a snapshot of the 10-year-old Vietnamese girl who makes my shoes" instead of the personalized shoes. When he emailed this correspondence to some friends, they sent it to friends where it spread across the internet and finally reached the press. Nike's stock price and revenues dropped.

An article in the *Financial Times*[13] points out two important lessons of Nike's case that illustrate modern reputation/boycott risks. The first is that the internet gives critics the ability to instantly communicate their campaign around the world. Information is becoming more available, and it is easier and less costly to disseminate than ever before. The second point is that the anti sweatshop campaign which was waged against Nike is extremely damaging to employee morale. No one wants to work for a company that is receiving embarrassing and negative publicity. Employees want to be proud of their employer and its business practices. Employees also realize that bad publicity can adversely impact the company and may imperil their jobs.

To their credit, Nike has done much to address these criticisms. Its first corporate responsibility report, published in October 2001, criticized its own practices and called for further improvements. Nike established a Code of Conduct, based on that of the Fair Labor Association (FLA), whose governing board includes representatives from industry, universities and NGOs.[14] Nike became the first large apparel company to disclose the locations of 42 plants in 11 countries, and they released complete audits of 600 plants that manufacture its shoes and apparel in 2000.[15] This was a critical decision because Nike and other corporations had maintained that disclosure would provide propriety information to competitors. As noted by Eric Brakken, organizer for United Students Against Sweatshops:

> "What Nike did is important, it blows open the whole notion that other companies are putting forward that they can't make such disclosures. Disclosure is important because it allows us to talk to people in these overseas communities—religious leaders, human rights leaders—who are then able to go and examine and verify working conditions."[16]

Brakken's comments proved on point as dozens of companies, including Jansport and Reebok, followed Nike's lead of partial disclosure.[17] In 2005, Nike disclosed for the first time the names and locations of more than 700 factories that produce its sneakers, apparel and other products.[18]

In 2003, Nike adopted the Reuse-A-Shoe program, which involves collecting shoes and grinding up the raw materials for use in soccer, football and baseball athletic surfaces and synthetic basketball courts, tennis courts and playground surfaces. They are also incorporating small amounts of organically grown cotton into their apparel and eliminating the use of toxic glues, solvents and other chemicals in most of the shoes they produce.[19]

Nike made a sizeable multimillion dollar grant to the International Youth Foundation to establish an organization called the Global Alliance for Workers and Communities. The Global Alliance produced a report which was critical of supervisors in nine Indonesian factories that make Nike products. Nike responded positively by increasing the training of factory managers and supervisors. Nike has set workplace standards that require workers to be 18 years old to produce footwear and 16 years old to produce apparel. The maximum work week has been set at 60 hours.

The controversy over working conditions in Nike's subcontracted factories was the subject of potentially significant litigation. California activist, Marc Kasky, brought a suit against Nike claiming that the statements Nike made in its defense of working conditions in their factories was false advertising under California law. Public statements normally have considerable free speech protection under the U.S. Constitution. Kasky held that Nike's statements were commercial speech, which enjoys less protection. The California Supreme Court agreed with Kasky by a 4-3 vote and the case went to the U.S. Supreme Court. Rather than deciding the case, the U.S. Supreme Court returned the case to California for trial. Nike and Kasky then settled for $1.5 million to be paid to the Fair Labor Association to improve reporting and monitoring standards for factory working conditions. The fact that the U.S. Supreme Court did not offer any guidance means that corporations are still vulnerable to similar suits. The case demonstrates how difficulties brought by boycott pressures can be compounded and produce further problems.[20]

The Nike case demonstrates the additional complexity and risk costs of globalization and out-sourcing the manufacturing process. As a company expands globally, increasing pressure is placed on monitoring and control programs. The negative publicity associated with sweatshop conditions, child labor and sexual harassment can adversely effect reputation, brand, and ultimately the bottom line. Such incidents can be particularly embarrassing and damaging to a company's reputation and even to the reputations of famous endorsers. Talk show host, Kathie Lee Gifford's public confession that she did not know that her Wal-Mart outfits were made by Honduran girls paid 31 cents per hour demonstrates this risk.

Pressure has been brought by groups like Oxfam Community Aid, an Australian based organization that is part of Oxfam International. Besides their dissatisfaction with Nike's efforts, Nike is an attractive target due to its profitable operation and its status as the market leader. Such pressure may have lead to the June 2003 decision by Nike, Reebok, Adidas, Levi Strauss and Liz Claiborne to post their factory labor audits on the website of the Fair Labor Association.[21] Companies with strong and successful business operations not only can face greater reputation/boycott risks, they are more apt to be targets of environmental and social justice related criticisms.[22]

Starbucks—Fair Trade Coffee

Starbucks is one of the most successful businesses in U.S. history. The number of Starbucks coffee stores is approximately 8,500, with more than one fourth in 34 countries outside the U.S. Their annual 2004 fiscal year sales exceeded $5 billion with profits of around $400 million. Its stock over the decade 1992-2002 rose more than 2,200 percent surpassing Wal-Mart, General Electric, PepsiCo, Coca-Cola, Microsoft and IBM in total return.[23] But since March 2001, Starbucks has been the focus of a boycott by Organic Consumers Association (OCA).

The boycott by OCA is over two principal issues. One issue is Starbucks use of recombinant bovine growth hormone and other genetically engineered ingredients in its brand-name beverages, baked goods, chocolates, frappuccino drinks and ice cream. The other issue involves pressure to have a greater use by Starbucks of fair trade, shade-grown, and organic coffee. While Starbucks does offer an organic milk alternative for an increased price, OCA feels that all GE ingredients should be removed from all its beverages and foods. Starbucks' use of GE ingredients raises many of the issues that will be discussed in Chapter 8, so the discussion here will focus on the fair trade issues of how coffee that Starbucks uses is grown and priced.

Businesses committed to fair trade agree to adhere to the following criteria:

1. Cooperative and healthy workplaces

2. A fair and living wage

3. Environmental sustainability practices

4. Consumer education and public disclosure

5. Respect for cultural identity

While fair trade principals can apply to many products, the production of coffee has probably been the commodity where it has been discussed and debated the most. The main reason for the focus on coffee production is the distressing economic plight of coffee farmers in Latin America, Africa, and Asia. Coffee farmers are suffering from the lowest coffee prices in 30 years. Oxfam, the British charity, produced a 2002 report, which documented that the global oversupply of coffee had pushed prices to their lowest levels in 100 years on an inflation adjusted basis. The report noted that farmers are paid roughly 24 cents a pound for beans, while companies that buy the beans are selling them for $3.60 a pound. Farmers' revenues amount to six or seven percent of the sales price of the coffee beans. Coffee farmers only receive one percent of the price of a cup of coffee sold at a coffee shop.[24] Out of the $55 billion generated by the sale of coffee worldwide, coffee growing countries that produce the beans only receive $8 billion.

According to the World Bank, over 600,000 coffee farmers and workers have lost their jobs in Central America alone due the recent coffee crises. Hundreds of families each week are leaving coffee farms and migrating north to earn a living. In other cases, farmers are forced to cut down the rainforest on their land to plant other crops or graze cattle. If coffee prices were higher, shade grown coffee could be raised, which saves the rainforest and all the accrued benefits such as watershed protection, carbon storage, biodiversity support, and medicinal plants. About 85 percent of fair trade certified coffee is shade grown and organic as small farmers have never had the money to purchase chemicals. For fair traded coffee, farmers receive $1.26 per pound, which is adequate to support themselves and their families, and protect the rainforests.

Given that U.S. coffee drinkers consume one-fourth of the world's coffee supply and Starbucks is the leading coffee shop corporation, it is a most visible target for OCA's boycott. Starbucks has responded by buying some fair trade, shade grown or organic coffee but OCA complains that these are token purchases. OCA would like Starbucks to buy more than its current one percent of total purchases and also to promote fair trade, shade grown or organic coffee as its coffee of the day at least one day a week. Buying more fair trade, shade grown or organic coffee would improve the working, living and economic conditions of coffee farmers and also help to decrease deforestation in the rainforests. Organizations like TransFair USA and the Rainforest Alliance provide labels, certification and verification that coffee is grown and produced under appropriate practices.[25]

Starbucks' need to grow, particularly in international markets, is drawing more general protests as a symbol of American corporate greed, much the same as has been targeted at McDonald's international expansion. The fact that Starbucks has experienced a continuing boycott by OCA for over four years, with all its accompanying negative publicity, gives fuel to the international protests. Starbucks has practical difficulties in not using milk without recombinant bovine growth hormone, particularly in the U.S. where milk is not separated into milk from cows using the hormone and those that do not. While Starbucks has taken a number of actions to support coffee farmers, Starbucks' reluctance to not purchase, promote and sell more fair trade, shade grown or organic milk is puzzling. As noted above its profitability has been unparalleled and a modest increase in price, especially for individual expensive drinks like lattes, would probably go unnoticed by customers. Customers could be told that the increase is for good reasons-to treat coffee farmers more fairly and equitably and to protect the environment. It should be noted that Starbucks total purchases only account for one percent of the world coffee supply and all coffee shop purchases together account for only about 5 percent of the world coffee supply. To produce a large impact, the big four multi-national companies, Sara Lee, Kraft, Procter & Gamble and Nestle, which purchase nearly half of the world's coffee supply, need to make meaningful contributions. Kraft's partnership with the Rainforest Alliance (RA), which is discussed in chapter 9, is one positive development. To protect its own interests, Starbucks might consider more cooperation with the Organic Consumers Association and other groups promoting fair trade practices. While their reputation has suffered, to date Starbucks sales and profitability have not suffered, but one wonders how long that might last.[26]

Citigroup—Financing Camisea Rainforest Project

Citigroup is the world's largest financial services company. It employs almost 300,000 people and its 2004 revenues and profits were $108 billion and $17 billion, respectively. Citigroup finances projects all over the world, and it is the financial advisor to a massive project to extract natural gas from the Camisea region of Peru, primarily for use in the United States.

The Camisea rainforest is located in the Urubamba Valley. It is one of the most ecologically diverse places on earth. Researchers at the Smithsonian Institute have found 200 bird species, 188 kinds of fish, 86 types of reptiles and over 100 different small mammals. Camisea is also home to some of the last un-contacted communities of indigenous people in the world.

The Rainforest Action Network (RAN) conducted a "Stop Citi" campaign to put pressure on Citigroup to stop financing large environmentally destructive projects like Camisea. Besides the natural gas project in Camisea, RAN cited Citigroup for financing other projects including those in:

Indonesia—Rainforest deforestation by funding palm oil plantations.

Chad and Cameroon—Rainforest deforestation by funding oil pipelines.

U.S.A.—Logging ancient redwoods by funding Pacific Lumber.

Venezuela—Environmental destruction in Orinoco River Delta by funding oil drilling.

RAN urged citigroup customers to cut up their credit cards and send them to RAN. While most of the work on the Camisea project is complete, RAN and other environmental groups like Amazon Watch, Conservation International, and the World Wildlife Fund, have concentrated on a fractionation plant on the coastal town of Paracas, which is only 20 percent complete. The Paracus plant is an important cog in holding and shipping the natural gas to destinations like the U.S.

Efforts by environmental groups have been successful in persuading international funding agencies to tie financing to strict environmental standards. For instance, in August 2003, the Export-Import Bank, a credit agency of the United States, rejected a $214 million loan for the Paracus project due to concerns about the environment. On the other hand, the Inter-American Development Bank did decide to extend an additional $75 million in financing. Reports from the Development Bank and the United States Agency for International Development have raised serious "concerns about a lack of transparency, about environmental studies that are called shoddy or insufficient, and a lack of knowledge of native groups in the region."[27]

Large scale projects, like the Camisea/Paracus natural gas project, provide economic opportunities and jobs for the country's individuals and businesses. Projects also provide energy sources like natural gas and oil. But these opportunities and jobs must be weighted against environmental destruction, biodiversity losses and adverse impacts on indigenous peoples. At a minimum if projects go forward, the costs of adequate controls to minimize environmental, biodiversity and human losses should be included in the project's costs. Past practices have tended to externalize these costs to the country and peoples where the project is located. In effect, profits are increased. Sustainability principles would require shifting some monies from profits to cover increased costs of preventing harm to the country's environment, biodiversity and peoples.

When I was first working on this chapter in 2003, I wrote that large lenders like Citigroup could partner with NGOs to set standards for environmental and social impacts in their loan application practices and to develop procedures for deciding which projects should be considered. In 2004, Citigroup formed a partnership with the Rainforest Action Network (RAN) and also participated in developing the Equator Principles to set up procedures for measuring environmental and social impacts (see chapter 9). Citigroup seemed to realize that long term boycotts and other anti Citigroup campaigns could damage its reputation and cost Citigroup financially in the long run.

A noteworthy appendum can be added to the Citigroup story. In April 2004, just three months after RAN partnered with Citigroup, RAN announced that it was ending one of the shortest campaigns in their history by reaching an agreement with the Bank of America. Bank of America agreed to forest protection, climate change policies, and protections for indigenous people's rights on the eve of RAN's launch date (April 22—Earth Day) of their "No Way B of A" campaign. This quick response by the Bank of America demonstrates not only the power of a threatened boycott, but also the pressure that a competitor's action can produce. It took another year, but RAN's pressure resulted in an agreement by J.P. Morgan to establish a comprehensive policy to take meaningful measures on climate change, forest protection, and indigenous rights.[28]

Andersen—Auditing Conflicts

The demise of Andersen, LLP, over their work with Enron is one of the most vivid examples of reputation damage in business history. While not involving sustainability risk issues of environmental quality and social justice, it very much dealt with the survival of its financial performance objectives. For decades, Andersen was the flagship of world accounting firms. Its practices set the standards for the field. Its ethics were impeccable. But within less than a year, reputation damage had destroyed the firm. Most of its principal customers had left. Any public companies who were still clients of Andersen were forced to leave because of its criminal conviction in a U.S. Justice Department obstruction of justice trial. It was in effect a defacto boycott against Andersen. Big chunks of its business were sold off to competitors. Its partners and other employees transferred to other firms or lost their jobs.

The Andersen situation and its disastrous involvement with Enron have encompassed entire books.[29] For the purpose of the discussion here, just a few of the main points will be covered. Andersen lost sight of the fact that it was an independent auditing firm on which many stakeholders relied, including customers, employees, investors, lenders, and regulators. That independence was compromised when Andersen auditors became too cozy with Enron management. The large fees that Andersen was collecting from Enron through its consulting services, as well as auditing services, set up a classic conflict of interest. A tough auditing stance may have compromised the consulting business with Enron, but protecting its consulting business compromised its auditing standards. While

Andersen claimed to have control walls in place to prevent conflicts, they clearly were not or could not be effective.

Enron was a huge enterprise, at one time the seventh largest corporation in the United States, and at the time of its collapse, it became the largest bankruptcy ever. So if big mistakes were made, big consequences could be incurred. The practices that Andersen used at Enron were used by Andersen at numerous other firms including Sunbeam, Waste Management, Global Crossing, World Com, Qwest, and Halliburton, and produced similar problems, indicating that their strategy had systemic characteristics and was not an isolated event. This fact resulted in limited sympathy from aggrieved parties. Andersen shredded tons of documents that gave the appearance that they had something to hide. The so called "little guys," like Enron employees, many innocent Andersen employees, and small individual investors, were hurt. The public outrage and resulting damage to reputation is particularly acute when innocent parties like employees and small investors are injured.

The Andersen/Enron case also demonstrates the fact that insurance is not going to save the firm or its top management in this type of catastrophic event. Andersen, like any accounting firm, had an errors and omissions liability insurance policy to cover claims for negligent acts in providing accounting services. While Andersen's policy limit was in the hundreds of millions of dollars, it was not adequate to cover all the expected claims and the cost of defending itself in the various liability suits. When insurance amounts were exhausted, the partnership capital was called upon. Typically, each partner has capital equal to hundreds of thousands to the millions of dollars. Often the capital is financed by the partner taking out a loan. All Andersen partners are expected to lose their equity capital, but they will still be responsible to repay the loans. Partners and employees directly found responsible for negligent acts and possibly others can be held liable for their personal assets under Andersen's form of limited liability partnership. Because the reputational damage to future revenues and profits was so severe, none of the partners or any of the employees for that matter will be able to recoup any of these lost monies by working at Andersen as it is effectively out of business. Since retirement income and health insurance benefits are financed by going concern revenues, the benefits of current and future Andersen retirees are threatened and indeed may be wiped out.[30]

What is particularly unique about Andersen, and is highly relevant to the ideas being expressed in this book, is that no one would have ever predicted that a firm of the size and reputation of Andersen could have effectively be forced out of business in a period of less that a year. Had Andersen officials been aware of the enormity and swiftness of these consequences, they almost certainly would have changed their business practices to reduce the apparent risks. As I have been arguing in this text, the potential reputation damages from sustainability risk situations can be cruelly swift and financially disastrous, as they were to Andersen in their accounting practices. After Andersen's demise, it would be fool-hearty to believe what happened to Andersen could not happen again to another firm. While I cannot predict when and to which particular firms an Andersen/Enron type catastrophe in the sustainability risk area will happen, it is clear to me that the conditions exist to make such events a virtual certainty. By adopting sustainability risk management practices, such catastrophic sustainability risk events can be avoided.

Merrill Lynch—Investment Conflicts

While not as devastating as the Andersen/Enron fiasco, Merrill Lynch suffered major reputation damage from another poorly monitored conflict of risk situation. Merrill Lynch is basically in two types of business. One type is retail brokerage that helps individuals manage and invest their money. The other type involves investment banking services for large firms. In the first type, Merrill will analyze and recommend certain stocks to their clients as to whether they are a good buy, should be held or should be sold. Conflicts can be raised between the two types of business when an analyst suggests selling the stock of a company (an indication that it is not a good investment), but the investment banking side of the business is collecting large fees from this company. A sell recommendation by the retail brokerage department may upset the management of the analyzed company and cause it to withdraw its investment banking business and their substantial fees. While Merrill and other firms in the business claim they have strong rules and fire walls to avoid conflicts, these conflicts can produce problems.

An investigation by the New York Attorney General, using the discovery process, turned up internal emails showing that Merrill employees were bad mouthing companies internally but were publicly recommending to their customers that they buy the stocks of these companies. Why would they do something that blatant? It was because the investment banking side was getting big fees from those companies. Investment managers were actually compensated for bringing companies to Merrill and keeping them by giving strong recommendations. As long as this does not become public, Merrill prospers, and investors on the outside just feel that sometimes stock recommendations do not turn out. But once these emails were made public through the investigation, there was incredible damage to Merrill's reputation. Investors that believed in Merrill's reputation of expertise and honesty in making stock recommendation now wonder if they should believe what Merrill says. What you might expect to happen did happen, Merrill's stock price decreased and customers left for other brokers. Like Andersen, it was in effect a defacto boycott.[31]

Once people lose trust in your firm and question your reputation, it is very difficult and takes a long time to regain that trust, if it ever can be regained. Some of the corrective actions taken by management, while understandable, seem a bit ridiculous. Merrill took out full page ads in the *Wall Street Journal*. These ads included statements like:

> Yesterday, we announced a series of measures designed to strengthen investor confidence in what's long been considered the pre-eminent research department in the industry. These ground breaking initiatives give our millions of clients around the word more reason than ever to put trust in Merrill Lynch. They set new standards for independence, objectivity and excellence in securities research.[32]

> Recently, we announced a series of measures designed to set new standards for investment research. These measures were in part an answer to criticisms leveled against Merrill Lynch, as well as against other financial institutions.[33]

My reaction when I read these ads was why would Merrill Lynch need "ground breaking initiatives" and "new standards for investment research" to "strengthen investor confidence" and "to put more trust in Merrill Lynch" to eliminate research analysts from knowingly promoting weak companies to gain investment banking fees from these companies? It would seem so utterly basic that a brokerage firm would not and should not promote weak companies to their investor clients no matter what the reason. This seems fundamental-indeed a minimum standard for any firm in the brokerage business. If Merrill Lynch needed to be caught to change and install these minimum standards, then I would just as soon switch to another broker. And if Merrill Lynch has violated what seems to be a minimum, basic standard, why should I have any confidence and trust that they will follow through with the changes suggested in the ads?

Andersen ran similar ads after its practices with Enron became public, and included statements such as:

> In December, Andersen committed to making fundamental changes in its business as a result of the issues raised by the Enron matter. These changes are already taking place. While not complete, we believe that these changes are

major steps toward reforming our U.S. audit practice and transforming our firm.[34]

Again, why would a competent accounting firm need "fundamental changes in its business" and "major steps toward reforming" their "audit practices?" If procedures and practices are seen as fundamental and major, they should have been part of the existing minimum standards of operating an accounting firm.

While the Andersen and Merrill situations do not involve environmental or social justice risk issues, they dramatically illustrate the reputation risk damage a firm can incur. Andersen paid the ultimate price with its swift demise. While Merrill suffered less initial reputation damage, both its stock price and business went down for a time and there still may be repercussions in the future. The management of other firms may believe that they will be given a second chance if they get caught in a situation like Andersen and Merrill. But as Andersen has shown, the reaction to their violation of trust and confidence may be so severe that the firm will not get a second chance.

In the environmental area, there is a great deal of feet dragging to make improvements in systems and products to produce less environmental damage. Similarly, managements are often reluctant to make changes to deal with their social justice risks. I think a common attitude often exists that businesses can resist changes until forced to by some outside disclosure or new regulation or NGO campaign or boycott. The problem with this strategy is that the accompanying violation of trust and confidence that a firm may encounter could produce such a severe public and regulatory reaction that the life and reputation of the firm is compromised or severely impaired. I think many firms are operating under the assumption that the public and regulators will be sympathetic and give them a second chance. The Merrill Lynch and particularly the Andersen cases suggest that this may be wishful thinking.

Eco-Labeling

The trend towards eco-labeling augments various boycott efforts. Companies may adopt an eco-label as part of an agreed upon strategy for ending pressure brought by NGOs, as we saw in the case of Home Depot and Lowe's switching to FSC certified wood. If a firm's competitors adopt eco-labels, then the lack of a firm's eco-label may take the form of a defacto boycott.

Eco-labeling dates back to 1977 with the introduction of the Blue Angel Label in Germany. This program currently certifies 3,700 products and is recognized by nearly 70 percent of German consumers. The Blue Angel eco-label raises environmental awareness, encourages market innovation, helps to limit pollution and promotes natural resource conservation. Today, more than 25 countries have some form of national eco-labels.[35] The Global Ecolabeling Network has members from 26 countries that support eco-labeling.[36]

An eco-label is a label, seal, logo, or marking on a product, which indicates that the product has met certain environmental and/or social justice standards. To use these labels, the firm must be certified by an independent third party organization, which is often the national government. In countries like the U.S., these organizations are typically NGOs. Some common eco-labels and their certifying organization are listed below.

Eco-Label	Certifying Organization
FSC	Forest Stewardship Council
Fair Trade Certified	Trans Fair USA, Fair Trade Labeling Organizations International
USDA Certified Organic	US Department of Agriculture
Free Farmed	Farm Animal Services—American Humane Association
Green Seal	Green Seal
MSC	Marine Stewardship Council
Rainforest Alliance Certified	The Rainforest Alliance
Salmon Safe	Salmon Safe, Inc.
Dolphin-Safe	National Marine Fisheries Services
GOA Certified Organic	Global Organic Alliance
LEED (Leadership in Energy and Environmental Design) Certified	Green Building Council

Today, more than 30 international bodies certify products.[37] The Consumer Union Guide to Environmental Labels at www.eco-labels.org and the Global Ecolabeling Network at www.gen.gr.jp are useful websites for these and many other eco-labels. A new book, *The Future of Eco-Labelling: Making Environmental Product Information Systems Effective,* by Frieder Rubik and Paolo Frankl, and published by Greenleaf Publishing, is another excellent source.

A firm which becomes the first in its industry to adopt an eco-label gains an immediate advantage over its competitors. A certain segment of customers will tend to purchase products from the firm with the eco-label. In the U.S. for the year 2003, 32 percent of consumers were significantly motivated in their purchases by concern for their health and the environment, according to the Natural Marketing Institute.[38] This competitive advantage may be lessened if the cost of certifying a company for an eco-label adds extra costs to their products.

If a firm does not qualify for an eco-label on its products, it faces the threat of being stigmatized. Companies without eco-labels make it easy to single them out. Sales and profits could suffer. Even if the firm eventually adopts an eco-label, the negative perceptions towards the firm may last far into the future and harm its business performance.

The lack of an eco-label, when other firms in an industry have adopted eco-labels, may expose the firm to a greater risk of liability. Recall in Chapter 2, the discussion of standards of care for determining negligence. If several firms have eco-labels, their level of care in manufacturing products may determine the reasonable and prudent person standard. If a firm with no eco-label is involved in a products liability suit, it may be easier to establish negligence. If injuries/damages are sustained and proximate cause is established, then liability can follow. If current trends continue, an increasing number of products will have eco-labels. Given these trends, sound sustainability risk management suggests that firms should move to qualify their products for eco-labels. Delays will only aggravate financial, reputation and liability costs.

Boycotts Expanding

A handful of well publicized boycotts have been discussed in this chapter to illustrate the risk of reputation damage. The boycott tool and its resulting reputation damage is alive, well and increasing. Several other prominent boycott examples include those against Nestles, McDonalds, Wal-Mart, Texaco, Levi-Strauss, Procter and Gamble, Adidas, PepsiCo, Gap, Taco Bell, World Bank, Altria (Phillip Morris), R.J. Reynolds, Dell, Coca-Cola, Dow, Monsanto, Ford, BMW, Mitsubishi, and Maxxum.[39] According to a Co-operative Bank research report, 52 percent of customers claimed to have boycotted at least one product in the last 12 months. Furthermore, customer boycotts are costing big business in the grocery trade some £2.6 billion ($5.0 billion) a year.[40]

The number and scope of boycotts has been made possible by the internet. A small group of individuals, indeed even one, can start and expand a boycott campaign by creating a website and spreading their message over the internet. By sending information to sympathetic groups, links can be made available to their members. Information can instantaneously be sent out worldwide. The use of the internet and websites not only minimizes costs, but it also generates tremendous speed and scope in spreading negative publicity on a corporation and its practices and products.

The pressures for increased disclosure and transparency almost surely will result in more damaging information becoming public. Newly disclosed information could act as a catalyst to initiate new boycotts or provide supplemental data to strengthen existing boycotts.

NGOs are often the source of boycott campaigns or lend them considerable support. Judy Rankin reports in *Strategic Reputation Risk Management* that the World Watch Institute estimates that the U.S. has 2,000,000 NGOs. India has about 1,000,000 grass-roots groups. She states "NGOs with operations in more than one country are estimated by the Yearbook of International Organizations to number over 26,000 up from 6,000 in 1990."[41] Other estimates put the number of international NGOs at 40,000.[42] Rankin also reports research showing that NGOs are the most trusted souce by the public on issues relating to pollution. Co-op America provides a "Guide to Researching Corporations," which includes information on a wide number of NGOs. While all NGOs do not necessarily deal with the environment quality and social justice issues, they are among the largest categories with the most members. Appendix A includes several websites of NGOs that are supporting boycotts or other campaigns or providing sustainability information as part of their mission.[43]

The Sooner the Better

Sound sustainability risk management requires a strategy for avoiding and responding to boycotts. Many of these strategies are discussed in Chapter 9 under sustainability risk control. While some boycotts may be unreasonable or unfair, many are not. The sustainability thinking of boycotting organizations is often ahead of corporate management. Rather than ignoring or resisting boycott pressure, and incurring financial losses and reputation damage, corporate management could take the opportunity to listen to the concerns put forth by the boycotting group. Better yet, management might work or partner with boycotting groups to establish strategies for cooperating and responding to concerns before the boycott is officially called.

Boycotts are inevitable and growing in importance. Actively participating in their own survival will require that corporate management develop sustainability risk management strategies for dealing with boycott risks. The sooner these strategies are incorporated, the better they will mitigate financial losses and reputation damage, improve a firm's competitive position, and ultimately lead to more profitable and sustainable operations.

CHAPTER 3—ENDNOTES

[1] James Allen and James Root, "The New Brand Tax," *Wall Street Journal,* September 7, 2004.

[2] Ibid.

[3] Grant Ledgerwood, "The Global 500, Big Oil and Corporate Environmental Governance," Chapter 12, *Greening the Board Room,* Sheffield, England: Greenleaf Publishing, 1997.

[4] Neela Banerjee, "BP Pulls Out of Campaign To Open Up Alaska Area," *New York Times,* November 26, 2002; Greenpeace Updates at www.greenpeace.org; Felicity Barringer, "ExxonMobil Becomes Focus of a Boycott," *New York Times,* July 12, 2005; www.exposeexxon.com.

[5] Greg Winter, "Timber Company Reduces Cutting of Old-Growth Trees: Move by Boise Follows Growing Pressure," *New York Times,* March 27, 2002.

[6] Ibid.

[7] Jim Carlton, "Boise Cascade Turns Green," *Wall Street Journal,* September 3, 2003.

[8] Dan Morse, "Home Depot Reviews Timber Policy," *Wall Street Journal,"* January 2, 2003.

[9] Joanna Sabatini, Marshall Glickman and Marjorie Kelly, "Making Change, One Share at a Time," *E Magazine,* March/April, 2004.

[10] John Carey, "The Enviros Try an End Run Around Washington," *Business Week,* December 16, 2002; Sierra Student Coalition and Ecopledge websites.

[11] Jim Carlton, "Big Business Oppose Logging in Alaska Forest, *Wall Street Journal,* August 25, 2003.

[12] Robert J. Samuelson, "The Tax on Free Speech," *Newsweek,* July 14, 2003.

[13] Michael Skapinker, "Corporate Social Responsibility Part II," *Financial Times,* May 7, 2002.

[14] David Drickhamer, "Under Fire," *Industry Week/IW,* June 2002.

[15] Louise Lee and Aaron Bernstein, "Who Says Students Protests Don't Matter?," *Business Week,* June 12, 2000.

[16] Steven Greenhouse, "Nike Identifies Plants Abroad Making Goods for Universities," *New York Times,* October 8, 1999.

[17] Louise Lee and Aaron Bernstein, "Who Says Students Protests Don't Matter?," *Business Week,* June 12, 2000.

[18] Rukmini Callimachi, Associated Press, "Responsible Nike—Sneaker giant opens book on overseas factories," *Capital Times,* April 15, 2005.

[19] www.responsibleshopper.org

[20] Information on this case from Linda Greenhouse, "Nike Free Speech Case is Unexpectedly Returned to California," *New York Times,* June 27, 2003; Robert J. Samuelson, "The Tax on Free Speech," *Newsweek,* July 14, 2003; and Stephanie Kang, "Nike Settles Case With an Activist for $1.5 Million, *Wall Street Journal,* September 15, 2003.

[21] Aaron Bernstein, "Sweatshops: Finally, Airing the Dirty Linen," *Business Week,* June 23, 2003.

[22] Information on Nike for this section from Michael Skapinker, "Corporate Social Responsibility Part II," *Financial Times,* May 7, 2002; Steven Greenhouse, "Anti-Sweatshop Movement in Achieving Gains Over Seas," *New York Times,* January 26, 2000; Louise Lee and Aaron Bernstein, "Who Says Student Protests Don't Matter," *Business Week,* June 12, 2000.

[23] Stanley Holmes, Drake Bennett, Kate Carlisle, and Chester Dawson, "Planet Starbucks," *Business Week,* September 9, 2002.

[24] Kim Bendheim, "Global Issues Flow Into America's Coffee," *New York Times*, November 3, 2002.

[25] "Making Trade Fair," *Co-op American Quarterly*, Spring 2003; and various issues of The Canopy produced by the Rainforest Alliance were used for parts of this section.

[26] Alison Maitland, "Bitter Taste of Success," *Financial Times*, March 11, 2002, was used for parts of this section.

[27] Juan Forero, "Energy Project vs. Environmentalists in Peru," *New York Times*, September 9, 2003; ED Solutions, Environmental Defense, Nov-Dec 2003, Vol. 34, No. 6.

[28] "RAN Breaks the Bank," Action Alert, RAN, Spring 2004; RAN Action Alert, Fall 2004; "Victory! J.P. Morgan Chase Adopts Green Policies," memo to members, RAN, May 10, 2005.

[29] Lynn Brewer and Matthew Scott Hansen, *House of Cards: Confessions of an Enron Execute*, College Station, TX: Virtualbookworm.com Publishing Inc., 2002; Bethany Mclean and Peter Elkind, *Smartest Guys in the Room: The Amazing Rise and Scandalous Fall of Enron*, Virginia Beach, VA: Portfolio, 2003; Mimi Swartz and Sherron Watkins, *Power Failure: The Inside Story of the Collapse of Enron*, 1st edition, New York, NY: Doubleday, 2003; Susan E. Squires, Cynthia Smith, Lorna McDougall and William R. Yeack, *Inside Arthur Andersen: Shifting Values, Unexpected Consequences*, 1st edition, Magna Park, Coventry Road, Lutterworth, Leics, LE17 4XH, United Kingdom: Pearson Education, 2003; Barbara Ley Toffler and Jennifer Reingold, *Final Accounting : Ambition, Greed and the Fall of Arthur Andersen*, 1st edition, New York, NY: Broadway, 2003.

[30] Information on Andersen from various newspaper and magazine accounts.

[31] Information on Merrill Lynch from various newspaper and magazine accounts.

[32] *Wall Street Journal*, May 22, 2002.

[33] *Wall Street Journal*, June 26, 2002.

[34] *Wall Street Journal,* Feb 6, 2002.

[35] Dave Wortman, "Shop & Save," *Sierra,* Nov/Dec, 2002.

[36] www.gen.gr.jp

[37] James Allen and James Root, "The New Brand Tax," *Wall Street Journal,* September 7, 2004.

[38] Katy McLaughlin, "Is Your Grocery List Politically Correct?" *Wall Street Journal,* February 17, 2004.

[39] Judy Larkin, *Strategic Reputation,* Risk Management, Houndmills Basingstroke, Hampshire, England: Palgrave MacMillan, 2003; www.boycotts.org; subjects of student papers in my Environmental Risk Management class.

[40] William Hall, "Customer boycotts cost business £2.6 billion," *Financial Times,* December 8, 2003.

[41] Judy Larkin, *Strategic Reputation,* Risk Management, Houndmills Basingstroke, Hampshire, England: Palgrave MacMillan, 2003; www.boycotts.org.

[42] Association of British Insurers, *Investing in Social Responsibility: Risks and Opportunities,* London, ABI, 2001.

[43] A central database, which tracks all existing boycotts, both nationally and internationally does not seem to be available. Boycotts in Action at one time provided this information at a website, but it is no longer in service.

4

SUSTAINABILITY RISKS FROM INVESTOR AND SHAREHOLDER ACTIONS

o o o o o o o o o o o o o o o o o o o o o o o o o o o o o o o o o

Corporate sustainability is a business approach to create long-term shareholder value. Sustainability leaders embrace opportunities and manage risks which derive from economic, environmental and social developments. As the importance of these trends increases, a growing number of investors integrate economic, environmental and social criteria into their stock analysis and use sustainability as a proxy indicator for innovative and future-oriented management.

—Dow Jones Sustainability Indexes

Sustainability risks can derive from several forms of investor and shareholder actions. One, a major environmental incident like a chemical or oil spill, or a social justice boycott entailing poor working conditions, may produce a drop in the involved firms' stock due to shareholders anticipating liability claims and decreased revenues. Two, if socially responsible investing screens result in significant numbers of shareholders selling the firm's stocks or in prospective shareholders not buying the stock, decreased demand may force the price of the stock down. Three, shareholder environmental/social justice resolutions may result in negative publicity and reputational damage. Finally, any of the above shareholder risks or some combination thereof may lead to shareholder litigation against directors and officers.

Environmental and Social Justice Incidents

Adverse environmental incidents, like a chemical or oil spill, litigation brought by injured customers and workers' exposures to dangerous substances, have deleterious impacts on a firm's financial position. Losses may be mitigated by insurance, but businesses frequently are not insured for a variety of environmental or social justice risks, including reputation damage.

Adverse environmental incidents often result in a drop of the price of the firm's stock because of anticipated financial losses. For instance, research conducted by Rory Knight and Deborah Pretty examined 15 major environmental incidents in the early 1990s. These incidents included Perrier's product recall of its water after benzene contamination, Union Carbide's Bhopal methyl-isocyanide gas leak, which killed thousands in India, the Exxon Valdez oil spill in Prince William Sound in Alaska and the Piper Alpha oil rig fire in the North Sea. Many of the incidents resulted in substantial direct financial losses, but there was also an immediate impact on the firm's stock price. In many cases, it was found that the share price recovered rapidly. The researchers reported that one factor common to companies, whose share price failed to recover, was that management was perceived to be at least partly responsible for the incident.[1]

Another study by Frooman found negative impacts on shareholder value when companies had engaged in illegal or socially irresponsible actions.[2] Both these studies would suggest the likelihood of liability claims against directors and officers, which would also tend to force the price of stock down.

A dramatic example of shareholder value loss in the area of harmful products involved the Firestone tire blowouts on Ford Explorers. Not only was Firestone being hit by liability suits from injured drivers and passengers, they also were being pressured by Ford legal teams who wanted to shift the blame from Ford Explorers to Firestone tires. Bridgestone Tire Company of Japan, which owned Firestone, saw their market capitalization plunge from $18.5 billion in January 2000 to $8.3 billion in January 2001, following its recall of 6.5 million Firestone tires.[3]

Socially Responsible Investment

Socially Responsible Investment (SRI) has a long history, but only recently has it had a measurable, significant impact. The Quakers, in the 1700s, were among the first groups to actively employ SRI by opposing investments in companies associated with slavery or military weapons. In modern times, such events as the Vietnam War and Apartheid in South Africa spurred growth in SRI by urging customers and investors to avoid those companies predominantly associated with the Vietnam War and Apartheid. In 1971, a Methodist group organized the PAX World Fund, the first SRI mutual fund, and in 1973, Dreyfus, a major marketer of mutual funds, launched its first SRI venture, Third Century Fund.

SRI funds grew modestly until the last half of the 1990s, when their growth surged. Table 4-1 illustrates this growth in the United States over the period 1995-2003. From 1995 to 2003, SRI funds grew by more than 240 percent, compared with 174 percent growth of the overall universe of assets under professional management. Of the 2003 total of $2.15 trillion in socially screened portfolios, $1.99 trillion are found in separate accounts (portfolios privately managed for individuals and institutions) and $162 billion is in mutual funds. Over 200 SRI mutual funds now exist, including Domini, Calvert, Citizens, KLD, TIAA-CREF, Parnassus, Third Avenue, AARP, Longview Collective, American Funds, Baron, Pioneer, New Covenant and Green Century.[4] SRI directed funds now comprise more than 11 percent of invested money under professional management in the United States. A study by the Association of British Insurers, entitled *Investing in Social Responsibility: Risks and Opportunities,* finds similar results with SRI funds comprising more than 10 percent of the U.K. stock market.[5]

Table 4-1
Summary of Socially Responsible Investing in the U.S.

Socially responsible investing embraces three strategies:
Screening, shareholder advocacy, *and* **community investing***.

	1995 ($billions)	1997 ($billions)	1999 ($billions)	2001 ($billions)	2003 ($billions)
Total Screening	$162	$529	$1,497	$2,006	$2,154
Total Shareholder Advocacy	$473	$736	$922	$897	$448
Both Screening and Shareholder*	N/A	($84)	($265)	($592)	($441)
Community Investing	$4	$4	$5	$7.6	$14
Total	$639	$1,185	$2,159	$2,320	$2,175

* *Some social investment portfolios conduct both screening and shareholder advocacy. These assets are subtracted out of the total to avoid double counting.*

Source: Social Investment Forum, Reports on Socially Responsible Investing Trends in the United States, 1995-2003

The SRI movement has the potential to have significant impacts on sustainability risk management strategy. First, a company whose stock is not purchased due to SRI screens may find its stock price drop due to a diminution of demand and the negative effects on its reputation. Second, a considerable body of research developed in the SRI area is reporting a positive, or at least break even, relation between corporate sustainability performance and financial results. Both of these SRI related impacts on sustainability risk management strategy will be examined below.

Shareholder Value and Reputational Losses Resulting from SRI

Early SRI directed funds primarily focused on employing negative screens. That is, companies or industries were excluded from SRI funds because of their involvement in a certain type of business or activity. Common areas included tobacco, gambling, weapons of war, nuclear power, and alcohol.

While still employing negative screens, more recent SRI strategies have had a broader and more positive focus. A company's record in the environmental and social justice areas is examined and evaluated. Those companies with positive evaluations are accepted as investment possibilities by SRI funds. Those companies with negative evaluations are not accepted. Whereas negative screens only affected a handful of specified industries, screens for positive environmental and social records can be employed in virtually any type of business or industry. As SRI screens expand, it is possible that less differentiation between SRI and general funds will result. Paul Hawken, noted sustainability expert and author, has criticized SRI funds for their lack of differentiation.[6]

The stocks of companies excluded from SRI funds will have fewer potential investment dollars that they can attract. This naturally results in less demand, which may lower stock prices. While lower stock prices might develop, little if any negative publicity or reputational damage would be done. SRI fund prospectuses list companies they invest in, but they typically do not list those companies they have excluded because of low environmental or social ratings. Only the most dedicated reader of prospectus forms would glean that some companies might be expected to be in the portfolio, except for their weak sustainability efforts.

Various types of SRI rating services and information sources are now developing systems that make it much more obvious which companies have poor records in sustainability. These rating services and information sources, like some of the SRI funds, take a broader look at companies' records on social, ethical, and human rights as well as environmental performance. More importantly, these services select a number of the top companies from a larger population to be included in their sustainability indexes and rank industry leaders. By examining the original larger population of companies, it becomes more obvious which are not in the index. Information provided by these sources clearly can impact a company's reputation, either negatively or positively. Prominent examples include the Dow Jones Sustainability Indexes launched in 1999 in the U.S., and the FTSE4Good Index launched in 2001 in the U.K.

Dow Jones Sustainability Indexes

The Dow Jones Sustainability Indexes (DJSI) were the first global indexes tracking the financial performance of the leading sustainability driven companies. These indexes were established in 1999 and are a cooperative effort of Dow Jones Indexes and STOXX Limited, two leading index providers, and Sustainable Asset Management (SAM), which specializes in sustainability investing. The DJSI STOXX group was launched in 2001 to provide sustainability benchmarks for European portfolios. The DJSI website offers a concise definition of corporate sustainability:

> "Corporate sustainability is a business approach to create long-term shareholder value. Sustainability leaders embrace opportunities and manage risks which derive from economic, environmental and social developments. As the importance of these trends increases, a growing number of investors integrate economic, environmental and social criteria into their stock analysis and use sustainability as a proxy indicator for innovative and future-oriented management."[7]

Sustainability indexes provide equity benchmarks and performance baselines of companies that have active environmental and social programs, as well as the traditional solid economic indicators. They provide an investment opportunity for various investor groups who desire to direct their dollars to companies that perform well in all three areas—economic, environmental and social.

In developing the DJSI World index, the starting universe is comprised of the 2,500 largest capitalized companies in the Dow Jones Global Index. The starting universe for the DJSI STOXX index is the Dow Jones STOXX 600 Index. These companies are categorized into 60 DJSI industry groups, and then are compared against their peers and ranked accordingly. For the DJSI World, the top ranked 10 percent of sustainability companies in each industry group are selected, and for the DJSI STOXX, the top ranked 20 percent are selected. In addition, the DJSI World seeks to cover 20 percent of the market capitalization in each sector of the Dow Jones World Index and, as a result, comprises a total of over 300 companies. The DJSI STOXX has a target market cap coverage of 45 percent of the Dow Jones STOXX 600 and includes about 170 companies.

Companies are assessed in terms of their sustainability efforts across 50 different criteria. Sixty percent of the analysis is based on general criteria, and 40 percent is allocated to industry specific criteria. An evaluation component examines various sustainability trends that will have a growing impact on the long-term successes of the rated companies. Sustainability trends include many of the trends that are discussed in this book, including global warming/climate change, diminishing fresh water supplies, agricultural and food systems, health issues like HIV/AIDS, and greater accountability and transparency in corporate governance.

In response to a question posed on the DJSI website, regarding the global nature of their indexes, they reply:

> "Drivers for business success become increasingly global. This is also true for the growing impact of sustainability trends and applies especially to the big multinational companies which we analyze for the DJSI family. We believe that the world's leading companies set global standards for themselves, thereby making the assessment criteria to be relevant no matter where the company is based. The competition is global."[8]

This statement supports arguments made in this book that global companies may want to develop sustainability programs based on the high denominator countries in which they operate.

A frequently mentioned advantage of corporate sustainability efforts is competitive advantage. The DJSI allows a direct comparison of competitors in a particular industry for 60 industry groups. It is totally transparent as to which top rated companies in an industry sector are on the list. For those familiar with the industry, the missing companies are obvious. Table 4-2 shows the 60 industry groups and the industry leaders, including ties. These rankings are not only guideposts for investors interested in sustainability focused companies, but they also provide positive and negative information, which can help or hinder a company's reputation. Thus besides investors, inclusion in the indexes may impact impressions and attitudes of other stakeholders, including employees, customers, suppliers and regulators.

Table 4-2
Industry Leaders
Dow Jones Sustainability Indexes

DJSI Industry Groups	Industry Group Leader(s)
Advertising	WPP Group Plc
Airlines	British Airways Plc, Deutsche & Lufthansa AG
Aluminum	Alcan Inc.
Aerospace	BAE Systems
Auto Parts & Tires	Denso Corp.
Auto Manufacturers	Toyota Motor, Volkswagen AG
Building Materials	Siam Cement Public Co. Ltd
Banks	Westpac Banking Corp.
Broadcasting	ITV Plc, British Sky Broadcasting
Biotechnology	Novozymes A/S
Beverage	SABMiller PLC, Allied Domecq Plc, Diageo Plc
Chemicals	DSM NV, Air Products & Chemicals Inc., BASF AG, Bayer AG, E.I. Du Pont De Nemours & Co., ICI, Praxair Inc.
Communications Technology	Nokia Corp., L.M. Ericsson, Motorola Inc.
Casinos	Hilton Group Plc
Heavy Construction	AMEC plc
Cosmetics	L'Oreal
Consumer Electronics	Koninklijke (Royal) Philips Electronics
Consumer Services	Stagecoach Group plc
Containers & Packaging	Temple Inland Inc.
Wireless Communications	mmO2 PLC
Pharmaceuticals	Novo Nordisk A/S, AstraZeneca PLC, GlaxoSmithKline, Novartis AG, Roche Holding AG
Electric Utilities	RWE AG, Enel, Grupo Iberdrola
Electric Components & Equipment	Daikin Industries Ltd.
Financial Services	Citigroup, 3i Group plc, Daiwa Securities Group Inc.
Food Retailers & Wholesalers	J. Sainsbury Plc
Food	Unilever, Cadbury Schweppes, Danisco A/S, Groupe Danone
Forest Products	UPM-Kymmene Oy
Furnishings & Appliances	Herman Miller Inc.
Fixed Line Communications	BT Group Plc, Deutsche Telekom AG, Telecom Italia SPA, Telefonica, S.A.
Gas Utilities	The Australian Gas Light Company, Centrica
Healthcare Providers	SSL International
Home Construction	Taylor Woodrow Plc
Household Products	Procter & Gamble Co. Henkel KGaA, Reckitt Benckiser
Industrial Services	Mitsubishi Corp., Premier Farnell Plc, Sumitomo Corp.
Industrial, Diversified	3M Company
Industrial Equipment	Metso Corp.
Insurance	Swiss Re, AGF, Allianz AG, Friends Provident, ING Groep N.V., Storebrand ASA
Advanced Industrial Equipment	Agilent Technologies Inc.
Mining	Anglo American Plc., BHP Billiton Group, Rio Tinto plc
Entertainment	EMI Group
Medical Products	Baxter International Inc. Coloplast
Oil Drilling, Equipment & Services	Noble Corporation
Oil, Gas and Coal Companies	Statoil, BP p.l.c.
Pipelines	TransCanada
Pollution Control	Tomra Systems ASA, Tetra Tech
Publishing	Pearson Plc., Yell Group Plc.
Real Estate	British Land Plc, Investa Property Group
Recreational Products & Services	Eastman Kodak Co., Fuji Photo Film
Restaurants and Lodging	Starbucks Corp.
Retail	Marks & Spencer p.l.c., Aeon Co Ltd., Ito-Yokado Co.Ltd
Semiconductors	Intel Corp.
Software	SAP AG Pfd, Cognos Inc.
Steel	Dofasco Inc.
Textiles & Apparel	adidas-Salomon AG, Nike Inc.
Technology Hardware & Equipment	Hewlett-Packard Co.
Toys	Mattel
Tobacco	British American Tobacco Plc
Industrial Transportation	BAA Plc, MTR Corp., Nippon Yusen KK
Technology Services	Unisys Corp.
Water Utilities	Severn Trent Plc

Source: www.sustainability-indexes.com as of September 20, 2004.

FTSE4Good Indexes

FTSE4Good Indexes were launched in 2001 in the United Kingdom. The Indexes encompass four tradable and four benchmark indexes representing Global, European, U.S. and U.K. markets. To meet the FTSE4Good inclusion criteria, companies must meet prescribed standards in:

- Environmental Sustainability
- Upholding and Supporting Universal Human Rights
- Developing Positive Relations with Stakeholders

The FTSE4Good indexes exclude companies involved in the tobacco, weapons and nuclear power industries.

Data used in assessing company's eligibility for inclusion in the FTSE4Good indexes is independently researched by Ethical Investment Research Services (EIRIS), a leading provider of data on companies to SRI fund managers, governments, and NGOs. FTSE has identified common themes from ten sets of declared principles, three of which are governmental and seven of which were created by either NGOs or business organizations. These principles were used to create the FTSE4Good selection criteria. The ten sets of principles are listed below:

Governmental Principles

    1. Universal Declaration of Human Rights

    2. The OECD Guidelines for Multinational Enterprises

    3. The UN Global Compact

NGO/Business Principles

    4. CERES (Coalition for Environmentally Responsible Economies)

    5. Amnesty International Human Rights Principles for Companies

    6. The Caux Round Table Principles for Business

    7. The Global Sullivan Principles

    8. Ethical Trading Initiative

    9. SA 8000

    10. Global Reporting Initiative Sustainability Guidelines

More than 1,600 companies are assessed for their compliance with social, environmental and humanitarian measures. Companies are evaluated and either included or rejected. The process is dynamic with companies being added and deleted from the inclusion list. As of October, 2004, 910 companies were in the FTSE4Good benchmark Index, an increase of 72 since October 2003. Companies on the list are not ranked relative to other companies, although they are placed in various industry groupings. Tradable indices cover the 50 largest companies by market capitalization in the benchmark index for the European tradable index and the UK tradable index. The 100 largest companies in the benchmark index are used for the U.S. tradable index and the Global tradable index.[9]

Like the Dow Jones Sustainability Indexes, FTSE4Good Indexes provide equity benchmarks and performance baselines of companies that have active environmental and social programs. They also provide direction, as well as direct investment opportunities, to institutional and individual investors, who wish to target their investments based on environmental and social justice criteria. Companies included in the indexes would be expected to have more favorable reputations because of their sustainability efforts.[10]

Financial Performance of SRI Stocks

General feelings existed that SRI stocks would not perform as well as other stocks. Investments in environmental and social initiatives were looked at as costs that would reduce a company's profits and result in lower stock prices. In addition, SRI funds, by eliminating various stocks, would have less diversification and therefore be subject to higher volatility in financial returns.

Recent studies are providing empirical evidence that SRI funds may not have lower returns—indeed some funds may have higher returns. An excellent and highly recommended book is *Environmental Finance* by Sonia Labatt and Rodney R. White of the University of Toronto. They report on a number of studies, completed in the period 1990-1999, which have analyzed the financial performance of SRI funds. Their overall conclusion found:

> Studies involving either individual companies and sectors or mutual fund performance figures illustrate that researchers have used an assortment of indicators, data sets, and techniques in the examination of the environment-finance nexus. The results of the examination of screened mutual funds consistently suggest that a balanced portfolio of good environmental performers has not harmed investment performance. The authors warn, however, that results should not be interpreted to mean that a "green premium" exists, but rather that there is not a "green penalty" associated with environmentally conscious investing.[11]

Another report, *Sustainability Pays,* commissioned by CIS, the UK's only co-operative insurer, and a leader in SRI, and conducted by the Forum for the Future's Centre for Sustainable Investment, also examined a number of studies, with some having more recent data.[12] The reader is encouraged to look at the complete report, but a summary discussion of their findings is presented below.

The authors of *Sustainability Pays* looked at a number of studies in the U.K. since 1992 and found that the returns of SRI or SEE (Social, Ethical, Environmental) screened funds were broadly similar to unscreened funds. In addition, the volatility or unpredictability of returns was not increased by the screening process. A 2001 study by Larry Chen of UBS Warburg found performance of FTSE4Good indexes were not markedly different than unscreened benchmark equivalents over the period 1996-2001.

A 2001 study by Auke Plantinga and Bert Scholtens, which looked at European screened funds over the period 1994-1999, found that SRI funds actually performed better than non SRI funds. Another 2001 study by Christopher Butz and Andreas Plattner demonstrated that environmental ratings "can explain a substantial part of the out performance or alpha of a portfolio of European stocks." The SRI effect was most significant in the pharmaceutical, chemical and construction industries, but also was important in a number of other industries.

The overall conclusion of the *Sustainability Pays* study stated:

> "The balance of evidence, then, suggests that any advantage that an investor gains from the 'SEE (Social, Ethical, Environmental) effect' is likely to be equaled by the costs of lower diversification. While this may not support the case for higher returns from SRI, it certainly shows that investing in line with his or her beliefs does not imply that an investor must accept lower returns—as is often assumed."[13]

In the United States, a number of studies, which compared the Domini Social Index (DSI) of 400 U.S. companies to the S&P 500 index, were also examined. All these studies showed the DSI outperforming the S&P 500 during the bull market of the 1990s. During the following bear market, the DSI did worse due to its heavy weighting in high-tech stocks. Other data showed that the Calvert Social Investment Equity Fund earned 6.98 percent a year over the 3 year period, April 26, 1999-April 26, 2002, while the S&P 500 lost an average 6.24 percent a year.[14] Through December 31, 2003, Calvert's five year annualized return was 7.6 percent versus 0.4 percent loss for the S&P 500. The Calvert Fund was named one of the nine best mutual funds in 2004 by *Business Week* magazine.[15] More recently, DSI's 10 year annualized return for the period ending May 31,

2005 was 10.9 percent and Calvert's was 10.4 percent versus 10.2 percent for the S&P 500.[16] Another group of studies of U.S. markets found little difference between SRI portfolios and unscreened portfolios.[17]

Some researchers argue that better performance by SRI funds is not produced by a firm's environmental or social values, but by the investment coincidence that many SRI funds were concentrated in certain industries that happened to do well, or had certain features, such as they were larger firms or were high growth companies. In response to these arguments, a study was conducted by H.B. Blank and C.M. Carty of QED International for Innovest Strategic Value Advisors. Innovest produces eco-efficiency ratings based on a company's environmental performance. Both the *Sustainability Pays* report and the study by the Association of British Insurers, *Investing in Social Responsibility: Risks and Opportunities,* referenced the Blank and Carty research. The researchers compared the financial performance of the top rated companies in environmental performance with those of a universal portfolio over the period 1997-2000. The top Innovest environmentally rated company stocks outperformed the universal portfolio in all 4 years with the annual returns of 12.4 percent versus 8.9 percent for the universal portfolio. The volatility of the top environmentally rated stocks was actually lower than the universal portfolio, indicating that Innovest's top rated companies do not derive above average returns by assuming above-average risks. Another stage of the research controlled for unintended concentrations in certain industries or ones with certain characteristics. Innovest's top environmentally rated stock portfolios still outperformed the S&P 500 in 1998-1999 on a 21.8 percent versus 17.2 percent annual return. The final stage compared the top environmentally rated Innovest companies with the lowest rated companies in environmentally sensitive industries, such as chemicals, utilities, forest products, mining and petroleum. Over the period 1997-2000, the portfolio of top rated companies had an 18 percent annual return and lower volatility versus a 10.2 percent annual return and higher volatility for the lowest rated companies.[18]

A study by Governance Metrics International produced similar results as the Innovest commissioned study. Governance Metrics, which began operations in April 2000, examines companies and gives them a corporate governance rating. Some 600 measures, including a company's labor practices, environmental activities, workplace safety, litigation history, independent directors, past poison pill provisions, and restatements of earnings, are considered in determining the rating. Governance Metrics looks at the stock performance of the higher rated companies versus overall average stock performance and versus the lowest rated companies. Over the period March 20, 2000-March 20, 2003, the top five rated companies' stocks averaged a 23.1 percent appreciation in value. The stock of the top 15 rated companies averaged a 3.4 percent increase. Alternatively, the 50 companies with the lowest scores saw their stock values fall an average of 28.2 percent. The un-weighted average of the stocks in the S&P 500 declined 2.3 percent over this three year period.[19]

An updated Governance Metrics study provided similar results. Over the 10 year period ending March 22, 2004, the top 10 percent of rated companies had an annualized rate of return of 12.0 percent versus a 0.2 percent annualized rate for the bottom 10 percent of companies. The average of all rated companies was 10.0 percent. Governance Metrics scores about 1,000 of the largest U.S. firms and just over 600 foreign corporations.[20]

While the Governance Metrics ratings include factors that go beyond sustainability measures used by SRI funds, the study does provide evidence that the stocks of top rated companies in corporate governance, (which include sustainability factors) outperform the stocks of low rated companies, as well as the overall market. In addition, the ratings compiled by Governance Metrics, which are primarily used by institutional investors, is another example of the increasing transparency that companies are facing in the sustainability and corporate governance areas.

The empirical evidence presented above makes a strong case that investing in SRI screened stocks does not penalize the investor by producing lower returns. The evidence indicates that the worst case result for SRI stock returns is that they perform about the same as the overall market. The more recent evidence suggests that SRI stocks are producing higher returns than the overall market. These results are consistent with a major theme of this book that environmental stresses and social justice pressures are exposing corporations to greater risks. For those firms with poor environmental and social records, their stock performance appears to be suffering relative to companies with better records.

With increased transparency of corporate environmental and social justice performance, this developing discrepancy between SRI screened stocks and non-screened funds will attract more investor interest in SRI funds. As these funds grow, the demand for stocks that are screened out will drop, putting further downward pressure on shareholder values in these stocks. The increased transparency provided by DJSI, FTSE4Good and other rating systems will transmit positive or negative impressions to stakeholders other than investors, including customers, employees, suppliers, legislators and local communities. Corporate reputations may suffer or be improved. Those companies with high or top ratings within an industry group will gain obvious competitive advantage. Boards of directors of low rated companies may be questioned about their fiduciary duties to shareholders. As noted by Matthew Kiernan, CEO of Innovest Strategic Value Advisors, in a *Financial Times* article:

> "The "prudent fiduciary" equation is being turned on its head. Since there is now evidence that superior environmental and social performance improves the risk profile, profitability, and stock performance of publicly-traded companies, fiduciaries can be seen to be derelict in their duties if they do not consider sustainability."[21]

Shareholder Resolutions

Shareholder resolutions involving sustainability issues pose another type of risk. Resolutions favored by company management do not present problems, but many are brought to change company policy and strategy, and are typically in opposition to the practices and wishes of management. Such resolutions produce a variety of risks.

One, if the shareholder resolution passes, it will require a resistant management to make changes in its operating policies. Two, even if the resolution does not pass, it indicates areas of conflict between management and the shareholders that voted for the resolution. Such conflict is an indication that there may be a fundamental weakness in management policy, or at least raises questions about management strategy. Particularly if such resolutions receive publicity, it can put the company in an unfavorable light and may adversely impact its reputation and/or stock price.

Three, a victory can be claimed by the supporting shareholders, even if the resolution does not pass, if a significant percentage of positive votes are cast. This is particularly true if the resolution involves a large corporation with millions of shareholders. Victories can also be claimed if the percentage of positive votes increases from one year to the next. The appearance of victories, even when resolutions fail, heightens the conflict and leaves a stronger impression that management may be shortsighted in its opposition.

Shareholders have been particularly active in presenting global warming resolutions over the past few years and illustrate the risks discussed above. The rationale of these resolutions is that global warming poses large potential financial risks to corporations and should be addressed by management. For companies that produce large amounts of greenhouse gases, a financial risk exists that a new government regulation or competitive pressure will force them to invest large amounts of money in a short period of time to take corrective actions.

Reports from the European Union and the United Nations have estimated that changes in climate brought about by global warming could cost the world $300 billion annually by 2050 from weather damage, pollution and industrial and agricultural losses.[22] Often the resolutions ask the companies to calculate and disclose their annual greenhouse gas emissions, and to draft a plan for reducing these emissions.

Investor Responsibility Research Center (IRRC), a proxy research firm, reported that 14 global warming related resolutions were pending against U.S. companies as of April, 2003, which was double the number that came to shareholder votes in 2002.[23] By May 29, 2003, the *New York Times* reported that shareholders had filed 31 global warming resolutions with 23 U.S. companies and 5 Canadian companies.[24] For 2004 and 2005, shareholders filed 22 and 30 resolutions, respectively.[25]

IRRC also reported that those resolutions that came to a vote in 2002 received an average of 19 percent support, double the support in 2001.[26] For resolutions that had come to vote in 2003, the average support level was 22.6 percent. The United States Public Interest Research Group reported that average support in 2003 was at more than 25 percent.[27] The 20-25 percent level is critical according to Meg Voorhes, director of IRRC's social issues service. She states, "In the 32 year history of shareholder activism on social issues, only board-diversity proposals have had average support levels of 20 percent."[28]

CERES and the Interfaith Center on Corporate Responsibility (ICCR), which represents 275 faith-based institutional investors with combined holdings of around $90 billion, have coordinated the filing of shareholder resolutions over the last 10 years. They filed 31 global warming resolutions against 28 companies in 2003, including the five largest U.S. utilities. Their support levels at three of these utilities were: American Electric Power Company—27 percent; TXU Corporation—24 percent; and the Southern Company—23 percent. Other notable support levels at non-utility companies were Chevron Texaco—32 percent; GE—23 percent; and ExxonMobil—22 percent.[29] The 2005 shareholder resolution at ExxonMobil was watched closely, and resulted in a 28 percent approval rate.[30]

According to the Social Investment Forum 2003 survey, only 20 percent of SRI money is used in shareholder advocacy. This is actually a decrease of 40 percent from 2001, but more resolutions were filed, 320 in 2003 versus 261 in 2001, and those introduced got more votes, 11.4 percent in 2003 versus 8.7 percent in 2001. Most of the resolutions, with which SRI monies were involved, dealt with environmental and ethical employment issues.[31]

Not all shareholder resolutions came up for a vote. The Social Investment Forum, using IRRC data, calculated that 348 shareholder resolutions on social and environmental issues were filed, but only 211 were pending as of March 11, 2005.[32] Some are omitted by the SEC. In other cases, shareholder groups may withdraw the resolutions after meeting with the company and receiving assurances that efforts are being made to address the issues raised in the resolution. This latter point is demonstrated by resolutions brought against Ford and GM, in 2003, regarding global warming emissions from plants and cars. The resolution against Ford was withdrawn when Chairman William Clay Ford and other top managers met with shareholder groups and agreed to work hard to reduce greenhouse gas emissions. GM was not as cooperative and their resolution was voted on, but only received six percent support.[33]

A recent change in SEC rules may bring mutual funds more into play. Mutual fund investors do not cast proxy votes—they are cast by the mutual fund group. Until the new SEC rules passed in January, 2003, mutual funds have kept their proxy voting records secret, with the exception of some SRI funds. Now mutual funds must make their voting records available to mutual fund investors. This new transparency may be particularly important since according to Douglas G. Cogan, a deputy director with IRRC, "Over the last ten years most major mutual funds have consistently voted their proxies against shareholder resolutions."[34] Armed with this new information, investors could apply pressure to their mutual funds by threatening to withdraw their funds.

Other Shareholder/Investor Actions

Shareholder advocacy is increasing beyond shareholder resolutions. Institutional Shareholder Services (IIS), Inc., an advisor to pension and mutual fund managers, switched and supported a global warming resolution against ExxonMobil in 2002—one that IIS had opposed in 2001.[35] The publication of the *Investor Guide to Climate Risk*, in August 2004, is a strong indication that these efforts will accelerate and be more organized. The guide is a new resource of the Investor Network on Climate Risk (INCR) and available at its website.[36] The INCR is an alliance of institutional investors launched in November 2003 and dedicated to coordinating investor engagement with companies and policy makers on climate risk. The guide was published and commissioned by CERES, which serves as the INCR Secretariat. The author is Douglas G. Cogan of IRRC. The *Investor Guide* assists money managers to implement recommendations of the Investor Call for Action on Climate at the United Nations, which was signed by investor groups representing over $800 billion in assets. The three action areas identified in the guide are:

1. climate risk assessment;

2. climate risk disclosure; and

3. support of government actions to promote investor certainty, including mandatory policies to achieve absolute reductions in greenhouse gas emissions.[37]

In May 2002, 35 institutional investors, including Allianz Dresdner, Credit Suisse, Munich Re, and Swiss Re, with combined assets in excess of $4,500 billion wrote to the world's 500 largest companies, and asked them to disclose what the financial impacts of global warming and climate change risks will be on their companies. These investors emphasize that they feel the risks are real and they want to know what measures are being taken by the companies to minimize them.[38] The type of questions asked are similar to the inquiries being put forth by shareholder resolutions on global warming.

The above survey of the Fortune 500 (FT500), known as the Carbon Disclosure Project, was sent out a second time in November, 2003, with 95 institutional investors, managing more than $10 trillion, supporting the effort this time. The response rate increased from 47 percent to 59 percent. The quality and diversity of the responses also improved. The report authors, Innovest Strategic Value Advisors, noted that it is clear that corporations are taking the survey process and the risks more seriously. As noted in the report:

> "More firms than last year consider climate change to present risks and opportunities to their business. More are quantifying GHG emissions and preparing to trade emissions. Corporate climate strategies are becoming more coherent and more comprehensive."[39]

Each subsequent survey will put more pressure on the world's largest corporations to respond. Data on corporate CO_2 emissions and risk management strategies will be increasingly more transparent. And no regulations are involved here. Investor and competitor pressures are combining to force corporations to disclose and to act.

Another call for greater transparency comes from a group of philanthropic foundations and investment managers, including The Rose Foundation for Communities and the Environment, the Rockefeller Family Fund, the Surdna Foundation, and the Richard and Rhoda Goldman Fund. The group is calling on the SEC to enforce regulations for requiring companies to more fully disclose environmental liabilities. Their investment concern is that hidden environment liabilities will cause unforeseen losses to their portfolios. The report argues that "disclosure is important to investors because environmental risks and liabilities represent a drag on shareholder value, while corporate environmental initiatives can cut costs and boost share prices."[40]

California's state treasurer, who is a trustee for two of three largest public pension funds, has suggested that the two funds should start considering corporate environmental actions when making investment decisions. The two funds are the California Public Employees' Retirement System (CALPERS) and the California State Teachers' Retirement System. While these funds have a long track record of shareholder activism on social issues, moving into screening environmental performance would constitute a new strategy.[41]

Several developments in the U.K. have accelerated investors and shareholders attention to sustainability risks. The government passed a 1999 amendment (effective July 2000) to the 1995 Pensions Act requiring all pension fund trustees to consider social, ethical and environmental issues in making their investment decisions. The amendment requires that in their annual statement of investment principles a comment on: "the extent, if at all, to which social, environmental or ethical considerations are taken into account in the selection, retention and realization of investments."[42]

The Turnbull Report, published in 1995, called for professional shareholders to pay more attention to social, ethical and environmental risks in their investment strategies, and for such risks to be managed in a similar manner as financial and hazard risks. The Report, which has become law, also introduced guidelines for the disclosure of sustainability risks in company reports.[43]

The Association of British Insurers (ABI) has issued investments guidelines to recognize the increasing corporate exposure to sustainability risks and the need to effectively manage these risks. The ABI urges that its members use these guidelines when investing policyholders' monies. Specifically, the guidelines call for each publicly traded company, in which ABI insurers invest, to state in their annual reports whether:

- Its board of directors takes regular account of the significance of social, environmental and ethical matters to the company's business.

- Its board has identified and assessed the significant risks to the company's long and short term value arising from such matters.

- Its board has received adequate information to make this assessment and whether it has taken account of social responsibility in the training of its directors.

- Its board has ensured that the company has effective systems for managing the risks.

With regard to policies and procedures, the annual report should:

- Include information on social, ethical and environmental risks facing the company.

- Describe policies and procedures for managing those risks.[44]

A worst case scenario for a board of directors, which resists a shareholder resolution or other action, would be a large financial loss caused by the failure of the board to respond to the shareholders' concerns. The loss might have been avoided had the resolution been passed. The directors and officers, who in all likelihood had opposed the resolution, would be particularly susceptible to litigation brought by the group of shareholders supporting the resolution. Their defense under the business judgment rule would depend on how seriously the board of directors had researched and examined the concerns raised by the resolution (see Chapter 5). Since many shareholder resolutions involve sustainability issues, it seems most prudent that the board be well informed on these issues and have adequate risk management systems in place to deal with them.

Corporate Governance

In the wake of the Enron, Andersen, WorldCom, etc. scandals, shareholder proposals on corporate governance have increased dramatically. The Corporate Library, a Portland, Maine research firm focusing on corporate governance issues, provides data that show shareholder proposals increasing from 358 in 2000 to 668 in 2003. More significantly, 159 (24 percent) of the proposals in 2003 received more than 50 percent of the votes cast versus only 54 (15 percent) in 2000.[45] With both corporate governance and environmental and social justice resolutions and proposals on the rise, SRI funds and other investor groups are naturally reinforcing each others efforts. For further information, Appendix B lists several organizations and their websites that are active in the SRI, shareholder resolution, and corporate governance areas.

The mutual fund scandals may also lead some investors to direct more monies into SRI funds. It would seem to be a reasonable assumption that SRI mutual fund companies would be more ethical in their general handling of investors' monies, and would not be involved in such tactics as late trading and market timing. Calvert, the nation's largest family of SRI mutual funds, commissioned Harris Interactive to conduct a survey of investors. The survey results demonstrate investors' growing concern about ethical standards at corporations and mutual fund companies. The survey found that investors set a clear link between good corporate governance and shareholder value:

- 85 percent of investors are more likely to invest in a mutual fund if it engages in ethical operations and reporting.

- 71 percent of those surveyed said that they either strongly agreed (35%) or somewhat agreed (36%) that companies with high integrity carry lower investment risk.

- 68 percent of those surveyed said that they either strongly agreed (31%) or somewhat agreed (37%) that companies with high integrity deliver higher investment returns.

Barbara J. Krumsiek, Calvert's President & CEO, observed:

> "The survey clearly shows that investors understand that corporate responsibility matters. It is increasing clear that investors believe that well-governed, socially responsible companies are better positioned to deliver long-term, sustainable value to their shareholders."[46]

Strengthen All Three Bottom Lines

NGOs and other groups, interested in greater corporate effects in the environmental and social justice areas, have always been asked to make the business case for these efforts. Of the three components of sustainability, namely, economic, environmental and social justice, traditional thinking held that environmental and social efforts came with a cost that negatively impacts the economic or financial performance of the firm. Sustainability efforts were thought to be a zero-sum strategy.

Empirical based studies in the investment area are now calling these traditional notions into question. More evidence is developing that greater corporate sustainability efforts actually lead to improved economic performance, financial returns and stock prices—a win-win result. The increasing transparencies brought about by investment groups like DJSI can enhance a company's reputation among investors and other stakeholders including customers, employees, suppliers, regulators and local communities. Greater transparencies can also result in competitive advantages for companies making the greatest sustainability efforts within their industry groups. The risks of shareholder resolutions, even litigation directed at directors and offices, are minimized through increased corporate sustainability efforts.

Reluctant companies will increasingly be forced to make the case that corporate sustainability efforts are not in the company's interest. Growing evidence suggests this task will be difficult to accomplish. For those corporations not making sustainability efforts, the risks of lower financial returns, reputation damage, competitive disadvantage and shareholder discontent will escalate.

Sustainability risk management leads to the increasingly obvious conclusion that reluctant companies need to consider changing their course of action and focusing on sustainability efforts. Lack of action may constitute a breach of fiduciary duty by the management and board of directors. Given the continuing stresses and pressures in the environmental and social justice areas, sustainability risks are only going to increase. Following SRI and other related strategies can be an integral component of sustainability risk management. Environmental and social justice risks are minimized and the stability of the firm's financial performance is improved. All three bottom lines, economic, environmental and social justice, are strengthened.

CHAPTER 4—ENDNOTES

[1] Rory Knight and Deborah Pretty, "The Impact of Catastrophes on Shareholder Value," Oxford Executive Research Briefing, Oxford University; reported in Association of British Insurers, *Investing in Social Responsibility: Risks and Opportunities,* London: ABI, 2001.

[2] J. Frooman, "Socially Irresponsible and Illegal Behavior and Shareholder Wealth," *Business and Society,* Vol. 3b, No. 3, 1997.

[3] Judy Greenwald, "Brand Risk Requires Careful Management," *Business Insurance,* November 19, 2001.

[4] Social Investment Forum, *2003 Report on Socially Responsible Investing Trends* in the United States, SIF, 2003.

[5] Association of British Insurers, *Investing in Social Responsibility: Risks and Opportunities,* London: ABI, 2001.

[6] Ilana Polyak, "Do Blue Chips Belong in a Social Purist's Portfolio?" *New York Times,* May 1, 2005.

[7] www.sustainability-indexes.com

[8] Ibid.

[9] www.ftse.com

[10] For parts of this section on sustainability indexes, information derived from Sonia Labatt and Rodney R. White, *Environmental Finance,* Hoboken, New Jersey: John Wiley & Sons, 2002.

[11] Sonia Labatt and Rodney R. White, *Environmental Finance,* Hoboken, New Jersey: John Wiley & Sons, 2002.

[12] Forum for the Future Centre for Sustainable Investment, *Sustainability Pays,* commissioned by CIS, 2002.

[13] Ibid.

[14] Susan Scherreilk, "Following Your Conscience Is Just a Few Clicks Away," *Business Week,* May 13, 2002.

[15] Lauren Young, "The Best Mutual Fund Managers 2004," *Business Week,* March 22, 2004.

[16] Data from Wiesenberger Thomson Financial and KLD Research & Analysis, Inc., May 31, 2005.

[17] Forum for the Future Centre for Sustainable Investment, *Sustainability Pays,* commissioned by CIS, 2002.

[18] Forum for the Future Centre for Sustainable Investment, *Sustainability Pays,* commissioned by CIS, 2002; Association of British Insurers, *Investing in Social Responsibility: Risks and Opportunities,* London: ABI, 2001.

[19] Gretchen Morgenson, "Shares of Corporate Nice Guys Can Finish First," *New York Times,* April 27, 2003.

[20] Governance Metrics International, March 22, 2004; Ken Brown, "Weak Boardrooms and Weak Stocks Go Hand in Hand," *Wall Street Journal,* September 9, 2003.

[21] Matthew Kiernan, "Taking Control of Climate," *Financial Times,* November 24, 2002.

[22] Katharine Q. Seelye, "Environmental Groups Gain As Companies Vote on Issues," *New York Times,* May 29, 2003.

[23] Jeffrey Ball, "Global Warming Threatens Health of Corporations," *Wall Street Journal,* April 16, 2003.

[24] Katharine Q. Seelye, "Environmental Groups Gain As Companies Vote on Issues," *New York Times,* May 29, 2003.

[25] CERES, "U.S. Companies Face Record Number of Global Warming Shareholder Resolutions On Wider Range of Business Sectors," February 17, 2005.

[26] Jeffrey Ball, "Global Warming Threatens Health of Corporations," *Wall Street Journal,* April 16, 2003.

[27] Katharine Q. Seelye, "Environmental Groups Gain As Companies Vote on Issues," *New York Times,* May 29, 2003.

[28] Ibid.

[29] Marilyn Berlin Snell, "Sister Action," *Sierra,* May/June 2003; Katharine Q. Seelye, "Environmental Groups Gain As Companies Vote on Issues," *New York Times,* May 29, 2003.

[30] CERES, "ExxonMobil Investors Give Record Voting Support to Climate Change Resolution," May 25, 2005.

[31] Marshall Glickman and Marjorie Kelly, "Working Capital," *E. Magazine,* March/April 2004.

[32] Social Investment Forum, "Social Shareholder Resolutions Close to 2004 Record," April 7, 2005.

[33] Jeffrey Ball, "Ford, GM Diverge in Reaction to Fuel-Efficiency Resolutions," *Wall Street Journal,* May 8, 2003.

[34] Marilyn Berlin Snell, "Do You Know What Your Mutual Fund Is Up To?" *Sierra,* May/June 2003.

[35] Jeffrey Ball, "Global Warming Threatens Health of Corporations," *Wall Street Journal,* April 16, 2003.

[36] www.incr.com

[37] CERES press release, August 12, 2004.

[38] Matthew Kiernan, "Taking Control of Climate," *Financial Times,* November 24, 2002.

[39] Mark Nicholls, "Disclose or be damned," *Environmental Finance,* June 2004; Reports available at www.cdproject.net.

[40] David Bank, "Groups Urge Enforcing Rules of Environmental Disclosure," *Wall Street Journal,* August 22, 2002.

[41] Jeffrey Ball, "State Aids Mull Pension Funds and Environment," *Wall Street Journal,* November 21, 2003.

[42] Association of British Insurers, *Investing in Social Responsibility: Risks and Opportunities,* London: ABI, 2001.

[43] Carolyn Aldred, "Reputation Risks Seen as Growing Exposure," *Business Insurance,* November 26, 2001.

[44] Ibid.

[45] Queena Sook Kim, "Corporate Gadflies Are the Buzz," *Wall Street Journal,* June 10, 2004.

[46] "SRI Perspectives," *Greenmoney Journal,* Spring 2004.

5

THE BUCK STOPS HERE: DIRECTORS AND OFFICERS LIABILITY

○ ○

The "prudent fiduciary" equation is being turned on its head. Since there is now evidence that superior environmental and social performance improves the risk profile, profitability, and stock performance of publicly-traded companies, fiduciaries can be seen to be derelict in their duties if they do not consider sustainability.

> —*Matthew Kiernan, CEO, Innovest Strategic Value Advisors*

It takes 20 years to build a reputation and five minutes to ruin it. If you think about that, you'll do things differently.

> —*Warren Buffet, CEO, Berkshire Hathaway*

Directors and officers will feel the legal ramifications of the various sustainability risk exposures discussed in Chapters 1-4. These risk exposures can be expected to cause disruptions in the corporate governance area and increase the exposure of directors and officers to liability actions. The firm will actually face two levels of potential risk. The first level will derive from liability claims brought by injured parties, and the financial and reputation disruption brought by customer boycotts and shareholder actions. The second level of potential risk will be liability actions brought against directors and officers primarily by shareholders, but also employees, regulators and competitors.

Directors and officers are responsible for the broad overall management of the corporation. While emphasis is certainly on economic management—profitability and the financial condition of the firm, directors and officers today must also focus on the other two components of corporate sustainability—environmental and social justice management.

Fiduciary Duties

In conducting their responsibilities, directors and officers are required to exercise certain fiduciary duties, as they occupy a position of trust for shareholders, the board of directors and the general public. These fiduciary duties include the duty of care, the duty of loyalty and the duty of disclosure. Failure to perform these duties can result in liability claims.

The Duty of Care

Directors and officers have a duty to exercise reasonable care in the performance of their corporate functions. The level or standard is measured by the degree of care exercised by reasonable and prudent directors and officers. Failure to maintain this level can result in claims of negligence being brought against the directors and officers. Directors and officers are not guarantors of the firm's performance. Managerial and strategy decisions must be made, such as the development of a new product or the acquisition of another company, and the results of the decisions may be positive or negative.

The business judgment rule insulates directors and officers against liability, as long as they exercise appropriate judgment in reaching their decisions. The standard is whether their level of judgment meets the level exercised by reasonable and prudent directors and officers. An important requirement of invoking the business judgment rule is that directors and officers have a duty to keep themselves informed of the facts, information, etc. on which to base reasonable and prudent decision making. Obviously, this requires regular attendance at board and committee meetings. Directors and officers need to review supporting documentation associated with these meetings and more importantly request additional information when it is not provided.

The Duty of Loyalty

Directors and officers have the duty of loyalty to their corporation and their shareholders. This means the corporation and shareholders come first. A director or officer cannot personally take advantage of a business opportunity that rightly belongs to the corporation. They should not own or operate a business that directly competes with the corporation. Directors and officers cannot use insider information to buy or sell stock of the corporation.

The Duty of Disclosure

Directors and officers have the general duty to disclose material facts to the appropriate parties that have a right to these facts, but would not otherwise be able to obtain them. These parties include directors, regulators, shareholders, bondholders, creditors, and potential investors.[1]

Exposures

When faced with sustainability risk exposures, the business judgment rule can protect directors and officers against litigation, but it also puts pressure on them to stay informed of relevant sustainability developments. For instance, U.S. corporations cannot just ignore the Kyoto treaty on reducing greenhouse gas emissions, despite the fact that the Bush administration does not support the treaty and the U.S. Senate has not ratified the treaty. Directors and officers need to consider arguments made by environmental groups, governmental organizations, other countries and even business groups in favor of supporting the treaty. They certainly need to consider the wishes of their shareholders to disclose information on the corporation's strategy for dealing with greenhouse gas emissions. Ignoring these warnings and requests may compromise the protection that directors and officers have under the business judgment rule. If business decisions were made without considering warnings and requests, and they contributed to unfavorable results, then directors and officers expose themselves to litigation.

Response to Outside Warnings

Sustainability presents a complicated myriad of risks. Generating all the necessary information internally to make good decisions can be overly burdensome. It would seem wise to at a minimum assemble and consider the information being provided by other groups and organizations. That is not to say that decisions have to be made according to what, for instance, an NGO environmental group desires. But management needs to provide evidence and justification as to why their decision is better and different than an NGO group would have made. Again, it is not just NGO groups—similar management and strategic planning information is coming from business groups, shareholders and regulators. And these groups might be right. At a minimum, management and the board need to document why these groups might be wrong.

Response to Boycotts

One of the critical duties of corporate directors and officers is to protect the reputation of the firm. Given the reputation damage that boycotts of the firm can produce, they must be treated very seriously. While it is often difficult to isolate the adverse financial effects of a boycott, there is certainly antidotal evidence that sales and profits suffer. Several examples of boycott campaigns are discussed in Chapter 3.

If a firm is incurring minimal or no measurable damages from a boycott, the temptation exists to do nothing in response to the boycott in terms of corporate changes in operations. This risk management strategy may backfire if a catastrophic or unexpected event occurs. For example, if a firm was being boycotted because of sweatshop conditions of its suppliers or factories, and say a serious fire killed and injured a number of workers, the adverse publicity could strengthen the boycott and result in decreased revenues and profits. The liability exposure could be increased as the firm had plenty of warnings and information from the boycott that their practices were putting the workers at an excessive risk.

Boycotts also tarnish a company's brand. As David Mair, risk manager of the U.S. Olympic Committee, noted:

> "If I'm a director of a major corporation today, one of the questions I want to ask is whether our risk management is looking at the brand risks we face as a result of the business we are in or the business practices we employ."[2]

Many corporations are discounting the effects of global warming and waiting for clearer data on the impact of climate change. They assume that if adverse consequences develop there will be ample time to make adjustments in their operations to reduce greenhouse gases. But what if the climate were to change abruptly giving them little time to make effective adjustments (see Chapter 7). Governments could also pass crisis legislation requiring immediate and costly responses. Again their reputation and financial performance could suffer, and their liability exposure will increase.

If directors and officers discount a boycott, they not only face immediate reputation damage and adverse financial effects, but if something goes wrong that could have been avoided by responding to the boycott, their personal liability could increase substantially. Their protection under the business judgment rule could be compromised, as they are required to avail themselves to all relevant information in an area before making decisions.

A delay in responding to a boycott may not only result in short term reputation and financial damages, it could hurt the firm in the long run. If the firm eventually responds to the boycott and makes the required changes in their operations and the boycott is lifted, customers and other stakeholders may be slow to excuse the firm's resistance to the boycott. The effects of the boycott may extend beyond the effective period of the boycott. This would be particularly true if other competitors in the industry had responded sooner to the boycott. Customers knowledgeable of the boycott might choose to buy from those firms that reacted more expeditiously. The prolonged adverse financial results may result in disgruntled shareholders and possibly even litigation.

New Exposure—Private Corporations

Directors and officers liability has primarily been a concern for public corporations, with suits typically brought by shareholders. A May 2003 ruling, in a case brought by creditors against directors and officers of a private corporation, has substantially increased their exposure.[3]

The case involves Trace International Holdings and the actions of its President, Marshall S. Cogan. Mr. Cogan was alleged to have siphoned off millions of dollars from the holding company through excessive executive compensation, illegal family compensation, unauthorized loans, and inappropriate dividend distributions when the company went insolvent. An action was brought by the bankruptcy trustee, John S. Pereira, against Cogan and the other directors and officers. Judge Robert W. Sweet of the Federal District Court in Manhattan held that the directors and officers could not simply rubberstamp whatever their boss decided—they have a fiduciary duty to the corporation. The judge effectively applied the same criteria for fiduciary responsibility to Trace's directors and officers as are used with public companies. With the exception of Mr. Cogan, the directors and officers were found to be liable even though they did not benefit personally. John Camps, a lawyer who represented the bankruptcy trustee, stated:

> "It clarifies that directors and officers of private companies will be held to the same standards as those at public companies in determining whether they have fulfilled their fiduciary duties. Creditors of bankrupt private companies can use the precedent to look to the directors and officers for recovery of damages caused by mismanagement."[4]

While this case does not deal with environmental and social justice issues, the precedents established here could impact future cases where such issues are at the heart of a case. Directors and officers of private corporations will be held to the same level of fiduciary duties as in public companies. Private corporations failing to adequately deal with environmental and social justice concerns will be exposed to the same degree of accountability as public companies. Private directors and officers will not be able to escape liability because of perceived lower standards.

Similar Exposure—Public Corporations

Another case involving a large public company, Walt Disney, illustrates a similar exposure for directors of public corporations. In June 2003, a Delaware judge ruled that a shareholder derivative lawsuit against Disney's CEO and directors could go to trial.[5] The case involves a lucrative compensation deal for Michael Ovitz, in which he received $38 million in cash and options valued at $100 million, for a 14 month engagement. The deal was negotiated by Disney's Chairman & CEO, Michael D. Eisner, with allegedly minimal involvement by the board of directors. Rather than shielding the board, their lack of involvement suggests that directors were "consciously indifferent" to the terms of the contract with Mr. Ovitz.

The decision was the first to allow a case against directors accused of failing to uphold their fiduciary duties, without any suggestions of self dealing or personal gain. It also marks the first time the Delaware Court of Chancery ever threatened directors with personal liability for decisions involving ordinary business matters. The business judgment rule may not protect the directors because of their failure to keep themselves informed. The suit sought repayment of monies from Ovitz and damages assessed against the company and its directors.[6] A case with similar issues involves legal action against the directors of Abbott Laboratories.[7]

In August 2005, Judge William B. Chandler ruled for Disney's board of directors. While concluding that the Disney's board, "fell significantly short of best practices of ideal corporate governance," he found that "Eisner's actions were taken in good faith." Since the events occurred 10 years ago, and before the Enron and WorldCom scandals, the judge reasoned that it would be unfair to apply today's standards to past conduct. But Judge Chandler suggested that courts, "may take a tougher stance related to more recent events."[8] This is of critical importance regarding directors' actions in the sustainability area, as most of these risks are expected to develop from current and future actions.

These two cases, one involving a private company and one involving a public corporation, illustrate the increasing exposure of directors when they fail to uphold their fiduciary duties. The precedents could easily be applied to sustainability risks. Indeed, the directors of many companies could be found to be "consciously indifferent" to environmental and social justice risks facing their firms. If damages to shareholders and other parties are determined to have been caused by such conscious indifference, directors may be found personally liable for these damages. It is worth repeating a quote in Chapter 4 by Matthew Kiernan, CEO of Innovest Strategic Value Advisors:

> "The "prudent fiduciary" equation is being turned on its head. Since there is now evidence that superior environmental and social performance improves the risk profile, profitability, and stock performance of publicly-traded companies, fiduciaries can be seen to be derelict in their duties if they do not consider sustainability."[9]

Social Justice Exposures

Another new case has the potential to substantially increase directors liability regarding human rights abuses in developing countries. If this case were to go to a jury trial, it would be the first case to do so. The case involves human rights abuses in Myanmar (formerly Burma), and the precedents could be applied to any U.S. multinational firm operating in any developing country.[10]

The specific issue involves whether Unocal, an energy company, should stand trial for human rights abuses that were perpetrated by the government of Myanmar during construction of a natural gas pipeline. The case is based on a 1789 law, the Alien Tort Claims Act (ATCA), which originally was intended to allow foreigners to sue international pirates in U.S. courts. The modern approach entails actions brought in U.S. courts against multinationals like Unocal that work with foreign governments in building large projects like the natural gas pipeline in this case. Unocal paid the military to provide security and supported the government, which is accused of engaging in torture, genocide and related abuses of local villagers in violation of international law. Unocal won an important victory in January 2004, when Superior Court of California judge Victoria Gerrard Chaney held Unocal blameless for human rights abuses, saying it was the company's subsidiaries that had been responsible for building the pipeline.[11] The case did not die as Earthrights, the lead plaintiffs attorneys, pursued other legal bases for holding Unocal responsible. A U.S. Supreme Court decision in June 2004, involving another ATCA case, affirmed that non-U.S. citizens may sue corporations for human rights abuses and assisted Earthrights' efforts (see Chapter 10).[12] In spring 2005, Unocal decided to settle the case. While monetary terms of the settlement were not made public, it is estimated that well over $60 million was paid by Unocal to Burmese villagers. The precedent set is extremely important as noted by one of the human rights lawyers in the case, Daphne Eviatar:

> "The standard disclaimers that they've used: that it wasn't our president physically torturing the villagers who worked on the pipeline, it was the government, our joint venture partner, doing this—the Unocal case established that they can't say that anymore."[13]

Similar cases have been brought against a dozen multi-national firms operating in developing countries. These include IBM and Citigroup for benefiting from apartheid in South Africa, Coca-Cola for allegedly hiring para-military units that murdered union organizers in Columbia, and ExxonMobil for allegedly hiring Indonesian troops who committed widespread human-rights abuses.[14]

Besides potential liability damages, the negative publicity and reputation damages of such cases are enormous and may result in cancellation of the project. A case involving charges brought against Talisman Energy for alleged abuses in Sudan resulted in negative publicity and a shareholder resolution that forced the company to sell its $770 million stake in an oil development project.[15] Similarly, for Unocal, a shareholder resolution in 2003 won 32.8 percent support to adopt new corporate principles covering fundamental rights, such as freedom from discrimination in employment, the elimination of child labor and freedom of association and collective bargaining.[16]

In another important case, ChevronTexaco is facing litigation in Ecuador, which may establish new legal precedents.[17] The lawsuit, originally begun in 1993, is being brought by indigenous Indian groups of the Amazon Basin of Ecuador for $1 billion in injuries, illnesses and deaths allegedly caused by Texaco's (Texaco merged with Chevron to create ChevronTexaco in 1991) failure to follow industry standards in disposing of wastewater, oil and toxic wastes from their oil drilling operations. The suit was filed on behalf of 88 plaintiffs, but the entire class action could expand up to 30,000 individuals who are affected by the waste.[18] One estimate of damages puts the ultimate liability at $5 billion.[19] In a related development, the Ecuadorian government passed legislation in 1999 that will require companies like Texaco to pay for past pollution obligations.[20]

What is paramount in this case is that the United States Court of Appeals in New York ruled that the lawsuit should be tried in Ecuador, but the court said that any final ruling and financial penalty imposed against ChevronTexaco would be enforceable in the United States. American multi-nationals typically prefer that lawsuits be tried and verdicts enforced in the developing countries, but this will not be the case in this litigation. The lawsuit contends that some 16 million gallons of oil, 50 percent more than spilled by the Exxon Valdez disaster, was spilled directly into the ground, rivers, and estuaries. While Ecuador did not have environmental laws governing waste disposal in the period of Texaco's operations, 1971-1992, plaintiff lawyers contend that the company ignored long-established practices of re-injecting waste back into the deep oil wells. This process has been used in the United States since at least the 1970s. Environmentalists estimate that Texaco's profits over its two decades of operations were more than $20 billion. It would have cost Texaco $5 billion to re-inject the waste back into the ground.[21] And of course, the oil was not used by the Ecuadorian Indians—it was used in the United States.

Besides the liability action, management faced a resolution asking Chevron Texaco to report on new initiatives to address its legacy of environmental damage in Ecuador, which gained nine percent support from shareowners.[22] This case, as others discussed above, demonstrates how sustainability risks can result in multiple consequences.

ChevronTexaco contends that the plaintiffs presented "no credible scientific evidence" that the oil company caused environmental damage or violated Ecuadorian pollution laws. The Ecuadorian government "released Texaco from further liabilities and obligations," upon the completion of a $40 million decontamination program in 1998.[23] Vice President and general counsel of ChevronTexaco's overseas division stated that the litigation:

> "was not a positive indicator to say this is a place we want to continue to do business. The threat of litigation adds a further element of risk and makes us less competitive."[24]

Many multinational corporations are currently facing pressure from human rights, labor and environmental groups regarding working conditions of suppliers and factories in developing countries, as well as environmental damages resulting from their operations. Actions like those brought against Unocal, ChevronTexaco and others bring an additional layer of pressure and potential liability. Corporations and directors will be held accountable when they are "consciously indifferent" to sustainability risk situations in their corporations. Ignoring these situations is done at the directors own peril. Directors have substantial incentives to adopt strong sustainability risk management strategies.

The cases discussed above also illustrate how risk costs in the environmental and social justice areas can reduce the financial or economic bottom line. In the words of J. Daniel O'Flaherty, Vice President at the National Foreign Trade Council:

> "Large jury awards will send a message that if you are going to do business in a country where the government is violating human-rights or labor standards, you may be sued."[25]

Business groups worry that plaintiffs' successes will stifle U.S. corporate activities around the world. That may be true if business as usual is preserved. But if corporate directors and officers consider all the sustainability risks and incorporate appropriate changes in their business strategies, ample opportunities will still exist, indeed may expand, and hopefully meaningful improvements will be made in countries in which they operate.

Sarbanes—Oxley Act

The Sarbanes—Oxley Act of 2002 will put additional pressure on directors and officers to properly disclose environmental and worker safety liabilities. The corporate CEO and CFO must certify that the company's quarterly and annual reports do not contain any material misrepresentation or misleading information with respect to the financial condition or results of operations of the company and that certain internal control standards are being met.

James Kendrick, President of the American Society of Safety Engineers (ASSE), notes that the Act requires an organization to report an operation that has a failure in a safety, environmental or property operation that may significantly impact the company's financial condition.[26] While details, criteria and standards are still being worked out, a report by the ASSE recommends that all environmental, health and safety personnel meet with top management so that their respective operations can be properly managed and reported under Sarbanes—Oxley.[27] Failures to do so may result in senior management as well as EH&S personnel being penalized under Sarbanes—Oxley.

The Sarbanes—Oxley Act also calls for new criminal penalties for

- securities fraud,

- destruction of documents
- corporate officers who certify statements while knowing that the period report accompanying the statement does not comport with Section 13(a) or 15(d) of the Securities Exchange Act of 1934.
- knowingly retaliating against a whistleblower.

These various criminal penalties could be associated with acts involving environmental or worker related events or disclosure of liabilities associated with these events. Officials prosecuting corporate officers for securities fraud may find the new criminal penalties under Sarbanes—Oxley work equally well in prosecuting environmental or worker related crimes.[28]

A major difference between the prosecution of corporate accounting and financial scandals and environmental and social justice crimes is that the latter is in an earlier stage of development. In my opinion, the public outrage and prosecution of environmental and social justice crimes are far below their potential peak. They will grow significantly in the future. For alert and enlightened officers and directors, there still is time to develop sound sustainability risk management practices to cope with these expanding risks.

Disclosure of Environmental Liabilities

Sarbanes—Oxley puts greater pressure on top management to adequately disclose their environmental liabilities. Studies have shown that corporations have historically done a poor job at disclosure.

- A 1996 study by Freedman and Stagliano of companies with known Superfund sites and involved in IPOs found a 54 percent non-reporting rate. Registered companies with known sites had a 61 percent non-reporting rate.
- A 1998 EPA study found a non-reporting rate of 74 percent for years 1996 and 1997 on the disclosure of environmental legal proceeding.
- The same 1998 EPA study showed 96 percent of publicly traded companies facing Resource Conservation and Recovery Act (RCRA) corrective actions failed to accurately disclose these liabilities.
- A 2001 EPA study stated that 96 percent of publicly traded companies facing federally imposed toxic cleanup costs failed to properly disclose there liabilities.[29]

Some companies would undoubtedly argue that these liabilities do not meet materiality tests, or FASB 5 tests for losses being "probable" and "reasonably-estimated" for reporting of loss contingencies, to require full disclosure. Even allowing for FASB 5, all indications are that environmental liabilities are widely undisclosed. A recent report by the U.S. Government Accounting Office, entitled, "Environmental Disclosure: SEC Should Explore Ways to Improve Tracking and Transparency of Information," is an excellent source document for the SEC's current thinking on environmental disclosure.[30]

Sarbanes—Oxley, with its requirement that the CEO and CFO must personally sign off on financial statements, will undoubtedly put more pressure on companies to disclose their environmental liabilities. To help the process along, EPA has begun identifying companies on its website that face environmental enforcement actions totaling $100,000 or more. SEC guidelines specifically require publicly held companies to disclose legal proceedings that might result in amounts of $100,000 or more. For those companies which have not disclosed their liabilities, SEC action may be forthcoming.[31]

Greg Rogers, who practices environmental law in Dallas, has written numerous articles on the impact of Sarbanes—Oxley on disclosure of environmental liabilities. Rogers argues that many companies are not properly reporting these liabilities.[32] He maintains that pollution risk oversight goes beyond financial reporting to include:

> "the legal responsibilities of directors to provide oversight of the corporation's compliance with environmental laws, financial reporting of environmental liabilities, and management of environmental risk."[33]

He notes that pollution risk oversight is the process by which board members attain reasonable assurance that the company's environmental related objectives will be met. These environmental related objectives are regulatory compliance, financial reporting and risk management. He defines environmental risk management as:

> "The company should identify environmental-related risks that could have a material adverse impact on achievement of its financial and operational objectives, and take timely and appropriate action to control and finance these risks."[34]

As more environmental liabilities are disclosed, some of these disclosures could result in significant adjustments in financial statements that may surprise shareholders. In some cases, litigation may be brought against the directors and officers. As noted in a paper by Kenn Anderson and Donna Ferrara of Arthur J. Gallagher:

> "As Sarbanes—Oxley's certification requirements remind us, laws governing financial disclosure have consequences for both the corporation and members of senior management. Failure to appropriately report environmental liability can lead to personal liability for directors and officers at every level of the corporate hierarchy."[35]

Need to Punish

Researchers say that acts of personal vengeance reflect a biologically rooted sense of justice. The urge to seek revenge is primed in the genes. As noted by Dr. Michael McCullough, a psychologist at the University of Miami:

> "The best way to understand revenge is not as some disease or moral failing or crime but as a deeply human and sometimes very functional behavior. Revenge can be a very good deterrent to bad behavior, and bring feelings of completeness and fulfillment."[36]

The need to catch and punish wrongdoers has evolved as a basic need in human based social organizations. A 2002 article by Ernst Fehr and Simon Gächer in *Nature* entitled, "Altruistic Punishment in Humans" speaks to this need.[37] The authors explain that punishment plays a key role in the development of human cooperation. Altruistic punishment means that individuals punish, although punishment is costly for them and yields no material gain. The authors conducted experiments with human subjects and found that without such punishment, cooperation breaks down. Cooperation and trust could not have evolved without a corresponding readiness to catch and punish those that cheat.

In an interview with Dr. Fehr reported in the *New York Times,* reporter Natalie Angier described Dr. Fehr making a particular important point:

> "As a rule, said Dr. Fehr, the more closely a society's economy is based on market rather than kinship ties, the more prevalent the use of altruistic punishment to bring others into line."[38]

As businesses and governments work to develop risk management systems for dealing with increasing environment and social justice risks, we can expect more pressure to punish those corporations who do not cooperate and share in the burden of managing these risks. These pressures to "punish the cheats" will not only come from individuals, NGOs and governments, they will come from businesses themselves. Again the world of corporate accounting and financial scandals provides insights.

WorldCom's bankruptcy with reported assets of $107 billion was the largest in history. Enron had held the bankruptcy record with reported assets of $67 billion. An accounting fraud of some $11 billion cost WorldCom investors, employees and creditors billions of dollars. After settling for $750 million, WorldCom's successor company, MCI, was moving smoothly through bankruptcy, entered in July 2002, and set to emerge as a debt free company. Two of its principal competitors, Verizon and AT&T, typically fierce competitors themselves, strongly agreed on one point—MCI had not been punished enough. Alerted by a whistleblower, the companies charged that MCI had disguised its calls to avoid paying access fees to use the lines of their rivals. William Barr, Verizon's general counsel and a former U.S. attorney general, stated:

> "There must be an outcome that doesn't allow WorldCom to profit from its wrongdoing and that is fair to the companies that have played by the rules."[39]

Mark Neporent, co-head of the MCI creditors committee, responded by saying: "Barr was very clear that his mission was to impose the corporate death penalty on MCI."[40] These efforts were successful in that the GSA suspended MCI from receiving a new contract, a $1 billion a year business for MCI; and the bankruptcy courts confirmation hearing on the company reorganization plan to emerge from bankruptcy was delayed.

One can argue that these pressures brought against MCI by Verizon and AT&T (and joined by SBC Communications) were actions brought by competitors to hinder a potential rival. Yet, these pressures to punish seem very familiar to the findings made by Fehr and Gächter in their research on punishment.

In a related development, Oklahoma Attorney General Drew Edmondson brought criminal charges against WorldCom/MCI, its CEO, Bernard Ebbers and five other defendants. The punishment motive is apparent in a statement by Edmondson:

> "I don't think this company has been punished. I think it has been rewarded for its bad acts, and I intend to prosecute them criminally."[41]

When Edmondson brought these charges in August, 2003, the actions against WorldCom to date had resulted in a $750 million settlement with the SEC for civil charges and four guilty pleas from former executives, who were awaiting sentencing. The fact that no one was in jail, Bernie Ebbers and WorldCom/MCI had not been indicted, and $180 billion in WorldCom stock had evaporated played a role in contributing to the Oklahoma's Attorney General's impatience.[42] Mr. Edmondson may be feeling better since Bernie Ebbers was indicted in March 2004 by federal prosecutors for securities fraud, conspiracy to commit fraud, and participation in filing false corporate records. Ebbers was later convicted and sentenced to 25 years in jail.[43]

The need to punish is a necessary, but not sufficient, condition to restore trust that has been lost in both the Enron and WorldCom scandals. A sampling of headlines, following the corporate scandals, on loss of trust speaks volumes:

"Can You Trust Anybody Anymore?" *Business Week,* January 28, 2002, by Bruce Nussbaum.

"Now Who Do You Trust?" *Newsweek,* May 27, 2002, by Jane Bryant Quinn.

"Americans Don't Trust Each Other," *Chicago Tribune,* reported in *Wisconsin State Journal,* June 8, 2003, by Greg Burns.

"Restoring Trust in CEOs," *Yale Alumni Magazine,* December 2002, by Bruce Fellman.

"There Are No Markets Without Trust," *Wall Street Journal,* March 27, 2002, by Holman W. Jenkins Jr.

"When Trust Goes Bust—Learning to Believe Again Can Be Difficult After Things Go Wrong," *South Florida Sun—Sentinel,* reported in *Wisconsin State Journal,* September 17, 2002, by Liz Doup.

"Once Bitten, Twice Shy: A World of Eroding Trust," *New York Times,* April 21, 2002, by Janny Scott.

Individuals need to feel that some sort of penalty or cost must be paid for illegal, unethical, or negligent behavior. If penalties or costs are not paid, then the trust that has been eroded will be difficult to recover. Trust and cooperation are necessary for the working of personal as well as business relationships. The failure to use appropriate punishments and deterrents in order to help to restore trust can result in enormous costs for business and society. That is why I foresee considerable liabilities and penalties, including criminal offences, being assessed against those individuals and businesses that have violated our trust in the environmental and social justice areas.

Criminal Liability

Our system of criminal punishment may well become more stringent for environmental and social justice crimes. When corporations knowingly put customers, workers or the public in danger, criminal prosecution can result. All the major federal environmental acts provide for criminal penalties, as illustrated in Table 5-1. Table 5-2 shows the number of federal environmental criminal actions initiated over the five year period 1998-2003 (fiscal year). Additional data on the number of referrals and defendants charged, length of sentences and total fines are also provided.

Looking to the future, it is my opinion that there will be more prison sentences assessed against corporate executives for environmental damages and unsafe working conditions. I find support for this opinion in the reactions to corporate/accounting scandals in the last few years. The fact that many of the responsible parties initially avoided prosecution produced a strong public reaction. Even articles in business publications like *Business Week*[44] and the *Wall Street Journal*[45] have called for more prison sentences.

Besides the $750 million settlement by WorldCom, mentioned previously, there have been some other hefty settlement payments in civil cases resulting from recent corporate scandals, as can be seen in Table 5-3. But when compared to their profit and capital bases, and to the billions of dollars that were lost by investors, employees, and creditors, some of the fines seem insignificant and their deterrent effects are questionable. The problem with monetary fines is that net deal for the corporation/individual assessed the fine is often positive. If you make $100 million from a questionable deal and have to pay a $50 million fine, you are still ahead $50 million. And in most of the settlements, corporations do not have to admit to any culpability.

Table 5-1
Criminal Penalties Under Environmental Acts

Act	Prison	Fine	Offense
CERCLA	Up to 3 years (5 years 2nd offense)	In accordance with applicable provisions of the federal criminal code.	Failure to report releases of reportable quantities of hazardous waste or false reporting.
RCRA	Up to 2-5 years (4-10 years 2nd offense)	Up to $50,000/day of violation.	Transport hazardous waste to an unpermitted facility; treat, store or dispose of hazardous waste without a permit or in knowing violation of any material condition of a permit or of interim status; material omission or false material statement in documents required to be filed or maintained under RCRA; generate, store, treat, transport, dispose, export, or otherwise handle hazardous waste or used oil and destroy, alter, conceal or fail to file required records, documents; transport without a manifest hazardous waste or used oil; export hazardous waste without consent of a receiving country or in violation of an applicable international agreement; transport, treat, store, dispose of or otherwise handle used oil in violation of applicable permit or regulations.
	Up to 15 years	$150,000 (individuals) $1,000,000 (organizations)	Knowingly transport, treat, dispose, store or export hazardous or used oil in violation of the above provisions who "knows at that time that he thereby places another person in imminent danger of death or serious bodily injury.
Clean Water Act	Up to 1 year (2 years 2nd offense)	$2,500-$25,000/day of violation ($50,000, 2nd offense)	Negligent violations of the act or permits issued under the act and negligent discharges into a sewer system, which the person knew or reasonably should have known could cause personal injury or property damage or which causes a sewage treatment works to violate its own permit.
	Up to 3 years (6 years 2nd offense)	$5,000-$50,000/day ($100,000, 2nd offense)	Knowing violations: felonies
	Up to 15 years	$250,000 (individuals) $1,000,000 (organizations)	Knowing endangerment: knowingly violates the act or a permit issued pursuant to the act who "knows at that time that he thereby places another person in imminent danger of death or serious bodily injury.
Clean Air Act	Up to 1 year (2 years 2nd offense)	$25,000 per day of violation ($50,000 2nd offense)	Knowingly violating an applicable implementation plan more than 30 days after notice, knowing violations of orders, knowing violation of new source performance standards, hazardous emission regulations and other enumerated violations.
	Up to 6 months	Up to $10,000	Knowingly making false statements or for tampering with monitoring devices.

Source: Rothenberg, Eric B., and Dean Jeffery Telego, <u>Environmental Risk Management A Desk Reference</u>, Alexandria VA: RTM Communications, Inc., 1991.

Table 5-2
U.S. Environmental Regulatory Acts
Criminal Enforcement Program

	FY 1998	FY 1999	FY 2000	FY 2001	FY 2002	FY 2003
Environmental Crime Cases Intiated	636	471	477	482	484	471
Referrals	266	241	236	256	250	228
Defendants Charged	350	322	360	372	325	247
Sentences (Years)	173	208	146	212	215	146
Fines (MIL)	$93	$62	$122	$95	$62	$71

Source: U.S. Environmental Protection Agency, Office of Compliance "FY 2003 End of Year Enforcement and Compliance Assurance Results, Washington, D.C.: USEPA, December, 2003.

Table 5-3
Settlement Payments

Amount	Corporations
$1.4 billion	Citigroup, Credit Suisse First Boston, Merrill Lynch, Morgan Stanley, Goldman Sachs, Bear Stearns, J.P. Morgan Chase, Lehman Brothers, USB Sarburg, Piper Jaffray for investor abuses – SEC and various other regulatory groups.
$250 million	Quest Communications for accounting practices – SEC
$600 million	Alliance Capital Management for improper mutual fund trading – SEC and New York Attorney General.
$300 million	Citigroup, JP Morgan Chase for Enron dealings – Manhattan District Attorney
$100 million	Merrill Lynch brokerage/investment banking conflicts – New York Attorney General
$350 million	Massachusetts Financial Services for improper mutual fund trading – SEC and New York Attorney General.
$225 million	Janus Capital Group for improper mutual fund trading – SEC and New York Attorney General.
$175 million	Strong Financial for improper mutual fund trading – SEC and New York Attorney General.
$675 million	Bank of America and Fleet Boston for improper mutual fund trading – SEC and New York Attorney General.
$2.6 billion	Citigroup – class action brought by investors in WorldCom
$2.0 billion	Citigroup – class action suit brought by investors in Enron
$2.2 billion	J.P. Morgan Chase – class action suit brought by investors in Enron
$2.4 billion	Canadian Imperial Bank of Commerce – class action suit brought by investors in Enron
$2.0 billion	J.P. Morgan Chase – class action suit brought by investors in WorldCom

Source: Various newspaper articles in *Wall Street Journal* and *New York Times*.

Prison sentences may be the only effective means of producing an effective deterrent in these situations. A person who commits an armed bank robbery netting a few thousand dollars will almost certainly go to prison, but a corporate official whose acts result in $100 million being loss by other parties can escape prison and even make money, if the money they make exceeds the fine. Scott Harshbarger, former Massachusetts attorney general and now in a private law practice, argues that strong jail sentences are a critical factor in persuading people to behave ethically in business. He states:

> "The predictability or the certainty of some measure of sanction is the crucial piece in getting deterrence and compliance in advance, particularly in white-collar crimes. You're simply saying, there are limits, there are lines, there are boundaries, and, hopefully, they're clear and bright. And when you cross that line, you risk a serious penalty."[46]

Two money managers, Anthony Ogorek, head of Ogorek Wealth Management and Gerald Cole, managing partner of Arbor Capital Management express similar feelings:

> "The best thing to restore investor confidence would be to see authorities aggressively pursue criminal cases against executives who went too far. A few high-profile convictions would go a long way toward putting things right again."[47]

When I started writing this book in the summer of 2003, only a few top managers had received jail sentences. The first CEO to go to jail, Sam Waskal, founder and CEO of ImClone Systems, was sentenced to 87 months, beginning in July 2003, for securities fraud, conspiracy, perjury and obstruction of justice in connection with stock trades he made for himself and his family.[48] In September 2003, Ben Glisan, a former Enron treasurer, pleaded guilty to conspiring to commit fraud. It was the first public admission of fraud by a former Enron Executive. He was sentenced to five years in prison and made to return $938,000 of improperly obtained funds.[49] The first guilty verdict handed down by a jury was in the case of Rite Aid's former chief counsel. In October 2003, Franklin C. Brown was convicted of conspiracy to obstruct justice, witness tampering, lying and other charges in a scheme to inflate the pharmaceutical chain's earnings so he and other executives could get big payouts.[50]

From fall 2003 through summer 2005, the pace of criminal indictments and convictions picked up substantially. Tables 5-4a and 5-4b include a number of these criminal convictions. Indictments have been brought against Enron's Kenneth Lay (former Chairman), Jeffery Skilling (former CEO), and Richard Causey (former Chief Accounting Officer) and their trial will begin on January 17, 2006. Observers of increased corporate criminal indictments and convictions, like Alex Berenson of the *New York Times*, notes:

> "Now the prosecutions may have reached a critical mass that will make executives think twice before lying to shareholders and federal officials, experts on white-color crime say. No one expects corporate executives to suddenly give up their pay packages and devote their lives to good works. But they may back away from the aggressive accounting practices and tax shelters that became common even among blue-chip companies in the last two decades, as well as some of their more egregious perks."[51]

Table 5-4a
Criminal Convictions

Name	Company	Title	Conviction	Prison Sentence
John Rigas	Adelphia Communications Corp.	Former CEO	Conspiracy, bank and securities fraud	15 years
Timothy Rigas	Adelphia Communications Corp.	Former CEO	Conspiracy, bank and securities fraud	20 years
Jamie Olis	Dynegy	Former Midlevel Executive	Accounting fraud	24 years
David Delainey	Enron	Chief Executive North American Unit and Energy Services	Insider trading	Up to 10 years
Andrew S. Fastow	Enron	Former CFO	Conspiracy	Up to 10 years
Kenneth D. Rice	Enron	Former Head of High-speed Internet unit	Securities fraud	Up to 10 years
Lea Fastow	Enron	Former Assistant Treasurer	Tax evasion	1 year
Mark Koenig	Enron	Former Head of Investor Relations	Aiding and abetting securities fraud	Up to 10 years
Dan Boyle	Enron	Former Executive in finance division	Conspiracy and fraud to inflate earnings at Enron	3 years, 10 months
Martin L. Grass	Rite Aid	Former Chief Executive	Accounting fraud, conspiracy	8 years
Eric Sorkin	Rite Aid	Former Executive Vice President	Accounting fraud	5 months
Franklyn Bergonzi	Rite Aid	Former CFO	Accounting fraud	2 years, 4 months
Philip Markovitz	Rite Aid	Vice President	Accounting fraud	1 month
Frank Quattrone	Credit Suisse Group's First Boston	Former Silicon Valley Investment Banker	Obstructing a probe of how IPO stocks were doled out	18 months
James Patrick Connelly	Fred Alger Management	Director of Sales and Marketing	Tampering with evidence in investigation of improper mutual fund trading	1-3 years
Daniel Bayly	Merrill Lynch	Former Head of Investment Banking	Conspiracy and fraud to inflate earnings at Enron	2 years, 6 months
James A. Brown	Merrill Lynch	Former Head of Structured-Finance Group	Conspiracy and fraud to inflate earnings at Enron	3 years, 10 months
Robert S. Furst	Merrill Lynch	Banker in Houston responsible for managing Enron relationship	Conspiracy and fraud to inflate earnings at Enron	3 years, 1 month
William Fuhs	Merrill Lynch	Banker who reported to Mr. Brown	Conspiracy and fraud to inflate earnings at Enron	3 years, 1 month

Source: Various newspaper articles in *Wall Street Journal* and *New York Times*.

Table 5-4b
Criminal Convictions (cont.)

Name	Company	Title	Conviction	Prison Sentence
Bernard J. Ebbers	WorldCom Inc.	Former CEO	Securities fraud, conspiracy, filing false corporate records with SEC.	25 years
Scott Sullivan	WorldCom Inc.	Former CFO	Conspiracy, securities fraud, bank fraud and filing false statements.	5 years
David F. Myers	WorldCom Inc.	Former Controller	Fraud, conspiracy, filing false financial documents.	1 year, 1 day
Buford Yates	WorldCom Inc.	Former Director of general accounting	Securities fraud, conspiracy	1 year, 1 day
Betty Vinson	WorldCom Inc.	Former accounting manager	Fraudulent book entries	5 months
L. Dennis Kozlowsky	Tyco	Former CEO	Grand larceny, conspiracy, violation of business law, falsifying business records.	Up to 25 years
Mark Swartz	Tyco	Former CFO	Grand larceny, conspiracy, violation of business law, falsifying business records.	Up to 25 years

Source: Various newspaper articles in *Wall Street Journal* and *New York Times*.

Kirby Behre, a white collar defense attorney, feels significant changes are occurring in executive behavior: "I think the effect is already incredibly profound. The wake-up call was sent and received in a huge way."[52] Besides criminal indictments and convictions, sources report renewed efforts by investors, shareholders, employees and regulators to make executives return some of their ill gotten gains.[53] Bernie Ebbers, former WorldCom CEO, surrendered his personal assets of $40 million to defrauded investors, and Scott Sullivan, former WorldCom CFO, forfeited his $10 million Florida mansion to fraud victims.[54]

Criminal liability can have a devastating impact on a corporation's reputation. Cases in the insurance industry involving Marsh's contingent commissions and Berkshire Hathaway's General Re dealing with AIG have taken a toll on the reputations of these firms. Warren Buffet, CEO of Berkshire Hathaway, has been particularly upset because of the high value he puts on reputation. He has referred to the importance of always having his actions pass the *"New York Times* test," and is reported to have told his son:

> "It takes 20 years to build a reputation and five minutes to ruin it. If you think about that, you'll do things differently."[55]

Another development coming out of the WorldCom and Enron scandals involves class action securities lawsuit settlements in which directors had to pay from their own personal funds. In the Enron settlement, 10 outside directors will contribute a total of $13 million from their personal funds.[56] In the WorldCom settlement, 12 directors will contribute a total of $24.75 million from personal funds.[57]

Committing an environmental or social justice crime may produce the same type of reaction as corporate accounting and financial scandals. Prison sentences or sizeable liability assessments may be the only effective deterrents. If only fines are considered, managers may feel that corporation will come out better financially by paying the fine and saving funds that might be spent on preventing environmental and social justice harm. But if managers face the threat of prison sentences and large liabilities, funds spent on prevention may indeed be less than the financial and personal costs of prison time and/or assessed liabilities. In addition, reputation damages must also be factored into the decision making process.

Summary

The liability exposure of directors and officers is clearly expanding. The principal catalyst has been the Enron and post-Enron financial and accounting scandals. While not directly related to sustainability risks, the calls for higher standards and greater diligence by the directors, increased transparency, and even criminal sanctions can impact all aspects of directors and officers liability. The bar has been raised for all areas of corporate governance, not just the financial and accounting areas. As environmental and social justice litigation issues press forward, increased pressure will be put on directors and officers to give more attention to sustainability risk management practices as part of overall corporate governance strategy.

For actions brought by parties injured by an environmental event, most corporations will not have liability coverage due to the pollution exclusions in standard liability policies. D&O policies have similar exclusions for litigation based on failure to disclose environmental liabilities (see Chapter 10). Corporations may also not have insurance coverage for social justice risks (also see Chapter 10). Liability losses incurred by the firm because of injured parties will be retained or self-insured by the corporation. If these losses are large, the drain on internal funds could be substantial. If liability actions increase, and management is found to not have enacted appropriate sustainability risk management mitigation strategies, then directors and officers are going to be held accountable by shareholders and others suffering losses. While management may be covered by directors and officers insurance, several restrictions and exclusions could comprise the coverage (see Chapter 10). If coverage is excluded, restricted or limits are inadequate, directors and officers could face unlimited personal liability. Particularly under the current atmosphere of increasing emphasis on proper corporate governance in the aftermath of the Enron, Anderson, World Com, etc., cases, managements that fail to respond appropriately will likely be shown little sympathy for their failure to take action.

CHAPTER 5—ENDNOTES

[1] Discussion of directors' duties from "Professional Liability Insurance, Part II," Chapter 10 in Donald S. Malecki and Arthur L. Flitner, *Commercial Liability Risk Management and Insurance,* 5th Ed., Malvern, PA: American Institute, 2001.

[2] Roberto Ceniceros, "Brands Used to Bargain in EPL Suits," *Business Insurance,* January 28, 2002.

[3] *Pereira v. Cogan,* 00 Civ. 619 (RWS), United States District Court for the Southern District of New York, 294 B.R. 449; 2003 U.S. Dist. LEXIS 7818, May 7, 2003, Decided, May 12, 2003, Filed, Counsel Amended May 20, 2003.

[4] Geraldine Fabrikant, "Private Concern, Public Consequences," *New York Times,* June 15, 2003.

[5] In Re *The Walt Disney Company Derivatives Litigation,* C.A. No. 15452 E Del. Ch. May 28, 2003.

[6] Parts of this section based on information from Patrick McGeehan, "Case Could Redefine Board Members' Liability," *New York Times,* June 14, 2003; Bruce Orwall and Joann S. Lublin, "Suit Against Disney Over Ovitz Severence Chills Boardrooms," *Wall Street Journal,* October 11, 2004.

[7] In Re *Abbott Laboratories Derivative Shareholders Litigation,* 325 F. 3d 795, 7th Cir. March 28, 2003.

[8] Bruce Orwall and Merissa Marr, "Judge Backs Disney Directors In Suit on Ovitz's Hiring, Firing," *Wall Street Journal,* August 10, 2005; Laura M. Holton, "Delaware Judge Rules for Disney in Firing of Ovitz," *New York Times,* August 10, 2005.

[9] Matthew Kiernan, "Taking Control of Climate," *Financial Times,* November 24, 2002.

[10] *John Doe I,...vs. Unocol Corporation,* United States Court of Appeals Ninth Circuit, 2002 WL 31063976.

[11] "Unocol Wins Myanmar Human Rights Ruling," *Business Respect,* January 24, 2004.

[12] Linda Greenhouse, "Human Rights Abuses Are Held to Fall Under U.S. Courts," *New York Times,* June 30, 2004.

[13] Savanna Reid, "Unocal's Historic Burma Settlement," *The Good News Roundup,* May 2, 2005, 222.gnn.tv/articles/1353/The_Good_News_Roundup.

[14] Paul Magnusson, "Making a Federal Case Out of Overseas Abuses," *Business Week,* November 25, 2002.

[15] Alex Markels, "Showdown for a Tool In Rights Lawsuits," *New York Times,* June 15, 2003.

[16] *Business Respect,* issue 52, March 15, 2003 at mallenbaker.net.

[17] *Gabriel Ashanga Jota…vs. Texaco,* United States Court of Appeals for the Second Circuit, 157 F. 3d 153, 1998 U.S. App. LEXIS 24615; 41 Fed. R. Serv. 3d (Callaghan) 1282: 29 ELR 20181.

[18] Abby Ellin, "Suit Says Chevron Texaco Dumped Poisons in Ecuador," *New York Times,* May 8, 2003.

[19] Marc Lifsher, "Chevron Would Face $5 Billion Tab For Amazon Cleanup, Expert Says," *Wall Street Journal,* October 30, 2003.

[20] Scott Wilson, "Showdown in the Ecuadorian Jungle," *Washington Post,* October 23, 2003.

[21] Juan Foreno, "Texaco Goes on Trial in Ecuador Pollution Case," *New York Times,* October 23, 2003.

[22] William Baue, "ChevronTexaco Faces Class-Action Lawsuit in Ecuador Over Environmental Damage," socialfunds.com, May 11, 2004.

[23] Marc Lifsher, "Chevron Would Face $5 Billion Tab For Amazon Cleanup, Expert Says," *Wall Street Journal,* October 30, 2003.

[24] Alex Markels, "Showdown for a Tool in Rights Lawsuits," *New York Times,* June 15, 2003; for an excellent source referenced in this article see Errol P. Mendes, *Global Governance, Economy and Law.*

[25] Paul Magnusson, "Making a Federal Case Out of Overseas Abuses," *Business Week,* November 25, 2002.

[26] James Kendrick, "Act has Safety Health, Environmental Impact," *Business Insurance,* August 11, 2003.

[27] ASSE, "Identification of Risks and Other Issues—Sarbanes—Oxley Act of 2002 Public Law 107-204," available at www.asse.org/ prac_spec_cops_issues13htm.

[28] Lisa S. Pogostin, "Sarbanes—Oxley Expands Potential Liability of Directors, Officers, Attorneys and Accountants," *XLRE Liability Bulletin,* Issue 2002-5, November 2002.

[29] Kenn E. Anderson and Donna Ferrara, "Disclosing Environmental Liabilities: Director, Officer and Insurance Issues," Arthur J. Gallagher & Co., August 2003.

[30] U.S. G.A.O., "Environmental Disclosure: SEC Should Explore Ways to Improve Tracking and Transparency of Information," GAO-04-808, July 14, 2004.

[31] Dave Lenckus, "Governance Law Hasn't Fueled Big EIL Interest," *Business Insurance,* June 6, 2003.

[32] Greg Rogers, "Uninsured and Undisclosed Environmental Liabilities Pose Risks for Directors," *Directors Monthly,* National Association of Corporate Directors, May 2003; Greg Rogers, "Environmental Transparancy: Areas For Concern," *Financial Executive,* June 2004.

[33] Greg Rogers, "Pollution Risk Oversight," *Directors Monthly,* National Association of Corporate Directors, February 2004.

[34] Ibid.

[35] Kenn E. Anderson and Donna Ferrara, "Disclosing Environmental Liabilities: Director, Officer and Insurance Issues," Arthur J. Gallagher & Co., August 2003.

[36] Benedict Carey, "Payback Time: Why Revenge Tastes So Sweet," *New York Times,* July 27, 2004.

[37] Ernst Fehr and Simon Gächer, "Altruistic Punishment in Humans," *Nature,* Vol. 415, 10 January, 2002.

[38] Natalie Angier, "The Urge to Punish Cheats: It Isn't Merely Vengence," *New York Times,* January 22, 2002.

[39] Almar Latour, Dennis K. Berman and Yochi J. Dreazen, "Getting Through: How Rivals' Long Campaign Against MCI Gained Traction; Drive by Verizon's Barr Leads to Probes, Delay of Bankruptcy Hearing; Seeking the 'Death Penalty'," *Wall Street Journal,* August 1, 2003.

[40] Ibid.

[41] Deborah Soloman, "Zealous States Shake Up Legal Status Quo," *Wall Street Journal,* August 28, 2003.

[42] Russel Gold, Almar Latour, Dennis Berman and Yochi Draegen, "MCI and Ebbers Are Charged in Oklahoma," *Wall Street Journal,* August 28, 2003.

[43] Barnady J. Feder and Kurt Eichenwald, "Ex-WorldCom Chief Is Indicted by U.S. In Securities Fraud," *New York Times,* March 3, 2004; Ken Belson, "WorldCom Head Is Given 25 Years For Huge Fraud," *New York Times,* July 14, 2005.

[44] Emily Thorton and Mike France, "For Enron's Bankers, A 'Get Out of Jail Free' Card," *Business Week,* August 11, 2003.

[45] Larry D. Thompson, "'Zero Tolerance' for Corporate Fraud," *Wall Street Journal,* July 21, 2003.

[46] Jeffrey L. Seglin, "The Jail Threat is Real. So, Will Executives Behave," *New York Times,* July 20, 2003.

[47] David Robinson, "Executives Cooking the Books are the Worst Terrorists," *Wisconsin State Journal,* July 28, 2002.

[48] Jeffrey L. Seglin, "The Jail Threat is Real. So, Will Executives Behave," *New York Times,* July 20, 2003.

[49] Kurt Eichenwald, "Former Enron Treasurer Enters Guilty Plea," *New York Times,* September 11, 2003.

[50] "Rite Aid Ex-Counsel is Convicted," Associated Press in *Wall Street Journal,* October 20, 2003.

[51] Alex Berenson, "Guilty Verdicts Give Executives A New Focus: Risk of Prison," *New York Times,* March 8, 2004.

[52] Ibid.

[53] Richard B. Schmitt and Henry Sender, "CEOs Wealth May Be at Stake In Investor Suits," *Wall Street Journal,* August 9, 2002; Joann S. Lublin, "Companies Seek to Recover Pay From Ex-CEOs," *Wall Street Journal,* January 7, 2004; Charles Forelle, "Seeking Restitution, Government Targets Tyco Duo's Fortunes," *Wall Street Journal,* June 30, 2005.

[54] Dionne Searcey and Almar Latour, "Ebbers to Surrender Assets to Settle WorldCom Suit," *Wall Street Journal,* July 1, 2005; Ken Belson, "Ex-WorldCom Executive Forfeits Florida Mansion, *New York Times,* July 27, 2005.

[55] Jesse Eisinger, "Buffet's Reputation Faces a Test," *Wall Street Journal,* March 31, 2005.

[56] Dave Lenckus, "D&O settlements get personal," *Business Insurance,* January 10, 2005.

[57] Michael Bradford, "WorldCom directors to settle claims from personal funds," March 28, 2005.

6

OLD SUSTAINABILITY RISKS: ASBESTOS AND SUPERFUND

o o o o o o o o o o o o o o o o o o o o o o o o o o o o o o o o o o o
It is estimated that $54 billion has been spent on asbestos litigation as of 2000, and future costs will range from $145 to 210 billion.

—*The Rand Institute for Civil Justice.*

The asbestos and Superfund litigations have huge implications for sustainability risk management. First, this litigation has been developing over the past 30 years, so much can be learned by examining these cases. Second, ultimate amounts paid for both asbestos and Superfund liabilities are expected to be in the $100 billions. Third, these liabilities were assessed against both corporate America and the insurance industry. Cumulatively these liabilities represent the two greatest single insured loss events for the world insurance industry. Fourth, these liabilities were accumulated over decades before corporations or their insurers were required to make any payments. While not recognized by the insurance industry as they accrued, these liabilities would represent enormous Incurred But Not Reported (IBNR) loss reserves. Finally, after three decades asbestos and Superfund litigations are still not settled. Indeed particularly in the case of asbestos, this litigation has actually witnessed a resurgence.

Both asbestos and Superfund provide enough material for a book, probably many books. My purpose here will be to succinctly describe the asbestos and Superfund situations and how these liabilities were assessed to corporations and the insurance industry. The financial impact of asbestos and Superfund litigation will be documented. Lessons that can be learned from these two important risk events to better formulate sustainability risk management strategies will be presented.

Asbestos

Asbestos claims have produced unprecedented liability, litigation, and compensation problems for corporate America and the insurance industry. Asbestos litigation is regarded as the first of the mass toxic torts, and established precedents that have influenced other mass toxic torts including DES, the Dalton Shield, hazardous waste (Superfund) and tobacco. Since the first lawsuit brought against the Johns-Manville Corporation in 1968, 750,000 claimants have sought recovery for their injuries through 2002, and 225,000 deaths will be attributed to asbestos through 2009, according to the Rand Institute for Civil Justice.[1] A study by the Environmental Working Group estimates that 10,000 Americans are currently dying each year from asbestos-related illnesses and the tread may be increasing.[2]

Asbestos use dates back to the turn of the last century. It actually is a very practical and functional product. It is fire resistant and an excellent insulator and was widely used in the construction industry. It also was utilized in the wrapping of pipes in ships and buildings, including homes. Its properties made it quite functional for employment in brake linings, floor tiles and roofing shingles. Unfortunately, asbestos would be found to seriously harm those workers and individuals who came in regular contact with it. Workers in the asbestos manufacturing, insulation, and ship building industries received substantial exposure and would constitute the first groups of injured parties to bring claims against the manufacturers of asbestos.

Early Litigation

Asbestos related diseases are divided into three main areas. The first is asbestosis, a progressive thickening and scaring of the lung linings. Asbestosis causes the lungs to lose their elasticity, which produces reduced breathing capacity and eventually leads to a stiffening of the lung that victims suffocate. The second is mesothelioma, a rare cancer of the lining of the chest and abdominal cavities. The third is lung cancer. It took many years to connect these diseases of workers to their exposure to asbestos. The most significant event was the studies of Dr. Irving Selikoff of Mt. Sinai School of Medicine in New York City in the 1960s. Selikoff came into contact with many workers that were diagnosed with asbestos related diseases. He was particularly curious about the high incidence of mesothelioma, which is a rare cancer in the general population. Selikoff apparently was also the first doctor/researcher to regularly ask the workers where they worked. What he found was that these workers worked in jobs where they had a high exposure to asbestos. As he pursued the connection between asbestos and various diseases, he came across some old union records of asbestos workers, which listed their deaths and causes. This discovery provided a richer data set for Selikoff in his studies.

The significance of Selikoff's research findings was enormous as it connected medically and scientifically the exposure to asbestos with resulting diseases/injuries. These findings also became public information. It would later be discovered through litigation that asbestos manufacturers had earlier indications of injuries to workers from asbestos exposure, but this information was not made public or available to workers for fear of litigation. Recent litigation against MetLife, the life insurance giant, is particularly noteworthy. MetLife is being accused of keeping studies, which they conducted in the 1930s, showing a relation between asbestos exposure and diseases. Documents introduced as evidence included a MetLife study of asbestos miners in Canada in the 1930s that found one in five had an asbestos related disease. Another document indicated that MetLife showed a 1935 study of the health risks to lawyers of Johns-Manville, the largest producer of asbestos.[3] To date, MetLife has paid out $180 million to settle claims and they currently face 112,700 suits. In March of 2004, the company upped its asbestos-liability reserves to $1.2 billion.[4]

Once the causal relationship between asbestos and diseases was established, attorneys could argue that asbestos was an inherently dangerous product and that the manufacturers were negligent in failing to warn workers. Initial suits were unsuccessful, but attorneys persisted, and finally, in 1973, in the *Borel v. Fiberboard Paper Products Corporation* case, the first successful suit by a worker injured by asbestos was accomplished. In 1985, Paul Brodeur serialized a four part article, entitled, "The Asbestos Industry on Trial," in *The New Yorker* magazine, which would be published in a book, *Outrageous Misconduct*.[5] The reader is recommended to these articles or the book for an extensive discussion of story of asbestos workers' injuries and the resulting early litigation.

After the *Borel* decision, more claimants brought litigation. The plaintiff lawyers also organized large legal complexes that specialized in bringing class action and individual asbestos suits. For instance, 10 law firms together filed 53 percent of all the claims filed against the Manville Trust in 2000.[6] Through the Internet, lawyers also created websites aimed at asbestos victims to offer their services. The number of claimants would eventually number in the hundreds of thousands and the dollar payouts in the tens of billions of dollars. While asbestos defendants and their insurers were certainly not pleased with the billions of dollars being paid out, there was a feeling that the number of claimants would eventually fall off as cases are settled and older asbestos workers died. There seemed to be a large but finite number of such claimants. In addition, a significant number of asbestos firms had gone into bankruptcy and many insurers had paid out the limits of their policies, so even if new claimants came in, new funds and insurer payouts would not be available.

Second Wave of Lawsuits

As law firms specializing in asbestos claims looked for a new class of defendants with new limits of insurance to tap, a second wave of asbestos suits was initiated in the late 1990s. One avenue for the new suits are mergers and acquisitions, where a large financially sound corporation purchases a smaller firm that has a liability exposure from asbestos. Prior to the merger, the smaller firm might not have been an attractive target, but after the merger claimants have access to the assets and the insurance policies of the larger acquiring firm. For example Halliburton, whose CEO at the time was Vice President Dick Cheney, acquired Dresser Industries in 1998 and inherited their asbestos liabilities. These liabilities turned out to be much larger than originally anticipated. Halliburton would subsequently agree to pay $5.1 billion to settle more than 400,000 asbestos claims.[7] Another merger case involved Dow Chemical's acquisition of Union Carbide. Union Carbide had operated an asbestos mine in California form 1963 to 1985. Prior to the merger in February 2001, court filings of asbestos claims against Union Carbide were averaging 31 a month. Some months after the merger, the court filings jumped to 400 in November and 905 in December 2001.[8] Other examples included media giant, Viacom's purchase of Westinghouse, which has previously merged with CBS, Georgia-Pacific's 1965 acquisition of Bestwall Gypsum and No.1 drug maker, Pfizer's 2000 deal with Warner-Lambert.[9]

Other suits looked to product manufacturers that have products containing asbestos. A good example would be claims brought against General Motors Corporation arguing the asbestos used in brake linings in its vehicles led to health problems for auto mechanics. General Motors is an attractive target as it has ultimate deep pockets through its huge asset base and insurance limits. Sears, Roebuck & Co. faces asbestos claims from its floor tiles and roofing products, going back to the 1940s.[10] General Electric has settled nearly 300,000 cases and has 140,000 outstanding claims from individuals who had contact with GE turbines insulated with asbestos.[11] Other tangentially related firms such as consultants, engineering firms, plant owners, and maintenance and construction contractors have been named as defendants. The bottom line is that the number of claimants and defendants has grown substantially. According to estimates of the Rand Institute, the total number of claimants in 1982 was 21,000 but has increased to 750,000 as of 2002. Similarly, the total number of defendants had increased from 300 to 8,000 over the same period.[12]

Bankruptcies

In 1982, the largest asbestos processor, Johns-Manville, filed for reorganization under Chapter 11 of the Federal Bankruptcy Act. At that time, Johns-Manville faced 16,500 outstanding asbestos related claims for $12.5 billion in damages and had paid out $50 million in claims. New suits were being filed at a rate of 500 per month. Johns-Manville estimated the present value of all future claims at approximately $2 billion, which exceeded its net worth of $1.1 billion. Johns-Manville's filing was unusual in that its business was generally sound; it had earned profits of $60 million on $2.2 billion of sales in 1981. Johns-Manville was attempting a new and unusual approach to controlling its asbestos liability claims. Johns-Manville's basic premise was that it could consolidate and settle all its asbestos claims, present and future, and emerge from bankruptcy in a healthier financial condition than it could by continuing to pay for claims in perpetuity.[13]

Johns-Manville would reorganize and eventually emerge from bankruptcy as the Manville Corporation in 1988. As part of the reorganization plan, Manville had to set up a trust fund for asbestos claimants. The trust fund consisted of $850 million in cash, bonds with a face value of $1.3 billion, 50 percent of Johns-Manville common stock, and a perpetual claim on 20 percent of the company's consolidated profits.[14] They are still making payments out of that trust, although the amounts of the compensation payments have been reduced from originally 100 percent of the liquidated value to 5 percent in 2001.[15] This reduction in per claimant payments was necessitated by the large increase in new claims, tripling from around 30,000 in 1995 to just under 90,000 in 2001.[16]

In 1982, only Johns-Manville and two other asbestos defendants had used bankruptcy as protection against asbestos liability claims. By 2002, bankruptcy has been used by 67 asbestos defendants according to the Rand Institute. Table 6-1 below shows some of the largest companies that have recently filed for bankruptcy because of asbestos liability claims.[17]

Table 6 – 1

Chapter 11 Bankruptcies Because of Asbestos Liability Claims.

	FILED FOR CHAPTER 11	CLAIMS SO FAR*	COST OF CLAIMS
Owens Corning	Oct. 5, 2000	460,000	$5.0 billion
Harbison-Walker Refractories†	Feb. 14, 2002	200,000	4.1§
Federal-Mogul	Oct. 1, 2001	365,000	2.1§
ABB	Feb. 17, 2003	204,326	2.1
W.R. Grace & Company	April 2, 2001	325,000	1.9
Babcock & Wilcox	Feb. 22, 2000	385,000	1.6
GAF	Jan. 18, 2001	500,000	1.5
Pittsburgh Corning	April 17, 2000	435,000	1.2
USG	June 25, 2001	250,000	1.1§
Armstrong World Industries	Dec. 6, 2000	455,000	N.A.
Kaiser Aluminum	Feb. 12, 2002	112,400	0.6

*Settled and pending   †A subsidiary   §Amount set aside by company to
                         of Halliburton   cover claims, which could go
                                            higher in some cases

Source: Alex Berenson, "Asbestos Accord Is Said To Be Near," *New York Times*, April 24, 2003.

Insurance Coverage Issues

Asbestos litigation has produced some very important precedents regarding insurance coverage issues. By far the most important was determining the trigger of coverage. When asbestos claims first started to come in, asbestos defendants naturally looked to their liability insurance carriers for indemnification and defense cost coverage. It was not immediately obvious which insurers would have to respond. In order to answer this inquiry, it is necessary to determine the trigger of coverage.

The term "trigger of coverage" is used to denote when an insurance policy responds to a loss, that is, when a policy is triggered. Typical wording in occurrence based liability insurance policies, the most widely used, requires that the bodily injury and/or property damage occur "during the policy period." In acute loss situations, like an automobile accident or a fire, the time and date of the injury or damage are clear and will fall within a particular insurer's policy period. When injuries occur undetected over time, such as in asbestos injury or pollution damage cases, the exact timing of when the injury or the damage took place, and which policy or policies are triggered, are more difficult to determine.

The question arose: If a worker is exposed to asbestos in 1945, but is not diagnosed for say asbestosis until 1975, which event triggers coverage? The resulting litigation initially produced two triggers of coverage:

(1) exposure trigger—those insurance companies with policies in effect when the worker was exposed to the asbestos must respond; and

(2) manifestation trigger—those insurers with policies in effect when the worker was diagnosed with asbestosis must respond.[18]

Both triggers produced reasonably short and definable loss periods and consequently a short and definable number of policy periods. Since in any particular case, only one trigger would be held to be the applicable trigger, the insurance industry's liability for asbestos injuries was, while not trivial, within limited bounds.

This situation was changed dramatically in 1982 by the famous, or infamous, depending on your viewpoint, decision in the *Keene vs. Insurance Company of North America* case. The lead attorney for the policyholder was Eugene Anderson, whose law firm was then, and still is now, one of the leading representatives of policyholders in insurance coverage litigation. Anderson's medical experts opined that asbestos injuries occurred progressively and continuously over the time period between exposure and manifestation. The judge in the Keene case reached the conclusion that not only should both the exposure and manifestation triggers apply, but a third trigger—the entire time period between exposure and manifestation, the so-called latency or residency period—should also apply. This became known as the triple or continuous trigger. It was devastating to the insurance industry, as it meant that all the insurance policies, in effect from the time of the initial exposure of asbestos to the time of manifestation of the disease, must respond. In an event like asbestos injuries, this can mean a period of 20 to 30, or even up to 40 plus years. The Keene decision would ultimately be upheld in what was probably the largest insurance coverage litigation ever, *in re Asbestos Insurance Coverage Cases* in the mid 1980s. The case involved a large number of asbestos companies and an even larger number of insurers. A San Francisco gymnasium was converted into a courtroom to handle the large number of litigants. Judge Ira Brown held for the asbestos companies and applied the triple or continuous trigger to asbestos claims.[19]

Superfund

The disposal of hazardous waste in the United States, like many environmental problems, was largely ignored until the 1970s. When the government decided to deal with the environmental problems of hazardous waste disposal, it faced two distinct problems. One was the problem of how to regulate the present and future disposal of hazardous waste. The second was the problem of how to handle the cleanup of old, often abandoned, hazardous waste sites. The solutions to these dual problems were set forth in two separate pieces of legislation. The Resource Conservation and Recovery Act (RCRA) was passed in 1976 to deal with the present and future disposal of hazardous waste. In 1980, the Superfund program was set up under the Comprehensive Environmental Response, Compensation, and Liability Act (CERCLA) to deal with the cleanup of old hazardous waste sites. As will be discussed below, these two Acts have had a substantial impact on both general liability insurance and environmental liability insurance markets and coverages.

RCRA

RCRA established a rigorous cradle-to-grave manifest control system to track and assign responsibility for current and future hazardous waste disposal. The manifest is a control and transport document that accompanies the hazardous waste at all times, from its point of generation to its point of disposal. RCRA imposes strict waste management requirements upon generators and transporters of hazardous wastes and upon hazardous waste treatment, storage and disposal (TSD) facilities. With its emphasis on current and prospective environmental problems, RCRA is more similar to the Clean Water and Air Acts than CERCLA.[20]

RCRA is one of the first federal laws to require proof of financial responsibility for environmental liabilities. Owners of TSD facilities are required to demonstrate their financial ability to pay for third-party claims resulting from a release of contaminants and for closure/post closure care costs. Owners of under-ground storage tanks are also required to demonstrate their ability to pay for third-party claims and cleanup costs associated with a release of contaminants. Financial responsibility requirements frequently are met by the purchase of environmental impairment liability (EIL) insurance. RCRA's requirements created a demand for EIL insurance and were important in the development of early EIL insurance markets in the late 1970s.[21]

Under RCRA, the risk management regulatory concept is that hazardous waste, if properly handled today, will not cause problems in the future. The costs of hazardous waste disposal are internalized to the generators, transporters, handlers, and disposers of hazardous waste, each paying their own cost of complying with RCRA's regulations.

CERCLA

The Superfund program was established by CERCLA to deal with coordinating and financing the cleanup of old hazardous waste sites. The costs associated with Superfund liabilities, and their financial impact on insurance companies, have been enormous. Although the total costs (cleanup, transaction, and administrative costs) of cleaning up hazardous waste sites is unknown, various studies have put the ultimate figure between $100 billion and $1 trillion. Some of the studies, which estimated these costs, are included in Table 6-2.

Since 1980, a total of nearly 44,418 sites have been assessed through the federal Superfund and related state programs. Through October, 2003, 33,106 (75 percent) sites have been removed from the Superfund inventory. The remaining 11,312 sites (25 percent) remain active with the site assessment program or are on the National Priority List (NPL). The NPL is intended to be a listing of the sites with the most serious and urgent cleanup problems. Since the Superfund program began, 1,560 sites have been put on or proposed for the NPL. As sites are cleaned up and removed from the NPL, new ones are added so the number of active NPL sites typically stays in the range of 1,200—1,300. As of October, 2003, 1,292 sites were on or proposed for the NPL while 267 have been completely cleaned up and removed from the NPL. Construction has been completed at another 583 NPL sites, so they are expected to be removed from the NPL in the not too distant future. Remedial investigations/feasibility studies are in process for most of the other NPL sites.[22]

In a 2001 study financed by Congress, Katherine Probst, senior fellow at Resources for the Future, estimated that 230 to 490 new Superfund sites may be added to the NPL, with a cost of at least $14 billion over the next decade.[23] A 1995 Standard and Poor's study estimates that eventually over 5,000 sites will be placed on the NPL.[24]

Table 6 – 2
Hazardous Waste Cost Estimates

Office of Technology Assessment (OTA)*	$500 billion
Standard & Poor's	$700 billion
Solomon Brothers	$1 trillion
Congressional Budget Office	$165 billion (Superfund only)
University of Tennessee*	$750 billion (all sites)
	$150 billion (Superfund only)
Academy of Actuaries	$100 billion (Superfund only)

*cleanup cost only

Sources:
American Academy of Actuaries, *Costs Under Superfund,* Washington, D.C., American Academy of Actuaries, August 1995.
Diane Dimond, "The $700 Billion Cleaning Bill," *Insurance Review,* January 1989.
David Foppert, "Pressure Mounts for Cleanup Reserves," *Best's Review,* P/C Edition, July, 1993.
Timothy Noah, "Clinton Today Begins An Attempt to Clean Up Big Toxic-Waste Problem: Superfund Law Itself," *Wall Street Journal,* February 3, 1994.
Office of Technology Assessment, Congress of the United States, *Coming Clean, Superfund Problems Can Be Solved,* U.S. Government Printing Office, Washington, D.C., October 1989.
Milton Russell, William E. Colglazier and Mary R. English, Hazardous Waste Remediation Project, *Hazardous Waste Remediation: The Task Ahead,* Knoxville, TN: The University of Tennessee, Waste Management Research and Education Institute, December 1991.
Milton Russell, William E. Colglazier, Mary R. English and B.E. Tonn, "The U.S. Hazardous Waste Legacy," *Environment,* 34, 1992.
Waste Management Research and Education Institute, *Hazardous Waste Remediation Project, The Superfund Process: Site-Level Experience,* Knoxville, TN: The University of Tennessee, Knoxville, December 1991.
Dan R. Anderson, "Development of Environmental Liability Risk Management and Insurance in the United States: Lessons and Opportunities," *Risk Management and Insurance Review,* Summer 1998, Vol. 2, No. 1, pp. 1-23.

The average cleanup cost per site has run in the range of $30-40 million. Between initial placement on the NPL and the final cleanup, there is roughly an average time lapse of over 10 years. Numerous states have state mini Superfund programs, which are designed to address the cleanup of the next level of waste sites, that are not serious enough to be placed in the federal Superfund program, but still require attention.[25]

Tax Financing

Funding for the Superfund program derived from two main sources: taxes and recoveries from potentially responsible parties (PRPs). Taxes were designed to pay for cleanup costs at abandoned or orphan sites, at sites where responsible parties cannot be identified or are unable to pay, at sites where responsible parties refuse to pay, and for emergency action. Taxes were paid into a trust fund, or Superfund, which gave the program its name. Taxes were originally assessed only against the chemical and petroleum industries, because they were the most obvious and largest industrial generators of hazardous waste. Under this arrangement, funding in the first five years of the program, 1980 to 1985, was $1.6 billion.

A general corporation tax was added to the chemical and petroleum industry taxes under the Superfund Amendments and Reauthorization Act of 1986 (SARA). The budget for the next five years, 1986 to 1991, was set at $8.5 billion. An additional $5.1 billion was authorized for the years 1992 to 1994. Funding was extended through September 30, 1995, the end of fiscal year 1995.[26]

There were also modest contributions from general tax revenues, which were designed to cover EPA administration and legal expenses, but the bulk of the money came from corporate taxes. For instance in 1994, general tax revenues paid $250 million or 17 percent of the budget, while Superfund taxes provided $950 million or 83 percent of the budget.[27] In the years 1993, 1994 and 1995, Superfund taxes generated more than $2 billion a year.[28] Part of these annual taxes would be used to cover most of the Superfund budget and the remainder would be deposited into the trust fund.

Efforts by the Clinton administration to reauthorize these taxes beyond September 30, 1995 were stymied by a Republican Congress. To date, these taxes have yet to be reauthorized, and the current Bush administration opposes them. The failure to reauthorize taxes has altered the funding philosophy of Superfund, which was based on the principle of "the polluter pays." When taxes were paid, the trust fund gradually built up a balance that maxed out just short of $4 billion. Since 1995, the trust fund balance has been drawn down. As the balance decreased, general revenues were tapped to make up approximately 50 percent of Superfund budget. When the Trust Fund ran out of money in 2004, 100 percent, less any recoveries from PRPs, of the Superfund budget is now financed from general revenues. The current annual budget is running around $1.2—1.3 billion. Thus for the monies spent on abandoned sites, taxpayers and not the oil, chemical and other industries are footing the bill. This development is particularly significant for the oil industry, as they were exempted from PRP liabilities, based partly on the rational that they were paying taxes in lieu of such liabilities.[29]

Not surprisingly, with less money coming into the Superfund program, a smaller number of sites are being added to the NPL. For instance, in the four years of the Clinton administration's second term, 34-45 sites per year were added to the NPL. In the first three years of the Bush administration, nine, 14 and 11, respectively, have been added.[30] In 1999 and 2000, construction was completed on 85 and 87 sites, respectively, while in 2001, 2002 and 2003, construction was completed on 47, 42 and 40 sites, respectively.[31] The Bush administration claims the reason for the lower number is that the added sites and recently completed sites are more complex and require more work to clean up. Critics charge that insufficient funding is causing the slow down and is just one more example of the low priority that the Bush administration puts on the environment. Government budget documents show a short fall in Superfund funding, for sites under or beginning construction, of $175 million and $250 million in fiscal years 2003 and 2004, respectively.[32]

PRP Recoveries

The second source of non-general tax revenue funding comes from recoveries from PRPs. These parties can include current and past owners and operators of hazardous waste sites, generators of hazardous waste and transporters of hazardous waste. Both private business and governmental units can be named as PRPs. PRPs can also include financial institutions, which through foreclosures or other means, become responsible for the property that contains hazardous waste. EPA attempts to persuade PRPs to carry out and pay for a site cleanup ("enforcement lead"). If a settlement cannot be reached, EPA will arrange to clean the site and then litigate against PRPs to recover costs.[33] Typically, most PRPs elect to conduct their own cleanup. Approximately 70 percent of Superfund sites are cleaned up by PRPs. Not only can PRP corporations control the costs, but the EPA can charge the companies three times the EPA's cost, plus penalties, if PRPs refuse to cooperate. EPA takes the lead on the 30 percent of sites where PRPs are not available ("fund lead"). For the life of the Superfund program through September 30, 2004, PRPs have funded more than $18 billion in remedial actions at NPL sites.[34]

Seeking recovery from PRPs follows "the polluter pays" principle, where the costs of an activity are allocated or internalized to those responsible for that activity, in this case hazardous waste disposal. Of course, those parties named as PRPs, who may not have polluted or feel they did not pollute, may disagree with this assessment. "The polluter pays" principle can also act as a powerful incentive to properly dispose of hazardous waste in the future.

Liability Rules

The designers of the Superfund program gave EPA considerable leverage in its efforts to recover cleanup costs from PRPs, either through settlements or litigation. PRPs' liability is based on retroactive, strict, and joint and several liability.

Retroactive liability means that even though past hazardous waste disposal met all existing regulations at the time of disposal, liability can still be assessed against those involved with the past disposal. In many cases, no regulations existed at the time of disposal.

Strict liability in the Superfund context means that negligence of PRP defendants need not be proven by EPA. It is only required that EPA show that PRP defendants disposed of the hazardous waste requiring cleanup. The burden of proof for EPA is less severe under strict liability.

Under the joint and several liability doctrine, any particular PRP that contributed part of the hazardous waste at a site can be held responsible for the entire cleanup cost. While there is little, if any, evidence that EPA has actually forced PRPs to pay an extremely imbalanced or disproportionate percentage of cleanup costs, joint and several liability gives EPA a strong tool to pressure PRPs to cooperate in settlements.[35] This would be particularly true of a "deep pocket" PRP, i.e., one with substantial financial resources that had contributed only a portion of the hazardous waste at the site. Of course, large PRPs may seek contribution from other potential PRPs.

These liability rules, particularly retroactive liability and joint and several liability, are subjects of considerable controversy. Alternatives to these rules are key components of various proposals to change the Superfund program and will be discussed later.

Insurance Industry Involvement

The insurance industry becomes involved with Superfund-mandated cleanup costs when PRPs attempt to have their insurance companies pay for these costs. Given the enormity of the potential costs for hazardous waste cleanup, it is not surprising that PRPs would seek other sources to assist in financing the costs. Similarly, it is not surprising that insurance companies would resist paying costs that they never anticipated covering. This situation set the stage for a high-stakes litigation contest. The central question being contested is: Do insurance policies cover Superfund-mandated hazardous waste cleanup costs?

The type of insurance policy that is typically involved in the litigation is the general liability insurance policy. This policy is carried by virtually all businesses. Hazardous waste claims typically come under the premises and operations coverage section. Excess and umbrella liability policies are also brought into insurance coverage litigation when primary limits are exhausted. While property insurance policies, particularly all risks forms, have also had claims brought against them,[36] most of the litigation has focused on general liability and related policies.

The affected policies are primarily older general liability policies, purchased before 1986 when an "absolute" exclusion for all hazardous waste, pollution, and related claims was placed in liability policies. Policies written before 1970, when not even the limited pollution exclusion for gradual pollution was in effect, are particularly vulnerable for insurers.

PRPs have conducted and are conducting extensive searches for older policies, because the actual policies are the most clear and convincing evidence that coverage was in effect. Many policies have been destroyed as part of regular records attrition management programs, so other evidence of coverage, e.g., correspondence, check stubs, etc., are sought to prove that coverage was in effect. The reconstruction of a PRP's past insurance program has given rise to a new consulting area called "insurance archeology."[37]

Financial Impact on the Insurance Industry

The financial impact of Superfund-mandated hazardous waste liabilities on the insurance industry depends on three factors: (1) total costs to clean up hazardous waste sites; (2) transaction costs (litigation and administration costs); and (3) the outcome of insurance coverage litigation with PRP/policyholders. The potential costs for hazardous waste cleanup costs are enormous. Although the total of cleanup, legal, and administrative costs are unknown, various estimates have been put forth. Six of these estimates are shown in Table 6-2 and range from $100 billion to $1 trillion. Estimation techniques typically extend these costs over a minimum of 30 years into the future.

No attempt is made in this book to evaluate the methodologies used by the above organizations, or to evaluate which total dollar estimate of costs associated with hazardous waste cleanups is most appropriate. At this time, it is probably safe to say that no one knows what the ultimate cost will be. Some of the estimates include total projected cleanup and transaction costs for Superfund and all other hazardous waste sites combined. It should be noted that most states have mini Superfund plans for sites that are not included in the federal Superfund program. Others, like the Tennessee study, give estimates for Superfund sites and all sites combined, but include only cleanup costs and not transaction costs. At a minimum, we are talking about financial liability risks in the hundreds of billions of dollars facing corporate America and the insurance industry.

The Superfund program has produced considerable litigation and other transaction costs, particularly in the early years of the program. There are two tiers of negotiation and litigation. The first involves the EPA's pursuit of PRPs to cleanup Superfund sites. The second encompasses the PRPs seeking indemnification and defense cost coverage from their insurers for Superfund liabilities. This double-edged, highly litigious environment has resulted in substantial transaction costs. For the first tier litigation, an analysis on the extent of these costs has been provided by the Rand Institute for Civil Justice. In a 1989 study conducted by Paul Acton, it was estimated that overall litigation and administration expenses were running at approximately 40 percent of total Superfund costs.[38] A second study, in 1992, by Acton and Dixon, estimated that transactions costs to date were approximately 36 percent of all Superfund related expenditures.[39] In a Rand Corporation 1993 study by Dixon, Drezner and Hammitt, PRP transaction costs were estimated at 32 percent of their total expenditures.[40] A 1995 study by the American Academy of Actuaries estimates that 30 percent of future Superfund costs will be for transaction costs.[41]

For insurers, transaction costs were even greater, especially in the early years. A Rand Corporation study by Acton and Dixon, which examined the experience of four key insurers, estimated that 88 percent of their total expenditures for all Superfund claims (open and closed) were for transaction costs.[42] The 1992 study estimated that 37 percent of the 88 percent transaction costs estimate went toward defending PRP policyholders, and 42 percent went toward insurance coverage litigation with PRP policyholders. For closed claims, 69 percent went for transaction costs. Even insurers like USF&G, who took an active claims management approach, still experienced a 50 percent payout rate for transaction costs.[43] Since transaction costs tend to be higher at the beginning of Superfund cases, a Rand spokesperson estimated that the ultimate proportion of total Superfund related costs would range from 19 to 27 percent, "with our best estimate at the upper end of this range."[44]

Insurance Coverage Litigation

The insurance coverage litigation between PRPs as policyholders and insurance companies has produced several key coverage issues involving the extent of covered damages, the pollution exclusion, the triggers of coverage, duty to defend provision, the number of occurrences, and the care, custody, and control exclusion. For the insurance industry, these coverage issues go far beyond the Superfund liabilities. As has been discussed throughout this book, developing environmental liabilities often are characterized by a long time lag between the occurrence of exposures/injuries/damages and the ultimate assessments of liabilities on defendants and their insurers. Insurance coverage precedents established in Superfund related cases, and the previously discussed asbestos cases, could apply to any number of future sustainability risk areas. Because of the importance of these insurance coverage issues to a wide variety of sustainability risk situations, I want to present a brief description of these issues.

Each coverage issue will be discussed from the viewpoints of both the PRP policyholders and the insurance companies. A complete and detailed examination of all the nuances of each coverage issue across various jurisdictions is beyond the scope of this book.[45] The purpose here is to give the reader a basic understanding of the key issues in the litigation.

1970 Pollution Exclusion

Prior to the early 1970s, no mention was made of pollution or hazardous waste in general liability policies. Without any other defense, coverage would presumably exist under the premises and operations section of the policy. In the early 1970s, insurers began to include an exclusion which limited coverage for pollution claims. An example of this standard partial pollution exclusion is included below:

> This insurance does not apply to bodily injury or property damage arising out of the discharge, dispersal, release or escape of smoke, vapors, soot, fumes, acids, alkalis, toxic chemicals, liquids or gases, waste materials or other irritants, contaminants or pollutants into or upon land, the atmosphere or any water course or body of water; but this exclusion does not apply if such discharge, dispersal, release or escape is sudden and accidental.[46]

Insurers argue that the purpose was to exclude all types of pollution claims, except those that resulted from "sudden and accidental" dispersals. Insurers were attempting to exclude the "gradual pollution" claims resulting from, perhaps, a slow leak that no one had bothered to trace and correct and which, over years, could result in a serious contamination problem, while still maintaining coverage for pollution that might occur from a sudden and accidental event, like an exploding chemical tank.

The term sudden and accidental has become the focal point of extensive litigation. Insurers claim that the event had to happen in an instantaneous or very short period of time. PRP policyholders claim that the term sudden and accidental only meant unintended or unexpected and does not connote any temporal quality. Some courts resorted to using dictionaries, which, depending on the particular meaning or set of meanings chosen, resulted in findings for insurers in some cases and for policyholders in others. Findings for policyholders have the effect of negating the exclusion, thus coverage becomes effective for both sudden and gradual pollution events. The situation is complicated for the fact that some insurance organizations, in arguing for the pollution exclusion, stated that the exclusion was merely a clarification of existing policy wording and not a restriction of coverage. Not surprisingly, these arguments have come back to haunt insurers, as policyholders use them to support their cases.[47]

1986 Pollution Exclusion

In the mid 1980s, the Insurance Services Office (ISO) began to file an expanded pollution exclusion that was aimed at excluding most types of pollution/hazardous waste claims, both sudden and gradual, from general liability policies. The 1986 ISO exclusion is included below:

This insurance does not apply to:

(1) "Bodily injury" or "property damage" arising out of the actual, alleged or threatened discharge, dispersal, release or escape of pollutants:

(a) At or from premises you own, rent or occupy;

(b) At or from any site or location used by or for you or others for the handling, storage, disposal, processing or treatment of waste;

(c) Which are at any time transported, handled, stored, treated, disposed of, or processed as waste by or for you or any person or organization for whom you may be legally responsible; or

(d) At or from any site or location on which you or any contractors or subcontractors working directly or indirectly on your behalf are performing operations:

> (i) if the pollutants are brought on or to the site or location in connection with such operations; or

> (ii) if the operations are to test for, monitor, clean up, remove, contain, treat, detoxify or neutralize the pollutants.

(2) Any loss, cost, or expense arising out of any governmental direction or request that you test for, monitor, clean up, remove, contain, treat, detoxify or neutralize pollutants.[48]

While insurers attempted to exclude most pollution claims in this so called "absolute" pollution exclusion, some situations were still covered. For instance, product liability claims involving environmental contaminations are not excluded.[49]

Covered Damages

According to the ISO language, the general liability insurance policy typically provides that the insurer will:

> pay on behalf of the insured all sums which the insured shall become legally obligated to pay as damages because of bodily injury or property damage during the policy period neither expected not intended from the standpoint of the insured.[50]

Insurers contend that government-mandated hazardous waste cleanup costs under Superfund are not, "sums which the insured shall become legally obligated to pay as damages," and thus, are not covered under liability policies. They argue that such costs are economic losses, and constitute equitable monetary relief rather than legal relief, i.e., monetary amounts awarded by a court of law. PRP policyholders counter that policy wording is unclear on the intent and should be interpreted as the common everyday definition of damages, which would include monies they must pay for cleanup costs.

A closely related aspect of the covered damages issue is the expectation or intention related to property damages. Liability policies have never been meant to cover intentionally caused or expected property damages, like arson. Both public policy considerations and specific policy wording requiring property damage be "neither expected nor intended from the standpoint of the insured" argue against such coverage.

When applicable, insurers contend that pollution/hazardous waste property damages are not covered, as they were either intended, or at least should have been expected by the policyholders. Policyholders counter by saying that either their actions were not intended, that is, they were accidental, or even if their actions were intentional, they did not intend or expect property damages to occur. Court decisions have been widely split on this issue. Intent and what the policyholder should reasonably have expected to happen, as indicated by the specific facts of the case, have largely decided the outcome.[51]

Trigger of Coverage

While the triple or continuous trigger rule has established a strong foothold in asbestos cases, the situation in hazardous waste litigation is not as clear. Not surprisingly, PRP policyholders argue for the more expansive triple or continuous trigger as it maximizes their coverage. For instance, in litigation involving the Shell Oil Company, Shell sued 260 liability insurers (primary and excess) that provided coverage from 1947 to 1983. Shell sued for one billion dollars in cleanup costs it was responsible to pay for cleanup at two hazardous waste sites in Colorado and California.[52] Insurers, in contrast, argue for either an exposure trigger (when the hazardous waste was disposed of) or a manifestation trigger (when a cleanup order or suit arises).[53] As is readily apparent, the final determination of the trigger issue has enormous significance for both PRP policyholders and insurance companies.

Duty to Defend

A standard feature of liability insurance policies is that the insurance company has the right and duty to defend the policyholder in any litigation resulting from actions covered under the policy. Defense costs include attorney fees, court costs, expert testimony, investigations, studies, and other costs associated with defending the policyholder.

When it is determined that the insurer's policy must respond, there is little debate that the insurer must provide defense cost coverage. There are other cases, however, where the insurer may be asked to defend. Generally, the insurer's duty to defend is broader than the duty to indemnify for bodily injuries and property damages. Typical policy wording is included below:

> The insurer shall have the right and duty to defend any suit against the
> insured seeking damages on account of such bodily injury or property dam-
> age, even if any of the allegations of the suit are groundless, false or fraudulent,
> and may make such investigation and settlement of any claim or suit as it
> deems expedient.[54]

PRP policyholders argue that insurers have a duty to defend and pay defense
costs for actions brought against them by EPA under Superfund, even if cleanup
costs may not be held to be covered property damages. In addition, policyholders
argue that a letter from the EPA, naming them as PRPs for cleanup costs, has the
same practical effect as a lawsuit and triggers an insurer's duty to defend.

Another more troublesome situation involves the amount or the limit on
defense cost coverage. In most general liability insurance policies, no specific dollar limit applies to defense costs. When defense costs are in addition to policy
limits (outside the limits), policy limits apply to bodily injuries and property
damages to establish maximum amounts payable by the insurance companies for
injuries and damages. Since 1966, insurers have typically included an explicit
clause in policies that states that defense cost coverage ceases when policy limits
for bodily injuries and property damages are exceeded. The standard ISO clause
in included below:

> the insurer shall not be obligated to pay any claim or judgment or to defend
> any suit after the applicable limit of the insurer's liability has been exhausted
> by payment of judgments or settlements.[55]

Similar issues regarding pre-and post-1966 policies and the duty to defend are
argued in asbestos litigation. In asbestos claims, as with Superfund cases, insurers
are particularly vulnerable for pre-1966 liability policies in terms of limiting their
payouts for defense.

When defense costs are inside the policy limits, bodily injury, property damage, and defense cost payments are all added together and applied to the limits.
For these types of policies, the issue of unlimited defense cost coverage is not a
problem. Once any combination of total payments for bodily injury, property
damage, and defense costs hits the limit, then coverage ceases.[56]

Number of Occurrences

Policy limits in liability policies are usually expressed as "X" dollars per occurrence (there may also be per injured person limits). Older policies had per accident rather than per occurrence limits. The basic idea is to establish a maximum

amount of money that the insurance company will pay in injuries or damages for a particular event or loss.

If a hazardous waste/pollution situation involves multiple claims, questions have arisen as to whether this should be considered one occurrence or multiple occurrences. For instance, in the 1984 *Jackson Township*[57] case, the court held that numerous claims, which arose from the seepage of landfill wastes into local drinking water, each constituted a separate occurrence. The result was an increase in the potential liability of the insurance company, as the full policy limit became available for each separate occurrence.

Since 1986, the premises and operations portion of the general liability policy has been subject to an annual aggregate limit. This type of limit stipulates the maximum liability of the insurance company for a particular year, regardless of the number of occurrences. Earlier policies, at least the primary policies (excess and umbrella policies usually have aggregate limits), did not have an annual aggregate limit on this portion of the coverage, from which pollution/hazardous waste claims arise. On these earlier policies, insurers may incur substantial liabilities in excess of their per occurrence limits. In addition, as new claimants come forward, policy limits may never be exhausted, and could also lead to claims for additional defense cost coverage.[58]

Care, Custody, and Control Exclusion

Liability insurance policies have an exclusion called the "care, custody, and control" exclusion, as shown below:

This insurance does not apply to property damage to:

(1) property owned or occupied by or rented to the insured,

(2) property used by the insured, or

(3) property in the care, custody or control of the insured or as to which the insured is for any purpose exercising physical control.[59]

The effect is to exclude coverage for damage to property that is in the care, custody, and control of the policyholder. Coverage for such damage is more appropriately provided by property insurance policies.

In the context of hazardous waste claims, coverage for hazardous waste cleanups, involving waste that was disposed of on the policyholder's property, would be excluded. If the waste is shipped off the insured's property to a waste site handled by another party, then the exclusion does not apply. Contested situations evolve when hazardous waste may contaminate the groundwater below the insured's property, or when monies are spent to prevent the spread of waste to an adjacent property. Insurers argue that these situations are not covered claims, while PRP policyholders say that coverage should apply.[60]

Outcome of Insurance Coverage Litigation

In a 1994 article, I discussed the various litigated coverage issues and measured the success rates of insurers and PRP policyholders in this litigation.[61] The results are shown in Table 6-3 from the study. On some issues, like the 1970 and 1986 pollution exclusions, court decisions favored insurers. On other issues, like covered damages and the duty to defend, court decisions favored PRP policyholders. Yet overall, based on the compiled data in that study, the success rates of insurers and policyholders across all the litigated coverage issues and various jurisdictions were nearly equal—48 percent for insurers and 52 percent for policyholders. While several caveats are in order (e.g., no trend analysis was performed and cases were equally weighted), my inescapable conclusion in 1994 was that insurance coverage litigation in the environmental area is very complex and far from being resolved in favor of either policyholders or insurers.

Table 6-3
Summary Insurance Coverage Litigation Issues

| | For Insurers | | For Policyholders | |
| | American Re | Oshinsky, Warin, and Serafin | American Re | Oshinsky, Warin, and Serafin |
Issue				
1970 Pollution Exclusion	67	37	40	27
1986 Pollution Exclusion	38	–	9	–
Covered Damages	27	7	59	27
Trigger of Coverage	21	25	19	25
Duty to Defend	15	11	19	21
Number of Occurrences	17	–	16	–
Care, Custody, and Control Exclusion	9	5	17	19
TOTAL	194	85	179	119
	52%	42%	48%	58%
Weighted Average	48%		52%	

Source: Dan R. Anderson, "Insurance Coverage Litigation and the Financial Impact of Superfund-Mandated Hazardous Waste Liabilities on the Insurance Industry," *Journal of Insurance Regulation,* Vol. 13, No. 1, Fall 1994, pp. 53-96.

When I conducted my study, one of the principal data sources I used was *Environmental Coverage Case Law,* published by American Re, a major U.S. reinsurer, which is now owned by the Munich Re Group. American Re's study examines each of the coverage issues as to how they have been resolved in various jurisdictions (federal, state, local) across all the states. The lack of resolution, as indicated by the data compiled by American Re, is complicated by the fact that insurance coverage issues cases rarely if ever reach the U.S. Supreme Court, because constitutional issues are not involved.

I was using one of their earlier editions, the fourth (1993), in my 1994 study, but American Re has continued to publish their research annually, with the most recent being the 15th edition (2004).[62] In this edition, for the first time, American Re assembled an index of state and federal decisions for each of the coverage issues. A perusal of the indexes of each of the coverage issues indicates that the lack of resolution of these issues across various jurisdictions and states that I found in 1994 still exists as of 2004. There may be resolution for a particular issue, in a certain jurisdiction, in a particular state. But corporate policyholders and insurers often operate across numerous states and may have a choice of jurisdictions. For these policyholders and insurers, predicting how a coverage issue will be interpreted on an aggregate basis is difficult if not impossible.

Ultimate Financial Impact: Asbestos and Superfund Liabilities

The ultimate financial liabilities for Superfund and asbestos will be in the hundreds of billions of dollars. Estimates for Superfund, from various studies shown in Table 6-2, range from $100 million to $1 trillion. The Superfund program has budgeted and spent over $30 billion since its inception. These monies were spent primarily on orphaned sites and others cleaned up by the EPA. EPA data indicate that the cumulative value of private party commitments over the program's life is slightly more that $18 billion. So approximately $50 billion has been spent to date on Superfund sites.

These figures refer only to Superfund sites, not state mini Superfund sites. The University of Tennessee study, cited in Table 6-2, estimates ultimate costs at non-Superfund hazardous wastes sites to be four times the Superfund costs. This could indicate $200 billion for these sites in addition to the $50 billion spent on Superfund. Even if non-Superfund sites cleanups cost the same as Superfund, the total estimated expenditures spent to date would be $100 billion. My purpose here is not to perform a detailed financial analysis of costs of Superfund and other hazardous waste sites; it is to demonstrate that at a minimum we are witnessing present and future expenditures in the hundreds of hundreds of billions of dollars.

The costs of resolving asbestos liabilities present numbers in the same general magnitude. In June, 2001, Tillinghast-Towers Perrin, a leading actuarial and risk management consulting firm, estimated total ultimate asbestos costs to be $200 billion.[63] The Rand Institute for Civil Justice, which has conducted a number of asbestos related studies, estimates that $54 billion has been spent on asbestos litigation as of 2000, and future costs will range from $145 to 210 billion.[64] It is estimated that up to 2.5 million more claims may materialize in the future.[65] Again, I believe it is safe to conclude that asbestos liabilities, like Superfund, will result in hundreds of billions of dollars in expenditures.

Insurer Liabilities

Tillinghast-Towers Perrin estimates that insurers are picking up around 61 percent of the costs of asbestos claims, with 30 percent paid by U.S. insurers and 31 percent by foreign insurers.[66] I have not seen a percentage for environmental claims, but based on my insurance coverage analysis above, I think 50 percent of what PRPs pay would be a reasonable estimate. Insurers and rating organizations have attempted to estimate environmental (mostly Superfund) and asbestos liabilities of the insurance industry. These estimates are included to create a combined category, environmental and asbestos (E&A) liabilities. Environmental and asbestos liabilities cause very similar problems for insurers, as they both involve huge costs, extend over a long time, trigger old policies, and the expectation exists that substantial payments will be required into the future.

A 1995 study by Standard & Poor's estimated insurers' future E&A costs to be $125 billion.[67] A 1997 study by the A.M. Best Company estimated insurers' ultimate (past and future) E&A costs to be $106 billion.[68] A more recent A.M. Best report puts E&A ultimate costs at $121 billion, with asbestos at $65 billion and environmental at $56 billion, as of May 2001. Approximately $44 billion have been paid through May 2001, with $77 billion still yet to be paid. A.M. Best notes that as of 2001, insurers were only carrying around $24 billion in loss reserves, or about one third, of the expected amount to be paid in the future.[69]

Loss Reserves

As asbestos and environmental costs have increased, insurers have been forced to increase their loss reserves for these liabilities. Loss reserves are an estimate of what the insurers expect to pay in the future for a set of risks. Loss reserves are carried as a liability on the insurers' balance sheets. Table 6-4 illustrates some major reserve adjustments by insurers in the mid 1990s. Figure 6-1 shows some major reserves adjustments by insurers in 2002. While not exclusively adjusted for increasing environmental and asbestos claims, most of the adjustments relate to these claims. In 2003, Hartford increased its loss reserves for asbestos claims by $1.7 billion[70] and Travelers strengthened their asbestos reserves by $2.4 billion.[71] In July 2004, St. Paul Travelers added $1.63 billion to reserves,[72] and followed that up with a $1.01 billion increase in March 2005.[73] Liberty Mutual increased its asbestos reserve by $1.1 billion in fall of 2004.[74] In January 2005, ACE increased its asbestos and environmental reserves by $788 million, and in May 2005, AIG boasted its reserves by $850 million.[75] Even with these adjustments, insurers still have not posted the ultimate expected loss reserves needed to cover ultimate environmental and asbestos liabilities.

Table 6 – 4
Loss Reserve Increases – mid 1990s

Aetna	$750,000,000
Allstate	400,000,000
CIGNA	1,200,000,000
ITT Hartford	510,000,000
Kemper	550,000,000
Fireman's Fund	800,000,000
Nationwide	1,100,000,000
Swiss Re America	700,000,000

Sources:
"Allstate Pumps Up Reserves for Environmental Coverages," *Business Insurance*, October 14, 1996.
Best, A.M., "The Industry at a Turning Point," *Best's Review*, P/C Edition, January 1996.
Best, A.M., "Choosing to Survive Or Thrive In a New Era," *Best's Review*, P/C Edition, January 1997.
"ITT Hartford Boosts Reserves," *Business Insurance*, April 10, 1995.
Sara Marley, "Swiss Re Ups U.S. Stake," *Business Insurance*, April 10, 1995.
Michael Quint, "A Superfund Plan Divides the Insurance Industry," *Wall Street Journal*, June 10, 1994.
Leslie Scism, "Fireman's Fund Doubles Its Reserves for Pollution Claims to $1.4 Billion," *Wall Street Journal*, June 23, 1995.
Leslie Scism, "Aetna to Boost Loss Reserves by $750 Million," *Wall Street Journal*, July 12, 1995.
Eric M. Simpson, W. Dolson Smith and Cynthia S. Babbitt, "Insurers Chip Away at E&A Liabilities," *Best's Review*, P/C Edition, April 1996.
Dan R. Anderson, "Development of Environmental Liability Risk Management and Insurance in the United States: Lessons and Opportunities," *Risk Management and Insurance Review*, Summer 1998, Vol. 2, No. 1, pp. 1-23.

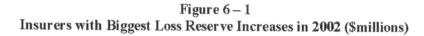

Figure 6 – 1
Insurers with Biggest Loss Reserve Increases in 2002 ($millions)

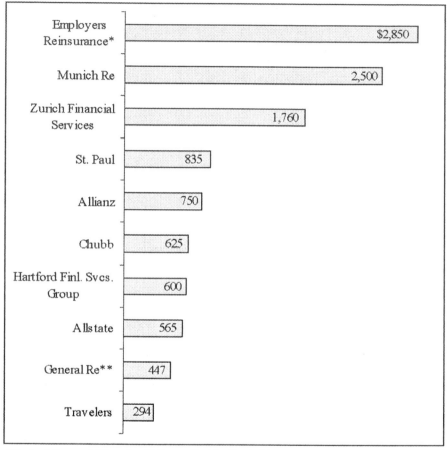

*Part of General Electric **Controlled by Berkshire Hathaway

Source: Christopher Oster, "Insurers Continue To Be Haunted By Past Messes," *Wall Street Journal,* December 5, 2002.

A recent court decision has created potential cash flow problems for insurers. Typically, environmental and asbestos claims take a long time to be paid out. Insurers refer to these type of claims payments as long tail. While an insurer may carry a sizeable loss reserve on its balance sheet, the amount actually paid in cash in the next year is a small percentage of the total amount that will eventually be paid. Until actually paid in cash, insurers have the use of these reserves for investment purposes. The 2002 court decision in question, *Fuller-Austin Insulations Co. v. Fireman's Fund Ins. Co.*,[76] involved the issue of when insurance payments for asbestos claims need to be paid into a trust fund created by Fuller-Austin's bankruptcy. Rather than paying into the fund as claims came in, the insurers were ordered to immediately make their total expected payments into the trust fund. For internal cash flow planning purposes, loss reserves are discounted for claims that are expected to be paid out over a long time. If payments need to be made immediately, then insurers will lose the time value of those monies. If this precedent holds up on appeal, the financial impact of asbestos claims, and possibly other long tail risks, will become more severe for the insurance industry.

Reorganizations

In addition to environmental and asbestos liabilities causing significant adverse financial consequences for insurers, some insurers have been forced to employ innovative re-organizational techniques to mitigate losses. The liability-based restructurings or related reorganizations of Lloyd's of London,[77] Home/Zurich Insurance,[78] CIGNA,[79] and Continental/CNA,[80] were accomplished in large part to relieve the financial pressures caused by environmental and asbestos liabilities.

The reorganization of Lloyd's of London is of particular note. Lloyd's is the oldest and probably most venerable insurance organization in the world. For 300 years, they had successfully provided insurance and reinsurance coverage for marine exposures, natural catastrophes, and numerous unique and difficult risks. But environmental and asbestos claims nearly forced Lloyd's into bankruptcy. In the latter half of the 20th Century, Lloyd's was a major market for insuring excess liability risks for large corporations or providing reinsurance for insurers writing excess liability. Lloyd's had a piece of excess liability exposure for hundreds, if not thousands, of corporations. When environmental and asbestos claims starting to roll in, excess coverage layers were pierced for an enormous number of claims. Many individual Lloyd's underwriters and syndicates were wiped out. Only a major reorganization in the late 1990s, which brought in corporate capital and consolidated all its environmental and asbestos claims in a runoff entity, Equitas, prevented Lloyd's from what seemed to be an inevitable insolvency.

Reinsurance

Weakness in the reinsurance sector of the insurance industry could also exasperate financial difficulties. Reinsurers provide insurance for insurance companies. When an insurance company writes a large risk, typically, part of the potential loss will be ceded to the reinsurance market. If the insurance company had to pay the entire loss, it could produce financial strains in its operations. For instance in 2002, St. Paul Insurance Company paid nearly $1 billion to settle litigation over asbestos coverage for Western McArthur.[81] Also in 2002, PPG Industries agreed to pay $2.7 billion to resolve all of its asbestos claims through the bankruptcy of Pittsburgh Corning Corporation. It is expected that insurers, including reinsurers, will pay for two-thirds of this amount.[82]

In these types of large loss situations, insurers rely on their reinsurers to contribute toward the amounts paid out. If reinsurers fail to respond, the entire loss must be paid by the insurers. A recent study by Standard & Poors entitled, "Insurers and Reinsurers: The Context for Conflict,"[83] points to some disturbing developments in reinsurance markets. S&P notes that reinsurers are not adjusting loss reserves upward for E&A liabilities. S&P credit analyst, Laline Carvalho, states that, "in 2003, reserve increases by reinsurers were nowhere near the levels of the previous two, and way below the colossal actions taken by primary companies since the fourth quarter 2002."[84]

The study also documents that the financial ratings of reinsurers are declining. From 2001 to 2004, 15 of the top 19 reinsurers were downgraded by Standard & Poor's. In 2001, five reinsurers had a top rating of AAA, but by 2004, only one, Berkshire Hathaway Re still had its AAA rating. Any weakness in the reinsurance markets, and their ability and willingness to pay, will aggravate the adverse financial consequences of environmental and asbestos claims on the insurance industry.

Losses Not Spread Evenly Over the Insurance Industry

The current allocation of environmental and asbestos liabilities to the insurance industry is not spread evenly over the industry. Since most PRPs or asbestos defendants are corporations, businesses, and other organizations, the involved insurers are commercial lines insurers who wrote general liability insurance. Since 1939, the A.M. Best Company has compiled statistics listing the leading writers of other liability insurance and published them in *Best's Review* and/or *Best's Aggregates and Averages*. Other liability insurance is predominantly made up of general liability insurance, but also includes some professional liability coverage.

In a previous study, using the Best data, I calculated the market share over the period 1939 to 1991 of the top five, the top 10, and the top 15 writers of other liability insurance. The top five writers for most of the years had approximately 25 to 30 percent of market share; the top 10 writers for most years had approximately 35 to 45 percent of market share; and the top 15 writers for most years had approximately 45 to 60 percent of market share. Table 6-5, compiled by Standard & Poor's, shows the composite share of the top 15 insurers equals 63.1 percent over the period 1948-1985. Periods beyond the mid 1980s are not considered by these studies as asbestos and environmental risks had been excluded from general liability policies by that time. The significance of these market share percentages is that a substantial amount of the asbestos and Superfund liabilities can be expected to fall on a handful of large commercial lines insurers.[85]

Table 6 – 5
Composite Share of "Other Liability"
Market 1948 to 1985* (in %os)

Aetna	6.8
AIG	5.6
Chubb	2.7
CIGNA	4.5
CNA	4.7
Continental	4.3
Fireman's Fund	3.4
ITT/Hartford	6.1
Liberty Mutual	4.2
Nationwide	3.5
State Farm	0.6
Allegan	4.4
Travelers	5.9
USF&G	4.4
Zurich/Maryland Casualty	2.0
TOTAL	63.1

*Based on premium income net of ceded reinsurance. Shares based on premium income of U.S. insurers only; data includes foreign business of U.S. insurers. Other liability includes CGL (general), E&O, and some professional liability lines.

Source: Standard & Poors

Uneven Distribution Impedes Federal Solutions

This uneven distribution complicates the picture when federal legislation is proposed to alter the current financing system. For instance, federal legislation was proposed in 1994 to reduce Superfund litigation and determine a process of allocating costs to the insurance industry. Under the proposed legislation, the insurance industry would submit to mandatory premium taxes or assessments if PRP policyholders would agree to settlements with insurers and cease litigation. Insurers would pay 40 percent, 50 percent, or 60 percent of the costs, depending on the specific state, and if 85 percent of the PRP policyholders agreed, a settlement without litigation would be reached.

While a number of issues may have scuttled the legislation, a principal roadblock resulted from the insurance industry's lack of agreement on how the premium taxes would be allocated. Large commercial insurers like Aetna, Hartford, and Travelers that historically wrote most of the general liability insurance (i.e., the ones currently paying for most of the costs), argued that a prospective tax on future premiums should be used. Other large commercial insurers, like AIG and Chubb, which currently have large market shares of the general liability business, opposed these plans and argued for a retroactive tax based on past market shares. When proposals called for surcharges to be spread over wider premium bases than just general liability insurance, large personal lines companies like State Farm, which write predominately automobile and homeowners insurance, objected.[86]

A similar situation has developed regarding legislative attempts to create more efficiency and certainty in asbestos liability payments. In 2003, 2004 and 2005, the United States Congress took up the issue of resolving asbestos claims in the Fairness in Asbestos Injury Resolution (FAIR) Act. The legislation would create a trust fund, from which asbestos claimants would be paid, to replace the tort system. Again, there are major issues that have stalled the legislation, such as the total size of the trust fund. An earlier version of the act proposed $154 billion, which was favored by labor and trial attorneys, but a more recent version, favored by insurers and asbestos defendants, arrived at a $114 billion fund. This $114 billion fund is to be financed by a total of $46 billion contributed by insurers over 27 years, and $58 billion to be contributed by corporate asbestos defendants over 23 years, and an additional $10 billion from defendants after 23 years, if the fund is not able to cover its obligations. Yet, even had agreement been reached on this later version, the insurance industry had still not agreed on the allocation of their $46 billion share. The allocation issues were similar to those in the proposed Superfund legislation. Should all the contributions be made by the large commercial insurers, which had historically insured asbestos defendants, or should there be a broader allocation to bring in other insurers? The issues of how much foreign reinsurers should contribute, and whether they could be made to contribute, were also raised.[87]

Lessons to be Learned from Asbestos and Superfund

A constructive effect of the asbestos and Superfund risk situations is that they provide valuable lessons that can be used to rationalize and develop sustainability risk management strategies. It may have been necessary for corporations, insurers and society to experience the difficulties of asbestos and Superfund liabilities in order to alter the manner in which we face future risks of a similar nature. If corporations do not formulate and implement sustainability risk management practices, in my opinion future liabilities, which evolve from environmental and social justice risks, will cause far greater problems for corporations and the insurance industry than those caused by asbestos and Superfund. A principal focus of this book has been to set forth and document why environmental and social justice risks are expected to be significant in the coming years and the enormous costs of ignoring these risks. The asbestos and Superfund risk situations provide further evidence of the potential costs of not paying attention to developing sustainability risks. Lessons from the asbestos and Superfund risks include:

One, environmental stresses, increasing exposure to chemicals and other harmful substances, and persistent inequitable working conditions are accumulating much like asbestos exposures and hazardous waste accumulated in the past. The longer these potential risks amass, the greater and more debilitating will be their eventual and inevitable financial and reputation costs. Had action been taken against asbestos exposures back in the 1930s, when evidence was first being compiled on the deleterious effects of asbestos, the costs that have been incurred over recent years by asbestos defendants and their insurers would have been greatly mitigated. Had Superfund been passed in the early 1960s, when Rachel Carson and others began raising concerns about exposure to chemicals, the costs being incurred by PRPs and their insurers would also have been greatly reduced. The longer corporations take to develop sustainability risk management strategies for present risks, the greater will be their future costs and possibly the costs to their insurers.

Two, even if businesses are not being held accountable today for creating or contributing to causing losses, it does not mean that their immunity to accruing liabilities will last in perpetuity. The costs of these risks may be postponed, but not avoided. A new study, a new law, an innovative legal theory, a discovered document, or the more obvious extent of the injuries/damages will at some point in the future open the door to these accruing liabilities and their financial and reputation consequences. Asbestos producers and hazardous waste disposers operated decades before they started to directly incur liabilities and pay claims. The same is true of insurers who wrote liability policies for these producers and disposers. But then their risk exposures were dramatically altered by an important event: the Selikoff studies for asbestos producers, Superfund law for hazardous waste disposers, and the *Keene* decision for insurers. For those businesses, who may be avoiding accountability today for their mistreatment of the environment and their workers, at some point they will not be able to further postpone their accountability and they will pay the costs. And at least some of these costs will be passed on to their insurers.

Three, the hundreds of billions of dollars of Superfund and asbestos liabilities have been substantial for many firms and fatal to some. In my opinion, the future potential costs of environmental and social justice risks will exceed Superfund and asbestos liabilities. Recall in Chapter 1 the estimated annual value of ecosystem services being set at a figure of $33 trillion. If only a fraction of these values work their way into corporate liabilities, the costs could be enormous. What kind of value would you put of the availability of water and quality air? If corporate negligent actions and activities are found to be the proximate cause of losses to our water and atmospheric systems, liabilities could be in the trillions of dollars, not just the hundreds of billions of dollars.

Four, sustainability risks, like Superfund and asbestos risks, result in liabilities being shifted to future generations. The management and shareholders of asbestos firms and hazardous waste disposers in the 1930s, 1940s, 1950s, 1960s and 1970s did not bear the costs that developed in later periods. It was the management and the shareholders of firms in the 1980s, 1990s and 2000s, as well as injured victims, that would bear these costs. Clearly, this is an inequitable situation and a failure in allocating costs to responsible parties. Corporations today that are conducting business to produce short term profits to shareholders, without regard to future costs being assessed against other stakeholders, may incur substantial sustainability risk costs. I believe that increased transparency and pressure by NGOs and shareholder groups, along with developing liability trends and government regulations, will cause this to happen.

Five, once the asbestos and Superfund situations reached a critical mass, they gained a certain momentum and inertia. We are into over 30 years with asbestos and 25 years with Superfund, and there is no foreseeable exit strategy in sight.

Asbestos defendants and PRPs and their insurers have experienced drains on their financial resources. In a number of cases, it has lead to bankruptcies. Attempts to design a long term exit strategy through federal legislation have reached impasses because of the conflicting interests of the parties, and even of the conflicting interests among members of the same party, as within the insurance industry. While it is too late to alter past asbestos and Superfund liabilities, we are still early in the process of incurring liabilities from evolving sustainability risks discussed in this book. By developing sound sustainability risk management strategies, corporations and their insurers can avoid a repeat of the asbestos and Superfund debacles. For those corporations and insurers that do not, as they say, history has a habit of repeating itself.

CHAPTER 6—ENDNOTES

[1] Susan Warren, "Asbestos Quagmire," *Wall Street Journal,* January 27, 2002; Shailagh Murray and Kathryn Kranhold, "Asbestos Factions Struggle to Settle Their 30-Year War," *Wall Street Journal,* October 15, 2003.

[2] Mary Carmichael, "Asbestos: Still Lurking," *Newsweek,* March 22, 2004.

[3] Richard B. Schmitt, "How Plaintiffs' Lawyers Have Turned Asbestos Into a Court Perennial," *Wall Street Journal,* March 5, 2001.

[4] Lorraine Woellert and Steven Baker, "Asbestos Clouds Over MetLife," *Business Week,* April 19, 2004.

[5] Paul Brodeur, *Outrageous Misconduct,* New York: Pantheon, 1985. The book was serialized in four issues of the *New Yorker* magazine in 1985 under the title, "The Asbestos Industry on Trial."

[6] Deborah Hensler, Stephen Carroll, Michelle White, and Jennifer Gross, *Asbestos Litigation in the U.S.: A New Look at an Old Issue,* Santa Monica, CA: Rand Institute for Civil Justice, August 2001.

[7] Russell Gold, "Halliburton Finalizes Settlement For $5.1 Billion Over Asbestos," *Wall Street Journal,* January 4, 2005.

[8] Joseph Chang, "Investors Turn Spotlight on Chemical Industry Environmental Liabilities," *Chemical Market Reporter,* New York, January 21, 2002, Vol. 261, Iss. 3.

[9] "The Asbestos Monster: How Scary for Halliburton?" *Business Week,* December 24, 2001.

[10] Richard B. Schmitt, "How Plaintiffs' Lawyers Have Turned Asbestos Into a Court Perennial," *Wall Street Journal,* March 5, 2001.

[11] Kathryn Kranhold, "GE Financial Exposure On Asbestos May Grow," *Wall Street Journal,* April 28, 2003.

[12] Susan Warren, "Asbestos Quagmire," *Wall Street Journal,* January 27, 2002.

[13] Dan R. Anderson, "Financing Asbestos Claims: Coverage Issues, Manville's Bankruptcy and the Claims Facility," *Journal of Risk and Insurance,* Vol. LIV, No. 3, September 1987.

[14] Daniel Gross, "Recovery Lessons From an Industrial Phoenix," *New York Times*, April 29, 2001.

[15] Deborah Hensler, Stephen Carroll, Michelle White, and Jennifer Gross, *Asbestos Litigation in the U.S.: A New Look at an Old Issue,* Santa Monica, CA: Rand Institute for Civil Justice, August 2001.

[16] Susan Warren, "As Asbestos Mess Spreads, Sickest See Payouts Shrink," *Wall Street Journal,* April 25, 2002.

[17] Susan Warren, "Asbestos Quagmire," *Wall Street Journal,* January 27, 2002.

[18] Dan R. Anderson, "Financing Asbestos Claims: Coverage Issues, Manville's Bankruptcy and the Claims Facility," *Journal of Risk and Insurance,* Vol. LIV, No. 3, September 1987.

[19] Ibid.

[20] Ridgway M. Hall, Jr., Tom Watson, Jeffery J. Davidson, and David R. Case, *Hazardous Waste Handbook,* 5th Edition, Rockville, MD: Government Institutes, 1984.

[21] David Dybdahl and Rod Taylor, "Environmental Insurance," *Commercial Liability Risk Management and Insurance,* 5th Ed., by Donald S. Malecki and Arthur L. Flitner, Malvern, PA: American Institute, 2001.

[22] EPA, Superfund Accomplishment Figures, Summary Fiscal Year (FY) 2003.

[23] Katherine Probst and David Konisky, *Superfund's Future: What Will It Cost?* Washington D.C.: EPA, Resources for the Future, 2001; Katherine Q. Seelye, "Bush Proposing to Shift Burden of Toxic Cleanups to Taxpayers," *New York Times,* February, 24, 2002.

[24] Standard & Poor's, "Environmental Liability Strains P/C Insurers," *Credit Week,* October 30, 1995.

[25] United States General Accounting Office, *Hazardous Waste Sites: State Cleanup Status and Its Implications for Federal Policy,* CAO/RCED-89-164, August 1989; Dan R. Anderson, "Financial and Organizational Impact of Superfund-Mandated Hazardous Waste Liabilities on the Insurance Industry," *CPCU Journal,* Vol. 49, No. 1, Spring 1996.

[26] Dan R. Anderson, "Financial and Organizational Impact of Superfund-Mandated Hazardous Waste Liabilities on the Insurance Industry," *CPCU Journal,* Vol. 49, No. 1, Spring 1996.

[27] Katherine Q. Seelye, "Bush Proposing to Shift Burden of Toxic Cleanups to Taxpayers," *New York Times,* February, 24, 2002.

[28] Carol Browner, "Polluters Should Have to Pay," *New York Times,* March 1, 2002.

[29] Tom Zeller, "The Future of Superfund: More Taxing, Less Simple," *New York Times,* March 24, 2002; Jennifer S. Lee, "Drop in Budget Slows Superfund Program," *New York Times,* March 9, 2004.

[30] Jennifer S. Lee, "Drop in Budget Slows Superfund Program," *New York Times,* March 9, 2004.

[31] *Superfund: Building on the Past, Looking to the Future,* Washington, D.C., USEPA, April 22, 2004.

[32] Felicity Barringer, "Polluted Sites Could Force Shortage of Cleanup Money," *New York Times,* August 16, 2004.

[33] Jan Paul Acton, *Understanding Superfund,* Santa Monica, CA: Rand Corporation, Institute for Civil Justice, 1989.

[34] *Superfund: Building on the Past, Looking to the Future,* Washington, D.C., USEPA, April 22, 2004.

[35] Joan T. Schmit, Dan R. Anderson, and Timothy Oleszczuk, "An Analysis of Litigation Claiming Joint and Several Liability," *Journal of Risk and Insurance,* Vol. LVIII, No. 3, September 1991.

[36] Carolyn Aldred, "Property Insurers to Reword Pollution Exclusion," *Business Insurance,* February 29, 1988.

[37] Dan R. Anderson, "Financial and Organizational Impact of Superfund-Mandated Hazardous Waste Liabilities on the Insurance Industry," *CPCU Journal,* Vol. 49, No. 1, Spring 1996.

[38] Jan Paul Acton, *Understanding Superfund,* Santa Monica, CA: Rand Corporation, Institute for Civil Justice, 1989.

[39] Jan Paul Acton and Lloyd S. Dixon, *Superfund and Transaction Costs,* Santa Monica, CA: Rand Corporation, Institute for Civil Justice, 1992.

[40] Lloyd S. Dixon, Deborah S. Drezner, and James K. Hammitt, *Private-Sector Cleanup Expenditures and Transaction Costs at 18 Superfund Sites,* Santa Monica, CA: Rand Corporation, 1993.

[41] American Academy of Actuaries, *Costs Under Superfund,* Washington, D.C., American Academy of Actuaries, August 1995.

[42] Jan Paul Acton and Lloyd S. Dixon, *Superfund and Transaction Costs,* Santa Monica, CA: Rand Corporation, Institute for Civil Justice, 1992.

[43] Robert H. Gettlin, "Getting Ahead of Superfund," *Best's Review,* P/C Edition, April 1, 1997.

[44] *Business Insurance,* November 8, 1993.

[45] For an extensive discussion of coverage issues, the reader is referred to Jerold Oshinsky, Roger Warin, and Catherine J. Serafin, *Environmental Insurance,* Washington, D.C.: Federal Publications, Inc., October, 1993.

[46] Insurance Rating Bureau, 1970.

[47] For an extensive discussion of the 1970 pollution exclusion the reader is referred to Robert N. Hughes, John MacDonald, and Eugene R. Anderson, "The Polluters Exclusion Was No Accident," *CPCU Journal,* Vol. 47, June 1994; and Richard C. Cavo, Edward Zampino, and Daniel G. Litchfield, "The Polluters Web: The Pollution Exclusion and the Question of Deception," *CPCU Journal,* Vol. 47, June 1994.

[48] ISO, CB00020286.

[49] Dan R. Anderson, "Insurance Coverage Litigation and the Financial Impact of Superfund-Mandated Hazardous Waste Liabilities on the Insurance Industry," *Journal of Insurance Regulation,* Vol. 13, No. 1, Fall 1994.

[50] Note that this is a composite phrase combining the insuring agreement and the definitions of occurrence, bodily injury, and property damage.

[51] Dan R. Anderson, "Insurance Coverage Litigation and the Financial Impact of Superfund-Mandated Hazardous Waste Liabilities on the Insurance Industry," *Journal of Insurance Regulation,* Vol. 13, No. 1, Fall 1994.

[52] *Shell Oil Co. v. Accident @ Casualty Co. of Winterthur,* 1988, California Super. Ct., San Mateo Cty., No. 278-953, December 19.

[53] A fourth trigger of coverage, injury-in-fact trigger, which lies somewhere between the manifestation and triple triggers, may also be claimed by policyholders. With this trigger, those insurers on the risk when the injury-in-fact occurred, not necessarily when it becomes manifested or was diagnosed, must respond.

[54] ISO, CK 809-2, 12-79.

[55] Ibid.

[56] Dan R. Anderson, "Insurance Coverage Litigation and the Financial Impact of Superfund-Mandated Hazardous Waste Liabilities on the Insurance Industry," *Journal of Insurance Regulation,* Vol. 13, No. 1, Fall 1994.

[57] *Jackson Township Municipal Utilities Authority v. American Home Insurance Co.*, 1984, No. L. 29236-81 (N.J. Law Div.).

[58] Dan R. Anderson, "Insurance Coverage Litigation and the Financial Impact of Superfund-Mandated Hazardous Waste Liabilities on the Insurance Industry," *Journal of Insurance Regulation*, Vol. 13, No. 1, Fall 1994.

[59] ISO, CK 809-2, 12-79.

[60] Dan R. Anderson, "Insurance Coverage Litigation and the Financial Impact of Superfund-Mandated Hazardous Waste Liabilities on the Insurance Industry," *Journal of Insurance Regulation*, Vol. 13, No. 1, Fall 1994.

[61] Ibid.

[62] American Re-Insurance Company, *A Review of Environmental Coverage Case Law*, 15th edition, Princeton, NJ: American Re, 2004.

[63] Deborah Hensler, Stephen Carroll, Michelle White, and Jennifer Gross, *Asbestos Litigation in the U.S.: A New Look at an Old Issue*, Santa Monica, CA: Rand Institute for Civil Justice, August 2001.

[64] Susan Warren, "Asbestos Quagmire," *Wall Street Journal*, January 27, 2002.

[65] Deborah Hensler, Stephen Carroll, Michelle White, and Jennifer Gross, *Asbestos Litigation in the U.S.: A New Look at an Old Issue*, Santa Monica, CA: Rand Institute for Civil Justice, August 2001.

[66] Ibid.

[67] Standard & Poor's, "Environmental Liability Strains P/C Insurers," *Credit Week*, October 30, 1995.

[68] A.M. Best, "Choosing to Survive or Thrive In a New Era," *Best's Review*, P/C Edition, January 1997.

[69] A.M. Best, "Largest Increase in A&E losses to Date seen in 2001," Special Report, October 28, 2002.

[70] Chad Bray, "Hartford Sets $1.7 Billion Charge To Boast Asbestos Reserve," *Wall Street Journal*, May 13, 2003.

[71] Business Wire via NewsEdge Corp, Jan 14, 2003.

[72] "St. Paul Travelers adding $1.63 billion to reserves," *Business Insurance*, July 26, 2004.

[73] "Reserving merry-go-round continues," *Reactions*, March 2005.

[74] Diane Dietz, "Liberty Mutual smoothes bumps with rising insurance premiums," Lexis Nexis Academic, *Knight Ridder/Tribune Business News*, October 26, 2004.

[75] Shaheen Pasha, "ACE Boasts Reserves by $788 Million," *Wall Street Journal*, January 7, 2005; Judy Greenwald, "Reserve boast raises concerns," *Business Insurance*, June 6, 2005.

[76] *Fuller-Austin Insulations Co. v. Fireman's Fund Ins. Co.*, No. BC 116835 [Cal. Super. Ct. LA Cnty., 2002]; Christopher Oster, "Payout Timelines for Insurers On Asbestos Claims May Shrink," *Wall Street Journal*, April 23, 2002.

[77] Stacy Shapiro, "Lloyd's Forecasts Return to Profitability," *Business Insurance*, May 29, 1995; Stacy Shapiro, "A Tough Juggling Act for Lloyd's," *Business Insurance*, August 28, 1995; Sarah Goddard, "Equitas Project is Top Priority," *Business Insurance*, August 28, 1995; Brendan Noonan, "Lloyd's Costly Victory," *Best's Review*, P/C Edition, December 1996; Stacy Shapiro, "Audit Questions Validity of Equitas' First Financials," *Business Insurance*, April 14, 1997.

[78] Meg Fletcher and Gavin Souter, "Zurich May Beef up Home Offer," *Business Insurance*, February 6, 1995; Gavin Souter, "Zurich's Plan for Home Viable," *Business Insurance*, April 10, 1995; Gavin Souter, "The Home in Supervision," *Business Insurance*, March 10, 1997.

[79] Dave Lenckus, "Court Hears Challenge to CIGNA Reorganization," *Business Insurance*, December 16, 1996; Dave Lenckus, "CIGNA Reorganization Plan

Unleashes Criticism," *Business Insurance*, December 23/30, 1996; Dave Lenckus, "CIGNA to Fight New Round of Hearings," *Business Insurance*, March 10, 1997.

[80] *World Corporate Insurance Report*, October 21, 1994; *Business Insurance*, September 19, 1994; *Business Insurance*, December 12, 1994.

[81] "The St Paul pays $1bn settlement," *Reactions*, July 2002.

[82] Susan Warren, "PPG Agrees to Pay $2.7 Billion To Resolve Asbestos Litigation," *Wall Street Journal*, May 15, 2002.

[83] Standard & Poors, "Insurers and Reinsurers: The Context for Conflict," January 29, 2004.

[84] Ibid.

[85] Dan R. Anderson, "Financial and Organizational Impact of Superfund-Mandated Hazardous Waste Liabilities on the Insurance Industry," *CPCU Journal*, Vol. 49, No. 1, Spring 1996, pp. 22-39.

[86] Ibid.

[87] Lorraine Woellert, "Why An Asbestos Deal May Go Up In Smoke," *BusinessWeek*, June 2, 2003; Shailagh Murray and Kathryn Kranhold, "Asbestos Factions Struggle to Settle Their 30-Year War," *Wall Street Journal*, October 15, 2003; Douglas McLeod, "Asbestos reform bid renewed amid debate over plan's terms," *Business Insurance*, February 2, 2004; Mark A. Hofmann, "Asbestos fund plan draws insurers' ire," *Business Insurance*, April 19, 2004; Mark A. Hofmann, "Doubts emerge as asbestos bill fails," *Business Insurance*, May 17, 2004.

7

NEW SUSTAINABILITY RISKS: GLOBAL WARMING/ CLIMATE CHANGE

o o o o o o o o o o o o o o o o o o o o o o o o o o o o o o o

There can no longer be genuine doubt that human made gases are the dominant cause of observed warming. This energy imbalance is the 'smoking gun' that we have been looking for.

> —James Hansen, head of NASA's Goddard Institute for Space Studies

This situation only strengthens our commitment to preserve sustainability as a key component of our corporate strategy. We have included the vital issues of water and climate in our Top Topics Management programme and actively contribute the reinsurer's perspective to the public debate on these topics. Throughout the whole Swiss Re Group, we are implementing sustainability as a business model in reinsurance, investment and internal operations, adding the entrepreneurial element to its broader socio-political realization. We are convinced that this initiative will increase our competitive strength in the long term, creating new business opportunities and enhancing our appeal, both as a sound investment and as an employer.

> —Walter Kielholz, CEO and Bruno Porro, Chief Risk Officer and Chair of the Steering Committee on Sustainability Swiss Reinsurance Company

Global warming refers to the gradual warming of the earth's atmosphere that has been documented over the last 150 years. Global warming can result from natural fluctuations in climate or can be induced by human causes. A principal cause of global warming is the increasing concentrations of greenhouse gases, which effectively trap solar heat in the atmosphere. The principal greenhouse gas is carbon dioxide, CO_2, but greenhouse gases also include methane and nitrous oxides. Greenhouse gases are produced primarily by burning fossil fuels like oil, coal and natural gas. Energy production (38 percent), automobiles, other transportation systems like airlines and ships (32 percent), manufacturers (20 percent) and households (10 percent) all burn fossil fuels and produce greenhouse gas emissions.[1] There has been considerable debate as to whether human activity in producing increased emissions and concentrations of greenhouse gases has been associated with the global warming trend. A second issue concerns the effects of global warming on climate change and the resulting effects of climate change on societies, properties, businesses and the environment.[2]

Human Activity Causing Global Warming

Regarding the first issue, scientific data clearly show that since the mid-1800s, global average temperature has increased by about 0.6°C (1°F). Since 1980, we have experienced 22 out of the 23 hottest years on record.[3] Sea ice has been shrinking over the past 40 years, glaciers are receding, and ice stays on lakes for shorter periods of time.[4] A U.S. Geological Survey study reported that the number of glaciers in Glacier National Park has dwindled from 150 in 1850 to 35 today. They project that within 30 years there will be no glaciers, which gave the Park its name. Another USGS survey indicates that glaciers are shrinking in all 11 of Alaska's glaciated mountain ranges. The ice fields of Mount Kilimanjaro may be gone in 15 years.[5] The Ward Hunt Ice Shelf, the largest in the Arctic, has broken up over the last couple years.[6] Arctic sea ice is thinning and decreasing in size.[7] Antarctic glaciers are thinning and moving faster into sea.[8] Glaciers are also retreating in the Alps, the Himalayas and South America. The retreat of the Andean glaciers is particularly troublesome as this could create severe water shortages in countries like Peru and Bolivia.[9]

Over the last 150 years, atmospheric CO_2, the greenhouse gas most associated with global warming, has increased from 280 parts per million on a volume (ppmv) basis to 379 ppmv in 2003.[10] Measurements from the Climate Monitoring and Diagnostics Laboratory on Mauna Loa on Hawaii recorded, in 2004, the 47th consecutive year in which CO_2 levels have increased.[11] The record of atmospheric changes stored in miles-deep ice cores show that CO_2 levels are higher in the atmosphere than at any time during the 400,000-year ice core record.[12] In addition, the current rate of increase in CO_2 concentration in the atmosphere is unprecedented during at least the past 20,000 years.[13]

While considerable debate has raged over whether increasing CO_2 concentrations are natural or human induced and associated with global warming, the overwhelming scientific evidence has gradually demonstrated that increasing greenhouse gas concentrations are largely human induced. For instance, studies by the Intergovernmental Panel on Climate Change,[14] the Committee on the Science of Climate Change of the National Academies[15] and the National Assessment Synthesis Team[16] clearly support the connection between human activity, increasing CO_2 levels and global warming. The American Geophysical Union, the world's largest organization of earth, ocean and climate scientists, in a position statement, states that it is now virtually certain that global warming is being caused by emissions of greenhouse gases and that the warming will continue.[17] Dr. Jerry Mahlman, senior researcher at the National Center for Atmospheric Research, has developed climate models that consistently show that CO_2 emissions are likely to cause global warming.[18]

Of possibly greater significance is the increased global warming over the next century. The IPCC Third Assessment Report estimates the full warming range over 1990 to 2100 to be 1.4°C (2.5°F) to 5.8°C (10.5°F), with the mid-range estimate being 3°C (5.4°F). The projected rate of warming is much larger than the observed changes during the 20th Century and is very likely to be without precedent during at least the last 10,000 years, based on paleoclimate data.[19] Without any control measures, human induced CO_2 concentrations are estimated to rise between two (560 ppmv) and three (840 ppmv) times its pre-industrial level of 280 ppmv by the end of the 21st century.[20]

Even the Bush's administration's Environmental Protection Agency released a report, which documented increased global warming and human activity in burning more fossil fuels as being the principal cause. This report entitled, *U.S. Climate Action Report—2002*, was sent to the United Nations.[21] Conservative political pressure caused President Bush to utter a dismissive response, "I read the report put out by the bureaucracy."

Two recent studies provide some of the strongest evidence to date that ties greenhouse gas emissions to global warming. Fourteen scientists from NASA, the Department of Energy and Columbia University reported, in an article in an April 2005 issue of *Science,* documentation for a global energy imbalance.[22] By taking readings of ocean temperatures, the study found that the earth is absorbing more of the sun's energy than it is radiating back to space as heat. This imbalance is warming the atmosphere and corresponds closely with increasing greenhouse gas emissions as specified in the researchers' climate model. As noted by the lead researcher, James Hansen, head of NASA's Goddard Institute for Space Studies, "There can no longer be genuine doubt that human made gases are the dominant cause of observed warming. This energy imbalance is the 'smoking gun' that we have been looking for."[23] The scientists also studied the thermal inertia of the earth's climate system and found that excess energy stored in the oceans will result in a .6°C (1°F) rise in atmospheric temperatures in this century, even if greenhouse gas emissions are capped today.

Their research corroborates yet to be published work done at the Scripps Institution of Oceanography. The Scripps scientists, like the NASA lead group, found that warming signals in ocean temperature could only have been produced by the build-up of man-made greenhouse gases. As noted by Professor Tim Barnett, leader of the Scripps project, "The debate over whether there is a global warming signal is over now at least for rational people."[24]

These two recent studies, following many other solid scientific reports, would seem to end one part of the global warming debate. Global warming is happening, will increase over the next century, and is primarily being caused by increased concentrations of greenhouse gases associated with humans burning more fossil fuels. While these points seem clear, what specific climate changes and resulting effects will be caused by global warming and what should be the appropriate responses to global warming are still very much in debate. The remainder of this chapter will focus on these issues.

Benefits of Global Warming/Climate Change

The rising concentrations of CO_2, which are causing global warming, principally come from energy production, automobiles, factories, homes, and deforestation. Rising CO_2 concentrations are a symptom of expanding economies, jobs and standards of living. Indeed, these economic benefits form the most frequently sited argument for resisting the Kyoto Treaty and other control techniques. For instance, President Bush stated in rejecting the Kyoto Treaty that it would "have a negative economic impact, with layoffs of workers and price increases for consumers."[25]

Some studies have indicated that agriculture and forestry will actually improve from global warming. For instance, the NAST report finds that US crop productivity is very likely to increase over the next few decades because of global warming. While benefiting consumers, falling crop prices and competitive pressures are likely to stress some farmers. The NAST report also found that forest productivity is likely to increase over the next several decades as trees respond to higher carbon dioxide levels. Milder winters should also reduce cold related stresses in some areas.[26] The Committee of the National Academies concurs with these benefit assessments.[27]

Risks of Global Warming/Climate Change

A wide variety of risks emanate from confirmed global warming and will be discussed below. A considerable amount of uncertainty and unpredictability exists as to precisely how global warming risks will develop over the next century.

Specific Risks

One of the more obvious specific risks associated with global warming is increasing property damages, resulting from storm intensification and rising sea levels. Munich Reinsurance Company reports that over the last 50 years, the number of weather-related natural disasters has been steadily rising, as have total losses and insured losses.[28] Since the 1960s, the frequency of weather disasters has tripled and insured losses have increased ten fold. For 2004, Munich Re estimated the total losses from natural disasters to be over $90 billion, with insured losses of $35 billion. These numbers in 2003 and 2001 were $60 and $35 billion for total losses, and $15 and $11.5 billion for insured losses, respectively.[29] In the last several years, the U.S. (August '92 hurricane Andrew), Poland (July '97 river floods), Canada (January '98 ice-storm), Australia (April '99 hailstorm), France (December '99 windstorms), China (Summer '98 floods), Central Europe (August '02 floods), and Korea (September '03 Typhoon Maemi) have all suffered record losses from weather events.[30] While it is too early to say with certainty that the increase in weather-related natural disasters is being caused by global warming, the inference of an association is quite compelling.

The NAST report estimates that, over the 21st Century, the amount of global rainfall is likely to rise; the observed trends toward an intensification of precipitation events are likely to continue; peak wind speed and rainfall intensity from hurricanes are likely to rise significantly; and sea levels are projected to increase 5 to 37 inches (13 to 95 cm) with a central estimate about 20 inches (50 cm).[31] The World Water Council reports that there is undeniable evidence that the world's water cycle is speeding up, causing more frequent and severe storms, floods and droughts. The Council cites climate experts as predicting changes in the next century that will lead to shorter and more intense rainy seasons in some areas and longer droughts in others.[32] Drought conditions, like those in the western states, can aggravate forest fire risks, as the California fires in 2003 and 2004 demonstrated.

Increasing storm intensity is particularly troublesome as the resulting damages are nonlinear. Increasing the speed of a 200 kpm storm by 10 per cent increases the damages by 150 percent.[33] Property insurers, catastrophe reinsurers, and risk managers and individuals with properties in vulnerable locations will need to be alert to increasing storm and flood damages.

Global warming increases heat-related stresses to human populations. The August 2003 heat wave in Europe impacted several countries with France reporting 14,802 deaths and total deaths estimated to be around 20,000-35,000.[34] Heat stress and smog-induced respiratory illnesses in major urban areas will increase. Warming of northern areas may spread diseases like malaria to larger populations. Global warming might also affect the incidence of diseases spread by insects, ticks, and rodents.

Discussions of global warming risks rarely involve liability. Establishing that the actions of a specific company were the proximate cause of global warming, which in turn caused injuries and damages to another party, would clearly be difficult. Making the proximate cause connection with an entire industry or a country as the negligent party may be a less difficult task. In Chapter 2, it was noted that Friends of the Earth International (FoEI) has studied the feasibility of bringing a lawsuit against fossil fuel companies and the U.S. to recoup financial damages caused by global warming.[35] Other environmental groups are also exploring litigation strategies.[36] Academics, like Widener University Law Professor Andrew Strauss, in a 2001 paper, "Suing the United States for Global Warming Omissions," discusses numerous possible litigation strategies.[37]

Island nations are particularly vulnerable to rising sea levels associated with global warming. Many have experienced severe flooding caused by storms and high tides in recent years. The Prime Minister of Tuvalu, Koloa Talake, announced in February 2002 that Tuvalu, along with Kiribati and the Maldives, are threatening to sue certain western nations and corporations for damages and loss of life and property.[38]

The Inuits (Eskimos) plan to seek a ruling from the Inter-American Commission on Human Rights that the United States is threatening their existence by contributing to global warming. The Inuits are being represented by Earth Justice and the Center for International Environmental Law. While the Inter-American Commission has no enforcement powers, a declaration that the United States is violating their human rights could create the basis for a subsequent lawsuit in international courts or against American companies in U.S. federal courts.[39] A statement by Sheila Watt-Cloutier, an elected leader of 5,000 year old Inuit peoples, captures their dilemma and portends future risks:

> "We've had to struggle as a people to keep afloat, to keep our indigenous wisdom and traditions. We're an adaptable people, but adaptability has its limits. Something is bound to give, and it's starting to give in the Arctic, and we're giving that early warning signal to the rest of the world."[40]

Before dismissing such efforts, recall the discussion of the asbestos and Superfund in the previous chapter, where resulting liabilities far exceeded anyone's expectations. It is also useful to remember that it was just in the last decade that the first successful lawsuit against a tobacco company was completed. This began a rapid chain of events leading to a U.S. $246 billion settlement by the tobacco industry with a consortium of states.

Cultural, Ethical, and Regional Disparity Risks

If the benefits and specific risks of global warming were bordered by defined areas, then those people benefiting from global warming would incur the risks. This is not the case. Industrialized nations overwhelmingly enjoy the economic benefits associated with increasing CO_2 levels and global warming. The risks of global warming are often spread to developing countries that have enjoyed few of the benefits. For instance, in October 1998, Hurricane Mitch hit Nicaragua with winds 180 miles per hour killing some 10,000 people in floods and mudslides. It was the first time in 100 years of observation that four Atlantic Hurricanes were raging at the same time. In February 2000, five straight days of unseasonable rain in Mozambique caused the worst flooding in history, with 100,000 being forced to flee their homes. A shortage of safe drinking water produced malaria and cholera outbreaks. In 1997, drought conditions in Indonesia greatly increased natural and manmade forest fires, resulting in respiratory problems and decreased food production.[41] According to the World Bank, the *per capita* cost of natural disasters in relation to GDP is at least 20 times higher in the developing world than in developed countries.[42] The Mozambique floods in 2000 resulted in a 45 percent decrease in their gross domestic product.[43]

Stephen Leathermann, director of National Healthy Beaches Campaign, notes that "Worldwide, 70 percent of beaches are eroding."[44] Small island states are especially vulnerable to global warming and global sea level rise. As noted in one study:

> Low-lying island states and atolls in the Caribbean, the Indian Ocean, the Pacific Ocean and the Mediterranean are particularly vulnerable to the impacts of sea level rise, including: the Bahamas, the Maldives, Kiribati, the Marshall Islands, Malta and Cyprus. These small island states could lose significant land area with sea level rise from 50 cm to 1 m. Many islands with higher elevations could also be seriously affected as their settlements and infrastructure are generally concentrated in the coastal zone.
>
> As climate changes and sea level rises, islands could experience increased freshwater shortages due to saline intrusion and/or changes in precipitation patterns. Health problems such as heat-stress, cholera, dengue fever and malaria would stress the already over-extended health systems of most small island nations. As the stresses mount and the land shrinks, so income from tourism—a major earner for many islands—is likely to fall.[45]

A region's or country's vulnerability depends not only on the climate change itself, but also on the sensitivity of the systems involved and the people's ability to adapt. An IPCC study of regional vulnerability shows that wealthier countries generally have the infrastructure to cope. Poor regions will suffer far more.[46] Developed countries have superior building standards, insurance and government disaster assistance programs to help mitigate natural disasters.

Even within defined areas like the United States, regional disparities in global warming effects may result. Some models project an increased tendency toward drought over semi-arid regions like the Great Plains.[47] Many crop distributions will change, which will harm some farmers while benefiting others. Small, locally based farmers could be especially hard hit. Regional droughts will increase the forest fire risk. Decreased snow pack and earlier season melting are expected. The western mountainous areas of the U.S., which are highly dependent on snow and the timing of the runoff, may incur losses. The western United States is entering its fifth year of a sustained drought with waters in the Colorado River basin at their lowest levels on record. Scientists at the U.S. Geological Survey say that the drought gripping the west could be the biggest in 500 years.[48] Other ecosystems, such as the Rocky Mountain meadows, and certain coral reefs and barrier islands are likely to disappear entirely.[49]

In Alaska, melting permafrost and the beetle infestation that is destroying spruce trees are both associated with warming temperatures. Mean temperatures have risen by five degrees in summer and 10 degrees in the winter since the 1970s, far in excess of average global temperature increases. Melting permafrost increases the erosion risk of coastal communities, particularly when the protection of sea ice is reduced. Frozen tundra and ice covered roads have become less reliable in the warming temperatures. Wild game migratory patterns are altered, which impacts the hunting-based culture.[50] Dr. Glenn Juday, an authority on climate change at the University of Alaska at Fairbanks, states, "We're experiencing indisputable climate warming. The positive changes from this take a long time, but the negative changes are happening real fast."[51]

The uneven distribution of global warming damages may aggravate liability claims against countries and industries associated with causing global warming. There is a sense of unfairness, of international outrage, that some peoples and countries, often the poorest with the least resources to respond, are suffering a disproportionate amount of damages from climate changes. Even if liability claims do not materialize, serious reputation damage, resulting in boycotts and shareholder actions, could be incurred in industries like the oil, coal, and automobile industries, and by the insurance industry, which both insures these industries and invests in them. Serious questions of ethics can also be raised against the industrialized countries, particularly the United States, whose citizens' consumption patterns and practices are disproportionately (less than 5 percent of world population, but produce nearly 25 percent of greenhouse gas emissions) responsible for these climate changes.

Ecosystem and Environmental Risks

Ecosystems are particularly vulnerable to global climate change. Rich nations will focus their resources and efforts on mitigating adverse effects on human populations and food and water producing systems. The predicted increase in precipitation in the U.S. will increase pollution run-off and change plant and animal habitat. Climate change will cause disruptions to many ecosystems such as wetlands, forests, grasslands, rivers and lakes. While ecosystems clearly have value and provide ecological services, causal associations are often indirect, less obvious, and under appreciated. Ecosystems in poor nations will be particularly vulnerable, and limited resources will impede the use of mitigation efforts for human populations and principal support systems.[52]

Large numbers of species extinctions are expected to be caused by global warming. An international group of 19 scientists analyzed research around the world and concluded that global warming presents a "very serious risk to huge numbers of species and at least ranks alongside habitat destruction." The paper, published in *Nature*, predicts that if present trends continue, 15 to 37 percent of the 1,103 species they studied will become extinct by 2050.[53] The warming trend, reported by the Arctic Climate Impact Assessment, threatens the existence of polar bears and ringed seals and the migratory patterns of caribou.[54]

A research report entitled, *The Implications of Climate Change for Australia's Great Barrier Reef,* concludes that the Great Barrier Reef is at risk of losing most of its coral by 2050 and could collapse by 2100, due to global warming. The 2004 study was conducted by economist Hans Hoegh-Guldberg and reef expert Ove Hoegh-Guldberg, and sponsored by the World Wildlife Fund Australia and the Queensland Tourism Industry. It is estimated that global average temperature increases must be kept below 2 degrees Celsius, in order for the Reef to recover from predicted damage. Under this best case scenario, coral cover will still be significantly reduced by 2100, but will recover in the following century as the global climate stabilizes.[55] Given that the IPCC study estimates the midrange temperature over the next century to be 3 degrees Celsius, the Reef will likely be destroyed unless major changes are made.

Destruction of ecosystems can also exacerbate global warming. The Amazon rain forest acts as a CO_2 sink. Extensive deforestation will reduce the Amazon's ability to sequester CO_2 and may turn the Amazon into a net emitter of CO_2.[56] Soil degradation can lead to the release of carbon, as soil acts as a sequester of carbon.[57] The cryptobiotic crusts of desert soils decrease light reflectance due to its darker color. Extensive disturbance of these crusts will increase light reflectance and raise the temperature of the air.[58]

The uncertainty and unpredictability factors associated with the effects of global warming are enormous. As stated in the NAST report:

> "There are also very likely to be unanticipated impacts of climate change during the 21st century. Such "surprises" may stem from unforeseen changes in the physical climate system, such as major alterations in ocean circulation, cloud distribution, or storms; and unpredicted biological consequences of these physical climate changes, such as massive dislocations of species or pest outbreaks."[59]

These large scale ecosystem risks present the possibility of fundamentally altering the environment in which we all live and which supports all living organisms. Some of the surprises may be uncontrollable and irreversible. The only way such surprises can be eliminated is to mitigate global warming, which is their potential driving force.

Customer/NGO Boycotts

The business risk that customers or NGOs may boycott or pressure firms contributing to global warming is real. Deciding which specific businesses are contributing to global warming, and choosing not to buy their products, is not as obvious. Yet, situations are developing that suggest this business risk could materially affect select businesses and industries.

Ford Motor Company belongs to an organization called the U.S. Council for International Business, which supports President Bush's decision to reject the Kyoto accord. Volvo, which is now owned by Ford, has publicly supported the Kyoto treaty before being acquired by Ford in 1999. Volvo is located in Sweden, which in general has strong environmental values. The environmental group, Greenpeace, has pressured Ford and Volvo, on their contradictory stances. On its website, another environmental group, Families Against Bush, lists Volvo as a "buy" on its website and Ford as a "don't buy." The threat that Ford may lose customer sales, over its stance on the Kyoto treaty, caused a company spokesperson to refer to the campaign by the two environmental groups as a "canary in the mineshaft."[60]

A similar campaign was brought by the two environmental groups against the Coca-Cola Company. Coke is also a member of the U.S. Council for International Business, but Coke's Spanish subsidiary has publicly supported the Kyoto Treaty. Again, Coke's location within the European Union was critical as the EU countries strongly support the Kyoto accord.[61] The national boycott against ExxonMobil, which was launched in July 2005, focuses on the company's lack of response to global warming risks (see Chapter 3).

These examples illustrate the potential business risk of global warming, namely that consumers may not buy a company's product because of its stance on treaties aimed at reducing greenhouse gas emissions. These examples also illustrate that the increased globalization of the world economy and consolidations of corporations from different continents will increase the business risks of global warming.

Kyoto Protocol and Regulatory Risk

The Kyoto Protocol, an international agreement, which calls for industrialized nations to reduce their emissions of greenhouse gases, was initiated in 1997 in Japan. The agreement calls for overall reduction of greenhouse gases to 5.2 percent below 1990 emissions. Individual countries have different specific reductions with the U.S. being 7 percent, the EU countries 8 percent, and Japan 6 percent. Developing countries, most importantly China and India, were exempted. In December 2000, delegates gathered in Hague, Netherlands to take the next steps leading to the ratification of the UN Kyoto Treaty on Climate Change. No agreement was reached. In spring 2001, President George Bush rejected the treaty, based on the argument that it would be too costly for the U.S. economy, and that scientific evidence of global warming was still lacking. Australia has also rejected the treaty.

In July 2001, an agreement was reached by 178 countries meeting in Bonn, Germany without U.S. participation. The key provision is still the 5.2 percent reduction in greenhouse gases by 2012 below levels measured in 1990. At least 55 industrialized nations and nations, which account for at least 55 percent of 1990 greenhouse gas emissions, must ratify the agreement for it to become binding.

In November 2001 in Marrakesh, Morocco, government ministers from around the world agreed to certain key details to make the Kyoto Protocol operational. Agreement was reached on several critical issues. Russia, Canada and Japan sought and gained substantial credit towards their gas targets for the ability of their forests to absorb carbon dioxide. These three countries also lead the fight for a trading mechanism for greenhouse gas emissions.[62]

In June 2002, the European Union and its 15 member completed en masse their ratification of the Kyoto Protocol. Japan followed suit a few days later. Before the end of the year, Canada ratified the treaty. When Russia ratified in November 2004, the required ratification limits of 55 participating countries and of industrialized nations that emitted 55 percent of the world's carbon dioxide in 1990 was met.[63]

Originally, there appeared little doubt that Russia would join. In December 2003, Russian President Vladimir Putin stated that Russia was skeptical about ratifying the treaty, using the Bush administration's rationale, namely that it would hurt the economy. In May 2004, President Putin switched his stance during negotiations with the European Union on Russia's entry to the World Trade Organization. After years of negotiations, Russia reached a deal with the EU on the terms of its entry to the WTO. While denying the connection to the EU negotiations, President Putin gave his most explicit endorsement yet of the Kyoto Protocol, "The EU has met us half way in talks over the WTO and that cannot but affect positively our position vis-à-vis the Kyoto Protocol."[64] Finally in November 2004, Putin signed the bill ratifying the Kyoto Treaty.

The Kyoto Protocol officially went into effect on February 16, 2005, having been ratified by 140 nations. Corporations and industries now face the regulatory risk that they will be required to reduce greenhouse gas emissions. Clearly this is the case for corporations in those countries ratifying the treaty. But what about corporations in those countries that do not ratify, particularly U.S. corporations?

Even if the U.S. does not ratify the Kyoto Protocol, corporations may be subject to various actions at the state level. California has recently passed a bill that will require cuts in tailpipe emissions of greenhouse gases by cars and light trucks, including SUVs, pickups and minivans. The bill directs the California Air Resources Board, appointed by the governor, to develop by 2005 a plan for the maximum feasible reduction in emissions of greenhouse gases from cars and light trucks. The plan will be reviewed by the legislature, and regulations will take effect for model year 2009, with the aim of reducing emissions by 30 percent by the end of 2015.[65] The most obvious change will be for automobile manufacturers to increase fuel efficiency, which will decrease gas use and also emissions. These emissions account for 40 percent of total greenhouse emissions in the state.[66]

California's action could spread to other states. Because California's original clean air regulations were instituted before the passage of the federal Clean Air Act in the 1970s, California was not only allowed to keep its own standards, but the 49 other states are permitted to follow California rather than federal standards. New York, Massachusetts, Vermont and Maine already follow California, and New Jersey, Rhode Island and Connecticut have said they intend to do so.[67] Even the Canadian government has indicated that Canada will follow California law.[68] The possibility of more states joining was heightened by a letter to President Bush, signed by the attorney generals of 11 states (Massachusetts, New York, Connecticut, New Jersey, California, Alaska, Maine, Maryland, New Hampshire, Rhode Island and Vermont), calling for strong federal measures to limit emissions of greenhouse gases.[69] In June 2003, Maine became the first state to pass a law calling for specific cuts in greenhouse gas emissions across the economy. It will reduce emissions to 1990 levels by 2010 and to 10 percent below 1990 levels by 2020, which even exceeds the Kyoto limit.[70] New Jersey and Illinois have established voluntary CO_2 reduction programs, and Massachusetts has set up CO_2 regulatory programs for utilities. Other states like New Hampshire, North Carolina and Florida are discussing legislation to reduce carbon dioxide emissions.[71]

The regulatory risk will be incurred by those corporations who take no actions to reduce greenhouse gas emissions. If the Kyoto Protocol is later ratified by the U.S., these companies will be behind and at a strategic disadvantage to their international competitors, and also to U.S. companies, who have instituted voluntary emission reductions. Lagging companies also face huge potential costs. A report by the Carbon Disclosure Project estimated that the market value of some heavy carbon emitters could be slashed by as much as 40 percent.[72] Another report by Innovest Strategic Value Advisors found similar results, with as much as 45 percent of earnings and 35 percent of market capitalization being at risk.[73] It is reports like these that have given rise to shareholder actions discussed in Chapter 4. Even without U.S. participation, regulatory risks raise problems for multinational corporations that operate across regulatory regimes such as those operating in both the U.S. and the EU.

Risk Management and Insurance Implications

The risk management and insurance issues associated with global warming risks are challenging. Developing risk assessment, risk control and risk-financing techniques to cope with global warming risks will again present substantial business challenges and opportunities.

The most obvious specific risk of global warming is the property risk. Risk managers with properties in areas vulnerable to hurricanes, storms, and floods, property insurers for both homeowners and commercial properties, federal flood insurance officials, catastrophe reinsurers, and property insurance brokers and consultants all need to be alert to changing conditions associated with global warming. Appropriate mitigation and financing strategies, as well as disaster planning schemes need to be put in place. Capital markets dealing with catastrophe bonds, catastrophe options and exchanges, weather derivatives and carbon trading mechanisms all will be affected by global climate change. While less obvious and clear, potential liabilities could develop, particularly if substantial damages and injuries are linked to global climate change. If litigation was brought against high emitters of greenhouse gases, liability insurers would need to respond. It is doubtful that greenhouse gases would be considered a pollutant, and therefore coverage would not be impacted by the pollution exclusion in general liability policies.

Another liability exposure could impact Directors and Officers (D&O) liability policies. At least one insurer, Swiss Re, has been gathering information on the climate change preparedness plans of corporate D&O policyholders, as part of its underwriting process. Of particular concern are those corporations that oppose shareholder global warming resolutions seeking information on climate change strategy and greenhouse gas emissions. If these corporations suffer financial losses related to their lack of response to the shareholder action, these same shareholders may initiate a derivative action suit against the directors and officers. While policies to date have not been surcharged or cancelled, the fact that Swiss Re is collecting underwriting information from corporate D&O policyholders on greenhouse gas emission strategies suggests such actions could be taken in the future.[74]

A 2002 CERES report, *Value at Risk*, found that climate change poses significant financial risks to a wide range of industry sectors. The report asserted that failure to address these risks could represent a breach of fiduciary responsibility by directors and officers. CERES has been active in the area of climate risks facing investors. Investor risks can become risks for directors and officers. Several publications are available at their website, including the *Investor Guide to Climate Risk* and *Investor Progress Report: Results Achieved Since the 2003 Institutional Summit on Climate Risk.*[75] This latter report was released at the May 2005 Institutional Investor Summit on Climate Risk at the United Nations. At the Summit, a 10 point action was released calling on:

> "U.S. companies, Wall Street firms and the Securities and Exchange Commission to intensify efforts to provide investors with comprehensive analysis and disclosure about the financial risks presented by climate change."[76]

Most of the global warming discussion in the insurance industry has centered around the property-liability sector. The life and health insurance industry could also be impacted. One of the principal potential impacts of global warming, which was listed and examined in the Bush Administration EPA report, was detrimental health outcomes in the United States. Negative health outcomes include water-borne diseases, heat stress, air pollution and diseases transmitted by insects, rodents and ticks.[77]

A study in *Science* found that climate warming is sparking disease epidemics in plants, animals and humans.[78] This study is based on existing global data and supports the frequently suggested scenario that pathogens and their carriers are able to spread farther and faster in warm weather. In addition, as cold winters, which normally help to control the populations, become warmer, more germs and parasites are able to survive.

The adverse health conditions will most certainly result in increased health and life claims. These increased claims could be particularly burdensome for health insurers, and for governments and employers that finance health coverage. These systems are currently under pressure and the aging population will apply even more pressure. If any of the adverse health effects from global warming were to develop into an epidemic, the situation could become particularly serious.

Ethical, business, reputational, and regulatory risks of global warming could be particularly debilitating to corporations and industries. These risks affect the heart and core of the business entity—its future revenues and profits. With the exception of directors and officers liability exposures, risk financing is difficult as these risks can rarely be transferred or hedged. Avoidance and loss control are the only effective risk management tools. This set of risks is greatly impacted by the increased globalization of the world economy. Corporations in the United States cannot make sustainability risk management decisions based solely on U.S. regulations, culture, and consumer preferences. Risk management strategies must incorporate the risks of all the countries and economic regions in which they operate.

Insurance Industry Response

Given that the insurance industry, particularly property insurers and reinsurers, may be at the front line in absorbing the adverse consequences of global warming, there has been a surprising level of indifference in the industry, particularly in the United States. A comprehensive survey and analysis of insurers' attitudes found "many insurers paralyzed by conflicting reports on the topic and skeptical about the political and scientific assessments of climate change." Of particular significance was the finding that "U.S. insurers have yet to publicly discuss the business opportunities that climate change avoidance/mitigation may offer to them and others in the business community."[79]

A major U.S. insurance trade association, the American Insurance Association (AIA), in a white paper, *Property-Casualty Insurance and the Climate Change Debate,* takes the position that "advocates of aggressive climate change action have overestimated the vulnerability of the U.S. property/casualty industry to climate change."[80] The author, Dave Unnewehr, senior research manager, states:

> "Most of the weather impact appears to be projected changes that the industry can adapt to through underwriting, claims management and support for efforts in mitigation and adaptation. Weather variability is an area that insurers are quite familiar with, as it is a basic part of underwriting property insurance."[81]

U.S. insurers have developed a wait-and-see attitude, not unlike that of the Bush administration. In the Administration's EPA report, while recognizing that global warming was indeed happening and may have considerable consequences, no action plan was proposed other than we will have to adapt to these changes as they happen. A paper by Dlugolecki and Keykhah supports the point that international insurers' primary focus has been on mitigation and adaptation.[82] An article in the *Economist* by Vijay Vaitheeswanran, referring to the problem of global warming, raises a fundamental point that rationalizes inaction:

> "...evidence of this problem would remain cloudy for decades; the worst effects might not be felt for a century; but the costs of tackling the problem would start biting immediately. That, in a nutshell, is the dilemma of climate change. It is asking a great deal of politicians to take action on behalf of voters who have not even been born yet."[83]

In contrast to the U.S. insurance industry, European insurers, under the leadership of Swiss Re, Munich Re, Storebrand, and Aviva, have taken a strong interest in global climate change.[84] For instance, "The Statement of Environmental Commitment by the Insurance Industry," adopted in 1995 under the United Nations Insurance Industry Initiative, has 86 corporate signatories plus five Associate members from 27 countries. Germany has 20, Switzerland and the United Kingdom have 10, Russia has eight, Sweden and Japan each have six signatories. By contrast, the United States has two—Employers Re and HSB Group. The UNEP Insurance Initiative developed a 1996 position paper on Climate Change, which calls for substantial reduction in greenhouse gas emissions.[85]

Swiss Re

Swiss Re is extremely active in the area of global warming/climate change. Examining their actions may produce a prototype of how the insurance industry can get more actively involved in this area. As one of the leading reinsurers in the world, Swiss Re has a clear incentive for interest in global climate change because of the distinct possibility of increasing frequency and severity in natural disasters. Yet, in addition to this obvious financial incentive, Swiss Re seems to possess a more enlightened, a more expanded view of the issues of global warming and global climate change, as well as sustainability issues in general.

Besides being active in global warming issues, Swiss Re has an overall corporate sustainability strategy. Swiss Re has been publishing an annual environment report since 1998. Its 2001 report, *Environmental and Social Report,* was expanded to include social responsibility, as well as environmental issues. The report is introduced and signed by Walter Kielholz, CEO and Bruno Porro, Chief Risk Officer and Chair of the Steering Committee on Sustainability. Swiss Re's environmental management strategy is a top-down approach, with support at the highest levels of management. A statement from the preface, by these two leading Swiss Re management officers, captures the overall importance of sustainability in its corporate strategy:

> "This situation only strengthens our commitment to preserve sustainability as a key component of our corporate strategy. We have included the vital issues of water and climate in our Top Topics Management programme and actively contribute the reinsurer's perspective to the public debate on these topics. Throughout the whole Swiss Re Group, we are implementing sustainability as a business model in reinsurance, investment and internal operations, adding the entrepreneurial element to its broader socio-political realization. We are convinced that this initiative will increase our competitive strength in the long term, creating new business opportunities and enhancing our appeal, both as a sound investment and as an employer."[86]

Swiss Re integrates a sustainability focus throughout its business operations. It is the leading reinsurer in the U.S. environmental liability insurance market. Approximately two percent of all Swiss Re stock is held in sustainability funds managed by ecologically or socially oriented institutional investors. Technical training modules in sustainability management are offered to its employees and clients. Swiss Re has implemented an internal group-wide management system to define, fulfill, and evaluate sustainability goals for all business activities and divisions, and to establish environmental and social reporting procedures. The MIERERGIE standard, for energy saving and CO_2 reductions, is applied whenever economically and technically viable for properties owned by Swiss Re Investors. Swiss Re is an active member of many national and international groups focusing on the environment and sustainability, including the World Business Council for Sustainable Development (WBCSD) and the United Nations Environment Programme (UNEP) Finance Initiatives.

Specifically, Swiss Re is very active in the global warming/climate change area. In 1995, Swiss Re formally adopted a corporate policy statement on climate risks, which is included below:

> We respond to the growing demand for reinsurance cover by relying on economic principles and taking due account of the risks associated with climatic developments, and we make available our experience in risk and claims management. We support a climate-friendly economy by making the appropriate economic and political commitments. We participate selectively in the build-up and transfer of knowledge regarding climate protection.[87]

Furthermore, it supports the following general strategies. Comprehensive protection plans must be implemented at the regional level, taking into account climate variability and the maximum possible extent of losses. Two strategies can be pursued to reduce the possible consequences to a manageable extent:

1. avoid the risk altogether.

2. introduce effective planning for the event of a loss.

The need to contain such potential consequences to a manageable extent calls for a precautionary global climate protection policy. Swiss Re is actively engaged in international climate negotiations and supports forefront measures to reduce greenhouse gas emissions. It is also closely involved in the United Nations Environmental Programme Insurance Initiative.[88]

Swiss Re's GHG Risk Solutions coordinates various types of financial solutions—investments, guarantees, project finance, and insurance in the area of greenhouse gas emissions reductions. Many of these financial solutions revolve around trading in carbon emissions, which Swiss Re estimates could grow to somewhere between $75-145 billion annually. Chris Walker, who heads up Swiss Re's GHG Risk Solutions, captures the strategic philosophy of his group:

> "It's our long-term risk management strategy. We've been given the opportunity to work anywhere in the organization where we see risk and opportunity as a result of climate change and emissions reduction."[89]

In October 2001, Swiss Re invited 130 participants from the political, scientific, industrial, and NGO communities to an international conference on "Reducing Greenhouse Gas Emissions."[90] In July 2002, it sponsored a follow up conference on "Emissions Reductions: Main Street to Wall Street—The Climate in North America."[91] In October-November 2003, Swiss Re sponsored another conference on "Beyond Carbon—Emerging Markets for Ecosystem Services." Swiss Re's first publication on the issue was in 1994 and entitled, *Global Warming: Element of Risk*.[92] It was followed in 2002 with the publication, *Opportunities* and Risks of Climate Change.[93] Swiss Re's most recent report, *Tackling Climate Change*, was completed in 2004.[94] These conferences and publications follow Swiss Re long-term efforts promoting dialogue on important issues facing the risk and insurance industry and society, as is evidenced by its *Sigma* publications.

Stabilization of Greenhouse Gas Emissions Does Not Stop Global Warming

A considerable number of U.S. corporations, insurers and individuals, as well as the federal government, seem to have the general attitude of "let's wait until things go bad and then make serious efforts to stabilize emissions of greenhouse gases and global warming." I would suggest that one of the greatest public misconceptions is that stabilization of greenhouse gas emissions will stop global warming.

Based on projections from the IPCC Special Report on Emission Scenarios (SRES), global warming range over 1990 to 2100 will be 1.4°C (2.5°F) to 5.8°C (10.5°F). The SRES scenarios and projections are depicted in Figure 7-1. The top end of the range, 5.8°C (10.5°F), results roughly from an assumption that we continue our economic growth without any efforts to reduce carbon dioxide (CO_2) emissions. Yet, even if we take drastic action and gradually reduce emissions to around 50 percent of current levels by 2100, the atmosphere will still warm to around 2.0°C (3.6°F) by the end of the century. Moving to gradual leveling off of emissions at higher levels will result in warming to about 3.0°C (5.4°F) by 2100, which is the midpoint of the IPCC estimates.

Figure 7-1

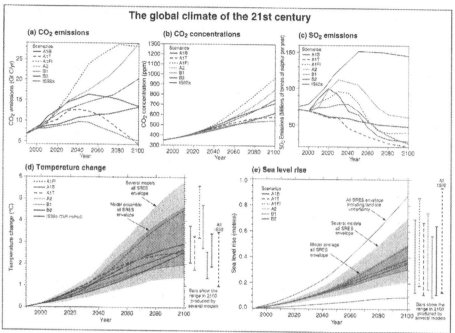

Source: IPCC, 2001: *Climate Change 2001: The Scientific Basis. Contribution of Working Group I to the Third Assessment Report of the Intergovernmental Panel on Climate Change* [Houghton, J.T., Y. Ding, D.J. Griggs, M. Noguer, P.J. van der Linden, X. Dai, K. Maskell, and C.A. Johnson (eds.)]. Cambridge University Press, Cambridge, United Kingdom and New York, NY, USA.

Emissions of CO_2 are different than concentrations of CO_2 in the atmosphere. Even if emissions are stabilized, concentrations of CO_2 in the atmosphere, along with global warming, will continue to rise for long periods into the future. The amount of current CO_2 emissions are approximately double the removal rate of CO_2 from the atmosphere. In order to stabilize CO_2 concentrations, it will actually be necessary to reduce CO_2 emissions to levels considerably below the Kyoto Treaty limits. In addition, even after CO_2 concentrations have stabilized, temperatures will still rise slowly for centuries because of thermal inertia in the climate system.

So waiting until something bad happens from global warming/climate change will be way too late. Whatever adverse consequences that are being produced will continue and in all likelihood worsen. The bottom line is we are going to get warmer and the climate will change. Our best realistic strategy is to slow the warming to allow us more time to adapt. Climate stabilization, but with warmer temperatures, can be accomplished but it will realistically take hundreds of years.

Abrupt Climate Change

Abrupt climate change would lessen the period for adoption and cause the most disruptions in societies and business systems. A compilation of recent research on past climate changes was assembled by the National Research Council (NRC) in a 2002 publication entitled, *Abrupt Climate Change: Inevitable Surprises.*[95] Data on climate changes in the past can be gathered from ice core borings, like those in Greenland, ocean and lake sediments, tree rings, and terrestrial sediments.

The NRC points out that this research has provided evidence, which "shows that major and widespread climate changes have occurred with startling speed." For instance, past changes of temperatures by 10°C (18°F) over a 10 year period on a local basis have been documented. Most notably:

> "roughly half the North Atlantic warming since the last ice age was achieved in only a decade, and it was accompanied by significant climatic changes across most the globe."[96]

Abrupt climate change can occur when gradual trends are pushed across some threshold. What is troublesome is that once this threshold is crossed, it becomes difficult, probably impossible, to get back to the other side. That is what makes the "let's wait until things go bad" strategy so risky. In addition, as the NRC points out, "faster earth-system changes...are likely to increase the probability of encountering a threshold that triggers a still faster climate rate."

The most developed theory to explain abrupt climate change is based on sudden changes in thermohaline circulation (THC). The global THC, or great ocean conveyer belt, is depicted in Figure 7-2. These alternating warm and cold ocean currents impact daily weather patterns. If global warming were to disrupt the THC, climate change, possibly abrupt climate change, could be triggered. Of particular interest is the warming effects of the North Atlantic THC, or Gulf Stream, which is associated with the milder than expected climates of Greenland, the United Kingdom, Scandinavia, and other western European countries. Surprisingly, Oslo Norway, Stockholm Sweden, and northern Scotland are at the same latitude as mid-Hudson Bay in the Northwest Territories, Canada, Anchorage, Alaska and central Siberia.

Figure 7-2

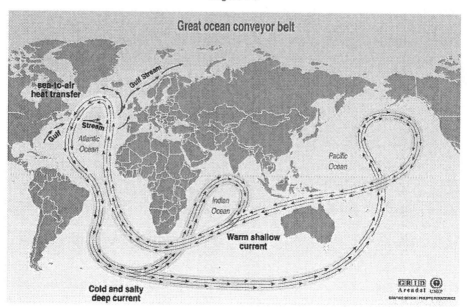

Source: Broecker, 1991, in Climate Change 1995, Impacts, adaptations and mitigation of climate change: scientific-technical analyses, contribution of working group 2 to the second assessment report of the intergovernmental panel on climate change, UNEP and WMO, Cambridge press university, 1996.

As can be seen in Figure 7-2, the Gulf Stream, which is fed from the warmer waters of the Pacific Ocean, moves along South America, the Caribbean, Southeast United States and circulates up into the North Atlantic. As the current moves northward it becomes colder, saltier and more dense, which causes it to sink south of Greenland. As it sinks it acts to pull the current behind it, much like an escalator or a conveyor belt. This deep ocean river of cold, salty water will eventually flow to the Pacific Ocean, where it warms to complete the cycle. The THC is maintained by these temperature, salinity and density contrasts in the world's oceans.

Global warming not only leads to warmer water in the North Atlantic, but by melting freshwater glaciers and ice sheets in the Arctic and Greenland, warming leads to less salinization in these waters. The warmer, less salty and lighter water may slow down the sinking motion the THC. Research data has established that these trends, warmer, less salty water and a lower sinking effect, are occurring across the North Atlantic. If the North Atlantic THC, or Gulf Stream, were to slow considerably or stop, the climate of Europe and the eastern coast of North America would change abruptly to much colder conditions. Severe drought conditions would also occur in some regions. Besides serious scientists studying this scenario, the U.S. Pentagon has conducted a recently released study analyzing the security concerns of large migrations of people moving into southern Europe to escape the cold conditions or from Mexico into the U.S. to escape drought conditions.[97]

The recent discovery that past climate changes from temperate to ice age conditions can occur over a period of years, not decades or centuries, is of particular concern. The most likely cause was a shut down in the great conveyor belt. As described by Thom Hartmann, author of *The Last Hours of Ancient Sunlight*, these changes:

> "resemble a light switch, which is off as you gradually and slowly lift it, until it hits a mid-point threshold or "break over point" where suddenly the state is flipped from off to on and the light comes on."[98]

So the movie, *The Day After Tomorrow*, while exaggerated at the extremes, is based on a scenario that is supported by both theoretical and empirical evidence.

An International Climate Task Force issued a report in January 2005. The report concluded that global warming is approaching the point of no return, in which widespread drought, crop failure and rising sea levels will be irreversible. The independent report was a joint effort by the Institute for Public Policy Research in Britain, the Center for American Progress and the Australian Institute. While no study can predict with certainty the point of irreversibility, the Task Force recommended a long term objective of preventing global average temperature from rising more than 2º C (3.6º F).[99] It might be noted that this rise in temperature is at the low end of the IPCC's estimate for increasing temperatures over the 21st century.

Recent studies on the Arctic and Antarctic regions add credibility to the concerns of the Task Force. In November 2004, The Arctic Climate Impact Assessment was released. The Overview Report, entitled *Impacts of a Warming Arctic* concludes:

> "The Arctic is now experiencing some of the most rapid and severe climate change on Earth. Over the next 100 years, climate change is expected to accelerate, contributing to major physical, ecological, social, and economic changes, many of which have already begun. Changes in arctic climate will also affect the rest of the world through increased global warming and rising sea levels."[100]

Arctic average temperature has risen at almost twice the rate as the rest of the world in the past few decades. In some areas, temperatures have risen as much as 2.2-4° C (4-7° F) over the last 50 years and are estimated to increase an additional 4-7° C (7-13° F) over the next century. These warming trends undermine the viability of traditional Arctic peoples, threaten the existence of polar bears, seals and other species, disrupt migratory routes and transportation systems, and increase sea levels due to the melting of sea ice and glaciers.[101]

Research in the Antarctic, and published in *Science* in fall 2004, shows that glaciers are thinning and moving faster into the sea.[102] Numerous ice shelves have collapsed over the last 10 years, including the Larsen A ice shelf in 1995, the Wilkins ice shelf in 1998, and the Larsen B ice shelf in 2002. The disintegration of these ice shelves can lead to glaciers moving faster into the sea, where they melt and add to rising sea levels. At this point, melting glaciers are a warning. But any significant weakening or collapse or excessive melting of the land based ice fields of West Antarctica would create calamitous sea level rises.[103]

Mitigation Strategies

Based on their acceptance of the Kyoto Protocol, most of the world agrees that slowing of global warming is an important mitigation strategy. Adopting Kyoto guidelines of reducing greenhouse gas emissions to 5.2 percent below 1990 levels will not stop global warming, but it certainly will slow the warming. Since it takes time, money and efforts to adapt to a changing climate, a longer period of adaptation, produced by mitigation efforts, will lessen stress and disruption.

Voluntary Reductions in Emissions by Corporations

Corporations and industries are facing the fact that their greenhouse gas emissions will be regulated. This is certainly the case for those corporations and industries operating in countries that have ratified the Kyoto Protocol. Even in the United States, state laws may impact businesses. A change in the composition or attitude of the federal government at the executive or legislative level could reverse the United States' stand on the treaty. Multinational corporations domiciled in the United States, which operate across multiple regulatory regions, could face difficult decisions in operating strategies.

A 2004 study by the World Resource Institute of nine corporations concludes that "'proactive work' by companies to measure emissions and minimize the costs of the coming rules could be much less expensive than 'reacting to events at a later date'."[104] One corporation, Johnson and Johnson, was cited for its energy efficiency projects and the fact that Johnson and Johnson has become the nation's second largest user of solar panels to product electricity.

For these reasons, many corporations have instituted voluntary CO_2 reduction plans. It makes particularly good sense for international companies to develop a uniform system for subsidiaries and divisions that operate both in the United States and the European Union or Japan. For instance, global oil producers including the Royal Dutch/Shell Group and British Petroleum, as well as power-generating companies like Cinergy, AEP and Entergy, all have moved to reduce their own emissions.[105] DuPont has reduced emissions of greenhouse gases from its factories worldwide more than 65 percent below its 1990 levels.[106] Alcoa has announced plans to reduce its greenhouse emissions by 2010 to levels 25 percent below those in 1990.[107] Xerox has cut CO_2 emissions through recycling and by increasing the energy efficiency of its copier machines by 50 percent.[108] Besides mitigating regulatory and reputation risks, these companies are also finding that energy costs have been reduced and efficiencies improved.

Despite these examples, many corporations have been slow to react. CERES commissioned a 2003 report, *Corporate Governance and Climate Change,* prepared by the Investor Responsibility Research Center, with Douglas G. Cogan as the author. The report found that most of the world's 20 largest companies have been lax in disclosure and formulation of strategies to reduce greenhouse gas emissions.[109] A 2003 survey by the Carbon Disclosure Project of the World's 500 largest companies found that while 80 percent see climate change as a financial risk, only 35 to 40 percent are taking action to mitigate the risks.[110]

One of the most effective programs was established by the Pew Center on Global Climate Change. The program was established in 1998 to support research and to provide information and innovative solutions relating to global climate change. Thirty-eight mostly Fortune 500 companies provide management expertise to the Center through the Business Environmental Leadership Council. Membership in the Council requires support of a statement of principles that focuses on: (1) acceptance of the scientific data that the consequences of global climate change are sufficient to act; (2) reduction of greenhouse gas emissions and investment in new, more efficient technologies; (3) support of the Kyoto agreement and further development of market-based mechanisms; and (4) climate changes consequences can be addressed while sustaining economic growth by adopting reasonable policies, programs, and transition strategies.[111]

Interestingly, even Republicans in the U.S. Congress, who have opposed efforts like the Kyoto Treaty and the McCain-Lieberman Climate Stewardship Act, are starting to become more concerned about the impact of global warming.

The above average warming in Alaska and the Arctic has caused concern for Alaska's two Republican Senators, Ted Stevens and Lisa Murkowski. Discussing the issue of reducing CO_2 emissions, Senator Stevens claimed, "It's the most difficult challenge I feel as a Senator from my state." Senator Murkowski made similar comments, "I need to be sensitive that there are changes going on right now. If that change is due in part to what man is contributing to the atmosphere, I think it would be prudent to look at."[112] Nebraska's Chuck Hagel, another Republican, who has opposed ratifying the Kyoto Treaty, introduced bills in 2005 that would provide financial incentives to companies that export or invest in equipment to reduce CO_2 emissions.[113]

While I am a casual observer of politics, I certainly am not an expert analyst. Yet, I am convinced that even if the Republicans hold on to the White House and both houses of Congress, a Kyoto type agreement to curb CO_2 emissions will be passed in the not too distance future. It will be very difficult to continue to ignore the accumulating evidence on climate change and its adverse impacts.

If the potential adverse consequences of global warming materialize over time, those companies and industries that have not instituted voluntary reductions in greenhouse gas emissions and have opposed regulatory limits could incur substantial damage to their reputations. Conversely, the reputations of those companies and industries that supported voluntary reductions and regulatory limits could be enhanced and might give them a substantial competitive advantage.

Avoiding Development in High Risk Zones

Virtually all the climate change projections call for increased, and intensification of, precipitation; higher peak wind speed and rainfall intensity from hurricanes; and rising sea levels. Areas such as the southeastern and gulf coastal regions of the United States will be particularly vulnerable. Prudence would suggest avoiding development in these areas. Unfortunately, just the opposite has been true.

A report by the National Oceanic and Atmospheric Administration calculates that 153 million people, approximately 54 percent of the total population, live in coastal areas of the United States. It is projected that 25 percent will live in California, Florida and Texas by 2030.[114] These three high-risk states grew at twice the average growth of the United States in the period 1980 to 1993, and continue to have above average growth.[115] A study by the American Geophysical Union found that population growth in high-risk states is disproportionably composed of wealthy individuals.[116] Such individuals would tend to build more expensive properties, which increases the exposure. In countries like the U.K.,

Japan, and Korea, virtually all of the population lives relatively close to the coast, and many of the world's leading urban areas are coastal cities.

Earlier in this chapter, it was noted that Munich Re data indicates total and insured losses from weather-related natural disasters have been increasing over the last 50 years. Douglas Collins, a consulting actuary with Tillinghast—Towers Perrin calculated the normalized insured hurricane damages adjusting actual damages to reflect inflation, housing density, wealth, and wind insurance coverage. Of these variables, the long-term increase in housing density near the coast emerged as the most important factor. Increasing coastal housing density was particularly found in Florida and it expected to continue for a least another 25 years.[117]

Property insurance and compensation programs for natural disaster caused property damage also exacerbates the situation in the United States. In a previous research article, I examined the ways in which the National Flood Insurance Program and Federal Disaster Assistance subsidize and help promote property development and rebuilding in high risk coastal areas.[118] State residual risk plans, which provide wind storm coverage for high risk coastal properties, have often sold policies at premiums below actuarially sound levels. Reasonable people can disagree on what level of coastal development should be permitted. But no rational justification or logic should allow these coastal property developments to not pay fair, equitable and actuarially sound premiums to insure these developments.

Figure 7-3 depicts a sobering picture of the long term potential consequences of building in coastal areas despite increasing global warming. The Florida Coastline is shown 20,000 years ago, today, and in the future if the West Antarctic ice sheet or the Greenland ice sheet were to melt. Even insurance policies would not help at this last stage, as they inevitably would have been cancelled.

Figure 7-3

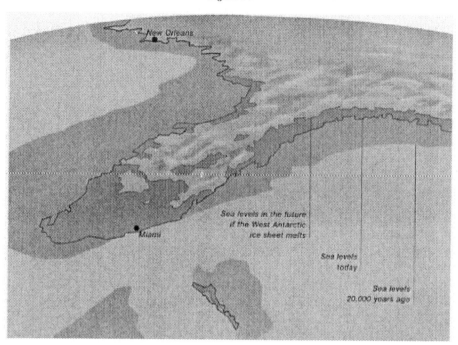

Source: Committee on Abrupt Climate Change; Ocean Studies Board; Polar Research Board; Board on Atmospheric Sciences and Climate; Division on Earth and Life Studies; and National Research Council, *Abrupt Climate Change Inevitable Surprises*, Washington DC, National Academy Press, 2002.

Business Opportunities

As we adapt to global climate change, mitigation opportunities will be substantial. According to the U.S. Secretariat for the International Decade of Natural Disasters, worldwide, only one dollar is spent on prevention for every U.S.$100 spent on rescue efforts.[119] Insurers and others in the risk management industry ought to be leaders in developing mitigation strategies, as they are the experts in disaster and crisis management.

Mitigation strategies will need to be flexible, since many of the consequences of climate change, as to exact time, place, peoples impacted, are unpredictable. It is likely that some aspects and impacts of climate change will be totally unanticipated, as complex systems respond to ongoing climate change in unforeseeable ways.[120]

Whole new industries and sectors will develop around mitigation strategies. A 2003 report by the Carbon Disclosure Project estimates that the renewable energy market will grow to around $1.9 trillion by 2020 from between $234 billion and $625 billion in 2010.[121] British Petroleum, at its new natural gas processing plant in Algeria, has developed a technology to inject one million tons of carbon dioxide back underground each year. This is equivalent to 500 megawatts of electricity produced by wind or solar systems, which emit no greenhouse gases.[122]

Carbon dioxide emissions trading is expected to create a number of opportunities in the financial markets, including insurance. Emissions trading is called for under the Kyoto Protocol. The European Union has enacted a plan that became operational in 2005. Caps on allowances will be set on thousands of individual factories and power plants in the EU. At first, the caps will only apply to around 12,000 facilities such as fossil fuel power plants, and energy intensive industries such as steel, oil, cement and paper. Together these sites represent about 45 percent of the CO_2 emissions in the EU.[123]

Once the caps are set, those companies whose emissions exceed their allowances can invest capital to upgrade their facilities to reduce emissions, or they can buy emissions credits from companies whose emissions are below their cap. Hence the market is created. The market acts to encourage the efficient development of technology to reduce emissions. By reducing total allowances, governments can also reduce total emissions. A similar trading scheme has been successfully in operation for years in the U.S. for sulfur dioxide (SO_2) emissions. This program was enacted under the 1990 amendments to the Clean Air Act to reduce the amount of acid rain from SO_2.

Based on estimates of 15 Euros per one ton CO_2 allowance, an annual 30 billion Euro market will be created in the EU.[124] Actually, a voluntary market is already in existence and resulted in 71 million tons of CO_2 of credits swapping in 2003.[125] Under the EU plan, this figure will jump to 2 billion tons, so the opportunities are obvious.

While no regulations for CO_2 exist in the U.S., the Chicago Climate Exchange for trading greenhouse gas emissions allowances was started by Richard Sandor in 2003 with the participation of 28 large corporations. The Exchange was started in the anticipation that the U.S. government will eventually enact an emissions reduction program.[126]

Under the Kyoto Protocol, trading is allowed in up to six industrially produced greenhouse gases. Emissions trading will become a major commodity market. Steve Drummond, managing director of a greenhouse gas brokerage COZE.com, a subsidiary of Cantor Fitzgerald, states, "The emissions market closely resembles the bond market. This is a serious business opportunity."[127]

As an example of insurance opportunities, Swiss Re GHG Risk Solutions has developed a new product called Contingent Cap Forward for Emissions Reduction Trades. It protects against price volatility in the emissions trading market by "guaranteeing that the cost of the emissions credits stays within a certain range and helping ensure that the credits are delivered, should the transaction apply to some future time period."[128]

An excellent article by Dlugolecki and Loster, in the *Geneva Papers*, summarizes a study by the UNEP Finance Initiative entitled, "Climate Change and the Financial Services Industry." This article and study discusses various business opportunities for the financial services sector, including the insurance industry.[129]

Conclusion

If ever there was a dynamic issue, global climate change certainly qualifies for this distinction. It is international in scope. It raises a myriad of risk issues that will impact people, governments, industries, and businesses. At the 2002 Davos World Economic Forum, business and government leaders described climate change as "the most urgent problem facing humanity."[130] Not developing sound sustainability risk management practices to respond to climate change could result in catastrophic consequences.

In the author's opinion, global climate change may be the leading risk area in sustainability risk management. Besides the traditional risks of property, liability, life and health, global climate change produces a broad array of additional risks, including ethical, cultural, business/boycott, reputation, and regulatory risks. Risk transfer, financing, and hedging mechanisms for this broadened array of risks are often limited, which puts additional pressure on avoidance, risk control, and other mitigation techniques. Global climate change risks have the potential to damage reputations which strike at the heart and core of business—generation of future revenues and profits.

To date, European reinsurers and corporations have assumed the leadership position in discussions on issues raised by global warming/climate change. Increasing pressure will be brought on U.S. insurers and reinsurers and their corporate policyholders, particularly now that the Kyoto Protocol has been ratified. As noted by Dr. Michael Schlesinger, Director of climate research at the University of Illinois, "the persistent uncertainty itself about big climate perils is precisely the reason to invest now in modest mandatory curbs on greenhouse gas emissions."[131] I feel that businesses will lead the way to some form of mandatory limits on greenhouse gas emissions, because they desire more certainty and a level playing field. Even if the United States refuses to ratify the Kyoto Protocol, multinational corporations may choose voluntary reductions in greenhouse gases because of competitive pressures. For both insurance and non-insurance firms, a proactive stance can bring substantial competitive advantages as well as business opportunities. As noted by Dr. Peter Forstmoser, Chairman of the Board of Swiss Re, at their 2001 Conference on Reducing Greenhouse Gas Emissions,

> "Environmental issues have changed and will continue to change the way business operates. Where there is change, there is opportunity."[132]

CHAPTER 7—ENDNOTES

[1] Entergy Corporation Chairman Bob Luft, September 10, 2003, in "Southern Utility Charges Ahead on Climate Issues," *In Common,* Fall 2003.

[2] I have explored global warming/climate change risk issues in two previous articles: Dan R. Anderson, "Global Warming/Climate Change: Implications for the Risk Management and Insurance Industry," *CPCU Journal,* Vol. 56, No. 1, January 2003; Dan R. Anderson, "Environmental Risk Management: A Critical Part of Corporate Strategy," *The Geneva Papers on Risk and Insurance,* Vol. 27, No. 2, April 2002. Some of the material from these two articles was used in writing parts of this chapter.

[3] Climate Research Unit at www.cru.uea.ac.uk

[4] C. Lazaroff, "Global Warming is Real, Council Tells Bush," *Environment News Service,* June 7, 2001; John L. Magnuson, et.al., "Historical Trends in Lake and River Ice Cover in the Northern Hemisphere," *Science,* 289, September 8, 2000.

[5] Lester Brown, "Earth's Ice Melting Faster than Projected," *Population Press,* April/May 2002.

[6] Andrew C. Revkin, "Huge Ice Shelf Is Reported to Break Up In Canada," *New York Times,* September 23, 2003.

[7] "Impacts of a Warming Arctic," *Arctic Climate Impact Assessment,* Cambridge, MA: Cambridge University Press, *2004.*

[8] Richard A. Kerr, "A Bit of Icy Antarctica is Sliding Toward the Sea," *Science,* Vol. 305, September 24, 2004; Robert Thomas, et.al., "Accelerated Sea-Level Rise from West Antarctica," *Science,* Vol. 306, October 8, 2004.

[9] Juan Foreno, "As Andean Glaciers Shrink, Water Worries Grow," *New York Times,* November 24, 2002.

[10] Charles J. Hanley, Associated Press, "Carbon Dioxide hits record level," *Wisconsin State Journal,* March 21, 2004.

[11] "As the World Turns—For the Worse," *Business Week*, April 18, 2005.

[12] NAST—National Assessment Synthesis Team, *Climate Change Impacts on the United States: The Potential Consequences of Climate Variability and Change*, Report for the U.S. Global Change Research Program, Cambridge, U.K.: Cambridge University Press, 2001.

[13] IPCC—Intergovernmental Panel on Climate Change, *Climate Change 2001: The Science Basis*, Third Assessment Report, Cambridge, U.K.: Cambridge University Press, 2001.

[14] Ibid.

[15] Committee on the Science of Climate Change, Climate Change Science: An Analysis of Some Key Questions, Washington D.C.: National Academy Press, 2001.

[16] NAST—National Assessment Synthesis Team, *Climate Change Impacts on the United States: The Potential Consequences of Climate Variability and Change*, Report for the U.S. Global Change Research Program, Cambridge, U.K.: Cambridge University Press, 2001.

[17] Antonio Regalado, "Global Warming Report Cites Gases," *Wall Street Journal,* December 17, 2003.

[18] Claudia Dreifus, "A Conversation with: Jerry Mahlman; Listening to the Climate Models, And Trying to Wake Up the World," *New York Times,* December 16, 2003.

[19] IPCC—Intergovernmental Panel on Climate Change, *Climate Change 2001: The Science Basis,* Third Assessment Report, Cambridge, U.K.: Cambridge University Press, 2001.

[20] NAST—National Assessment Synthesis Team, *Climate Change Impacts on the United States: The Potential Consequences of Climate Variability and Change*, Report for the U.S. Global Change Research Program, Cambridge, U.K.: Cambridge University Press, 2001.

[21] U.S. Environmental Protection Agency, U.S. Climate Action Report—2002, *Third National Communication of the United States of America Under the United Nations Framework Convention on Climate Change,* www.epa.gov/globalwarming/publications/car/index.html, May, 2002.

[22] James Hansen, et.al., "Earth's Energy Impalance: Confirmation and Implications," *Science,* April 28, 2005.

[23] "'Smoking Gun' on humans and global warming claimed," MSNBC News Service, April 28, 2005.

[24] Clive Cookson, "'Global warming real' says new studies," *Financial Times,* February 18, 2005.

[25] D. Sanger, "Bush Will Continue to Oppose Kyoto Pact on Global Warming," *New York Times,* June 12, 2001.

[26] NAST—National Assessment Synthesis Team, *Climate Change Impacts on the United States: The Potential Consequences of Climate Variability and Change,* Report for the U.S. Global Change Research Program, Cambridge, U.K.: Cambridge University Press, 2001.

[27] Committee on the Science of Climate Change, Climate Change Science: An Analysis of Some Key Questions, Washington D.C.: National Academy Press, 2001.

[28] E. Mills, E. LeComte and A. Peara, *U.S. Insurance Industry Perspectives on Global Climate Change,* Berkeley, CA: Lawrence Berkeley National Laboratory, MS90-4000, February 2001; Munich Re, *Annual Review of Natural Catastrophes,* 2000, Munich, Germany: Munich Re Group, 2001.

[29] www.munichre.com

[30] www.ECES.org, "New research finds that the droughts and record floods that have ravaged Central Europe in the last few years will become more common due to global warming," February 19, 2003; Vijay Joshi, Associated Press, "Powerful typhoon slams South Korea's Coast: Thousands flee as worst storm in century hits," *Seattle Times,* September 14, 2003; A.F. Dlugolecki, "Climate Change and

the Insurance Industry," *The Geneva Papers on Risk and Insurance,* Vol. 25, No. 4, 2000.

[31] NAST—National Assessment Synthesis Team, *Climate Change Impacts on the United States: The Potential Consequences of Climate Variability and Change,* Report for the U.S. Global Change Research Program, Cambridge, U.K.: Cambridge University Press, 2001.

[32] www.ECES.org, "Water Council report...," February 27, 2003.

[33] A.F. Dlugolecki, "Climate Change and the Insurance Industry," *The Geneva Papers on Risk and Insurance,* Vol. 25, No. 4, 2000.

[34] Pamela Sampson, Associated Press, "Heat wave in Europe killed more than 19,000, *Wisconsin State Journal,* September 26, 2003; Anita Weier, "Prof warns of global warming health impacts," *The Capital Times,* February 22, 2005.

[35] B. Hansen, "Friends of the Earth Considers Legal Action to Curb Global Warming," *Environmental News Service,* September 15, 2000.

[36] K.Q. Seelye, "Global Warming May Bring New Variety of Class Action," *New York Times,* September 6, 2001.

[37] Andrew Strauss, "Suing the United States for Global Warming Omissions," Red Conference, London, July 10, 2001.

[38] Kim Moore, "Turning up the Heat," *Reactions,* July 2002.

[39] Andrew C. Revkin, "Eskimos Seek to Recast Global Warming as a Rights Issue," *New York Times,* December 15, 2004; "The Inuit Struggle for Survival," *In Brief,* Earth Justice, Spring 2005.

[40] "The Inuit Struggle for Survival," *In Brief,* Earth Justice, Spring 2005.

[41] O. Cowell and J. Karas, *Gathering Storm: The Human Cost of Climate Change,* Amsterdam, The Netherlands: Friends of the Earth, September 2000.

[42] J. Linnerooth-Bayer and A. Amendola, "Global Change, Natural Disasters and Loss-sharing: Issues of Efficiency and Equity," *The Geneva Papers on Risk and Insurance*, Vol. 25, No. 2, 2000.

[43] ECES.org, "Water Council Report....," February 27, 2003.

[44] Don Harrison, "It's No Day at the Beach," *Parade*, June 6, 2004.

[45] O. Cowell and J. Karas, *Gathering Storm: The Human Cost of Climate Change*, Amsterdam, The Netherlands: Friends of the Earth, September 2000.

[46] IPCC—Intergovernmental Panel on Climate Change, *The Regional Impacts of Climate Change*, Cambridge, U.K.: Cambridge University Press, 1998.

[47] NAST—National Assessment Synthesis Team, *Climate Change Impacts on the United States: The Potential Consequences of Climate Variability and Change*, Report for the U.S. Global Change Research Program, Cambridge, U.K.: Cambridge University Press, 2001.

[48] "Drought in West tops Dust Bowl," *Capital Times*, June 18, 2004.

[49] U.S. Environmental Protection Agency, U.S. Climate Action Report—2002, *Third National Communication of the United States of America Under the United Nations Framework Convention on Climate Change*, www.epa.gov/globalwarming/publications/car/index.html, May, 2002.

[50] John J. Fialka, "Senators Warm Up to Emissions Curbs," *Wall Street Journal*, February 22, 2005.

[51] Timothy Egan, "Now, in Alaska, Even the Permafrost is Melting," *New York Times*, June 16, 2002.

[52] Committee on the Science of Climate Change, Climate Change Science: An Analysis of Some Key Questions, Washington D.C.: National Academy Press, 2001.

[53] C.D. Thomas, et al., "Extinction Risk from Climate Change" *Nature*, 427, 145-148, January 8, 2004.

[54] "Impacts of a Warming Arctic," *Arctic Climate Impact Assessment*, Cambridge, MA: Cambridge University Press, 2004.

[55] Hans Hoegh-Guldberg and Ove Hoegh-Guldberg, *The Implications of Climate Change for Australia's Great Barrier Reef*, World Wildlife Fund Australia and the Queensland Tourism Industry, 2004.

[56] Larry Rohter, "Deep in the Amazon, Vast Questions about the Climate," *New York Times*, November 4, 2003.

[57] David Barboza, "Plan Gives Farmers a Role in Fighting Global Warming," *New York Times*, November 24, 2003.

[58] Elizabeth Royte, "Don't Spoil the Soil," *Onearth*, Fall 2003.

[59] NAST—National Assessment Synthesis Team, *Climate Change Impacts on the United States: The Potential Consequences of Climate Variability and Change*, Report for the U.S. Global Change Research Program, Cambridge, U.K.: Cambridge University Press, 2001.

[60] J. Ball, "Global-Warming Treaty Opens Corporate Rifts, and Activists Jump In," *Wall Street Journal*, August 27, 2001.

[61] Ibid.

[62] A.C. Revkin, "Deals Break Impasse on Global Warming Treaty," *New York Times*, November 11, 2001.

[63] Eileen Claussen, "The Global Warming Dropout," *New York Times*, June 7, 2002; Steven Lee Myers, "Putin Ratifies Kyoto Protocal of Emissions," *New York Times*, November 6, 2004.

[64] Guy Chazan, "EU Backs Russia's WTO Entry As Moscow Supports Kyoto Pact," *Wall Street Journal*, May 24, 2004.

[65] Danny Hakim, "At the Front on Air Policy," *New York Times*, July 3, 2002.

[66] Fred Krupp, "Cars Can Get Much Cleaner," *New York Times,* July 20, 2002.

[67] Danny Hakim, "Several States Likely to Follow California on Car Emissions," *New York Times,* June 11, 2004.

[68] Danny Hakim, "Canada Says It May Emulate California on Auto Emissions," *New York Times,* March 12, 2004.

[69] James Sterngold, "State Officials Ask Bush to Act on Global Warming," *New York Times,* July 17, 2002.

[70] Jeffery Ball, "States Feel Heat on Global-Warming Steps," *Wall Street Journal,* November 23, 2003.

[71] John J. Fialka, "States Are Stepping in to Reduce Levels of Carbon Dioxide," *Wall Street Journal,* September 11, 2001.

[72] CNN.com, "Climate Change to thump markets," February 17, 2003.

[73] Matthew Kiernan, "Taking Control of Climate," *Financial Times,* November 24, 2002.

[74] Inside Washington Publishers, "Insurance Industry Worries Climate Resolutions Will Prompt Suits," Clean Air Report vs News Edge Corporation, February 12, 2004.

[75] www.ceres.org

[76]"2005 Summit Press Release," Institutional Investor Summit on Climate Risk, at United Nations, May 10, 2005.

[77] U.S. Environmental Protection Agency, U.S. Climate Action Report—2002, *Third National Communication of the United States of America Under the United Nations Framework Convention on Climate Change,* www.epa.gov/globalwarming/publications/car/index.html, May, 2002.

[78] C. Drew Harvell, Charles E. Mitchell, Jessica R. Ward, Sonia Altizer, Andrew P. Dobson, Richard S. Ostfeld and Michael D. Samuel, "Climate Warming and Disease Risks for Terrestrial and Marine Biota," *Science*, Vol. 296, June 2002.

[79] E. Mills, E. LeComte and A. Peara, *U.S. Insurance Industry Perspectives on Global Climate Change*, Berkeley, CA: Lawrence Berkeley National Laboratory, MS90-4000, February 2001.

[80] AIA—American Insurance Association, *Property-Casualty Insurance and the Climate Change Debate: A Risk Assessment*, 1999.

[81] Ann Deering and Jared Wade, "Climate Control: Global Warming Hits the Insurance Market," *Risk Management*, August 2002.

[82] Andrew Dlugolecki and Mojdeh Keykhah, "Climate Change and the Insurance Sector: Its Role in Adaptation and Mitigation," *Greener Management International*, Greenleaf Publishing, Issue 39, 2002.

[83] Vijay Vaitheeswaran, "A Survey of the Global Environment," *The Economist*, July 6, 2002.

[84] E. Mills, E. LeComte and A. Peara, *U.S. Insurance Industry Perspectives on Global Climate Change*, Berkeley, CA: Lawrence Berkeley National Laboratory, MS90-4000, February 2001.

[85] E. Mills, E. LeComte and A. Peara, *U.S. Insurance Industry Perspectives on Global Climate Change*, Berkeley, CA: Lawrence Berkeley National Laboratory, MS90-4000, February 2001; Saria Labatt and Rodney R. White, *Environmental Finance*, Hoboken, NJ, John Wiley & Sons, 2002.

[86] Swiss Re, Environmental and Social Report, www.swissre.com, 2001.

[87] Swiss Re, "Corporate Policy Statement on Climate Risks," www.swissre.com, 1995.

[88] Ibid.

[89] Joanne Wojcik, "Reinsurers aiding efforts to address climate change," *Business Insurance,* September 1, 2003.

[90] Swiss Re, *Reducing Greenhouse Gas Emissions,* Swiss Re Conference Report, www.swissre.com, 2001.

[91] Swiss Re, *Emission Reductions: Main Street to Wall Street,*—"The Climate in North America" at The American Museum of Natural History in N.Y., www.swissre.com, July 17-18, 2002.

[92] Swiss Rc, *Global Warming: Element of Risk,* www.swissre.com, 1994.

[93] Swiss Re, *Opportunities and Risks of Climate Change,* www.swissre.com, 2002.

[94] Swiss Re, *Tackling Climate Change,* www.swissre.com, 2004.

[95] National Research Council, *Abrupt Climate Change: Inevitable Surprises,* Washington D.C.: National Academy Press, 2002.

[96] Ibid.

[97] David Stipp, "The Pentagon's Weather Nightmare," *Fortune,* February 9, 2004.

[98] Thom Hartmann, "How Global Warming May Cause the Next Ice Age," CommonDreams.org, January 30, 2004.

[99] The Institute for Public Policy Research, The Center for American Progress, and the Australian Institute, *Meeting the Climate Challenge: Recommendations of the International Climate Change Task Force,* January 2005.

[100] Arctic Climate Impact Assessment, *Impacts of a Warming Arctic,* Arctic Council and the International Arctic Sciences Committee, Cambridge: Cambridge University Press, 2004.

[101] Ibid.

[102] Richard A. Kerr, "A Bit of Icy Antarctica is Sliding Toward the Sea," *Science,* Vol. 305, September 24, 2004; Robert Thomas, et.al., "Accelerated Sea-Level Rise from West Antarctica," *Science,* Vol. 306, October 8, 2004.

[103] Larry Rohter, "Antarctica, Warming, Looks Ever More Vulnerable," *New York Times,* January 25, 2005.

[104] John J. Fialka and Jeffery Ball, "Companies Get Ready for Greenhouse—Gas Limits," *Wall Street Journal,* October 26, 2004.

[105] A.C. Revkin and N. Banerjee, "Energy Executives Urge Voluntary Greenhouse-Gas Limits," *New York Times,* August 1, 2001.

[106] "A Wake-up call from the Arctic," *Solutions, Environmental Defense,* Jan-Feb, 2005.

[107] K. Bradsher and A.C. Revkin, "A Pre-emptive Strike on Global Warming," *New York Times,* May, 15, 2001; Douglas G. Cogan, *Corporate Governance and Climate Change,* CERES, IRRC, June 2003.

[108] Katrin Bennhold, "New Limits on Pollution Herald Change in Europe," *New York Times,* January 1, 2005.

[109] Barnaby J. Feder, "Report Faults Big Companies on Climate," *New York Times,* July 10, 2003; Douglas G. Cogan, *Corporate Governance and Climate Change,* CERES, IRRC, June 2003.

[110] CNN.com, "Climate Change to thump markets," February 17, 2003.

[111] Pew Center on Global Climate Change, www.pewclimate.org.

[112] John J. Fialka, "Senators Warm Up to Emissions Curbs," *Wall Street Journal,* February 22, 2005.

[113] Ibid.

[114] "Buffet Warns of Mega—Catastrophes Threat to Reinsurer, Insurers," *Advisen Front Page News,* March 8, 2005.

[115] George B. Jones, IV, "Alternative Reinsurance: Using Catastrophe Bonds and Insurance Derivatives as a Mechanism for Increasing Capacity in the Insurance Markets," *CPCU Journal*, Vol. 52, No. 1, Spring 1999.

[116] American Geophysical Union, "Why the United States Is Becoming More Vulnerable to Natural Disasters," *EOS*, November 3, 1998.

[117] Douglas J. Collins, "So Much for Global Warming," *Contingencies*, March/April 2002.

[118] Dan R. Anderson, "Catastrophe Insurance and Compensation: Remembering Basic Principles," *CPCU Journal*, Vol. 53, No. 2, Summer, 2000.

[119] J. Linnerooth-Bayer and A. Amendola, "Global Change, Natural Disasters and Loss-sharing: Issues of Efficiency and Equity," *The Geneva Papers on Risk and Insurance*, Vol. 25, No. 2, 2000.

[120] NAST—National Assessment Synthesis Team, *Climate Change Impacts on the United States: The Potential Consequences of Climate Variability and Change*, Report for the U.S. Global Change Research Program, Cambridge, U.K.: Cambridge University Press, 2001.

[121] CNN.com, "Climate change to thump markets," February 17, 2003.

[122] Jeffery Ball, "Deep in the Sahara, BP Tries to Put Dent in Global Warming," *Wall Street Journal*, February 4, 2005.

[123] Jeffery Ball, "In Europe, Clues to Kyoto's Impact," *Wall Street Journal*, October 10, 2003.

[124] Ibid.

[125] John J. Fialka, "Emissions Credits see Brisk Trading Tied to Kyoto Pact," *Wall Street Journal*, December 5, 2003.

[126] "The Chicago Climate Exchange," *Economist New Paper Limited*, October 17, 2002.

[127] Otto Pohl, "U.S. Left Out of Emissions Trading," *New York Times,* April 10, 2003.

[128] Joanne Wojcik, "Reinsurers aiding efforts to address climate change," *Business Insurance,* September 1, 2003.

[129] Andrew Dlugolecki and Thomas Loster, "Climate Change and the Financial Services Sector: An Appreciation of the UNEPFI Study," *The Geneva Papers on Risk and Insurance,* Vol. 28 No. 3, July 2003; UNEPFI, "Climate Change and the Financial Services Industry," 2002. Work carried out by Innovest Strategic Advisers with Andrew Dlugolecki as advisor.

[130] Matthew Kiernan, "Taking Control of Climate," *Financial Times,* November 24, 2002.

[131] Andrew Revkin, "Deciding How Much Global Warming Is Too Much," *New York Times,* February 1, 2005.

[132] Swiss Re, *Reducing Greenhouse Gas Emissions,* Swiss Re Conference Report, www.swissre.com, 2001.

8

NEW SUSTAINABILITY RISKS: GENETICALLY MODIFIED CROPS

o o o o o o o o o o o o o o o o o o o o o o o o o o o o o o o o o o o o o

You don't mess around with the genetic base of a food production system as fundamentally as some of these biotech applications are, without causing some things to change. It is really scientific hubris to think that we understand all that, because we don't. This stuff is just horrendously complicated.

—Charles Benbrook, former Director of the Board of Agriculture for the National Academy of Sciences.

It is not clear what liabilities there are in this issue and whose they would be, because it is a completely new situation.

—Spokesperson for NFU Mutual, which insures two-thirds of U.K. farmers

Genetically Modified (GM) crops are the leading edge of the developing biotech industry of life sciences. In an article in the *Harvard Business Review*, Enriquez and Goldberg state:

"Advances in genetic engineering will not only have dramatic implications for people and society, they will reshape vast sectors of the world economy. The boundaries between many once-distinct businesses, from agribusiness and chemicals to health care and pharmaceuticals to energy and computing, will blur, and out of their convergence will emerge what promises to be the largest industry in the world: the life-science industry."[1]

GM crops are also at the center of the storm of a debate over their benefits versus their risks. Risk managers, brokers, insurance officials, and consultants of the affected business sectors obviously must be attuned to the risks of this emerging technology. But lessons can be learned, by all those involved in the risk management and insurance industry, from the complexity and importance of the issues and potential loss exposures deriving from GM technology.

An analysis of GM technology risks go far beyond product liability and recall risks. GM technology involves business and reputational risks, as well as environmental, ethical, cultural, social, and even religious questions and issues. The GM debate has been heightened by the globalizing of the world economy, raising World Trade Organization conflicts and pitting the European Union countries against the United States. The management of GM risks is one of the more vivid examples today of the expanding scope of sustainability risk management.[2]

Basics of Genetic Modification

Cells of living organisms have sets of chromosomes that control the organism's life. Chromosomes are made up of genes, each of which is a piece of DNA that contains a code to make a specific protein, which in turn tell the cells what to do. For centuries, farmers have selectively bred plants and animals to arrive at better gene combinations for increasing their yield or their resistance to disease. With the experiments and studies of Austrian monk and botanist Gregor Mendel in the mid 1800s, breeding efforts took on a more scientific basis. Mendel's experiments with garden peas resulted in the formulation of the basic laws of heredity and initiated the science of genetics. In the 1900s, the development of hybrids of corn and other staple crops would become increasingly important and commercially successful. Yet, all these efforts involved the exchange and varied combinations of genes in the same or closely related living organisms.

When James Watson and Francis Crick discovered the molecular structure of DNA, the door was opened to genetic engineering or modification. Dr. Martha Crouch, Associate Professor of Biology at Indiana University, defines genetic engineering as:

> "...the process of manipulating the pattern of proteins in an organism by altering genes. Either new genes are added, or existing genes are

changed...[and] because the genetic code is similar in all species, genes taken from a mouse can function in a corn plant."[3]

It is this ability to transfer genes from one species to another that is so appealing and creates a virtually unlimited potential for modified living organisms. Organisms can be made to exhibit new characteristics. Crops can be made resistant to pests, drought and even herbicides to improve their performance. Defective genes in plants, and even humans, could be repaired to ameliorate or eliminate the adverse effects of a disease.

It is also this ability to cross biological boundaries that creates the greatest fears. We are tampering with natural evolutionary development that has produced living organisms over millions of years. Disturbing this process may produce unforeseen and potentially catastrophic risks. The problem is we just do not know, but by the time we do know, it may be too late to reverse or control the consequences of these unknown risks. It sounds like science fiction, but this is the real world as it exists, and the risk management community, indeed all of society, will need to confront and deal with the risks of genetic engineering. As stated by Dr. Bruce Currie, professor of animal science at Cornell University:

> "The biggest concern is the degree of uncertainty in manipulating genes. Especially when dealing with pleiotropic genes—those which have multiple actions—there can be surprising side effects. There is no simple formula for anticipating these intangibles."[4]

Experiments are being conducted to examine whether GM crops could be used as a way to inexpensively produce certain pharmaceutical drugs and chemicals. The recent completion of the mapping of the human genome extends potential benefits and risks into the human realm. The human genome refers to the sequencing of DNA in the approximately 30,000 genes contained in human cells. It will take some time before human genes are actually manipulated, but today genes are being manipulated in plants, as will be discussed below. By examining the benefits and risks of GM crops, much can be learned not only about GM crops, but also about potential applications in humans, pharmaceuticals and chemicals.

GM crops were introduced in 1997, lead by the efforts of Monsanto. Virtually all of the worldwide GM crops are composed of soybeans, corn, cotton and canola. In 2003, over 160 million acres of GM crops were planted worldwide, with the United States share being around 100 million or 62 percent. Argentina has over 20 percent of world GM acreage. Other countries where GM crops are grown include Canada, Brazil, China, South Africa and Spain. In the United

States, more than 85 percent of soybeans and slightly less then 80 percent of cotton is genetically engineered. Over 40 percent of the corn crop relies on GM technology. The global market value of GM crops is estimated to be as much as $4.75 billion. While considerable experimentation is being conducted, GM crops today are basically of two types—pest resistant and herbicide resistant—as will be explained in the next section.[5]

Benefits of GM Crops

GM crops are marketed by seed companies and used by farmers for their superior characteristics over traditional crops. These characteristics include pest resistance and less chemical use. Two particularly successful GM crops are Bt corn and Roundup Ready soybeans.

Bt corn was developed by genetically modifying corn to resist pests, specifically the corn borer. Inserting a gene for the soil bacterium, *Bacillus thuringiensis* or Bt, into corn gives it resistance. The obvious benefit is the reduction of chemicals used to control the corn borer. Later versions of Bt corn have been developed for the bollworm and rootworm. Bt, a naturally occurring soil organism, is also approved for direct use by organic farmers. A Bt cotton has also been developed. If only benefits are considered, Bt crops clearly are environmentally friendly.

One problem with applying herbicides and pesticides is to kill the weeds and pests without damaging the crops. Chemicals have to be applied at different times, and not necessarily at the optimal time, in order to avoid damaging the crops. Through gene manipulation, Monsanto developed soybeans with a built-in immunity to glyphosphate, the active ingredient in Monsanto's herbicide Roundup. With these GM soybeans, farmers can control weeds with a single application of Roundup, which previously would have been lethal to the crop. This reduced the need to employ more toxic and long-lasting herbicides and also reduced soil-damaging tillage. Roundup Ready soybeans became so popular with farmers in the United States that by 1999, just three years after their introduction, over one half of the soybean crop was genetically modified.[6] A herbicide resistant corn product has also been developed.[7]

There are a number of other GM examples. The Flavr-Savr tomato has a gene that is altered to slow the aging process and extend shelf life. Another GM tomato involves inserting an antifreeze gene from a flounder into tomatoes to make them frost resistant.[8] Future health benefits could be gained from cholesterol-lowering cheese, allergen free peanuts, and immunity-boosting bananas as a substitute to syringe-injected vaccines.[9] Again the possibilities and potential benefits seem virtually unlimited.

Because of the large and often rapidly increasing populations in developing countries, GM crops hold the potential for considerable benefits. It is estimated that 800 million people in the world are chronically malnourished and this number is increasing rapidly.[10] Built-in resistance to drought, pests, and poor soils, could increase food production and reduce chemical use. Potential benefits could also include the insertion of vaccines into foods and the development of more nutritious food. A frequently cited example is golden rice, a GM rice that includes vitamin A supplements to fight blindness. A 2004 report, "Agricultural Biotechnology Meeting the Needs of the Poor," by the United Nations Food and Agriculture Organization called for the increased use of GM crops in developing countries.[11]

Risks of GM Crops

There are risks in the development of GM crops, which will be documented and discussed below. As with benefits, future potential risks greatly exceed documented risks. With both benefits and risks, we are working in the realm of the potential and the unknown. Huge uncertainty and unpredictability are present, which of course create risks within themselves. In addition to the typical risks of injuries and property damages, potential risks of GM crops include cultural, ethical, and religious ramifications, the unpredictability and irreversibility of environmental genetic pollution, as well as reputation and regulatory risks and the business risk that consumers may refuse to buy GM products.

Specific Risks

A frequently referenced specific risk is allergenic reactions. This could occur from consumption of a product, which includes genes from another species. A study, reported in the *New England Journal of Medicine* by Dr. Julie Nordlee of the University of Nebraska and colleagues, found that soybeans modified to contain genes from Brazil nuts triggered allergic reactions.[12] In another study at York Nutritional Laboratory in England, researchers found a substantial increase in soy allergies in conjunction with the introduction of GM soybeans in that country.[13]

In the previous section on the benefits of GM crops, Roundup Ready Soybeans and Bt corn and cotton were discussed. There are potential downsides to these GM crops that have been frequently cited. If the herbicide resistant characteristics of Roundup Ready Soybeans spread to a weedy relative, a "superweed" might be created.

While Bt corn eliminates the corn borer, it might also harm beneficial insects. As Bt corn is tilled into the soil, its toxins may alter the chemistry and essential organisms of soil. Indeed, no one knows the long-term effect of eating Bt crops on human health. When organic farmers or others use Bt as a natural bacteria to spread on a crop, it is killed by sunlight and any residues can be washed off. But with GM crops, the Bt gene is engineered into the DNA of the crop and is not affected by sunlight or washing. The wide spread planting of Bt crops also increases the likelihood of the evolution of "superbugs" resistant to the toxin. This possibility is particularly upsetting to organic farmers, as they use Bt as a natural pesticide. Organic farmers could be put in serious jeopardy if Bt were rendered ineffective against Bt resistant pests.

In May 1999, entomologist John Losey, behavioral ecologist Linda Rayor, and biologist Maureen Carter, published a study in the journal *Nature* that found the pollen of Bt corn is lethal to the monarch butterfly caterpillar.[14] The study prompted immediate concern for monarchs in the field because the annual migration of the butterflies takes them right through the U.S. corn belt. The monarch caterpillars would encounter the Bt corn pollen on the leaves of their favorite food, the milkweed, which grows in and around cornfields.

This study was important and received a great deal of publicity, because it was the first evidence that pollen from a GM plant can harm non-pest species. It also provided evidence that GM crops could have unforeseen effects on the environment. Subsequent studies have indicated that the risks may be minimal.[15] For instance, Mark Sears of the University of Guelph in Ontario found that Bt pollen does not travel far beyond the cornfields, and monarch caterpillars are unlikely to get sufficient doses of Bt corn pollen in the out of doors to be lethal.[16] In September of 2000, the EPA issued a preliminary report concluding that Bt corn is unlikely to pose a serious threat to monarch butterflies. This was followed by a final report released in July 2001 with the same conclusions.[17] Similar findings were reported in the *Proceedings of the National Academy of Sciences* in October 2001.[18]

In July 2004, a report entitled, *Safety of Genetically Engineered Foods: Approaches to Assessing Unintended Health Effects,* by the National Academy of Sciences was released. The report found that GM crops do not pose health risks that cannot also arise from conventional crops. The authors concluded that special food safety regulations were not needed, but noted that GM techniques could result in unintended harmful changes to the composition of food.[19]

Cultural Risks

As previously mentioned, the production of GM crops is concentrated in North America. Significant portions of all crop production in North America are exported. U.S. farmers export more than 25 percent of the corn, soybean and cotton they produce, and more than 50 percent of their wheat and rice.[20] Therefore, the manner in which these crops are produced will impact other cultures. The European Union countries have largely refused to import GM crops or have made importation difficult. At least one reason for their refusal is cultural differences. For instance, in France the ingredients, preparation, and consumption of food constitute a way of life. The French refer to their culinary sovereignty, so when you alter their food you affect their culture. In India, bollworm infestation in cotton plants has caused havoc. In Indian field tests, a GM cotton variety, modified to control bollworms, was showing promising results. Yet farmers, disturbed that their livelihoods may be threatened by these corporate biotech developments, burned the test plots in protest.[21]

While the potential benefits of GM crops for developing countries is appealing, critics charge that food production is not the problem; rather it is poverty and lack of adequate resources to purchase food that leads to famine and malnourishment. The world today produces more food per inhabitant than ever before. Enough is available to provide 4.3 pounds of food to every person every day: 2.5 pounds of grain, beans and nuts, about a pound of meat, milk and eggs, and another pound of fruits and vegetables.[22] The problems are distribution systems, the lack of financing to move food to regions needing it, and the inability of many individuals to purchase foods due to low incomes. Farmers in developing countries often would not be able to afford GM products made in developed countries.

There are also worries about corporate concentration and control of the seed and agricultural industries. The terminator technology that produced sterile seeds heightened these concerns despite the fact that Monsanto cancelled its efforts with this technology.[23] Issues still exist as to whether saving seeds for next year's crops violates licensing, patent and intellectual property rights. Monsanto has won millions of dollars from farmers in lawsuits and settlements. A statement by one farmer being sued by Monsanto captures the essence of the farmers' side of the litigation:

> "It's a God-given right that farmers were given when they were born to save seeds. All we are is farmers trying to scrape a living out of this dirt."[24]

Monsanto has had particularly difficult problems in Argentina, and more recently in Brazil. Argentina is the largest GM soybean market after the United States. Regulations have been quite lax in Argentina, where farmers save GM soy seeds and cut into Monsanto's sales.[25] In Brazil, the situation is complicated by the fact that until September 2003 Brazil has had a ban on GM crops, but black market sales and loose enforcement results in significant quantities of GM soybeans being grown.[26] Permission to use GM crops was granted in 2003 from a temporary decree issued by President Luiz Inácio Lula de Silva.[27] In March 2005, Brazil's lower house passed legalizing GM crops, following the Senate's approval in December 2004. With the President's signature, the bill becomes law.[28]

In poor countries, multiple nutritional deficiencies will dilute the benefits of GM crops like golden rice. Critics contend that these deficiencies will impede the effectiveness of vitamin A enhanced golden rice, and will also produce other nutritional problems.[29] Questions have been raised as to whether the profits generated by marketing GM crops to developing countries are sufficient to maintain commercial development. Products to date has been almost exclusively in big money crops, like soybeans, cotton, corn and canola, that are mostly of use to big commercial interests, and not necessarily the most useful crops for small local growers in developing countries.

A report in May 2004, by the United Nations Food and Agricultural Organization, on genetically modified crops noted that:

> "The technology, despite its promise, was not yet doing much to help feed the world's poor because it was not being applied to the sorts of crops grown in developing countries—like potatoes, cassava, rice, wheat, millet and sorghum."[30]

Others have countered that GM crops should be avoided altogether, and emphasis should be put on local, sustainable, cultural-compatible agricultural development, as is captured in a statement by an African delegation to the United Nations:

> "We do not believe that such companies or gene technologies will help our farmers to produce the food that is needed in the 21st century. On the contrary, we think it will destroy the diversity, the local knowledge and the sustainable agricultural systems that our farmers have developed for millennia and that it will thus undermine our capacity to feed ourselves."[31]

Ethical and Religious Risks

Genetic engineering raises the ethical issue of whether we should be altering nature. While conventional breeding techniques produced improved hybrid crops, these hybrids could have developed naturally. With GM crops, biological species boundaries are crossed. In natural circumstances, Bt bacteria genes would not move into corn plant cells and fish genes would not cross into tomatoes. This can occur only in the biotech laboratory with gene gun technology. Since GM crops are developed in the laboratory, questions of whether and how they fit into the natural world are being pondered. Many individuals and organizations are questioning whether, on an ethical basis, this should be done at all.

Even religious issues are being raised regarding GMOs. Many religions hold to the sanctity of the natural world—that humans are a part of the natural world and should fit harmoniously into it and should not artificially alter it. Pope John Paul II urged those who are developing new biotechnologies to keep a "healthy balance" with nature to avoid putting people's lives at risk. He urged rigorous scientific and ethical controls to avoid possible "disaster for the health of man and the future of the Earth" from new agricultural technologies. He further stated:

> "If the world of most refined techniques doesn't reconcile itself with the simple language of nature in a healthy balance, the life of man will run ever greater risks of which already we are seeing worrying signs."[32]

Environmental Genetic Pollution Risks

Genetic pollution of the environment is probably the biggest unknown with GM technology. Conventional types of pollution, like a chemical spill, can be cleaned up. A product like an automobile, which is defective, can be recalled. But if some unknown, unpredictable adverse effect results from GM crops, the effect could be uncontrollable, permanent and irreversible. The defective GM product would be out in the natural world and in all likelihood be unrecoverable.

Some adverse consequences can be tested in the laboratory or in a controlled experiment. For instance, Australian scientists accidentally discovered they could create a virus that kills mice by crippling their immune system. The scientists were attempting to make the mice infertile by adding a gene in the mouse's immune system to make the mouse immune to the pox virus. The experiment, which was controlled, had the unanticipated effect of making the virus deadly for mice normally resistant to the disease. The scientists were further surprised because past research had indicated that GM viruses were less virulent than their natural progenitors.[33]

If the adverse effect is delayed or unanticipated in a laboratory testing, it may occur when the GM product is used in the natural environment where its effects could be uncontrollable and irreversible. As noted by Charles Benbrook, agricultural consultant and former director of the board of agriculture for the National Academy of Sciences:

> "You don't mess around with the genetic base of a food production system as fundamentally as some of these biotech applications are, without causing some things to change. It is really scientific hubris to think that we understand all that, because we don't. This stuff is just horrendously complicated."[34]

Current research is beginning to produce evidence about problems that may exist with environmental genetic pollution. A British government field study of GM crops was released in the fall of 2003. The results "reveal significant differences in the effect on biodiversity when managing genetically herbicide tolerant crops as compared to conventional variety," according to Les Firbank, a co-coordinator of the project. Specifically, the study found that "the farming of some biotech crops could lead to significantly lower numbers of insects, an important link in the wildlife food chain."[35]

A report entitled, "Biological Confinement of Genetically Engineered Organisms," by the National Research Council of the National Academy of Sciences, was released in January 2004.[36] The report, which was commissioned by U.S. Department of Agriculture, examines bioconfinement methods for genetically engineered organisms. The research concludes that none of the methods to date appear to be completely effective. As noted by Professor Anne R. Kapuscinski, a member of the Committee from the University of Wisconsin:

> "One of our big messages throughout the whole report is that there are very few bioconfinement methods that are well developed."[37]

In February 2004, the Union of Concerned Scientists released a report that detected tiny quantities of GM seeds in bags of unmodified corn, soybean and canola seeds.[38] The mixings might have been done by farmers or seed companies, or from cross pollination of seed crops from nearby GM crops. The director of the study, Margaret Mellon, noted that the biggest health risk would occur if crops being tested for pharmaceutical producing genes were to get into seeds for food crops. As noted by Dr. Mellon:

"If the door to the seed supply is open to contamination, it is likely that drug genes will be able to pass through it, right to our breakfast tables."[39]

In commenting on the report, Frederick Kirschenmann, director of the Leopold Center for Sustainable Agriculture at Iowa State University, noted that organic farmers are experiencing difficulties obtaining seeds free of GM contamination. He further stated:

"If the current rate of seed contamination continues, then farmers that supply niche markets that do not allow any genetically modified materials will simply lose those markets."[40]

The problem of GM varieties spreading to unmodified varieties took a new turn with a study published in the September 2004 *Proceedings of the National Academy of Sciences*. The study measured the distances that pollen from the first developed GM grass could travel. The results found that GM bent grass pollinated test plants of the same species were 13 miles downwind, the furthest distance that was measured. Natural growths of wild grass of different species were pollinated at a distance up to nine miles. These results were totally unexpected in that previous studies had shown the maximum pollination distance to be one mile.[41]

In a report in the April 2004 issue of *New Scientist* magazine, researchers concluded that GM Soya in Argentina was causing an environmental crisis, damaging soil bacteria needed for breaking down vegetable matter and allowing herbicide resistant weeds to grow out of control. Ironically, farmers are now using twice as much herbicide for the herbicide resistant soya than for conventional soya. Most disturbing is that large farm groups, the main users of GM soya, have driven some 150,000 small farmers off the land. Production of needed local staples as milk, rice, maize, potatoes and lentils has fallen.[42]

Business Risks—Customers Won't Buy It

From a commercial development standpoint, all the risks discussed above may collectively augment the business risk that customers and markets will refuse to buy GM food products. Customers' refusal to buy a product is essentially the same as a product boycott. European consumers have been skeptical of GM foods since their early days of development. Just as GM foods were initially being cleared for import into European markets, the first mad cow disease scare hit in 1996. While GM foods are not related to mad cow disease, it generated new consumer anxieties about food safety. The scare also undermined consumer trust in regulatory and scientific opinion, as U.K. public health officials had given consumers assurances that there was no danger in eating beef from diseased animals.[43] While mad cow disease, or Bovine Spongiform Encephalopathy (BSE), had been discovered in Britain in the 1980s, it was not until 1996 that it was publicly announced that a possible connection may exist between BSE in cattle and Creuzfeld-Jacob Disease (CJD), a rare but fatal disease found among humans.[44] The problem of mad cow disease has spread to other European countries, as well as Canada and the United States, and currently is causing considerable consumer consternation and market disruptions.

In May of 1999, it was discovered that Belgium farm animals had been given dioxin-contaminated feed. This discovery resulted in the removal of Belgian chicken, eggs, pork and beef from the entire EU market. And in June of 1999, hundreds of French and Belgian residents were ill after drinking contaminated Coca-Cola. Recently, foot and mouth disease in cattle, while not posing a danger for humans, has raised further concerns among Europeans. Given this history and experience of food scares, it is not surprising that Europeans may be skeptical of any type of tampering with food, including genetic modifications. The scares have also seriously eroded the confidence of Europeans in their food-safety authorities.[45]

Consumers in the United States have been rather indifferent to GM foods, particularly compared to Europeans. For instance, in the United States, 70 percent of processed foods contains GM ingredients. Americans also have more confidence in governmental food regulators like the FDA.[46] But with the anti-GM foods activities and regulations in other countries gaining more and more attention, it seems likely that U.S. consumer attitudes could change.

Reputation Risks

Closely related to the business risk that customers will not buy GM foods is a firm's reputation risk. Firms and groups exposed to reputation risks include the GM technology companies, farmers, grain handlers, and food processors, manufacturers and retailers. Reputation is important to any organization, but food companies with strong brand power can suffer exceptional losses from reputation risks.

When customers consume a food product, particularly from a sealed package, bottle or can, they assume it is safe to eat. If one contaminated batch injures consumers, the adverse publicity and reputation damage can be severe. Recall the bankruptcy several years ago of the Bon Vivant Company following botulism poisoning in a batch of their canned soups. More recently, the contaminated Coke fiasco in Belgium and France mentioned above, particularly the effects on schoolchildren, tarnished Coke's worldwide image and reputation. While not a food company, the reputation damage to the Firestone and Ford Companies, from SUV rollover accidents caused by defective tires, demonstrates the considerable financial damages and the tarnishing of two of the oldest, most recognized brands in the U.S. that such an incident can cause.

While such potential GM risks as the "superbug," or "superweed," or severe allergic or toxic reactions, or other serious genetic pollution have not actually materialized on a large scale, the adverse effects on the reputation of any firms associated with such developments would be catastrophic. The fact that considerable warnings, criticism, and opposition will have preceded any such development will only aggravate reputation and potential liability losses.

Regulatory Risks

Companies face the regulatory risk that GM products may be prohibited or tightly controlled. Regulations of GM products in the United States has been relatively benign, particularly compared to Europe. In May of 1992, the FDA issued a policy statement: "The agency is not aware of any information showing that foods derived by these new methods differ from other foods in any meaningful or uniform way." The effect was that corporations would not need government approval to sell the crops they were developing. GM crops are considered to be "substantially equivalent" to those produced by conventional hybrid methods.[47]

Because of the increasing public debate on GM foods, the FDA, in January, 2001, proposed rules to make safety reviews of new GM foods mandatory before bringing the foods to the market. The rules stop short of mandatory approval of those reviews. The proposed rules should not impose many new burdens on the companies because they are already notifying and providing testing data to the agency voluntarily. Guidelines were also issued on how food companies could voluntarily label products that employ genetic engineering. While these proposed rules and guidelines represent a step up in regulation, many stakeholders argue for stronger requirements like mandatory approval, not just review, of new GM foods and mandatory labeling.[48]

Farmers and food producers in the United States have rigorously opposed labeling of GM foods. Their fear is that consumers will be reluctant to purchase foods with a GM label. Bob Callanan, a spokesman for the American Soybean Association states: "We think that's the equivalent of putting a skull and crossbones on the packages, saying these things are bad."[49] On the other hand, U.S. consumers strongly support labeling. A 2001 poll commissioned by the Pew Initiative on Food and Biotechnology found that 75 percent of people wanted to know whether their food contained products that were genetically altered.[50]

In contrast to the United States, European Union Directives have required both mandatory approval of GM crops before they can be planted (1990 EU Directive) and mandatory labeling of all packaged food that contains GM corn and soy (1998 EU Directive). The United Kingdom went even further, requiring the restaurants, caterers, and bakers list all GM ingredients or face fines up to $8,400. In April 1998, the EU stopped approving new GM crops for use in, or imported into, the EU.[51] Cultural differences, less trust in government regulators, and food-related scares discussed above contribute to greater societal pressure in EU countries than the United States to regulate GM crops and foods.

For the past several years, the EU has been working on a stricter set of regulations for GM products. The EU has been under considerable pressure from the United States and other countries that export GM crops to lift the moratorium on new GM products. In May, 2003, the United States filed a formal complaint with the World Trade Organization. Corn growers in the U.S. were particularly upset, as the National Corn Growers Association estimates losses of $300 million in annual GM corn exports to Europe. Soybean farmers were not as seriously affected as some types of GM soybeans had been approved before the moratorium went into effect. Finally, on April 18, 2004, new legislation was approved, which lead to the lifting of the ban on May 19, 2004. The new legislation calls for a stricter labeling requirement and a tough tracking system for GM products. A warning label is required for products on supermarket shelves if 0.9 percent or more of the ingredients comes from bioengineered food. Farmers and food packagers will have to track and maintain records on GM foods if they are destined to become ingredients for consumption in Europe.[52]

Tough regulatory stances are also present in a number of other countries. Japan and Korea have tightened approval procedures for GM varieties and require mandatory labeling of genetically modified seeds and foods. Australia and New Zealand announced in 1999 that they would require labeling of all GMO derived foods.[53] Thailand declared in mid-1999 that GM seeds would not be brought into the country until proven safe for human consumption. Some three dozen countries outside the EU have established a labeling system for GM products.[54] A number of developing countries support more restrictions on GM foods, as they fear that large corporations will develop too much power and control over seed technologies. Terminator crops that produce sterile seeds, and prevent farmers from saving seeds for next year's crops, is a case in point.

The Cartagena Protocol on Biosafety refers to the January 2000 agreement at the Montreal Round of international negotiations on the Convention on Biological Diversity (CBD). Most observers feel the agreement favors environmentalists and opponents of GM products over the U.S. and its allies, particularly with inclusion of the precautionary principle in the agreement. The precautionary principle holds that a country may restrict imports generally, and in this case GM imports specifically, if the country fears they could be harmful to biological diversity, and by extension to human health.[55] No GM products will be approved for trade until it is first proven safe. The burden of proof to show the product is safe is on the exporter, which in the case of GM products, is predominantly U.S. corporations and farmers. The European Union used the precautionary principle to justify decisions to ban imports and require labeling, as discussed above.

Interestingly, the precautionary principle is just the reverse of the World Trade Organization (WTO) rule, which forbids any nation from banning imports, unless it can be proven to a "scientific certainty" that products are unsafe. The burden of proof is on the importing country to show that the product is unsafe.[56] In the Montreal agreement, it is stated that national rejection of an imported GM product must be based on credible scientific evidence, and that the intention behind the agreement is not to supersede the WTO rules.[57] But clearly there will be further discussions/arguments to reconcile the seemingly contradictory positions of the Cartagena Protocol and WTO rules.

Risk Management and Insurance Strategies

The risk management and insurance issues associated with GM risks are challenging. The above discussion has demonstrated the expanded scope of GM risks. These risks have the potential of creating significant long-tail liability events. Innovation and creativity will be needed to address the risk assessment, control and financing issues associated with GM risks, and will provide substantial business opportunities.

In dealing with GM products, risk assessment and control techniques are critical. GM risks include potential consequences that have been described as unknown, irreversible and uncontrollable. While the U.S., EU, CBD, and WTO debate use of the precautionary principle, the author would suggest that risk managers across these forums reach fundamental agreement that the use of the precautionary principle is most appropriate in managing GM risks. CEOs of companies dealing with GM products should have sustainability risk management as a critical part of their overall development strategies.

Avoidance

Avoidance is a risk management control tool that often cannot be utilized for obvious practical reasons. For instance, if you are a manufacturer of automobiles, you cannot avoid the product liability risk if you are going to be in automotive business. The only way to avoid the risk would be not to manufacture automobiles, which of course would eliminate your entire concept of being in this business. On the other hand, avoidance can be a very practical tool for developers and users of GM technology, as firms have a choice.

In response to concerns related to GM foods and grains, several companies have chosen to avoid their use to eliminate potential damages, particularly from reputational risks and business risks. Gerber and then Heinz announced in the summer of 1999 that they would use only non-GM products in their baby foods.[58] In January 2000, Frito-Lay announced that it would stop using GM corn in its Fritos, Doritos, and Tostitos chips.[59] In Spring 2000, McDonald's began quietly telling their french fry suppliers to stop using potatoes from Monsanto, the only firm to commercialize a GM spud.[60]

Additional examples include Japan's two major breweries, Kirin and Sapporo, food giants Unilever, Nestle, and Seagrams, and Grupo Maseca, Mexico's largest tortilla maker.[61] In the United Kingdom, major food manufacturer and retailer, Sainsbury's, introduced the policy in 1999 of eliminating GM ingredients in its brand products. Marks and Spencer, also in the United Kingdom, ordered a total ban in 1999 on GM foods in all its stores.[62] Three of the largest natural food chains in the United States, Wild Oats Markets, Whole Foods Markets, and Trader Joe's, also plan to eliminate GM ingredients from their store brand products.[63] In all these situations, reasonable options exist as comparable non-GM ingredients are available.

In addition to food manufacturers and retailers, the U.S. agricultural sector has been reluctant to expand GM varieties of other crops. For example, Monsanto has developed a GM variety of wheat, Roundup Ready wheat, but decided not to introduce it due to concerns of wheat growers. Wheat farmers encountered resistance from both domestic and foreign customers. Jim Bair, Vice President of the North American Miller Association, expressed concern that "Biotech wheat offered plenty of risk for flour and bread makers, and retailers."[64] The risk is that consumers of bread and other wheat based products will not buy these products if made with GM wheat. The U.S. exports about one half of its wheat crop.[65] Concern about GM wheat from major import markets, including Japan and the EU, resulted in groups like the U.S. Wheat Association, an export marketing farmer funded trade group, to praise Monsanto's decision. Some wheat buyers indicated they would not buy GM wheat, while others threatened not to buy any wheat because it would be impossible to keep the GM and non-GM wheat from intermingling.[66]

Andrew Pollack, reporter for the *New York Times,* has reported extensively on GM crops. He points out that the GM industry has had difficulty marketing GM crops beyond the four main GM crops, soybeans, corn, cotton and canola. Pollack notes that "These crops are also largely used for animal feed, clothing or to make oil and other ingredients for processed foods rather than eaten directly—something that has helped them gain acceptance." Wheat on the other hand is largely used for food. The same is true of a wide variety of fruits and vegetables that have GM varieties developed in laboratories and field trials, but have not been introduced into markets because of potential customer resistance.[67]

Risk Financing

The impact of GM risks on risk financing can only be estimated as few claims have been filed. The Aventis/StarLink corn and Advanta/rape cases, the two most prominent GM risk events, will be discussed below. A few generalizations can be made. A substantial portion of GM risk financing will be retained rather than transferred/insured by GM firms. Most firms would carry product liability insurance, although deductibles/SIRs for larger firms could be in the millions of dollars. If GM seeds, crops, or foods cause bodily injuries or property damages, it would seem that, absent some nonstandard exclusion, these claims would be covered by products liability insurance. While products recall insurance is available, most firms do not carry this coverage so few of those claims would be insured. No insurance exists for the risk of customers not buying GM products. Neither are damages to a firm's reputation insured.

The case of StarLink corn is the most dramatic example of adverse financial and risk-related effects that can arise from the commercialization of GM products. Costs are estimated to be in the hundreds of millions of dollars. Several liability suits have been initiated. Executives have been fired and the reputation of Aventis, which developed StarLink, has been adversely impacted.

StarLink corn is a GM crop with a genetically inserted pesticidal bacterial protein known as Cry9C. It is similar to Bt corn in that it has been genetically modified to produce its own insecticide. The EPA approved StarLink corn only for animal consumption. The EPA decided in 1997 that Aventis' technology should be kept directly out of human food production because laboratory tests indicated that the protein might cause food allergies.[68] StarLink is the only GM corn that is not approved for use in U.S. food consumed by humans.

In the fall of 2000, StarLink corn was discovered in Taco Bell brand taco shells and other products of at least two food manufacturers, Kraft Foods and Mission Foods. The discovery was actually made in laboratory tests at Genetic ID, which were paid for by the Friends of the Earth. It was announced at a September 18, 2000 press conference covered by Genetically Engineered Food Alert, a coalition of environmental and consumer groups.[69] After these discoveries, the two manufacturers recalled their taco shells and other corn products from grocers' shelves. Several corn millers were forced to suspend operations to clean their facilities.[70] The Kellogg Company closed several lines at a cereal manufacturing plant in Memphis, Tennessee because a supplier could not guarantee its corn was free of a GM-modified grain.[71] Some 35 reports of adverse health effects from StarLink corn, experienced by 44 consumers, came in a two-month period following the discovery of StarLink in Kraft Foods taco shells.[72]

Aventis Crop Science, a U.S. subsidiary of Aventis, the French pharmaceutical and agricultural company, is incurring substantial costs related to its StarLink corn. While Aventis received less than a million dollars in licensing fees on StarLink, it is estimated that its cost to resolve the issue would be in the hundreds of millions of dollars. No future revenues are forthcoming as Aventis has withdrawn its license for future sales.[73] Farmers whose crops were contaminated are being reimbursed under a U.S. Department of Agriculture program in 17 states that is funded by Aventis. Aventis has promised to find markets for StarLink corn and farmers are being offered a 25-cent premium per bushel over the market cost of corn. Aventis also has pledged to compensate grain elevator owners and grain handlers for expenses related to the effort to keep StarLink corn out of the food chain.[74]

Aventis faces substantial costs in the future. A class action suit, involving several hundred thousand farmers who produced clean corn, but contend they lost overseas revenues because of damage to the U.S. corn supply, has been filed.[75] Another group of farmers who did not plant StarLink corn, but whose corn was contaminated by StarLink corn, is suing for damages.[76] In June 2004, a class action lawsuit against Aventis was concluded with a settlement of $112 million to some of the affected farmers.[77] Consumer suits have also been filed alleging allergic-type injuries from the StarLink corn.[78] Nearly every major food and agricultural company is testing for Cry9C from StarLink, so further recalls and expenses could result.

Aventis sought temporary approval of StarLink from the EPA to mitigate further recall and testing costs. A hearing and report by a federal advisory panel of scientists found there was a medium likelihood that StarLink is a potential allergen. It recommended more tests, which the EPA said would be conducted, so any approval at best is in the future.[79] Finally, Aventis fired the head of its U.S. crop-science division and two other top managers in the wake of the StarLink debacle.[80]

The StarLink corn case has several risk financing implications. Unless Kraft Foods and Mission Foods had products recall insurance, their substantial recall costs would not be insured. Kraft and Mission may file actions against Aventis, but Aventis products liability coverage is questionable because of restrictions in the definition of the property damages, and the impaired property exclusion. Voluntary payments by Aventis to farmers and grain owners/handlers, because of the mixing of StarLink corn with non-StarLink corn, would not seem to fall under products liability or products recall coverage. Consumer suits for allergic-type injuries would be the most obvious products liability covered claims. Farmers' claims that their non-StarLink corn crops were contaminated by a neighboring farmer's StarLink crop could be covered under the neighboring farmer's premises and operations coverage or Aventis' products liability insurance. The Kraft recall of StarLink corn-contaminated taco shells is the first of its kind in the United States, so clearly we are at the beginning of sorting out and resolving the risk financing issues.

Advanta/rape, the most prominent case in Europe, also happened in 2000, and involves a situation similar to the StarLink developments. Advanta, a Dutch seed supplier, announced on May 17, that some batches of its non-GM varieties of oilseed rape, also know as canola, imported from Canada tested positive for a very low-level presence—less than one percent—of Monsanto's RT73 GM rape. The seeds had already been sown in rape fields in the United Kingdom, Sweden, France, and Germany. The Swedish and French governments ordered farmers to destroy affected crops, while food retailers in the United Kingdom refused to stock products made from the affected rape. The British government has said that farmers will not be able to sell the crop. A spokesman from NFU Mutual, which insures two-thirds of U.K. farmers, stated that, "It is not clear what liabilities there are in this issue and whose they would be, because it is a completely new situation." An Advanta spokesman stated that, "We are continuously talking to our insurer, but this is new territory."[81]

These statements re-emphasize that, from the standpoint of risk financing and liability insurance, we are in brand new, unchartered waters. Farmers would seem to have an action against Advanta, although whether Advanta's products liability coverage applies is questionable. Products recall may be impossible as the seed is already in the ground. The farmers' case against Advanta could be complicated by the fact that the rape seed contained less than one percent GM rape, which is the minimum standard for required labeling. Advanta, of course, may have an action against Monsanto. Again, there are a number of liability and insurance coverages issues that will need to be worked out.

Long-Tail Genetic Pollution Risks

Long-tail genetic pollution risks may be the most potentially damaging risks from a risk financing standpoint. Genetic pollution differs from chemical and oil spills in that the consequences may be irreversible and uncontrollable. The worst-case scenario would be the occurrence of a superbug or superweed or some other deleterious form of genetic pollution, but one that took a long time to be discovered. The risk financing claims could be enormous. The asbestos and Superfund risk situations, which were examined in a previous chapter, provide an indication of what might happen in the case of a serious case of genetic pollution.

The GM technology firm would be subject to extensive discovery actions with their own data/records serving as the basis of a liability suit as happened in the tobacco litigation. Once the event has happened, it would be reasonably easy to establish foreseeability to determine negligence by the GM firm, given the considerable opposition, warnings and questions raised about GM products. Insurers may be somewhat protected by claims-made policies, which would limit the time period in which they must respond. Given that many of the GM technology firms are chemical and pharmaceutical firms they may already have claims-made rather than occurrence based coverage in force.

The damage to a GM technology or user firm from a major liability case involving serious genetic pollution could be enormous. It could result in bankruptcy, particularly given the limitations on the various insurance coverages discussed above. Clearly, there is no insurance for the damage to a firm's reputation, but the financial losses could be considerable. D&O coverage may apply if it is held that the action of the directors and officers, in getting involved in GM technology, was a wrongful act that caused stockholders or customers losses. Given the newness of all these risk situations, the defense costs, both insured and uninsured, would be expected to be considerable.

The Future

Risk management of GM technology is a dynamic process. Additional information, data, and evaluations will be required before the risks and benefits of GM crops can be fully measured. In the past few years, three scientific studies, which have not yet been discussed here, were produced. In April 2000, the National Research Council of the National Academies of Sciences and Engineering released a report entitled, *Genetically Modified Pest-Protected Plants: Science and Regulation.*[82] In December 2000, Dr. LaReesa Wolfenbarger, an ecologist at the EPA, and Dr. Paul Phifer, a conservation biologist at the State Department, published a study in *Science*[83] that some scientists say is the first comprehensive review of the published scientific data on GM crops. In February 2001, a huge decade-long study on environmental risks of GM crops, led by Dr. Mick Crawley, an ecologist at Imperial College London, was published in *Nature.*[84] While the reader is encouraged to review these studies, their principal message is that the documented risks to human health and to the environment to date are minimal. But all three studies called for further research, review, and monitoring. In essence, while significant GM risks to date have not materialized and been documented, it cannot be concluded that risks will not develop in the future.

It has frequently been suggested that had governments and producers of GM foods and crops clearly defined benefits to consumers, particularly in developed countries, they might have been more successful. But the benefits to date have gone largely to GM firms and farmers, so when perceived risks are presented to customers, it is easy for them to switch to non-GM foods. In developing countries, if the choice was between GM crops and starvation, the benefits would clearly exceed perceived risks.

With the exception of the Aventis/StarLink corn and Advanta/oilseed rape cases, no other significant risk events have materialized involving GM products. As discussed above, both these cases are largely unresolved regarding liability and insurance coverage issues. While some insurance coverages will most likely be available, it is expected that a substantial portion of the financial losses will be uninsured. Risk managers of GM technology and user firms will need to monitor these two events and others that may develop. Risk managers or their staff also need to monitor studies on GM risks, such as the three noted above.

The regulation of GM products, both domestically and internationally, is also a fluid process. The National Academies' report, referenced above, called on the EPA, USDA, and FDA to quickly come to an agreement on each agency's role in regulating GM products. The USDA decision that GM foods could not carry the label "organic" is a proxy for GM-free labeling. Legislation to require labeling of GM foods has been introduced in Congress and some state legislatures.[85] International regulations will put further pressure on labeling requirements. In addition, a panel of international experts, called the U.S.-EU Biotechnology Consultative Forum, recommended safety reviews and mandatory labeling for GM foods.[86]

The old adage that the "consumer is king" will be important in the development and regulation of GM products. The reluctance of Europeans to use GM products has been noted. Lydia Zepeda, a consumer science professor at the University of Wisconsin, reports that U.S. organic sales are soaring in large part because of the demand by consumers for foods free of GM ingredients. She also called for consistent international labeling standards, which she feels will help both GM and non-GM products.[87] As in all areas, risk managers need to be aware of changing regulations and their impact on the firm's risk management strategies.

The lessons and issues involving the risk management of GM products should be applied to related biotechnology areas like pharmaceuticals and the human genome. GM technology in pharmaceutical development and human gene manipulation present more obvious benefits to consumers than GM foods. Elimination of life threatening/debilitating diseases or reduction of their consequences clearly are benefits. Yet the risks also achieve a higher dimension. Among these risks are the direct adverse human side effects of a new drug and the ethical risks associated with manipulation of human genes. In addition, injuries can result from gene therapy, as shown by the death of a patient at the University of Pennsylvania's Institute for Human Gene Therapy.[88]

Sustainability risk management of biotechnology risks involves traditional risk areas like products liability and product recall. But it also deals with an expanded scope of potential risks that delve into ethical, cultural, even religious issues. The potential environmental risk of genetic pollution differs from say chemical and oil spills in that consequences may be irreversible and uncontrollable. Traditional cleanup and restoration techniques may not be effective against genetic pollution. Reputation and business risks impact all businesses, but they take on an extra dimension in biotechnology firms.

Biotech risks must be managed from a global perspective. Various international trade rules and protocols must be observed. Biotech firms face both domestic and international regulations. Finally, biotechnology is a dynamic and evolving scientific and business endeavor. As biotechnology is at the cutting edge so too must sustainability risk management efforts respond with innovative solutions and strategies.

CHAPTER 8—ENDNOTES

[1] Juan Enriquez and Ray A. Goldberg, "Transforming Life, Transforming Business: The Life-Science Revolution," *Harvard Business Review,* Vol. 78, March/April 2000.

[2] I have explored the risk management of GM crops in two previous articles: Dan R. Anderson, "Biotechnology Risk Management: The Case of Genetically Modified Organisms (GMOs)," *CPCU Journal,* Vol. 54, No. 4, Winter 2001; Dan R. Anderson, "Environmental Risk Management: A Critical Part of Corporate Strategy," *The Geneva Papers on Risk and Insurance,* Vol. 27, No. 2, April 2002. Some of the material from these two articles was used in writing parts of this chapter.

[3] Phillip Frazer, "The Genetically Engineered Food Fight," *News on Earth,* December 1998.

[4] "Risk Reporter: Trendy Genes," *Risk Management,* Vol. 45, No. 11, November 1998.

[5] Parts of this section from Andrew Pollack, "Narrow Path for New Biotech Food Crops," *New York Times,* May 20, 2004; Scott Miller, "EU's New Rule will Shake Up Market for Bioengineered Food," *Wall Street Journal,* April 16, 2004.

[6] Robert Paarlberg, "The Global Food Fight," *Foreign Affairs,* Vol. 79, May/June 2000.

[7] Scott Miller, "EU's New Rules Will Shake Up Market for Bioengineered Food," *Wall Street Journal,* April 16, 2004.

[8] Niki Denison, "Harvesting the Double Helix," *On Wisconsin,* Fall 1999.

[9] Joanne Jacobs, "Fear Is Killing the Future of Food," *Wisconsin State Journal,* March 8, 2000; Andrew Pollack, "We Can Engineer Nature. But Should We?" *New York Times,* February 6, 2000.

[10] David Stipp, "The Voice of Reason in the Global Food Fight," *Fortune,* Vol. 141, February 21, 2000.

[11] United Nations Food and Agriculture Organization, "Agricultural Biotechnology Meeting the Needs of the Poor," 2004.

[12] Julie A. Nordlee, Steve L. Taylor, Jeffrey A. Townsend, Laurie A. Thomas, and Robert K. Bush, "Identification of a Brazil-Nut Allergen in Transgenic Soybeans," *The New England Journal of Medicine*, Vol. 334, No. 11, March 14, 1996.

[13] Niki Denison, "Harvesting the Double Helix," *On Wisconsin*, Fall 1999.

[14] John E. Losey, Linda S. Rayor, and Maureen E. Carter, "Transgenic Pollen Harms Monarch Larvae," *Nature*, Vol. 399, May 20, 1999.

[15] Carol Kaesuk Yoon, "Biotech Corn Isn't Serious Threat to Monarch Butterflies," *New York Times*, September 26, 2000.

[16] "Biotech Foes Experience a Setback," *Wisconsin State Journal*, November 8, 1999.

[17] U.S. Environmental Protection Agency, "Bt Plant-Pesticides Biopesticides Registration Action Document," Washington D.C.: USEPA, July 2001.

[18] Mark K. Sears, et. al., "Impact of Bt corn pollen on monarch butterfly populations: A risk assessment," *Proceedings of the National Academy of Sciences*, Vol. 98, No. 21, October 9, 2001.

[19] Andrew Pollack, "Panel See No Unique Risk From Genetic Engineering," *New York Times*, July 28, 2004; Institute of Medicine and National Research Council of the National Academies, *Safety of Genetically Engineered Foods: Approaches to Assessing Unintended Health Effects*, Washington D.C.: The National Academies Press, 2004.

[20] Robert Paarlberg, "The Global Food Fight," *Foreign Affairs*, Vol. 79, May/June 2000.

[21] Ibid.

[22] Peter Rosset, "Why Genetically Altered Food Won't Conquer Hunger," *New York Times,* September 1, 1999.

[23] "The Outcry Over 'Terminator' Genes," *Business Week,* July 14, 2003.

[24] Adam Liptak, "Saving Seeds Subjects Farmers to Suits Over Patent," *New York Times,* November 2, 2003.

[25] Tony Smith, "Argentina Soy Exports Are Up But Monsanto Is Not Amused," *New York Times,* January 21, 2004.

[26] Alan Clendenning, "Brazilian farmers get rich using illegal soybean seeds," Associated Press printed in *Wisconsin State Journal,* December 21, 2003.

[27] Larry Rohter, "Planting-Time Soy Quandary for Brazil," *New York Times,* October 13, 2004.

[28] Todd Benson, "Brazil Passes Law Allowing Crops with Modified Genes," *New York Times,* March 4, 2005.

[29] Andrew Pollack and Carol Kaesuk Yoon, "Rice Genome Called a Crop Breakthrough," *New York Times,* January 27, 2001.

[30] Andrew Pollock, "Narrow Path for New Biotech Food Crops," *New York Times,* May 20, 2004; United Nations Food and Agricultural Organization "Executive Summary: Report of the Expert Consultation on Environmental Effects of Genetically Modified Crops," Rome, Italy, 16—18 June 2003.

[31] Statement of 24 African delegates to the Food and Agriculture Organization of the United Nations, June 1998.

[32] Frances D'Emilio, "Pope Is Wary of Bio-Farming," *Wisconsin State Journal,* November 13, 2000.

[33] William J. Broad, "Australians Create a Deadly Mouse Virus," *New York Times,* January 23, 2001.

[34] Niki Denison, "Harvesting the Double Helix," *On Wisconsin,* Fall 1999.

[35] Scott Miller, "Biotech Crop Study May Stir Critics," *Wall Street Journal,* October 17, 2003; L. G. Firbank, "The Farm Scale Evaluations of spring-sown genetically modified crops: Introduction." *Philosophical Transactions of the Royal Society of London B* 358, Nov. 29, 2003.

[36] National Research Council of the National Academies, "Biological Confinement of Genetically Engineered Organisms," Washington D.C., The National Academies Press, 2004.

[37] Andrew Pollack, "No Foolproof Way Is Seen To Contain Altered Genes," *New York Times,* January 21, 2004.

[38] Union of Concerned Scientists, "Genetically Engineered DNA Found in Traditional Seeds," February 23, 2004.

[39] Andrew Pollack, "Modified Seeds Found Amid Unmodified Crops," *New York Times,* February 24, 2004.

[40] Ibid.

[41] Lidia S. Watrud, et.al., "Evidence for landscape-level, pollen-mediated gene flow from genetically modified creeping bentgrass with *CP4 EPSPS* as a marker," *Proceedings of the National Academy of Sciences,* September 24, 2004; Andrew Pollack, "Genes From Engineered Grass Spread for Miles, Study Finds," *New York Times,* September 21, 2004.

[42] Paul Brown, "GM Soya Miracle turns sour in Argentina," *The Guardian,* April 16, 2004.

[43] Robert Paarlberg, "The Global Food Fight," *Foreign Affairs,* Vol. 79, May/ June 2000.

[44] Mark A. Pollack and Gregory C. Shaffer, "Genetically Modified Organisms: Why the United States Is Avoiding a Trade War," *LaFollette Policy Report,* Vol. 11, No. 2, Fall 2000.

[45] Ibid.

[46] "Business: Hybrid Rigour," *The Economist,* London, Vol. 352, September 11, 1999.

[47] Federal Drug Administration, Policy Statement on GM Products, May 1992.

[48] Andrew Pollack, "F.D.A. Plans New Scrutiny in Areas of Biotechnology," *New York Times,* January 18, 2001.

[49] Elizabeth Becker, "Battle Over Biotechnology Intensifies Trade War," *New York Times,* May 29, 2003.

[50] Lee Bergquist, "More genetically modified foods cropping up," *Milwaukee Journal,* April 27, 2003.

[51] Robert Paarlberg, "The Global Food Fight," *Foreign Affairs,* Vol. 79, May/June 2000.

[52] Parts of this section from Scott Miller, "EU's New Rules Will Shake Up Market for Bioengineered Food," *Wall Street Journal,* April 16, 2004; Andrew Pollack, "Narrow Path for New Biotech Food Crops," *New York Times,* May 20, 2004.

[53] Mark A. Pollack and Gregory C. Shaffer, "Genetically Modified Organisms: Why the United States Is Avoiding a Trade War," *LaFollette Policy Report,* Vol. 11, No. 2, Fall 2000.

[54] Bill Lambrecht, "Food & Gene Giants Dread New EU Labeling Laws on GMOs," *St. Louis Post—Dispatch,* April 18, 2004.

[55] "Global Deal on GM Food Trade," *Geographical,* Vol. 72, April 2000.

[56] Ron Sullivan, "Biosafety Protocol Compromise," *Earth Island Journal,* Vol. 15, Summer 2000.

[57] Frederick H. Buttel, "The World Trade Organization and the New Politics of GMOs: Will GMOs Be the Achilles' Heel of the Globalization Regime?" Pre-

sented at the annual meeting of the Rural Sociological Society, Washington, D.C., August 2000.

[58] Gerald C. Nelson, et.al., "The Economics and Politics of Genetically Modified Organisms in Agriculture: Implications for WTO 2000," University of Illinois at Urbana-Champaign, College of Agricultural, Consumer and Environmental Sciences, Office of Research, Bulletin 809, November 1999.

[59] David Barboza, "Modified Foods Put Companies in a Quandary," *New York Times,* June 4, 2000.

[60] Scott Kilman, "McDonald's, Other Fast-Food Chains Pull Monsanto's Bio-Engineered Potato," *Wall Street Journal,* April 28, 2000.

[61] Mark A. Pollack and Gregory C. Shaffer, "Genetically Modified Organisms: Why the United States Is Avoiding a Trade War," *LaFollette Policy Report,* Vol. 11, No. 2, Fall 2000.

[62] Gerald C. Nelson, et.al., "The Economics and Politics of Genetically Modified Organisms in Agriculture: Implications for WTO 2000," University of Illinois at Urbana-Champaign, College of Agricultural, Consumer and Environmental Sciences, Office of Research, Bulletin 809, November 1999.

[63] David Stipp, "Is Monsanto's Biotech Worth Less than a Hill of Beans?" *Fortune,* Vol. 141, February 21, 2000.

[64] Bill Tomson, "Retreat on Gene-Altered Wheat Relieves U.S. Millers, Exporters," *Wall Street Journal,* June 1, 2004.

[65] Scott Kilman, "Monsanto Drops Plans for now to make Bioengineered Wheat," *Wall Street Journal,* May 11, 2004.

[66] Andrew Pollack, "Monsanto Shelves Plan for Modified Wheat," *New York Times,* May 11, 2004.

[67] Andrew Pollack, "Narrow Path for New Biotech Food Crops," *New York Times,* May 20, 2004.

[68] Barnaby J. Feder, "Company Says Tracing Problem Corn May Take Weeks," *New York Times,* November 24, 2000.

[69] Matt Crenson, "StarLink Just Slid Through Cracks," *Wisconsin State Journal,* December 3, 2000.

[70] Phillip Brasher, "Biotech Corn Clearance Urged," *Wisconsin State Journal,* October 26, 2000.

[71] Lisa Collins, "Cereal Production Cut," *Wisconsin State Journal,* October 22, 2000.

[72] Andrew Pollack, "Plan for Use of Bioengineered Corn in Food Is Disputed," *New York Times,* November 29, 2000.

[73] David Barboza, "Gene Altered Corn Changes Dynamics of Grain Industry," *New York Times,* December 11, 2000.

[74] Michael Bradford, "Farmers Sue over Modified Corn," *Business Insurance,* January 1, 2001.

[75] Ibid.

[76] David Barboza, "Negligence Suit Is Filed over Altered Corn," *New York Times,* December 4, 2000.

[77] "U.S. Farmers to Get $112 Million for GE Starlink Corn Contamination," www.organicconsumers.org, July 16, 2004.

[78] Betsy McCay, "Cost of StarLink Corn Recall May Reach Hundreds of Millions as First Suit Is Filed," *Wall Street Journal,* November 3, 2000.

[79] Andrew Pollack, "Federal Panel Is Wary on Gene-Altered Corn," *New York Times,* December 6, 2000.

[80] Vanessa Fuhrmans, "Three Top Officials of Aventis Division in U.S. Are Fired," *Wall Street Journal,* February 12, 2001.

[81] Carolyn Aldred, "Tainted Seed Uproar Yields New Questions on Liability," *Business Insurance,* June 5, 2000.

[82] National Research Council, National Academies of Sciences and Engineering, *Genetically Modified Pest-Protected Plants: Science and Regulation,* Washington, D.C., National Academy Press, 2000.

[83] L.L. Wolfenbarger and P.R. Phifer, "The Ecological Risks and Benefits of Genetically Engineered Plants," *Science,* Vol. 290, No. 5499, December 15, 2000.

[84] M.J. Crawley, S.L. Brown, R.S. Hails, D.D. Kohn, and M. Rees, "Transgenic Crops in Natural Habitats," *Nature,* Vol. 409, February 8, 2001.

[85] Brian Mattmiller, "Labeling Genetically Modified Food Could Boost U.S. Farm Economy," *Wisconsin Week,* February 28, 2001.

[86] Sarah Lueck and Scott Kilman, "Gene-Altered Food Needs Labels, Safety Reviews, Committee Says," *Wall Street Journal,* December 19, 2000.

[87] Brian Mattmiller, "Labeling Genetically Modified Food Could Boost U.S. Farm Economy," *Wisconsin Week,* February 28, 2001.

[88] Chris Adams, "Gene-Therapy Death Sparks Investigations," *Wall Street Journal,* January 24, 1999.

9

SUSTAINABILITY RISK MANAGEMENT

○ ○

Negligence is described as doing the same thing over and over even though you know it is dangerous, stupid or wrong. Now that we know, it's time for a change. Negligence starts tomorrow.

— *Bill McDonough and Michael Braungart, authors of* **Cradle to Cradle**

Interface will be environmentally sustainable. But our mission is larger. We will also be financially sustainable, for the simple reason that our corporation must survive and that we must assure the livelihood of our associates and the investment of all our stakeholders. We will be socially sustainable, respecting the communities in which we work, positively influencing all those whose lives we touch, and taking care not to deplete the human spirit on which we depend... Our sustainability goals-financial, social and environmental-are inextricably bound together, which is why we make such a point of doing well by doing good.

— *Ray Anderson, CEO, Interface*

Developing and implementing a sustainability risk management program is a challenging process. Risk managers have traditionally dealt with more reasonably defined risks. For instance, risk management actions might include constructing a building to meet HPR (Highly Protected Risks) standards to lower the danger of fire damage, or incorporating work safety systems to hold down workers compensation costs, or requiring a defensive driving course to reduce automobile accidents. When managing sustainability risks, one often has to deal with hugely complicated problems like the effects of greenhouse gas emissions on climate change, the consequences of small exposures of a chemical on human health, the working conditions of employees in a developing country, or the impact of reducing biodiversity in ecological systems. These are long term, multidisciplinary, global, and difficult risk situations. There are no straightforward checklists or flow charts that a firm and its risk management department can use for sustainability risk assessment, control and financing. Each firm will need to devote the time and energy to develop systems to meet their own particular circumstances.

The strategy in the next two chapters will be to provide general guidelines for developing sustainability risk management systems. Numerous examples, information sources and facilitating organizations will be presented. The objective is to present an overall framework for sustainability risk management that can be employed by risk managers and others involved parties to develop sustainability risk management systems for their respective firms. The present chapter will focus on the risk management process, including sustainability risk assessment and risk control. The next chapter will be devoted to sustainability risk financing, including insurance and other alternative risk financing techniques.

Sustainability Risk Management Process

Environmental and social justice risks were largely ignored by both business and society until roughly the last 35 years. In the environmental area, natural resources were extracted without limits and businesses polluted at will. The general attitude was that natural systems had an inexhaustible capacity to supply resources and to absorb pollutants and waste. No accountability existed for the costs of environmental damages. Environmental costs were externalized. There was a virtual zero cost of production and a zero cost of risk regarding the maintenance of environmental quality. Environmental risk management was for all practical purposes non-existent.

Similarly in the social justice area, human rights abuses of workers by foreign governments, working conditions and pay levels of employees in the factories of overseas suppliers, differences in pay and promotions between men and women, and the absence of corporate responsibility efforts beyond making a profit, generally did not produce risk consequences for businesses. Many of these issues were felt to be the responsibility of the government and not business. A near zero cost of risk existed for social justice concerns and social justice risk management was essentially non-existent.

Today, the significance of risks associated with environmental quality and social justice has clearly come to the forefront of concern for risk managers, their insurers, top executives and boards of directors. Corporations are faced with incredible challenges in responding to the need to develop and implement sound sustainability risk management systems for dealing with these risks. But with challenges comes enormous opportunities for both risk managers and the companies for which they work.

The risk management process is ideally suited for dealing with the various sustainability risks discussed in this book. While the risks are not new, the realization that corporations are going to be held accountable and pay for the consequences of these risks has only recently been accepted. Responding to this challenge provides a huge opportunity for risk managers. If they can help lead the efforts, as they should, in developing effective sustainability risks management systems, their responsibility and stature within their firms will undoubtedly rise. Given their expertise, risk managers are the best equipped to deal with mitigating sustainability risk costs. Insurers, brokers, and consultants, who provide risk services and products to businesses and organizations, will also find considerable business opportunities.

It will be important for risk managers and others to be creative and take the initiative to involve themselves in developing sustainability risk management systems. A large number of risk managers seem to be out of the environmental loop. As reported in the 1997 *Cost of Risk Survey,* risk managers have primary responsibility for environmental risk control/engineering (claims management) in only 31 percent (39.7 percent) of those firms surveyed; for safety/security departments in only 23 percent (12.8 percent) of firms surveyed; for operations departments in only 27.6 percent (12.4 percent) of surveyed firms; and for the legal area in only 11 percent (26.6 percent), of the surveyed firms.[1]

The experience of David Dybdahl, past managing director of Willis' Environmental Risk Management Services, and currently a leading environmental risk consultant, confirms these results, namely that risk managers are often not involved in the environmental area.[2] Even if risk managers are not directly involved in the environmental and social justice areas in their corporation, I would argue that risk managers still have the responsibility to anticipate all risks that may adversely impact the firm, not just the ones for which they have primary responsibility. But with this responsibility comes an enormous opportunity for risk managers to become more involved with the overall strategic management of the corporation.

Corporations that take the lead in dealing effectively with sustainability risks will gain competitive advantage, minimize reputation damage, decrease costs and increase long-term profits. Sustainability requires running businesses much differently than before. New production, distribution, manufacturing and marketing systems will all be needed. Developing and implementing sustainability risk management systems can produce win-win business opportunities. Corporations can maintain long-term growth and profitability, and environmental quality and social justice conditions can be improved.

Sustainability Risk Assessment

Risk managers employ risk assessment techniques to identify and evaluate potential losses facing the firm. Risk assessment is the first step in the risk management process. If potential loss situations are not properly identified and evaluated, then loss control and financing tools cannot be used to mitigate these risks. Risk managers are trained to employ such risk assessment techniques as flow charts, fault tree analysis, questionnaires, checklists financial statement, inspections, interviews, and records of past losses. Along with top executives, risk managers often have the best understanding of the scope and diversity of the corporation's operations.

Assessing environmental and social risks will require a great deal more creativity. As a starting point, sustainability risks must become a priority in the risk assessment process. As noted by an Association of British Insurers study, *Investing in Social Responsibility: Risks and Opportunities,* "Social, ethical and environmental (SEE)) risks are part of that management challenge, but they have typically not been systematically included in established risk assessment work in most companies."[3]

New tools will be needed beyond those that have been used for assessing more conventional risks. It might be prudent to review the first five chapters of this book. In Chapter 1, I was focusing on the deteriorating conditions of some of the earth's major ecosystems, like the oceans, fisheries, fresh water, and forests. I also examined biodiversity losses, exposures to chemicals and social justice risks. Chapters 2, 3, 4 and 5 examine emerging liability risks, boycott risks, investment and shareholder related risks, and directors and officers risks, respectfully. While all businesses are impacted by these evolving risks, risk managers, at least initially, should concentrate on assessing those risks areas that will most directly impact their own corporation's financial condition and reputation. Risk managers should also pay attention to their competitors and other related companies. There is an old saying in risk assessment that if a new unexpected loss happens, you hope it happens first to another business.

Chapters 6, 7 and 8 might also be reviewed to assess old risks like asbestos and Superfund and new evolving risks like global warming/climate change and genetically modified crops, as to their applicability to a specific corporation's operations. It would be expected that most firms would be impacted by hazardous waste disposal decisions (Superfund), and global warming/climate change risks. The many examples, studies and references discussed in these three chapters should prove helpful to risk managers in their risk assessment efforts.

As environmental and social justice risks increasingly become internalized to the firm, they need to be worked into the risk assessment process. Ideally, this should be accomplished before losses have been incurred, but sometimes it is not accomplished until after the loss occurs. In one infamous loss situation, Union Carbide, following the disastrous Bhopal catastrophe, instituted a "Root Cause Analysis" on all significant spills and accidents to help prevent recurrence of such an event.[4]

In other situations, potential losses may develop more slowly giving risk managers more time to react and plan. George Reider, a retired insurance executive and past insurance commissioner, offers sound advice:

> "The second question, as to how the industry gets a quicker handle on newly arising liability issues, is the most difficult to address. Many liability issues over the past several decades have arisen and evolved quietly, rather than with a bang. This has been true to some extent in a number of the environmental areas. The answer may well be to actually explore and scan the horizon for the unforeseen, and to quickly study and evaluate every issue which could potentially prove troubling. This not only allows time for developing a defense approach, but perhaps more importantly, a preventive approach."[5]

As Mr. Reider notes, the luxury of time before risk situations materialize into actual losses can allow the risk manager and the firm to discover and anticipate problem areas so that preventive actions can be taken before they become actual losses. This description certainly characterizes sustainability risks. I might add that one of the purposes of writing this book is to help risk managers and insurance companies realize the vast potential for losses arising from sustainability exposures and to assist them in taking risk preventive actions.

In assessing the likelihood of an event occurring and its resulting consequences, it is possible in some risk situations to use high-powered mathematical models to analyze complex systems. An example would be probabilistic risk assessment that analyzes low probability, high severity events like nuclear accidents, hurricanes, earthquakes, or spacecraft losses. These techniques not only estimate the overall chances of a failure, but also compare the many ways the event might develop, which assists engineers to direct their resources to the most effective use of prevention efforts.[6]

Risk assessment involving chemical and other harmful substances can be extremely complicated. Such assessments require professional expertise provided either in house or by an outside consulting firm. A good general description of these types of risk assessments is included in Curtis Haymore's article, "Risk Assessment Process," in *Environmental Risk Management*.[7] Two important books on the effects of chemical exposures, *Our Stolen Future* and *Living Downstream*, would also prove most useful in assessing these different risks. Risk managers for any manufacturing firm or corporation that handles, distributes, or sells products, which contain synthetic chemical compounds, should be alert to scientific discoveries that are uncovering a multitude of risks associated with synthetic chemicals. If liability suits are brought, it will be increasingly difficult to employ a defense that evidence is lacking as to the harmful nature of these substances. In the past, such a defense could often be used, but future reliance on this defense will not be sound nor effective risk management.

A problem with any risk assessment involving chemicals and other harmful substances is that there is a lot we do not know. Most of the scientific work has been done on the effects on animals and humans. In terms of effects on the environment, much less has been done, causing Mr. Haymore to conclude, "Well-tested, easily administered, and commonly accepted measures of ecological damage do not exist."[8] A five year study by the H. John Heinz Center for Science, Economics and the Environment, entitled, "The State of the Nation's Ecosystems," found that about half the data needed to assess the health of ecosystems is not adequate. Environmental systems are extremely complex, so there will be continuing questions on the effects of chemicals and other harmful substances and the degree of environmental damage.[9]

Risk managers may also employ expert organizations in environmental risk assessment. For instance, the International Society of Exposure Analysis was established in 1989 "to foster and advance the science of exposure analysis related to environmental contaminants, to human populations and activities, and to ecosystems."[10] Risk managers could employ the technical knowledge emanating from such groups to enhance their risk assessment efforts.

In the products area, corporations can employ Life Cycle Assessment (LCA) and Design for Environment (DfE) to assess adverse environmental effects throughout the entire life of a product from raw material extraction, through manufacturing and distribution, and on to recycling or disposal. T.E. Graedel and B.R. Allenby, authors of *Industrial Ecology*, state that LCA "determines where products, processes or facilities are less than environmentally meritorious and ranks the environmental impacts of these specific situations."[11] Stuart Hart, writing in the *Harvard Business Review*, describes DfE:

> With DfE, all the effects that a product could have on the environment are examined during its design phase. Cradle-to-grave analysis begins and ends outside the boundaries of a company's operations-it includes a full assessment of all inputs to the product and examines how customers use and dispose of it. DfE thus captures a broad range of external perspectives by including technical staff, environmental experts, end customers, and even community representatives in the process.[12]

Qualifying for ISO 14001 certification obliges the firm to establish a risk assessment procedure. For instance, certification requires the "organization to identify the environmental aspects of its activities, products and services and to determine which of these represent potentially significant environmental impacts."[13] Considerable synergies are present in connecting ISO 14001 certified operations to environmental risk assessment. ISO 14001 certification can also be useful in assessing risks in a firms' supplier network. Many corporations today are requiring that their suppliers be ISO 14001 certified. These include Ford, GM, IBM, Xerox, and Bristol-Myers Squibb.[14] Such corporations can then be assured that their suppliers have been certified as following the ISO risk assessment features outlined above.

Qualifying for membership in such organizations as CERES (Coalition for Environmentally Responsible Economies), the International Chamber of Commerce's Business Charter for Sustainable Development, and the World Business Council for Sustainability Development, (see later sections below) allows corporations to network with other businesses and learn of their experiences in sustainability risk assessment. Specific industry programs such as The Responsible Care Program, established by the Chemical Manufacturers Association,[15] and Strategies for Today's Environmental Partnership, set up by the American Petroleum Institute,[16] may prove even more useful for companies in these industries.

An effective sustainability risk assessment strategy is to prepare a sustainability report. The increased use of sustainability reports was discussed in Chapter 2 under increased transparency. These reports typically examine various sustainability risks of the corporation preparing the report, as well as risk control systems. Just the process of going through the preparation of a report helps to assemble and organize sustainability data and efforts within the firm. As reports are prepared over the years, benchmarking can measure the progress of the corporation overtime and also relative to competitors and leading companies. Excellent sources that can be utilized include *The KPMG International Survey of Corporate Sustainability Reporting*, and The Corporate Register, which provides access to 9,000 corporate non-financial reports.[17]

Sustainability risk assessment is a dynamic process. As new scientific studies, legal developments and regulations emerge, risk managers will need to incorporate this information into their risk assessment methods. Once sustainability risks are assessed and prioritized, then the risk management process moves on to risk control.

Sustainability Risk Control

Risk control involves the prevention and reduction of loss causing situations. In an uninsured program, risk control is the only available tool to mitigate losses. If an insured program is in place, assuming reasonable risk control costs, it is almost always better to prevent the loss from occurring rather than incurring the loss and then collecting insurance. Even if losses are completely covered by insurance, there still is the inconvenience and disruption accompanying the loss, the time spent is assisting in loss adjustment, and emotional costs that may be incurred. I often tell my students, "I hope to never use my insurance," because in order to use my insurance, I must be hit by a loss. Of course, even with the best loss control systems, it is not possible to prevent all losses, so insurance is still needed as a risk management tool.

Risk control systems are varied and often require engineering and behavioral expertise. Some examples might include:

- Highly Protected Risk (HPR) risk structures which greatly reduces the fire risk

- Industrial hygiene systems to protect workers from toxic materials, noise, dusts and other harmful substances

- Machine guards

- Defensive driving programs

- Ergonomics

- Product quality programs

- Crisis management planning

A substantial amount of loss control is mandated by legislation. Noted examples in the U.S. would include:

- Occupational Safety and Health Act

- Consumer Product Safety Act

- Motor Vehicle and Highway Safety Act

- Flammable Fabrics Act

- Homeland Security Act

Consulting firms and insurance companies provide risk control services. With insurers, the cost is often loaded into the premium. Corporations also have in house employees working in the safety and security areas. There is no shortage of reading material on risk control ranging from standard college texts, to elaborately published volumes provided by consulting and insurance organizations, to corporate safety and security manuals.

In the environmental area, risk control is heavily driven, particularly in the early years, by regulations, including the Clean Water and Air Acts, RCRA, CERCLA (Superfund) and the Toxic Substances and Control Act. While some aspects of these regulations have been discussed in this text, I do not plan to describe the risk control systems mandated by these laws. Interested readers can refer to texts like *Environmental Risk Management* by Rothenberg and Telego and the *Environmental Law Handbook* published by the Government Institutes. Other legislation deals with social justice risks including workers compensation laws, OSHA and unemployment benefits. Again, interested readers might consult *Workers' Compensation Resources* by John Burton, *Workers' Compensation and Work-related Illnesses and Diseases* by Peter S. Burth and H. Allan Hunt, *Safety and the Work Force* by John D. Worrall, and *Social Insurance and Economic Security* by George E. Rejda.

Some companies and consultants have been developing sustainability risk control techniques that go beyond environmental quality and social justice compliance standards. The focus of my discussion is going to be on some of these newer sustainability risk control techniques and programs. I do not plan to get into the engineering and operational details. The discussion instead will be presented on a conceptual and general informational basis with a large number of real world examples. Each company needs to develop its own sustainability risk control programs according to the specific nature of their business. I am hoping that my presentation below will provide the strategic framework and risk management rationale to encourage corporations to develop and improve their own sustainability risk control strategies.

Implementing sustainability risk control programs will cost money. I will show that the reduction in future environmental, social justice and reputation risk costs will in most cases exceed the cost of putting these programs in place. Examples in this chapter will show the cost savings from greater efficiencies often exceed the cost the risk control programs themselves, even before the reduction in risk costs are considered. For additional information on a wide variety of examples and methods for implementing these cost saving systems, the interested reader is referred to *Natural Capitalism*, by Paul Hawken, Amory Lovins and Hunter Lovins, and *Driving Eco-Innovation* by Claude Fussler and Peter James.

A critical point in sustainability risk control is the synergistic relation between reducing sustainability risk costs and a positive strategic plan towards maintaining environmental quality and addressing social justice concerns. Establishing environmentally friendly products and operations, and treating workers and other stakeholders in a fair and equitable manner, reduce the risks of incurring liability suits, boycotts, negative publicity, shareholder actions and reputation damage. Since it is the general duty of top management, and the specific duty of risk managers, to reduce overall risk costs, including sustainability risk costs, these duties can be fulfilled by developing and implementing strong environmental quality and social justice risk management programs. Or more simply, sound sustainability risk management leads to improvements in environmental quality and social justice conditions, and implementing effective strategies to reduce environmental harm and inequitable treatment of workers and communities will bolster the effectiveness of the firm's sustainability risk management practices. The two go hand in hand in a mutually reinforcing cycle that strengthens the triple bottom line.

Corporate Attitude Towards Sustainability

The general corporate attitude towards sustainability is an important determinant of a successful risk control program. Take for instance, the petroleum industry and three of its major players, Shell, British Petroleum-Amoco (BP), and Exxon-

Mobil. As discussed earlier in this book, Shell was hit in the mid 1990s with the Brent Spar incident and accusations of its support of the repressive government in Nigeria. These twin events were the catalyst for a turnaround for Shell as regards its attitude towards environmental and social justice risks. Shell is a leader in their industry on sustainability issues. While not as public as the Shell event, BP ran into difficulties with its alleged support of a repressive government in Columbia where it was drilling for oil. BP, as the leading oil company at Prudhoe Bay, was also part of the oil industry's lobbying efforts that called for drilling in the Artic National Wildlife Refuge (ANWR) and questioned whether global warming was indeed occurring. Today, BP has taken a very different approach, as is evidenced by its attitude towards global warming. Sir John Browne, BP's CEO, was the first petroleum company CEO to publicly admit that the global warming is indeed occurring and is most likely related to human activities. BP pulled out of the industry lobbying group, the Global Climate Coalition, which has argued against the prevailing science that global warming was occurring. BP also pulled out the lobbying group that was pushing for drilling in the ANWR. Finally, BP is developing solar power services and currently has 10 percent of the world market,[18] and expects revenues from its solar investments to reach $1 billion before 2010.[19] BP along with Shell are petroleum industry leaders in sustainability efforts.

Contrast their efforts to ExxonMobil, which at least publicly is making few if any sustainability initiatives. In 2002, ExxonMobil did give a $100 million grant to Stanford University in support of Stanford's global energy and climate research project, but it is difficult to find other evidence of a commitment to sustainability. They are still fighting the large punitive damage award resulting from the Exxon Valdez spill, which spilled 11 million gallons of crude oil into Prince William Sound in 1989. That suit was brought by 32,000 fishermen, Alaska natives, landowners, small businesses and cities impacted by the spill. Federal district Judge Russell Holland, has most recently, in January 2004, set punitive damages at $4.5 billion, after the Ninth circuit Court of Appeals had sent back previous awards of $5 billion and $4 billion for review. Exxon has appealed this most recent decision. Exxon has paid $3 billion in cleanup and other costs, and reached a $900 million civil settlement with the federal government and the state of Alaska. Yet, ExxonMobil could pay less than half of its $21 billion in 2003 profits, or just its 2004 fourth quarter profits of $8.4 billion, to cover all its losses from the spill, including the $4.5 billion punitive damage award.[20] One could argue that additional funds are due, given a December 2003 study in the journal *Science* that showed damages from the spill are continuing in the Sound.[21] While

I am not in any way a petroleum industry expert, my hunch is that Shell and BP's sustainability efforts will begin to translate into demonstrable financial and competitive advantages over ExxonMobil in the years to come.

Supply Chain Initiatives

In the risk assessment section, the use of ISO 14001 certification to assist in identifying corporate sustainability risks deriving from suppliers was discussed. ISO 14001 certification can also assist in sustainability risk control. Procedures for establishing objectives and targets require that the organization consider six factors: "the environmental policy, legal requirements, potentially significant impacts, business considerations, technological options, and the views of interested parties."[22] Dealing with suppliers that are ISO 14001 certified by an independent outside party gives the organization a level of assurance that sustainability risks associated with their suppliers will be reduced.

Some firms are taking more direct control in raising the sustainability efforts of their suppliers. John Elkington, Chairman of Sustainability, Europe's leading sustainability consulting firm and author of *Cannibals with Forks,* offers numerous examples, including Volvo and Sainsbury's. The Swedish manufacturer, Volvo, has instituted an environmental supplier challenge program. Under this program, environmental care is given equal priority along with two long-established Volvo core values-safety and quality. In announcing the program, Han-Olov Olsson, Vice President of marketing at Volvo, noted that now all three factors-safety, quality, and environmental care with be used in Volvo's audits of it suppliers.[23]

Sainsbury's, the large food company in the UK, uses 6,500 suppliers worldwide. Its tuna products operations require that fish are caught using dolphin friendly techniques. Sainsbury's also brings pressure on its suppliers in areas such as "energy efficiency, integrated crop management, organic produce, animal testing, animal husbandry, timber and forest products, and peat."[24] Cost savings for supplier operations can help to reduce Sainsbury's' costs. In addition, not only has Sainsbury's mitigated potential reputation damage, its actions have improved its reputation.

Home Depot was discussed in Chapter 3 as being the focus of NGO protests and boycotts over their past use of wood from old growth forests. Not only did Home Depot change their practices and switch to buying FSC certified wood, they have been actively putting pressure on their suppliers. Part of their strategy was practical, as they realized that their demand could not be met with only FSC certified wood. They began approaching wood suppliers around the world to alter their forest damaging methods. When suppliers did not respond, such as in Indonesia and Gabon, Home Depot cancelled their purchases. Home Depot even helped to broker a deal between environmental groups and two of the largest Chilean lumber companies, Arauco and CMPC, to work together to reach a forest accord. While working on the accord, "the logging companies agreed to enact stronger conservation measures and the environmentalists agreed to stop targeting Arauco and CMPC in their boycott campaign."[25]

Research in business schools has documented that sustainability supply chain management not only benefits society in general, it can also have a positive impact on the firm's performance. Craig Carter of the University of Maryland and Marianne M. Jennings of Arizona State University examined logistics social responsibility along five dimensions: environmental issues, diversity, human rights and quality of work life, philanthropy, and safety. Positive outcomes of logistics social responsibility practices include improved trust with supplier and customer stakeholders, increased performance by stakeholders, and potentially improved financial performance. Survey data on purchase decisions and financial performance show a significant relationship of logistics social responsibility to cost of goods sold and net income.[26]

Hazardous Waste Reduction

Waste reduction is a strong sustainability risk control technique. Recalling the discussions of Superfund, any waste that is removed from operating systems will not have to be disposed and cannot produce future cleanup liabilities. Bill McDonough and Michael Braungart in their path breaking book, *Cradle to Cradle*, list the first step in the five step process to eco-effectiveness, as being: "Get free of known culprits." In designing products or manufacturing systems, one should make every effort to remove such materials as PVC, cadmium, lead and mercury. As an example, they point out that, when all mercury-based thermometers are eliminated, over four tons of mercury, the amount estimated to produce a one year's supply of thermometers for hospitals and consumers in the United States, will be removed from the product cycle.[27]

Several prominent corporations have made major reductions in waste and pollution. As an example, DuPont reduced toxic releases 74 percent from 1987 to 1993, halved its landfill waste, and cut its $1 billion per year waste treatment bill by $200 million.[28] DuPont also cut its emissions of cancer-causing chemicals by almost 70 percent since 1987.[29] Another example is 3M's Pollution Prevention

Pays program, launched in 1975, one of the first corporate-wide efforts to avoid waste from the start rather than clean it up later. In the first 20 years, 3M eliminated more than 1.5 billion pounds of air, land, and water pollution for a total cost savings of $790 million.[30] The giant chip maker, Intel, halved its hazardous waste over a 10 year period. This was accomplished during the same period that Intel was increasing its revenues by nine fold.[31]

Linda Bagneschi, an environmental consultant, emphasizes that "from a risk management standpoint, source reduction is preferred to recycling and treatment options because it is likely to pose the lowest environment risk."[32] While the impetus for these efforts may have been to reduce environmental risk costs, they also produced general cost savings for DuPont, 3M and Intel.

Waste Management

It is logical to concentrate on hazardous wastes first in a waste management program. If all waste, hazardous and non-hazardous, could be managed effectively, organizations could accrue huge savings. According to some estimates, more than 90 percent of materials extracted to make durable goods in the United States becomes waste almost immediately. The products themselves average only five percent of the raw materials involved in the process of making and delivering them. In their book, *Cradle to Cradle*, Bill McDonough and Michael Braungart reference these estimates as arguments for developing more effective waste management systems. They begin at the design phase of products, packaging and systems "to eliminate the concept of waste...to design things from the very beginning on the understanding that waste does not exist."[33]

McDonough and Braungart describe two metabolic cycles on earth, the biological metabolism, or the cycles of nature, and the technical metabolism, or the cycles of industry. Nature's systems are totally cyclical. Any effluents or emissions are totally absorbed and used in the system-there is no waste. McDonough and Braungart would design industrial systems so that so that any material not used in a product would cycle into a biological or technical cycle. Materials cycling into a biological cycle would be biodegradable and become a biological nutrient, such as biodegradable packaging. Other materials would stay in the technical cycle, which would produce a closed-loop system.[34] Similar ideas and concepts are included in Janine Benyus' fascinating book, *Biomimicry,* in which she explores adapting nature's methods for human use.[35]

McDonough and Braungart also talk about employing more upcycling and less downcycling. Downcycling reduces the quality of a material over time. For example, when plastics are recycled, they are mixed with different plastics to produce a hybrid of lower quality. This lower quality hybrid is then molded into a cheaper product than the product in which the original plastic was used. With upcycling, the final product is of the same or even superior quality. They give as an example the pages of their book, which are not made of paper and can be dissolved and remade as a polymer of high quality.

McDonough and Braungart describe an amazing example from a client's actual project. The Rohner textile mill in Switzerland was experiencing substantial costs is disposing of its upholstery fabric trimmings, which were defined as hazardous waste under government regulations. The authors as consultants set out to create a fabric that could meet regulations and be safely disposed of as a biological nutrient when it was worn out. The base material that was chosen was a mixture of safe, pesticide-free plant and animal fibers consisting of wool and ramie. The dyes, finishes and other process chemicals provided the biggest challenge. They eliminated thousands of potential chemicals, and ended up using 38 ingredients that had no mutagens, carcinogens, endocrine disrupters, or persistent toxins. This mix was actually cheaper than the mill had previously used.

When regulators later came to the mill to test the water effluent, they were shocked to find that their instruments could not detect evidence of any pollutants, not even elements that they knew were in the water when it came into the factory. In essence, the water coming out of the factory was as clean or even cleaner than the water going into the factory. They had designed an upholstery fabric that was safe to compost as a biological nutrient when its use was finished, and the factory effluent was actually safe enough to drink.[36]

This project provides an excellent example of the synergistic effects between sustainability risk management and financial performance. The final product was cheaper, more profitable and safer with no undesirable hazardous waste. The process of making this product is better for the environment and also reduces the risk costs of disposal and potential product liabilities. Employees are working in a safer environment, reducing workers compensation costs. Regulatory costs are reduced. Except for occasional monitoring there would need to be no regulation.

Remarkably, a business situation has been created that makes top management happy, makes the risk manager happy, makes the employees happy, makes environmentalists happy, makes regulators happy and makes the customer happy. It would seem that even members of opposing political parties would agree that they could jointly support this type of effort.

The possibilities for these types of design changes in manufacturing, product and distribution processes are endless. It just requires a new type of thinking.

Consultants like McDonough, Braungart and Elkington, as well as Paul Hawkin, Amory Lovins and Hunter Lovins (authors of *Natural Capitalism*), could be hired or a corporation could rely on the creativity of it own workers to come up with innovative solutions. The key is to incorporate fundamental principals into the beginning stages of the design process. The advantages, specifically noted above, and more generally set forth by McDonough and Braungart are:

- It would produce no useless and potentially dangerous waste

- It would save manufacturers billions of dollars in valuable materials over time

- It would diminish the extraction of raw materials and the manufacture of potentially disruptive materials, and eventually phase them out, resulting in more savings to the manufacturer and enormous benefit to the environment[37]

And I might add it would substantially reduce sustainability risk costs.

Promising Discoveries Become Known Culprits

Chlorofluorocarbons (CFCs), dichlorodiphenyltrichloroethane (DDT) and poly-chlorinated biphenyls (PCBs) are examples of environmentally harmful substances that have been removed from business processes and products. Their removal required direct regulation because it was so difficult to identify the specific responsible parties with the harm to the environment and human health. The story of CFCs, DDT and PCBs provides a number of sustainability risk management insights.

CFCs

Thomas Midley, Jr. was the first to synthesize CFCs in 1928. Midley developed CFCs as a safer alternative to the toxic and flammable chemicals used as coolants in refrigerators. He was presented in 1941 with chemistry's highest award for his efforts, the Priestley Prize. CFCs were felt to be safe and testing confirmed that they did not appear to break down into toxic compounds that might harm people or the environment.

In the late 1940s, James Lovelock, who would later become known for the Gaia hypothesis, invented the electron capture detector, which increased the sensitivity of the gas chromatograph a thousand fold. As he traveled and took readings with his new instrument, he discovered that DDT and CFCs and other compounds like dieldrin were in the atmosphere in virtually every place he tested from the Artic to the tip of South America.[38] Testing by others would find these chemicals in the breast milk of mothers around the world and in the fat of Antarctic penguins.[39]

In 1974, stimulated by Lovelock's findings, two chemists, Sherwood Rowland and Mario Molina, published a paper in *Nature*, for which they were awarded the Nobel Prize in 1995, which described how CFCs would permeate from the lower atmosphere to the stratosphere and attack ozone.[40] Ozone protects us from ultraviolet-B radiation. Their research was validated with the appearance of the now famous ozone hole over Antarctica and other countries in the southern hemisphere.[41]

International cooperation manifested itself in the ratification of the Montreal Protocol in which 35 countries signed an unprecedented agreement in 1987 to phase out CFCs and other ozone-depleting chemicals.[42] Phasing out CFCs also demonstrated that industry is capable of enormous changes, even though it may adamantly resist these changes. A World Resources Institute study examined the transition. It estimated that $100 billion worth of equipment relied on CFCs, with the United States using a third of the world's production. Yet, alternatives were developed for virtually all CFC applications. The report concluded that in most cases, "firms have eliminated CFCs faster, at a lower cost, or with greater improvements than ever imagined."[43]

DDT

The developer of DDT, Paul Müller, also was awarded the Nobel Prize in 1948. The pesticide kills insects, including mosquitoes that carry malaria, and would save hundreds of thousands if not millions of lives. For many years, DDT did not seem to pose a direct threat to humans. Rachel Carson's research, presented in her 1962 book *Silent Spring,* would alter this perception. The toll that DDT and other synthetic chemicals took on bird populations and her concern of links to cancer in humans shattered the notion that DDT was not harmful. Later research by the National Cancer Institute would find higher incidence of liver tumors in mice exposed to DDT. In 1972, William Ruckelshaus, the head of the Environmental Protection Agency, restricted most use of DDT.[44]

While DDT was banned in developed countries, including the United States, in the early 1970s, it is still being used in several developing countries in Latin America, Africa and tropical Asia. In those countries, DDT is often used for the control of malaria spread by mosquitoes. While industrialized countries used DDT to control mosquitoes, malaria was never the concern, so the banning of

DDT was an easier decision. It is important, in reducing the use of DDT in developing countries, that alternative methods of controlling malaria be adopted.

PCBs

PCBs were first created in 1929. This time no awards or Nobel Prizes were awarded. The variety of uses for PCBs is enormous, far exceeding those for CFCs and DDT. PCBs are nonflammable and extremely stable. One of their most common uses is as an insulating coolant for electrical equipment like transformers. They are also used as lubricants, hydraulic fluids, cutting oils, and liquid seals. PCBs help to make wood and plastic products nonflammable. They become ingredients in paints, varnishes, inks, pesticides, and carbonless copy paper.

Like PCBs and DDT, early tests did not indicate any hazardous effects associated with PCBs. Later testing would discover associations between exposure to PCBs and a variety of physical and neurological problems, including reproductive difficulties, compromised immune systems, and learning problems. PCBs are persistent and ubiquitous, found virtually in any part of the world, again like CFCs and DDT. In 1976, the United States banned the manufacture of PCBs and other industrialized countries would eventually follow.[45]

The stories of CFCs, DDT, and PCBs provide a number of common points.

- All three were major discoveries and developed for good purposes. Their uses improved the safety of products and contributed to the welfare of people.

- All three were felt to be harmless when first developed, without any documented toxic effects on humans and animals.

- All three would later be found to have spread throughout the world and to be harmful to humans and animals. These characteristics were not anticipated when they were developed and in their early use.

- All three would eventually be banned in the United States and other industrialized countries. Due to their persistency, they continue to be a problem in these countries. In countries where they continue to be used, their harmful effects remain as major concerns.

The development of CFCs, DDT, and PCBs cannot reasonably have been expected to be prohibited. Yet, any future development of similar synthetic chemicals should either not be permitted or should only be done after careful testing and in situations where less harmless substitutes are not available. Maximum risk control techniques should be employed. The words of Bill McDonough and Michael Braungart in *Cradle to Cradle* succinctly capture the essence of the required sustainability risk management strategy: "Negligence is described as doing the same thing over and over even though you know it is dangerous, stupid or wrong. Now that we know, it's time for a change. Negligence starts tomorrow."[46]

Redesign to Eliminate Monstrous Hybrids

In their book, *Cradle to Cradle*, McDonough and Braungart discuss their strategy of eliminating monstrous hybrids. They offer the conventional leather shoe as an example of a monstrous hybrid, and describe it follows:

> At one time, shoes were tanned with vegetable chemicals, which were relatively safe, so the wastes from their manufacture posed no real problem. The shoe could biodegrade after its useful life or be safely burned. But vegetable tanning required that trees be harvested for their tannins. As a result, shoes took a long time to make, and they were expensive. In the past forty years, vegetable tanning has been replaced with chromium tanning, which is faster and cheaper. But chromium is rare and valuable for industries, and in some forms it is carcinogenic. Today shoes are often tanned in developing countries where few if any precautions are taken to protect people and ecosystems from chromium exposure. Manufacturing wastes may be dumped into nearby bodies of water or incinerated, either of which distributes toxins, often disproportionately in low-income areas. Conventional rubber shoe soles, moreover, usually contain lead and plastics. As the shoe is worn, particles of it degrade into the atmosphere and soil. It cannot be safely consumed, either by you or by the environment. After use, its valuable materials, both biological and technical, are usually lost in a landfill.[47]

In the process of producing a shoe, which is a useful product and provides a necessary service to the customer, a whole array of environmental and social justice risks are created. The authors also describe such products as being products plus. With products like a shoe, a polyester shirt or a plastic water bottle, you get the "item or service you want, plus additives that you didn't ask for and did not know were included and may be harmful to you or your loved ones."[48]

McDonough and Braungart stress that products need to be designed properly to avoid producing monstrous hybrids or products plus. Design must consider and eliminate the use of harmful inputs and outputs, must produce a product that is safe to workers and customers, and must include a strategy at the product's end life for recycling or properly disposing of the product. McDonough and Braungart's emphasis on good design has immediate risk control results. Removing harmful substances and processes throughout a product's life will also remove that the risks of being liable for any resulting injuries and damages. Workers compensation costs are lowered. Boycott and reputation damages are also eliminated, as are any related shareholder actions. Good design is good risk management.

McDonough and Braungart also note that good design lessens the need for regulation. Regulation the authors note "is a signal of design failure....it is what we call a license to harm: a permit issued by the government to an industry so that it may dispense sickness, destruction and death at an 'acceptable rate'." Good design eliminates such sickness, destruction and death, and their resulting risks to the corporation. Indeed, as they note "good design can require no regulation at all."[49]

Life Cycle Assessment and Design for Environment

Life Cycle Assessment (LCA) and Design for Environment (DfE) were discussed previously as risk assessment tools. These strategies are also closely related to the emphasis on good design thinking of McDonough and Braungart. The objective of LCA is to assess the environmental or social costs during the whole life cycle of the product or service. Five stages are examined: raw material manufacturing, product fabrication, packaging and transport, use, and waste management. Increased efficiencies in material usage and the employment of recycling strategies play an important role in LCA.[50]

Elkington again provides salient examples like Procter and Gamble. Procter and Gamble is one of the world's leaders in the use of LCA. Statements of Peter Hindle, director of P&G's environmental affairs in Europe, captures the essence of LCA and illustrates the strong sustainability risk management component of this strategy:

> "Society expects that the products and services that it buys and uses will be safe for people and for the environment. It also expects that those involved in making the products or providing the services will work in safe conditions and that the production processes will not injure the environment.
>
> For everyday consumer goods such as laundry, detergents, dishwashing liquids, baby diapers, shampoos, toothpaste, skin cream and color cosmetics, people expect the products to be safe under conditions of use and reasonably

foreseeable misuse. This includes worker safety, user safety and environmental safety."[51]

Design for Environment (DfE) is a similar program. Graedel and Allenby, in *Industrial Ecology*, state that DfE programs are the second focused activity of industrial ecology, the first being pollution prevention. DfE strategies "refer to generally meritorious actions or considerations, and encourage their incorporation into product or process design activities."[52] Stuart Hart, in the *Harvard Business Review*, describes DfE as a "tool for creating products that are easier to recover, reuse, or recycle, (which) is becoming increasingly important."[53] All the effects that a product could have on the environment are examined during its design phase, including an assessment of all inputs to the product and how customers use and dispose of the product.

Good design efforts are stressed by a variety of individuals concerned with sustainability risks. For instance in their book, *The Natural Step for Business*, Nattrass and Altomare write:

"Today, more and more people throughout the world are becoming concerned that the basic design of our entire industrial society is both faulty and inadequate for the long-term voyage that is the dream of humanity."[54]

The authors note that business and society does not have to choose between maintaining profits and diminishing sustainability risks.

"There need be no conflict or compromise between commercial profits and the environmental health and well-being of humanity and other life forms if the design of commerce is aligned with the inherent design of the natural world."[55]

In their concluding chapter of *Our Stolen Future*, Colborn, Domanowski and Myers posit:

"The task that confronts us over the next half century is one of redesign. When forced by the phase out of CFCs to reconsider the use of solvents when manufacturing electronic circuitry, one research effort in the United States found a way to eliminate the need for CFCs or any other solvent by redesigning the soldering process. Following such examples, we need to redesign not only lawns, food packaging, and detergents, but also agriculture, industry, and other institutional arrangements spawned by the chemical age. We have to find better, safer, more clever ways to meet basic human needs and, where possible, human desires. This is the only way to opt out of the experiment (with synthetic chemicals)."[56]

Products liability has been one of the largest loss producing risks for corporations. Products quality control programs to deal with products liability risks are a key component of risk management systems. It seems reasonable that a products liability control program could be coordinated with good design, LCA, and DfE programs to produce products that minimize both products liability claims and environmental and social justice risks. Risk managers would obviously have to rely on experts in these fields like McDonough and Braungart, Elkington, Graedel and Allenby, and others.[57] But at a minimum, risk managers can and should be part of design teams. Risk managers' substantial expertise in the products liability area could make a major contribution to effective product and service life cycle design programs. And of course as has been shown above, good design programs add immeasurably to controlling sustainability risks.

Service Rather than Product Orientation

Providing service benefits rather than selling a product is another approach that can reduce a firm's risk exposure. The floor covering/carpets industry is a good example. When carpets and particularly commercial floor coverings are purchased, one is concerned with the look, feel, comfort, warmth characteristics and service benefits of that covering. With certain exceptions like Oriental rugs, when a carpet is worn out it will be discarded and a new floor covering will be purchased. In order to maximize recycling and efficiency efforts, some floor covering companies lease the floor covering for a period of time, and then when it needs to be replaced they come and get old floor covering and replace it with a new one. Their customers get the continuing service benefits of the floor covering and the company obtains the reuse value of the old floor covering. Some of the material is recycled and some may have to be disposed, but it is in the control of the company and not the customer. This process saves energy, raw material and disposal costs, and reduces the potential risk costs associated within these areas for both the customer and the carpet/floor covering manufacturer. Sustainability risk costs are reduced by using materials in manufacturing the floor coverings that are environmentally and people safe.

Emphasizing the providing of services rather than the product promotes recycling and the efficient reuse of the materials that go into the product. When combined with take back laws, the benefits of providing services are spread to entire industries. Take back laws began with packaging waste in Germany and have been expanded to automobiles, household durables, electronic products and computers throughout the European Union. Under these laws, product manufacturers are required to take back their products when customers are ready to part with them. In effect, the manufacturers become responsible for the recycling or disposal of the products. The process works similar to providing product services except that the customers own rather than lease the product when it is in their possession. As with providing product services, take back laws give manufacturers tremendous financial incentives to design products that can be more effectively recycled or are safer for deposal.

The story of Interface, Inc, provides an inspiring example of a company providing services as a critical part of an expanded sustainability strategy. The commercial floor covering company was founded by Ray Anderson in 1973 and by 1996 it had reached annual sales of $ 1 billion. Interface is commercially successful, but it has also been one of the best examples of a sustainable operation. I heard Anderson give a talk at a meeting of The Natural Step about his conversion to sustainability. He had been asked for input on a report about the efforts of his company in maintaining environmental quality. In thinking about his response, he decided to read Paul Hawken's book, *The Ecology of Commerce*, and as he described it-he had a veritable epiphany. He set out with the goal of making Interface a truly sustainable company. He describes environmental sustainability as "taking nothing from the Earth that is not renewable and doing no harm to the biosphere."[58]

In building a sustainable company, Interface developed the concept for the Evergreen Lease, which converts carpet as a product of material into a product of service. Customers lease the carpet system without taking ownership or liability for ongoing maintenance and the eventual disposal or recycling of the carpet. Interface then set out to eliminate waste from operations, to remove any toxic inputs or outputs in the carpet manufacturing process, to maximize recycling efforts, and to improve transportation and energies efficiencies. Interface also set up a number of programs to improve the working conditions and culture of its employees through its "putting people first" program.

These programs minimize sustainability risk costs for both customers and Interface. Customers are relieved of any use and disposal liabilities associated with the carpets. Interface's efforts reduce its workers compensation, disposal and social justice risk exposures. All parties reduce or eliminate their long-term liability risk exposures.

Roy Anderson was not content to just improve Interface's sustainability efforts. He gives about 100 talks a year to a variety of companies and groups to share his experience and encourage others to make sustainability efforts. Words from one of his speeches portray a number of salient points of his corporate philosophy:

> "Interface will be environmentally sustainable. But our mission is larger. We will also be financially sustainable, for the simple reason that our corporation must survive and that we must assure the livelihood of our associates and the investment of all our stakeholders. We will be socially sustainable, respecting the communities in which we work, positively influencing all those whose lives we touch, and taking care not to deplete the human spirit on which we depend...Our sustainability goals-financial, social and environmental-are inextricably bound together, which is why we make such a point of doing well by doing good."[59]

For a more extensive examination of the story of Interface readers are referred to *The Natural Step for Business* by Brian Nalltrass and Mary Altomare.[60] This book presents four cases, including Interface, Ikea, Scandic Hotels and Collins Pine Company. All four companies are building sustainable operations and reducing sustainability risks. Further corporate examples are provided in a second book by the authors entitled, *Dancing with the Tiger.*[61] The Natural Step process has played an instrumental role in their sustainability efforts of all these companies.

The Natural Step

The Natural Step is an environmental not-for-profit organization, which was founded in Sweden in 1989 by Dr. Karl-Henrik Robèrt. Dr. Robèrt is a medical doctor and cancer-treatment researcher. Prior to starting The Natural Step, Dr. Robèrt was generally concerned with environmental deterioration and more specifically upset by the large number of cancer-diseased children he was treating. In his mind, the declining state of the environment was unsustainable and he pondered the relation between environmental stresses and the increasing number of cancers in children. He wondered what changes would need to be made and how these changes might be accomplished.

Dr. Robèrt decided that the place to begin was with the setting forth of a universal set of fundamental conditions or a framework of first order principles that are necessary to produce a sustainable system. I heard him describe, at a seminar held by The Natural Step, how he wrote to a number of leading scientists and knowledgeable individuals and asked them whether they could agree on a set of fundamental conditions needed for sustainable development. After several drafts were circulated to the group, he arrived at a set of four critical conditions or principles that were agreed upon by his working group to be necessary to produce sustainable systems. The four system conditions and brief descriptions are shown in Table 9-1. These four system conditions became the foundation on which The Natural Step was established.

Table 9-1
Summary of the Rationale Behind the TNS System Conditions

	System Condition	Meaning	Rationale
1. STORED DEPOSITS	In a sustainable society, nature is not subject to systematically increasing concentrations of substances extracted from the Earth's crust.	This means substituting certain minerals that are scarce in nature with others that are more abundant, and using all mined materials efficiently.	If this condition is not met, the concentrations of substances in the ecosphere will increase and eventually reach limits – often unknown – beyond which irreversible changes occur. *Nothing disappears and everything disperses.*
2. SYNTHETIC COMPOUNDS AND OTHER SOCIETALLY-PRODUCED MATERIAL	In a sustainable society, nature is not subject to systematically increasing concentrations of substances produced by society	This means substituting certain persistent and unnatural compounds with ones that are normally abundant or break down more easily in nature, and using all substances produced by society efficiently.	If this condition is not met, the concentration of substances in the ecosphere will increase and eventually reach limits – often unknown – beyond which irreversible changes occur. *Nothing disappears and everything disperses.*
3. ECOSYSTEM MANIPULATION	In a sustainable society, nature is not subject to systematically increasing degradation by physical means.	This means drawing resources from only well managed eco-systems, using those resources efficiently, substituting unnecessarily area-consuming activities with others and exercising general caution in all kinds of manipulation of nature.	Our health and prosperity depend on the capacity of nature to reconcentrate and restructure wastes into new resources. *Human activities need to work in harmony with the cyclic principle of nature.*
4. SOCIO-ECONOMICS	In a sustainable society human needs are met worldwide.	This means using all our resources efficiently, fairly and responsibly so that the needs of all our stakeholders – customers, staff, neighbours, people in other parts of the world, and people who are not yet born – stand the best chance of being met.	Unless basic human needs are met world wide through fair and efficient use of resources, it will be difficult to meet conditions 1-3 on a global scale.

Source: Brian Nattrass and Mary Altomare, *The Natural Step for Business,* Gabriola Island, BC, Canada: New Society Publishers, 1999.

Dr. Robèrt understood that both regulation and involvement by private corporations would be necessary to accomplish the changes that had to be made in the current system to meet The Natural Step (TNS) system conditions. Dr. Robèrt began in his home country by obtaining the support of the King of Sweden to mail his ideas to every household in Sweden. The first corporation to incorporate TNS systems conditions in its strategic development was IKEA, the giant home products and furnishings company, which is based in Sweden. From its origins in Sweden, The Natural Step would expand throughout the world, including the United States, Canada, Australia, Japan, New Zealand, UK, and South Africa. A large and varied number of major corporations have molded TNS thinking into their strategic planning. The experience of a number of these corporations including IKEA, Interface, Scandic Hotels, Collins Pine Company, Nike, Starbucks, Home Depot, Norm Thomson Outfitters, and "CH2Mhill, as well as the cities of Whistler, Seattle and Santa Monica, are detailed in two books by Brian Nattrass and Mary Altomare, *The Natural Step for Business* and *Dancing with the Tiger.* Karl-Henrik Robèrt has also authored his own text, *The Natural Step Story.*[62]

What makes TNS system conditions attractive is they give the firm a solid framework for developing sustainable strategies. In its simplest form, every business decision, process, and product is approached from the standpoint as to whether they meet the four system conditions. If they do not, then changes have to be made to arrive at sustainability. The organization is given total freedom, creativity, and flexibility for making the required changes and developing the appropriate strategies for its particular operations. While there are TNS techniques and methods for assisting the firm in making changes and developing strategies, in the end it is the firm and its employees and stakeholders who must arrive at the final decisions that produce sustainable systems.

The Natural Step is certainly not the only management strategy for arriving at sustainable development, but its combining of a fundamental set of principles with the creativity of management and stakeholders makes it a very useful and practical approach. The Natural Step is also about companies making profits-all three components of the triple bottom line are emphasized. Indeed, a company that makes contributions to environmental quality and social justice conditions will not be able to have lasting impacts without maintaining its economic viability. For a corporation asking the question, "How do we get started in developing sustainable strategies?" or "How do we take our sustainability initiatives to the next level?," The Natural Step provides substantial direction and assistance.

The framework of The Natural Step provides an excellent example of how sustainability strategies and sustainability risk management are mutually reinforcing. Maintaining the TNS system conditions will clearly result in improvements in environmental quality and social justice conditions. In addition, environmental and social justice risk exposures will be substantially reduced. The first system condition reduces extractions of substances from the Earth's crust to a sustainable state. Extractive industries like mining and oil drilling have generally been high-risk industries with substantial worker injuries, high pollution levels and large accumulations of wastes. These industries also deplete raw materials, many of which are in limited supply. Reducing the extraction rates of these industries will reduce the sustainability risks associated with these industries.

The second system condition calls for stabilizing the increasing amounts of harmful substances produced by society. Emphasis is on persistent substances, particularly dangerous ones that do not naturally break down. Many like asbestos, lead, mercury, DDT, PCBs, CFCs, cadmium, PVCs and assorted substances at hazardous waste sites have been discussed, along with their associated risks, in this book. Requiring that the concentrations of these substances are not systematically increasing will clearly reduce the various environmental and human health risks associated with these substances.

The third system condition requires that natural ecosystems not be subject to systematically increasing degradation. The first chapter in this book was partly devoted to numerous examples of degradation of ecosystems and the associated risks of this degradation. Employing sustainability strategies, which restore and maintain natural ecosystems, will reduce the various risks that derive from their degradation.

The fourth system condition of a sustainable society requires that human needs are met worldwide. If inequities in resource consumption and general conditions of living are horribly out of balance across countries and peoples, then societal instability, liability suits, boycotts and other reputation damaging risks will continue to increase. With greater considerations of equity and fairness among the various stakeholders throughout the world and future generations, these social justice risks will be more effectively controlled.

As demonstrated here and throughout the book, improving environmental quality and social justice conditions will help to control sustainability risks. The corollary is also true that by instituting sound sustainability risk management systems, a corporation will not only control its sustainability risks, but also its products and systems will be more environmentally friendly and conducive with social fairness and equity.

Take Back Laws

Sustainability risk management efforts can be supported by creative regulation. A good example is take back or extended producer responsibility laws. These laws have been extremely effective in reducing toxic waste, increasing recycling, promoting the redesign of products to curb pollution, and increasing the efficient use of resources. While corporations may not like these laws, they represent an effective strategy where the government sets mandatory minimum requirements, and then allows the creativity and inventiveness of corporations to figure out the details of meeting the requirements. The key is that once manufacturers know that they will be responsible for taking the product back at the end of its life, they have strong financial incentives to reduce the amount of waste and toxicity in their products and to increase the amount of reusable material in their products. LCA, DfE and service orientation strategies, discussed earlier, can support initiatives necessitated by take back legislation.

Europe and Asia

Extended producer responsibility legislation was first introduced in Germany in 1991 through its "Green Dot," or *Ordinance on the Avoidance of Packaging Waste*, package recycling law. Other nations, including Sweden, Switzerland, and the Netherlands, followed suit. The European Union passed a *Directive on Packaging and Packaging Waste* in 2000. Today, 25 European nations and eight Asia countries have packaging laws. The EU Directive requires its Member States "to establish waste packaging recycling targets and allocate recycling costs to packaging raw material suppliers, packaging manufacturers and producers, distributors, and retailers of packaged goods-but not customers or taxpayers."[63] These package recycling laws have reduced the amount of packaging used, produced lower cost packaging and reduced environmental impact.

The EU *Directive on End-of-Life Vehicles* in 2000 expanded take back concepts to automobile manufacturers, following earlier initiatives in France, Germany, Italy, and the Netherlands. This Directive requires automobile manufacturers to reuse or recycle 85 percent of an automobile by weight at the end of its life by 2006, and this percentage will increase to 95 percent in 2015. The costs of recycling for cars built before 2002 must be paid by the automakers, while cars built after 2002 will include a tax to fund recycling at the end of their life.[64] While obviously automakers were not pleased with the retroactivity feature of the law, which requires that recycling costs of pre-2002 built cars be absorbed by the automakers, it is another example that corporations cannot expect that new legislation will allow them to be exempted through grand fathering provisions. Take back laws are an application of the polluter pays principle, which calls for the "polluters and users of natural resources to bear the full environmental and social costs of their activities."[65]

Japanese laws have even higher goals. Currently about 80 percent of an automobile is already recycled for spare parts and scrap value. Japan wants to focus on the other 20 percent by recycling the vehicle shredder dust, air bags, and ozone-depleting gases from air conditioners. The shredder residue or 'fluff' is composed primarily of plastics and fibers and creates major problems for solid waste landfills.[66]

The newest and most comprehensive take back legislation focuses on electronic equipment and waste. The EU Directive on *Waste Electrical and Electronic Equipment (WEEE)* became effective on February 13, 2003, calling for the 15 member states to implement this directive by August 13, 2004. Similar legislation has been promulgated in Japan, Taiwan and Korea. The tremendous growth of computers, monitors, TVs, cell phones, calculators, appliances, etc., has put enormous pressure on landfills and the environment, particularly because of the toxic materials that are contained in electronic equipment waste. Currently, over 90 percent of this waste goes to disposal facilities rather than being reused or recycled.

The WEEE Directive is very broad in scope, covering virtually all electrical and electronic equipment used by consumers or intended for professional use, including products sold in the EU from abroad and products sold electronically. The ten categories of products are included below:

1. Large household appliances (refrigerators, washing machines, stoves, etc.)

2. Small household appliances (vacuum cleaners, toasters, hair dryers, etc.)

3. Information and telecommunications equipment (computers and peripherals, cell phones, calculators, etc.)

4. Consumer equipment (radios, TVs, stereos, etc.)

5. Lighting (fluorescent lamps, sodium lamps, etc.)

6. Electrical and electronic tools (drills, saws, sewing machines, etc.)

7. Toys, leisure, and sports equipment (electric trains, video games, etc.)

8. Medical devices (ventilators, cardiology and radiology equipment, etc.)

9. Monitoring instruments (smoke detectors, thermostats, control panels, etc.)

10. Automatic dispensers (appliances that deliver products such as hot drinks).[67]

Producers are financially responsible for taking back their own products at end of life and managing them in accordance with the directive. A principal feature of proper management requires that waste electrical and electronic equipment be collected and deposed of separately from other wastes. Mandatory recovery rates range from 70 to 80 percent and reuse/recycling rates range from 50 to 75 percent across the 10 categories. For instance, computers and related equipment have a minimum required 75 percent recovery rate and 65 percent reuse/recycling rate. These target rates are to be met by end of the year 2006, but that date may be extended. Retailers are required to provide free take back on an "old for new" basis, i.e., a customer buying a new computer can bring back an old computer.

To guard against producers exporting their waste to other countries, in order to avoid the costs of meeting the directive, any exports of waste electrical and electronic equipment for treatment must comply with EU regulations. This calls for the exporter to prove that the waste treatment methods used in the importing country meet the requirements of the directive, in order to count toward the recovery and reuse/recycling target rates.

The costs of the WEEE Directive are internalized to the producers. For products put on the market before August 13, 2005, the costs of waste management are to be shared. Producers may impose a separate "visible" fee to cover these costs for eight years (10 years for large household appliances), which can be passed on to end users other than households. For new products put on the market after August 13, 2005, producers have individual responsibility of paying the cost of managing their own products. No visible fees are permitted to fund the management of waste for these new products.

To facilitate the waste management of new products, they must be labeled as being put on the market after August 13, 2005, verifying that they will be separately collected and bear the name of the producer. Producers must provide information to customers to facilitate the collection process. When producers put a new product on the market, they must provide a financial guarantee that waste management of the product will be paid for. Producers can meet this financial guarantee by participating in a producer responsibility organization, paying for recycling insurance or setting up a bank account for this purpose.

At the same time that the WEEE Directive was passed, a companion directive was also passed, called the Directive on the Restriction of the Use of Certain Hazardous Substances in Electrical and Electronic Equipment (RoHS). The same products are covered by both directives. The rational of the RoHS Directive is that even if all the recovery, reuse and recycling targets of the WEEE Directive are met, the toxic content of the waste would still pose risks to individual health and the environment. The directive calls for safer materials to be substituted for toxic materials. Specifically, by July 1, 2006, no new electronic or electrical equipment put on the market may contain lead, mercury, cadmium, or hexavalent chromium (date may be extended). Two types of flame retardants, polybrominated biphenyls (PBBs) and polybrominated diphenyl ethers (PBDEs), are also prohibited. A few exemptions to the new directive are permitted including some uses of mercury in fluorescent bulbs, lead in the glass used in CRTs, and lead in the solder used in such applications as servers and other network infrastructure.[68]

United States

The United States has not participated in this surge of take-back legislation in Europe and Asia. Three states, Florida, Minnesota and New Jersey, have passed laws that require the manufacturers take back and manage the disposal of the rechargeable batteries that they produce. Manufacturers of rechargeable batteries in Rhode Island and Vermont must ensure that a collection, transportation, and processing system to handle the disposal of their batteries is in place. A voluntary program for recycling rechargeable batteries was started by the five largest battery manufacturers. The program established the Rechargeable Battery Recycling Corporation (RBRC), to coordinate the system. Since it is not mandatory, questions have been raised about its effectiveness, due to lack of awareness among clerks at retail stores, where the batteries are dropped off.[69]

While several states, including California, Massachusetts, Minnesota, Rhode Island, Texas, Vermont and Washington, have introduced legislation dealing with electronics recycling, only California has actually passed a law imposing a $6-10 electronic waste recycling fee on the sale of new monitors and televisions and requiring manufacturers to inform consumers how to recycle or dispose of these products.[70]

This dichotomy between the United States and Europe and certain Asian countries will raise difficult challenges for U.S. multi-national companies, which sell both in the U.S. and abroad. When U.S. companies sell products abroad, these products will be subject to the requirements of extended producer responsibility legislation. They will have to decide whether to make two products, one for the U.S. and one for sale abroad, or make one product that meets take back standards for all markets. The initial reaction might be to make two products because of the higher costs associated with redesigning a product so that it meets take-back standards. These higher costs, if added on to their products in the U.S., could result in higher and less competitive prices for their products in the U.S. On the other hand, several corporations, like Volvo, Mercedes, and BMW have found that their redesigned vehicles have actually saved money, reduced waste and created additional jobs for their workers.[71] In addition, the risk of future liabilities resulting from injuries and damages associated with improper disposal of toxic materials are greatly diminished by following the higher standards of WEEE and RoHS Directives.

Several corporations and organizations in the United States are experimenting with design changes, setting up partnerships with recyclers and developing programs for their customers to voluntarily move their products and processes towards the goals of take back legislation. For instance, Gateway offers a $50 rebate off the purchase of one of its new computers if customers donate their old computer to a charity or a recycler. Apple Computer is designing its products to reduce the cost of disassembly and recycling. Canon, Hewlett Packard, Sony, and Toshiba have sponsored WEEE collection events at Best Buy stores, a major retailer of consumer electronics. Dell offers a recovery service in which it packs up old computers from its stores and ships them directly to recyclers. Dell and other corporations like Nokia and other Hewlett-Packard have set up partnerships with reputable recyclers to assure that old computers are disposed of properly. IBM operates its own recovery center in which it accepts computers from any source and then refurbishes, donates or recycles them. The Electronic Industry Alliance, a consortium of U.S. trade associations, reports that product designers of electronics are attempting to reduce the end of life environmental risks of their products through various design changes.[72]

In the automobile industry, Ford and General Motors have instituted recycling and bumper take back programs. In the Ford program, a partnership has been formed with General Electric to provide and recycle the plastic used in bumpers on Ford cars.[73]

From a sustainability risk management standpoint, all these changes represent sound risk control approaches. Future human health, environmental and product liability risks are being reduced. These efforts, particularly when they are not legislatively mandated, result in favorable publicity and reputation enhancement. Boycotts that might result would tend to concentrate on those companies that have not taken any action. Many companies are finding that overall costs are actually reduced by these efforts. Xerox was way ahead of the game with its program of taking back their photocopiers and refurbishing their components for reuse, which produced millions of dollars in savings.[74]

Finally, take back legislation may be passed in the future in the United States. Those companies, which have been making efforts to reduce waste and toxicity in their products and to make them more reusable, recyclable and disposal friendly, will be way ahead of competitors in meeting the requirements of any new legislation.

In a previous section on redesigning monstrous hybrids, several references were made to the fact that inadequacies in design were the cause of many health and environmental risk problems. What was needed was an entire new approach to design. Extended producer responsibility laws promote huge incentives for better designed products to lessen their environmental and health risks at their end of life. Focusing requirements on the end of life of products is a strong and efficient policy strategy because "many recycling and disposal costs are functions of the materials used in products and their assembly techniques, decisions made during product design and engineering."[75] More importantly, manufacturers are given certain target or parameter requirements to meet, but they maintain the freedom to employ their creativity and resourcefulness in making the various design decisions to make their products and processes more efficiently meet these requirements. As pointed out by the Explanatory Memorandum accompanying the EU's *Proposal for a Directive on Waste Electrical and Electronic Equipment,*

> "Producers of electrical and electronic equipment design the product, determine its specifications and select its materials. Only producers can develop approaches to the design and manufacture of their products to ensure the longest possible product life and, in the event that it is scrapped, the best methods of recovery and disposal."[76]

The principal objectives of take back regulations, the reduction of toxic waste materials, the improvement in human and workers' health, the increased use of recovery and recycling methods, and the lessening of environmental damage by products at the end of life, are all sound risk control goals of sustainability risk management. The risk of future liability suits is reduced, boycott risks are lessened along with potential reputation damage, and shareholder actions are minimized. Take back laws illustrate how the costs of an environmental and health risk area, which in the past have been externalized, can suddenly become internalized to businesses, even on a retrospective basis. While corporations and individuals can argue about the costs of meeting the requirements of take back laws, no reasonable company or person can argue that take back laws do not improve the quality of the environment and the health of its workers and citizens, and have not increased resource use efficiency. Realistically, because of the problem of free riders and other constraints, and the need to act now without long delays, the objectives of take back regulations necessitate that they be mandatory and not voluntary. In keeping with sound sustainability risk management, it would be my simple advice that corporations design, manufacture and take care of their products at the end of their lives as if take back laws were in effect. In my opinion, it is only a matter of time before EU type legislation will be passed in the United States.

Testing Chemicals for Health and Environmental Risks

Another EU Directive is being proposed that supports sustainability risk management strategies. The proposed directive is called Registration, Evaluation and Authorization of Chemicals (REACH). It calls for the testing, registering and authorizing of thousands of chemical substances. The original draft proposals called for around 30,000 chemicals to be included in the regulations. Heavy lobbying from the chemical industry and the governments of the United States, Germany, France, and Britain reduced this number by excluding polymers (most commonly found in plastics), and having less scrutiny for chemicals whose world production is less than 10,000 metric tons (may impact some two-thirds of all chemicals). Still, even this reduced number of approximately 10,000 chemicals represents a far greater testing program in scope than is currently in existence.

Current regulations in the EU and the U.S. have resulted in a relatively small percentages-one to two percent-of chemicals in use being thoroughly tested for their harmful effects. Under current EU rules, chemicals that were introduced after 1981, or new chemicals, must be registered with public authorities in the home country of the manufacturer. Some 3,000 new chemicals have been registered, but since 1993 only about 140 have actually been singled out for risk assessment. There are no automatic checks on the 75,000-100,000 that were in existence before 1981. Under the Toxic Substance Control Act and other regulations in the United States, around 1000-1500 chemicals have been tested for their harmful effects. The U.S. permits the use of about 30,000 chemicals that predate testing requirements under the Toxic Substances Control Act of 1976.

The proposed rule applies to chemicals produced in the EU countries and chemicals imported into the EU, so the U.S. and Asian companies that do business in Europe are impacted. Responsibility and costs for testing shifts to manufacturers from the government. The current estimate of these costs for the chemical industry is 2.3 billion euros or $2.8 billion over 11 years, a substantial reduction from the original cost estimate of 12.0 billion euros. The estimated costs for chemical users are 2.8 billion to 3.6 billion euros ($3.4 billion to $4.4 billion). So total estimated costs are in the range of 5.1-5.9 billion euros ($6.2-7.2 billion). The proposed regulation uses precautionary principle logic, which essentially puts the onus on producers of proving that chemicals are safe and do not harm individuals or the environment, rather than on the government having to prove that the chemicals are unsafe.

The arguments brought by the chemical industry and some governments are that the proposed law will result in excessive costs, will establish a large government bureaucracy, will force specialty companies out of business and will stifle innovation. Costs may be higher than currently estimated if changes have to be made to eliminate toxic substances from products. The business of making and importing chemicals in the European Union involves large amounts of money. The EU is the world's largest chemical producer, with about 28 percent of the world output. It is the third largest manufacturing industry in Europe. The U.S. chemical industry, America's largest exporter, exports $20 billion annually of its $460 billion in total revenues to EU countries.

The proposed directive must be approved by the 15 member countries in the EU and the European Parliament. The review and approval process is expected to take two years to around the end of 2005. While the industry has time to plan and adjust, it is generally expected that the rule will eventually be approved.

The main objective of the proposed REACH Directive is to protect and improve the health of individuals and the environment by identifying and phasing out some of the worst chemicals currently used in products and for other purposes. Previous sections in this book have discussed the adverse health and environmental effects of chemical exposures including increasing cancers, disruptions of the endocrine systems, reproductive problems and the fact that many chemicals are persistent and have spread to virtually all corners of the world. Previously referenced works, including, *Silent Spring, Our Stolen Future* and *Living Downstream*, as well as other studies have documented these adverse effects. Some of the costs have been assessed to chemical producers and users through liability suits and legislation like the Superfund program. Yet, most of the costs have been externalized and are being absorbed by the affected individuals, the environment, the life and health insurance industries and government social programs. Supporters of the directive would argue that present market mechanisms are not internalizing enough of these costs to create an incentive for chemical producers to voluntarily do what the directive requires.

So what would sound sustainability risk management strategies suggest for chemical companies and other potential businesses impacted by the REACH Directive? A sound strategy would be to support the directive. Ignoring the costs of complying for a moment, I think that everyone can agree that the directive will improve the health of individuals and the environment by phasing out the worst chemicals. If everyone agreed that the directive's objective of improving individual and environmental health is important, then the proposed directive does produce a strong risk control and prevention system. While the chemical industry may assert that they can do the job better with a voluntary system, past history is not supportive of such an assertion, and the problem of free riders ignoring voluntary compliance would still exist.

If the chemical industry is successful in derailing the directive, then they will only be delaying the time when they will have to pay for the costs of impairing the health of individuals and the environment. Without a government mandated system, a high probability exists that future liability suits and consumer boycotts will develop to assess these costs to the industry. And the assessment process will in all likelihood be more expensive and less efficient that the proposed regulatory system. The European commissioners have estimated that the benefits of the proposed regulation, mostly through lower health care costs, will be 18 billion to 54 billion euros ($20.6 billion to $61.7 billion) over a 30 year period. These estimated benefits far exceed the estimated costs to the chemical industry of 2.3 billion euros ($2.8 billion) of complying with the regulation. Even if additional costs to chemical users of 2.8-3.6 billion euros ($3.4-4.4 billion) are considered, it still seems that benefits will far exceed costs.

Without the regulation, the loss of these estimated benefits potentially become damages in liability suits. The tobacco litigation has strong parallels here. Tobacco industry executives long maintained that tobacco was not hazardous to health and fought regulations. But the end result was an enormous settlement of approximately $250 billion in litigation brought by several states in the United States. And the $250 billion primarily represented health care costs paid by the states as the result of treating tobacco related injuries. Whether or not one agrees with the outcome in this litigation, I would argue that a considerable probability exists that similar litigation could be brought against the chemical industry in the absence of the proposed regulation. The chemical industry might be more supportive of the proposed regulation if they looked at their estimated costs of 3.0 billion euros or $3.7 billion as being a premium for an option spread over 11 years to substantially reduce the risks of future litigation. Their risks will be reduced by mitigating the injuries to individuals and damages to the environment, and if they demonstrated a cooperative, supporting attitude, it would not only lessen the risk of reputation damage, it would also improve their chances of successfully defending future liability suits.

Contrast this strategy with what may occur if the regulation is not passed, or significantly watered down, and individual and environmental health continues to deteriorate from exposure to chemicals. A considerable amount of science currently exists, and has been referenced in this book, and more will certainly be developed in the future, that chemical exposure to humans and the environment is deleterious. Failure to deal with the situation now will only delay the inevitable, with far worse risk consequences in the future. And these consequences will fall not only the chemical industry but also on the politicians and governments that are working to defeat or weaken this legislation.

While individual chemical companies cannot necessarily control what other companies and governments do, they are in control of their own strategies. As has been repeatedly recommended in this book, enormous advantages exist to corporations who take the lead in dealing with sustainability risk exposures. While present costs may increase, these will almost certainly be less than the eventual and inevitable future costs of delaying to take action now. Enormous competitive advantage is gained through increased good will and reputation enhancement. Finally, given the seemingly inevitable passage of future legislation, early action will give corporations a head start on the necessary redesign in manufacturing, products, and other processes to eliminate the worse chemicals currently being used.[77]

Partnerships

Partnerships between corporations and various stakeholders can be an effective sustainability risk control strategy. Corporations and NGO environmental/social justice groups have traditionally been in separate camps and locked in states of confrontation. Corporations could afford to ignore NGO arguments, until recent boycott pressures and other techniques have had a material negative impact, giving NGOs more leverage and power. A number companies are working with NGO sustainability groups to try to find common ground. NGOs have to be careful of being co-opted, but in many cases a common ground has been found that results in a win-win situation for both parties. The best way to illustrate this risk control trend is to examine a number of constructive examples. These partnerships lessen the probability of liability suits and help to insulate the participating companies from boycotts and shareholder actions, with resulting reputation damage. They make contributions to sustainability efforts and often cost savings result.

McDonald's—Environmental Defense

Environmental Defense, a leading environmental group, has worked with several companies including General Motors, S.C. Johnson, and McDonald's. With

McDonald's, the world's largest buyer of meat, Environmental Defense worked to set up a program to reduce the use of antibiotics as growth promoters in poultry, beef and pork. Medical studies have shown that overuse of antibiotics in agriculture can lead to the development of drug resistant strains of bacteria that could impair human health. By working with Environmental Defense to reduce antibiotic use, McDonald's not only gains favorable publicity and a boast to their reputation, but the risk of future litigation is diminished. McDonald's also worked with Environmental Defense to reduce its waste and to increase its recycling.[78]

Alliance for Environmental Innovation

Environmental Defense has also worked with the Pew Charitable Trusts to form the Alliance for Environmental Innovation. The Alliance's purpose is to build on the partnership approach developed by Environmental Defense and McDonald's. The Alliance incorporates several core strategies including defining new environmental best practices, greening the supply chain, paving the way for stricter controls, and demonstrating the business benefits of environmentalism. Current Alliance business partners and developing projects include:

- Bristol-Myers Squibb—MERGE-ing the Environment into New Product Development
- Citigroup—Reducing the environmental impacts of copy paper
- FedEx—Creating the delivery truck of the future
- Norm Thompson Outfitters—Improving catalog paper practices
- SC Johnson—Implementing design-for-environment
- Starbucks Coffee Company—Re-inventing how to serve coffee
- United Parcel Service—Re-designing overnight shipping packaging[79]

Kraft Foods—Rainforest Alliance

Kraft Foods, the largest branded food and beverage company in the United States, announced in October, 2003 a new partnership with the Rainforest Alliance, an international conservation group, to support the development of sustainable coffee production in Mexico, Columbia, Brazil and Central America. Kraft will purchase and sell coffee certified as environmentally and socially sustainable by the Rainforest Alliance. Kraft will also fund technical assistance and training to improve living and working conditions on coffee farms. With this strategy, Kraft heads off boycott risks, receives favorable publicity and could gain an important marketing advantage on it main competitors. While Kraft has supported sustainable coffee initiatives for over the decade, the new partnership has taken this support and molded it into an important part of its overall strategic planning. For two groups that may have been at odds in the past, quotes from the directors of the new partners illustrate the new level of cooperation and mutual respect:

> "We are delighted to partner with the Rainforest Alliance and link our sustainability efforts to a widely respected organization with an established certification protocol and a strong local presence in major coffee growing areas." Anne Mieke, Kraft Foods Senior Director of Commodity Sustainability Programs.

> "This commitment by Kraft Foods is powerful evidence that the concept of sustainable coffee, once limited to niche markets, is ready to enter the mainstream market. Our partnership is an extraordinary step forward in advancing sustainable coffee farming and we are pleased to partner with Kraft Foods on this important initiative." Tensie Whelan, Executive Director of the Rainforest Alliance.[80]

Office Depot—Nature Conservancy, NatureServe and Conservational International

Office Depot, in March 2004, announced an alliance with three conservation groups, the Nature Conservancy, NatureServe, and Conservation International. The purpose of the newly formed Forest and Biodiversity Conservation Alliance is to promote research into forest management and endangered species protection. The results of the research will be used to strengthen Office Depot's procurement policy, which states that the Office Depot makes efforts to avoid procuring products made with fiber from forests that are of exceptional conservation value.[81]

Home Depot—Nature Conservancy, et.al.

The Home Depot had been the subject of a boycott and pressures to reduce their use of wood from old growth forests. In what was felt to be an act of conciliation and even appreciation, Home Depot ran a full page ad in the *Nature Conservancy* with a simply stated message:

> "The seed has been planted. It's with sincere thanks that The Home Depot recognizes those listed here. People helping us change the way we buy wood.

People who for the past two and a half years have educated and helped guide us toward even more responsible forestry. Our cause is growing. Thanks."

At the bottom of the ad page, 19 groups were listed including, The Nature Conservancy, Rainforest Alliance/SmartWood Program, World Wildlife Fund, World Resources Institute, Certified Forest Products Council, Conservation International, The Natural Step Environment Foundation, Tropical Forest Trust, USDA Forest Service International Programs, and Yale Forest Forum. Home Depot's action resulted in the boycott, and the resulting loss of sales, being called off. Since then Home Depot has been very active in their sustainability efforts (see earlier section in this chapter and chapter 3). Future generations who are able to enjoy old growth trees may reward the Home Depot with their purchases for helping to preserve these ancient forests.

KB Home, Staples and Hayward Lumber—Natural Resources Defense Council

Another novel partnership involving old growth trees brought the Natural Resources Defense Council (NRDC) together with home builder KB Home, office supply company Staples, and Hayward Lumber, a big supplier of building materials. Following pressure from environmental groups and shareholders, these three companies worked with the NRDC to formulate policies to reduce the amount of wood they used from old growth virgin forests. The NRDC persuaded the three companies to send letters to the Bush Administration opposing new road building and logging in Alaska's Tongass National Forest. Excerpts from letters sent by company representatives to the U.S. Forest Service illustrate the enormous distance that at least some companies have come in their new attitudes on supporting sustainability and reducing sustainability risks.

"Ample supplies of wood products can be found elsewhere; and we need not violate our most precious natural assets." Andrew Henderson, KB Home's Director of government and public affairs.

"National treasures such as the Tongass are a national trust which must be preserved for future generations." Mark Buckley, Staples Vice President

"Builders, developers and material suppliers continue to be cast as exploiters and plunderers and, given past actions, this characterization is not entirely unwarranted." Steven Brauneis, Hayward Lumber's Director of Sustainability.[82]

Unfortunately, their efforts and others were not successful as the Bush Administration went ahead and excluded the Tongass National Forest from a prohibition against building new roads. While the affected area is only five percent of the Tongass' total acres (but around 15 percent of the forested area), it contains much of the Tongass' oldest trees.

Looking long term, the prevailing attitude of many timber companies, including the U.S. Forest Service in the present administration, that we should continue to cut down old growth, virgin trees is puzzling. These areas are not realistically renewable as the trees are many hundreds and sometimes thousands of years old. Old growth areas have substantial tourist value, provide valuable habitat and offer aesthetic and even spiritual experiences for those that choose to visit them. With our present policies, we are essentially taking these experiences from our children and future generations. Those that have a financial interest in removing the trees favor continued cutting, but at some point in the relatively near future that financial opportunity will cease as these trees will be gone. The financial problems of timber companies in ceasing operations today will be exactly the same in the future when they are forced to stop because no more trees exist. By stopping today, we preserve in perpetuity these old growth areas and their considerable values, with the only cost being the loss of short-term financial gain by the timber industry. Clearly, financial assistance needs to be made available to workers, local communities, and companies that may suffer from a cessation of cutting old growth trees. But these funds could partly be provided from the savings that will be made from foregoing the expense of road building and other costs that are incurred by the government to facilitate the cutting of the old growth trees. By following the partnership and sustainability efforts of corporations like Home Depot, Office Depot, Kraft, KB Home, Staples, Hayward Lumber, Lowe's, Wickes Lumber, Home Base, Kinko's, L.L. Bean, and Patagonia, more sensible strategies could be employed that would preserve old growth trees and reduce sustainability risk costs.

Easements and Land Trusts

A related partnership involves the use of easements being negotiated between NGO environmental groups and timber companies. Easements can be used to sell development rights on land, which preserve forestlands for hunting, fishing, camping, hiking, and even limited logging. For example, Potlatch Corporation, a timber company out of Spokane, Washington sold the development rights of 600,000 acres of private forest to the Trust for Public Land for $40 million. The Great Northern Paper Company, a Maine based mill operator, sold development rights on 200,000 acres of privately held Maine forestlands to the Nature Conservancy. The Nature Conservancy also agreed to purchase and restructure $50 million of existing loans to keep the company's mills operating. Without this restructuring, Great Northern may have been forced to sell land to developers. The Conservation Fund paid $9.5 million to International Paper for development rights on 75,000 acres of private forests on the Tennessee's Cumberland Plateau. Under the arrangement, a private organization, Renewable Resources, bought the timber rights for $9.5 million and transferred the land to the control of the state. A group of national and local environmental organizations and land trusts has been particularly active in California's coastal areas. In 2003, 53,000 acres of coastal land was preserved according to the California Coastal Conservancy, a state agency that provided $168 million of seed money.

The Land Trust Alliance estimates that 2.6 million acres of U.S. land has been protected through conservation easements. This represents a five-fold increase over a decade ago. As part of these pacts, timber companies often agree to employ environmentally sound land use practices, such as limiting clear cutting and maintaining a buffer zone between cutting and stream beds. Financing from private NGO groups is often supplemented by federal funds through the Forest Legacy Program, which allocates up to $65 million a year for conservation easements. State board initiatives were passed in 2000 and 2002 that authorized $11.1 billion in state bonds to buy land for open space preservation, restore wetlands and wildlife habitat and create new urban parks.[83]

World Resources Institute

The World Resources Institute (WRI) is an independent non-profit think tank organization, founded in 1982 by James Gustave Speth, that "creates solutions to protect the Earth and improve people's lives."[84] WRI partners with 400 corporations, governments, and NGOs in 50 countries around the world. WRI's work focuses on four key goals:

- Protect Earth's living systems
- Increase access to information
- Create sustainable enterprise and opportunity
- Reverse global warming

WRI is active with business schools through its Business—Environment Learning and Leadership (BELL) program and its *Beyond Grey Pinstripes* Survey.

The BELL Program works with business school professors to provide them with educational tools in sustainable enterprise. WRI surveys graduate business schools and ranks their efforts in environmental and social impact management. The results are published in *Beyond Grey Pinstripes Preparing MBAs for Social and Environmental Stewardship.*[85]

The World Resources Institute brought a dozen major U.S. companies together in 2001 and persuaded them to pledge that, by 2010, at least 1,000 megawatts of the power they use will come from renewable sources such as wind, solar, landfill gas, and hydrogen fuel cells. Some of the companies include General Motors, Dow Chemical, DuPont, Johnson & Johnson, IBM, Kinko's and Staples. Some 10 percent of the electricity used by the latter two companies, Kinko's and Staples, currently comes from renewable sources. In the United States, around two percent of electricity comes from renewable sources.[86] Besides making a commitment to use non-renewable energy sources and lessening global warming pressures, employing renewable energy sources acts as a diversification strategy to reduce risk by hedging against widely fluctuating natural gas prices, possible oil supply disruptions arising from international conflicts, and the inevitable exhaustion of the resources at some time in the future.

Sierra Club Brands

Corporations have partnered with the Sierra Club to sell environmentally friendly products under the Sierra Club brand. Participating companies include Isda and Pillowtex and involve such products as hats, gloves, jackets, bedding and coffee. A frequent problem with environmentally friendly products is their extra cost. A marketing expert, Kurt Aschermann, cites studies that have shown that three-quarters of consumers will pay more for a product if it is associated with a nonprofit group they care about.[87] This partnership demonstrates a marketing strategy which sells products, but in an environmentally friendly manner. Besides having an outlet for their products, corporations partnering with the Sierra Club are also reducing potential liability and boycott risks that may accompany the selling of products which are harmful to the environment.

Citigroup—Rainforest Action Network

Citigroup reached an agreement with the Rainforest Action Network (RAN), in January 2004, to establish a new framework for evaluating its project financing for environmental impacts. The agreement will set higher standards that those under the Equator Principles that were backed by Citigroup and nine other major banks in 2003. The agreement guidelines call for Citigroup to not finance any project located in critical natural habitats unless the borrower demonstrates that the project "will not significantly degrade or covert the critical natural habitat." Citigroup will also not finance any commercial logging operations for use in tropical forests or for any illegal logging.[88] Citigroup has increasingly come under pressure from NGO sustainability groups for its financing strategies (see Chapter 3). The compact reached with RAN, which has been one of its most serious critics, should reduce future pressures and their negative impacts. Shortly following Citigroup, the Bank of America, in April 2004, also reached an agreement with RAN in the areas of stabilizing the earth's climate, protecting endangered forests and respecting the rights of indigenous people's rights.[89] As might be predicted RAN shifted its pressure to J.P. Morgan Chase, the largest U.S. based bank still operating without a comprehensive environmental policy and a non-signor of the Equator Principles. The bank partnerships with Citigroup and the Bank of America gave considerable leverage to RAN to pressure a competing bank. In April 2005, J.P. Morgan Chase reached an agreement with RAN to establish a comprehensive policy to take steps on climate change, forest protection, and indigenous rights.[90]

Certification and Standards Programs

The development of sustainability risk management practices can be bolstered through certification and standards programs. Such programs require that a business have certain minimum standards and procedures in place to control environmental and social justice risks. As noted above, these certifications and standards can be most useful in screening suppliers in a firm's supply chain for meeting certain levels of environmental and social performance. Three of the more well known programs, ISO 14001, Social Accountability 8000 and AccountAbility 1000, will be briefly described below.

ISO 14001

ISO 14001, which has been previously discussed, is a standard created by the International Organization for Standardization for developing environmental management systems. An environmental management system is defined as "the part of the overall management system that includes organizational structure, planning activities, responsibilities, practices, procedures, processes and resources for developing, implementing, achieving, reviewing and maintaining the environmental policy."[91]

Since its beginning in 1996, at least 36,765 companies have been ISO 14001 certified in 112 countries.

Companies in compliance with ISO 14001 must develop:

- An environmental policy
- An assessment of environmental aspects
- An assessment of legal and voluntary obligations
- A management system
- A series of periodic internal audits and reports to top management

While popular and useful for evaluating environmental commitment, it has been criticized for its lack of performance criteria. This criticism helped to give rise to the Eco-Management and Audit Scheme (EMAS), which was developed in 2001 by the European Parliament and the Council for the European Union. While similar to the ISO 14001, EMAS includes the requirement of public reports on environmental performance, which are verified by an independent verifier.[92]

Social Accountability 8000

Social Accountability (SA) 8000 is system for measuring corporate social accountability. It is a global and verifiable standard, which combines management systems of the ISO with conventions of the International Labor Organization. Its principal purpose is to make the workplace more humane. The certification standard was developed and is monitored by trade unions, corporations, NGOs and academics. The requirement of management systems means that social issues are integrated into all aspects of corporate policies and operations. Certifications have been granted in 36 industries in 36 countries, which impact 171,307 workers. As with ISO 14001, SA 8000 certification assists corporations in making appropriate decisions as to suppliers in its supply chain. The majority of companies seeking SA 8000 certification are those in problematic industries such as garments, shoes, toys, and the agricultural sector.[93]

AccountAbility 1000

AccountAbility (AA) 1000 defines best practice in social and ethical auditing, accounting and reporting. AA 1000 was developed as a framework in 1999 by the Institute for Social and Ethical AccountAbility, a professional membership group committed to promoting accountability as a means for achieving sustainable development. In 2003, the Institute developed the AA 1000 Assurance Standard.

Like SA 8000, multiple stakeholders formulated the standard, which increases its creditability. Corporate responsibility has often been a fuzzy concept, which is difficult to measure. AA 1000 brings discipline, professional qualifications, training and specific methods for developing quality systems.[94]

Business Associations

A number of business associations have been established over the last 10-15 years to promote environmental, social justice and sustainability efforts. These voluntary groups are particularly helpful to companies that are in the early stages of developing sustainability strategies. By sharing experiences and striving towards common goals, these groups can facilitate progress in sustainability risk management.

CERES

The Coalition for Environmentally Responsible Economies (CERES) is a non-profit organization, established in the United States in 1989, which sets forth 10 environmental principles for member organizations. Some of these principles have direct application to sustainability risk management, including reduction and disposal of wastes, risk reduction, and safe products and services. The CERES Principles were originally known as the Valdez Principles, as they were established after the Exxon Valdez oil spill in Alaska. The titles of the 10 principles are included below:

- Protection of the Biosphere
- Sustainable Use of Natural Resources
- Reduction and Disposal of Wastes
- Energy Conservation
- Risk Reduction
- Safe Products and Services
- Environmental Restoration
- Informing the Public
- Management Commitment
- Audits and Reports

CERES has been particularly active in responding to global warming risks through research, partnerships and support of shareholder resolutions (see Chapters 4 and 7). Members of CERES include General Motors, Ford, American Airlines, Con Edison, ITT, Nike, Bethlehem Steel, Polaroid, BankAmerica, Cocacola, and the Body Shop.[95]

ICC

The International Chamber of Commerce (ICC) created the Business Charter for Sustainable Development in 1991 in Rotterdam. Sixteen principles for environmental management are set forth by the Charter, which has been published in over 20 languages, including all the official languages at the United Nations. The ICC encourages member companies to express their support and implement the Charter and its principles.[96]

WBCSD

The World Business Council for Sustainable Development (WBCSD) is a coalition of over 120 international companies united by a commitment to the environment and to the principles of economic growth and sustainable development. Its members are drawn from thirty-five countries and more than twenty major industrial sectors. It has a global network of fifteen national business councils, as well as regional business councils and partner organizations in development countries.[97]

Equator Principles

One of the more recent business association programs centers around the formulation of the Equator Principles in 2003. This association was initiated by 10 of the world's largest banks to address the social and environmental impacts of large projects that they finance. As of September 2004, a total of 27 of the world's banks have joined the group, which account for around 80 percent of all project financing in the world. The signatories agree to a series of guidelines for assessing project finance deals, based on the Safeguard Policies used by the International Finance Corporation, the World Bank's private finance arm. Much of the motivation came from the damage done to their reputations by several high-profile projects such as the Ilisu Dam in Turkey.[98] Such projects have attracted negative NGO campaigning and resulted in huge environmental and social costs.[99]

United Nations Programs

The United Nations has developed some of the oldest sustainability programs in the world. Since the early 1970s, the UN has initiated a number of voluntary programs, in which participating companies agree to follow various environmental, sustainability, and social responsibility principles, standards and guidelines. Joining and supporting these programs can augment sustainability risk management strategies.

United Nations World Heritage Program

The United Nations World Heritage Program, founded in 1972, designates and helps to preserve cultural or natural sites for their "outstanding value to humanity." Once a site has been designated, 170 countries pledge to help protect it. Because of budget and enforcement difficulties, corporations can still bring pressure to develop in the designated areas. In August 2003, Royal Dutch/Shell and the International Council on Mining and Metals, which represents the world's 15 largest mining companies, pledged that they will not explore or extract resources from World Heritage sites. Of particular interest in the case of Shell is the Artic National Wildlife Refuge in Alaska, which is currently being evaluated as a World Heritage site by Unesco, the UN agency that controls the program. An investment group official, Rob Lake, director of corporate governance at Henderson's Global Investors in London, comments, "Shell and the mining companies have decided there is more shareholder value to their reputation than the resources they could tap in World Heritage sites."[100]

United Nations Environmental Programme (UNEP)

The United Nations Environmental Programme created the Industry and Environment Centre (UNEPIE) in 1975. UNEPIE works with business and industry, national and local governments, international groups, and nongovernmental organizations. The program "acts as a catalyst, providing a platform for dialogue and helping to move from confrontation to cooperation, from words to concrete actions." The goals of UNEPIE are to:

- Build consensus for preventive environmental protection through cleaner and safer industrial production and consumption

- Help formulate policies and strategies to achieve cleaner and safer production and consumption patterns, and facilitate their implementation

- Define and encourage the incorporation of environmental criteria in industrial production

- Stimulate the exchange of information on environmentally sound technologies and forms of industrial development[101]

Global Reporting Initiative

The Coalition for Environmentally Responsible Economies (CERES), along with the Tellus Institute, worked with UNEP to develop the Global Reporting Initiative (GRI) in 1997. In 2002, the GRI was launched as a permanent global institution. The Global Reporting Initiative pioneered sustainability reporting by establishing guidelines for economic, social and environmental reporting. The mission of the GRI is "to elevate the quality of reporting to a higher level of comparability, consistency and utility."[102] Indeed, GRI aims to elevate sustainability reporting to equivalency with financial reporting. Some 10,000 stakeholders from more than 50 companies were engaged in preparing the GRI guidelines. Consequently, considerable support is received from companies and NGOs around the world. Through 2003, 313 companies in 31 countries issue GRI reports, with the majority being located in Europe. The transparency, consistency, inclusiveness and audit ability of the GRI reports give the companies increased creditability with NGOs, shareholders and other stakeholders that may be interested and concerned about their sustainability progress.[103]

While possibly providing information that may be subject to criticism, GRI reporting companies would also seem to be given the benefit of the doubt by their critics, particularly if the companies are working to improve their sustainability performance. GRI reporting is voluntary, so the act of participating lends some creditability. Sustainability risks associated with liability litigation, boycotts, shareholders actions and reputation damage should be lessened through GRI reporting. GRI can be used in conjunction with Social Accountability (SA 8000) and AccountAbility 1000(AA 1000) discussed earlier in this chapter.

Universal Declaration of Human Rights

The Universal Declaration of Human Rights (UDHR) covers human rights broadly to include political, economic and social rights. It was adopted in 1948 by the General Assembly in the early years of the United Nations. A growing number of multinational corporations, including AVIVA, BP, British Telecommunications, and Shell, refer to the UDHR in their statements of principles. Because the UDHR includes political, as well as social and economic issues, it is challenging to incorporate the Declaration into business principles. The Danish Centre on Human Rights is working with companies and stakeholders to translate the articles of the UDHR into business principles.[104]

Global Compact

The UN Global Compact was established in 2000. The Compact works to ensure that corporate activities conform to basic environment, human rights and workers' rights standards. The Global Compact was initiated by UN Secretary General Kofi Annan, and marks the first effort on corporate responsibility aimed at companies to emerge from the Secretary General's office. From 50 charter members, more than 1,700 companies over the world participate by communicating through external reports (e.g., annual reports, sustainability reports) their progress in implementing the nine principles of the Compact. Around 25 global NGOs and labor groups have joined, making the Compact the world's largest voluntary corporate citizenship group according to a recent McKinsey & Co. study. Some 20 financial institutions have pledged to consider environmental and social justice practices in their equity evaluations. The nine principles are derived from the Universal Declaration of Human Rights, the ILO's Fundamental Principles on Rights at Work and the Rio Declaration on Environment and Development, and are included below:

Human Rights

- **Principle 1:** Businesses are asked to support and respect the protection of international human rights within their sphere of influence: and

- **Principle 2:** make sure their own corporations are not complicit in human rights abuses.

Labour

- **Principle 3:** Business are asked to uphold the freedom of association and the effective recognition of the right to collective bargaining;

- **Principle 4:** the elimination of all forms of forced and compulsory labour;

- **Principle 5:** the effective abolition of child labour; and

- **Principle 6:** the elimination of discrimination in respect of employment and occupation.

Environment

- **Principle 7:** Business are asked to support a precautionary approach to environment challenges;

- **Principle 8:** undertake initiatives to promote greater environmental responsibility; and

- **Principle 9:** encourage the development and diffusion of environmentally friendly technologies.

While the Global Compact has been a huge success from a membership growth standpoint, several NGOs are raising questions on its effectiveness. Since there is no transparent system for NGOs to verify company claims and few clear standards to measure performance, questions arise that some companies may be using Compact membership as a corporate public relations gimmick.[105]

Responsible Investment Initiative

In July 2004, the United Nations Environment Programme (UNEP) announced it was working with fund managers to establish the Responsible Investment Initiative. This Initiative will have a series of guidelines for socially responsible investment, which cover social, environmental and corporate governance issues. These guidelines are intended for use by brokers and asset managers, particularly pension fund managers whose portfolios are impacted by long term environmental and social developments. The foundation for the initiative was based on a 14 month study completed in June 2004 entitled, *The Materiality of Social, Environmental and Corporate Governance Issues to Equity Pricing.* The report was comprised of 11 sector studies performed by brokerage house analysts at the invitation of the UNEP Finance Initiative Asset Management Worker Group. Among the key findings of the study:

- There was agreement that environmental, social and corporate governance issues affect long-term shareholder value. In some cases those effects may be profound.

- The majority of analysts noted difficulties in comparative analysis due to the range of reporting practices for environmental, social and corporate governance risks and opportunities.

- Financial research was greatly aided by clear government positions with respect to environmental, social and corporate governance issues. In some cases analysts were not able to provide in-depth reports due to a lack of certainty regarding government policy.[106]

Furthermore, the authors stated, "These results provide strong independent support for the thesis that effective management of these issues will contribute to growing shareholder value. We therefore feel that they should be taken into account in fundamental financial analysis and thus investment consider- ations."[107] The fund guidelines are due to be completed by September 2005.

In writing the sections on some of the certification programs, business associa- tions and UN programs discussed above, I found that Deborah Leipziger's book, *The Corporate Responsibility Code Book*, was most useful. Her book of course is referenced in the text and the notes at the end of this book, but I wanted to alert the reader in the main text about this book. Anyone with responsibility in the sustainability risk management area would want to have this book on their shelves.

Reputation Risk Management

Protecting and enhancing a company's reputation is a critical part of an overall risk management strategy. Jim Kartalia, President of SeNet Corporation defines reputation as "a compilation of views held by all the firm's stakeholders-investors, clients, customers, employees, suppliers, partners, vendors, media, financial ana- lysts, special interest groups, politicians, labor unions, shareholder activists and regulators."[108]

Reputation is often captured by the value of the company's brand or corporate brand equity. This value can be considerable and is estimated by such organiza- tions as Interbrand. Recall Figure 3-1 that illustrates the brand values vs. market capitalization values for the top 10 brand companies in the world. For Coca- Cola, the corporation with the highest brand value, its brand value of $68.9 bil- lion equals 61 percent of it market capitalization of $113 billion. For Ford and McDonald's, the eighth and ninth highest valued brands, their brand value as a percentage of market capitalization is 66 and 71 percent, respectively.

Since the corporation's reputation depends on the views of so many different parties, adverse events, which impair a company's reputation, tend to lower those views. Such adverse events might include a failure in the product's performance that results in injuries to customers, such as the Firestone tires destructing at high speeds. Boycotts are another example. Boycotts often do not focus on the quality of the product so much as how the product manufacturing process may adversely impact the environment or its workers. Adverse events are almost always accompanied by negative publicity. When a corporation's reputation is imperiled, financial consequences can be serious. A typical consequence is a loss of sales and the resulting profits. These losses in turn decrease the price of the corporate stock and lower shareholder value.

In managing reputation risk, the luxury of having insurance, which is often available for other financially damaging adverse events, is not available. One cannot buy insurance to protect against the loss of sales, profits, and shareholder values associated with a decrease in reputation. The lack of financial backup provided by insurance is troubling as sometimes reputation losses can be swift and catastrophic, as was shown in the demise of the Andersen accounting firm. The absence of insurance puts more pressure on the risk management tools of risk assessment and risk control. Fortunately, the protection of a firm's reputation is a top priority of top management. A study conducted by Hill and Knowlton/ Yankelovich for the *Chief Executive Magazine*, and reported in Judy Larkin's *Strategic Reputation Risk Management*, found that 96 percent of CEOs feel that reputation is very important.[109]

I mentioned in the early sections of the book that one of my purposes is writing this book is to provide executives in the risk management and insurance industry and other interested parties with a wide variety of information sources on sustainability risk management. In reputation risk management, an excellent book by Judy Larkin entitled, *Strategic Reputation Risk Management*, was published in 2003. This book should be an important source for building sound reputation risk management practices as an overall part of formulating sustainability risk management strategies.

Managing reputation risks is a critical part of managing sustainability risks. Most sustainability risks, which have been discussed in this book, place a heavy burden on a corporation's reputation. This should act as a strong incentive not only for the risk manager but also for top corporate management to develop and maintain sound sustainability risk management practices.

Summary

This chapter has focused on sustainability risk management strategies that can be utilized by risk managers and corporate management. The information and strategies discussed here are quite different than those found in standard risk management texts. Previous chapters have documented increasing sustainability risk costs. This chapter examines methods of assessing and mitigating these risk costs.

Environmental and social justice risks are often ignored or minimized in the risk assessment process. Such omissions could prove to be costly mistakes. While some obvious effort will be required, risk managers certainly can accomplish this job, given their expertise in risk assessment. Some new methods discussed above will be needed, but the positive results of incorporating environmental and social justice risks into the risk assessment process will be well worth the effort.

This book does not provide a detailed blueprint or methodology as to setting up the specifics of sustainability risk assessment and control processes. Each company will need to construct their own specific sustainability risk assessment and control methods and techniques. Consultants like William McDonough, Michael Braungart and John Elkington would clearly provide considerable value to the effective development and implementation of sustainability risk assessment and control strategies, methods and techniques. Even accounting firms, like PricewaterhouseCoopers and KPMG, through their sustainability services practices, are entering the sustainability risk management consulting area.

The importance of the attitude and support of top management was discussed in this chapter. For those companies reluctant to get more involved in sustainability efforts, hopefully the information and strategies presented in this book and specifically this chapter will serve as a motivator for management to do so. Recall that the business judgment rule, which helps to insulate directors and officers from litigation, requires that directors and officers stay informed by seeking relevant and available information. Avoidance and ignorance of the vast amount of material that can be employed in developing sustainability risk management strategies will result in the loss of the business judgment rule protection. In addition, with increasing transparency, failure to take action will be more apparent to various stakeholders.

While considerable debate has revolved around the use of the precautionary principle, I have been totally comfortable with the concept. Indeed I think that most individuals schooled in risk management would incorporate the precautionary principle into their strategic thinking—I certainly do. The precautionary principal is an integral part of and imbedded within sustainability risk management systems. The key elements of the precautionary principle are one that regulators can take action based on evidence that harm may result from a particular substance or action; and two, the burden of proof shifts from the regulator proving a product/action is unsafe to the corporation proving that its products/actions are safe and will not result in harm. I would suggest readers consult a recent book, *The Precautionary Principle in the 20th Century*, edited by Poul Harremoës, et.al.

for an excellent examination of the principle with a number of real world examples.[110]

The precautionary principle is increasingly being applied as demonstrated by the EU's REACH directive, discussed in this chapter, and in EU regulations for GM crops (see Chapter 8). I anticipate that regulatory and competitive pressures will result in its expansion particularly in the United States. The need to incorporate the precautionary principle into corporate strategy augments the importance of developing sustainability risk assessment and control strategies. Sustainability risk costs will be reduced and firms will enjoy increased profits, improved reputations, and stronger competitive positions.

CHAPTER 9—ENDNOTES

[1] *Cost of Risk Survey, 1997,* Stamford, CT: Tillinghast, 1997.

[2] David J. Dybdahl, Managing Director of Willis Corroon's Environmental Risk Management Services, interview, 1997.

[3] Association of British Insurers, *Investing in Social Responsibility: Risks and Opportunities,* London: ABI, 2001.

[4] Paul A. Hilton and Alice Tepper Marlin, "The Role of the Nonprofit in Rating Environmental Performance," *Corporate Environmental Strategy,* 1997.

[5] George M. Reider, "Liability Claims-A Point in Time," *Insurance Economics,* Geneva: Geneva Association, January 2003.

[6] Seth Schiesel, "What Are the Chances?" *New York Times,* February 6, 2003.

[7] Curtis Haymore, "Risk Assessment Process," *Environmental Risk Management,* editors Eric B. Rothenberg and Dean Jeffery Telego, Alexandria, VA: RTM Communications, Inc., 1991.

[8] Ibid.

[9] www.heinzcenter.org; Jon Christensen, "Fiscal Accountability Concerns come to Conservation," *New York Times,* November 5, 2002.

[10] ISEA, 1998: www.iit.edu/~butler/isea.

[11] T.E. Graedel and B.R. Allenby, *Industrial Ecology,* Englewood Cliffs, New Jersey: Prentice Hall, 1995.

[12] Stuart Hart, "Beyond Greening: Strategies for a Sustainable World," *Harvard Business Review,* January-February, 1997.

[13] James H. Schaarsmith, "ISO 14001 Lowers Environmental Risks," *Business Insurance,* July 10, 2000.

[14] Ibid.

[15] M.S. Baram, "Multinational Corporations, Private Codes, and Technology Transfer for Sustainable Development," *Environmental Law Reporter,* 24, 1994.

[16] STEP, *American Petroleum Institute Environmental, Health and Safety Mission and Guiding Principles,* 1996.

[17] *The KPMG International Surveyof Corporate Sustainability Reporting,* KPMG; www.corporateregister.com, 2002.

[18] Catherine Arnst, John Carey, Stanley Reed, Gary McWilliams, and De'Ann Weimer, "When Green Begets Green," *BusinessWeek,* November 10, 1997.

[19] Ross Gelspan, "A Good Climate for Investment," *Atlantic Monthly,* June 1998.

[20] Thaddeus Herrick, "Judge Tells Exxon to Pay $4.5 Billion," *Wall Street Journal,* January 29, 2004; "Time for Exxon to Pay," *New York Times,* January 30, 2004; www.exxonmobil.com.

[21] Charles H. Paterson, et.al. "Long-Term Ecosystem Response to the Exxon Valdez Oil Spill", *Science,* Vol.302, December 19, 2003.

[22] James H. Schaarsmith, "ISO 14001 Lowers Environmental Risks," *Business Insurance,* July 10, 2000.

[23] John Elkington, *Cannibal with Forks,* Gabriola Island BC, Canada: New Society Publishers, 1998.

[24] Ibid.

[25] Jim Carlton, "Once Targeted by Protestors, Home Depot Plays Green Role," *Wall Street Journal,* August 6, 2004.

[26] "Socially Responsible Management of the Supply Chain," Robert H. Smith School of Business-University of Maryland, Research@Smith, Spring 2003, vol. 3, No. 2.

[27] William McDonough and Michael Braungart, *Cradle to Cradle*, New York: North Point Press, 2002.

[28] Catherine Arnst, John Carey, Stanley Reed, Gary McWilliams, and De'Ann Weimer, "When Green Begets Green," *BusinessWeek*, November 10, 1997.

[29] William McDonough and Michael Braungart, *Cradle to Cradle*, New York: North Point Press, 2002.

[30] Catherine Arnst, John Carey, Stanley Reed, Gary McWilliams, and De'Ann Weimer, "When Green Begets Green," *BusinessWeek*, November 10, 1997.

[31] John Elkington, *Cannibal with Forks*, Gabriola Island BC, Canada: New Society Publishers, 1998.

[32] Linda Bagneschi, "Pollution Prevention, The Best-Kept Secret in Loss Control," *Risk Management*, July 1998.

[33] William McDonough and Michael Braungart, *Cradle to Cradle*, New York: North Point Press, 2002.

[34] Ibid.

[35] Janine M. Benyus, *Biomimicry*, New York: Perennial, 1997.

[36] William McDonough and Michael Braungart, *Cradle to Cradle*, New York: North Point Press, 2002.

[37] Ibid.

[38] Theo Colborn, Dianne Dumanoski and John Peter Meyers, *Our Stolen Future*, New York: Plume Penquin, 1997.

[39] John Elkington, *Cannibal with Forks*, Gabriola Island BC, Canada: New Society Publishers, 1998.

[40] Sherwood Rowland and Mario Molina, "Stratospheric Sink for Chlorofluoromethanes: Chlorine Atom-Catalyzed Destruction of Ozone," *Nature,* June 28, 1974.

[41] Theo Colborn, Dianne Dumanoski and John Peter Meyers, *Our Stolen Future,* New York: Plume Penquin, 1997.

[42] Ibid.

[43] Elizabeth Cook (editor), *Ozone Protection in the United States: Elements of Success,* World Resources Institute, 1996; reported in John Elkington, *Cannibal with Forks,* Gabriola Island BC, Canada: New Society Publishers, 1998.

[44] Theo Colborn, Dianne Dumanoski and John Peter Meyers, *Our Stolen Future,* New York: Plume Penquin, 1997.

[45] Ibid.

[46] William McDonough and Michael Braungart, *Cradle to Cradle,* New York: North Point Press, 2002.

[47] Ibid.

[48] Ibid.

[49] Ibid.

[50] John Elkington, *Cannibal with Forks,* Gabriola Island BC, Canada: New Society Publishers, 1998.

[51] Ibid.

[52] T.E. Graedel and B.R. Allenby, *Industrial Ecology,* Englewood Cliffs, New Jersey: Prentice Hall, 1995.

[53] Stuart Hart, "Beyond Greening: Strategies for a Sustainable World," *Harvard Business Review,* January-February, 1997.

[54] Brian Nattrass and Mary Altomare, *The Natural Step for Business,* Gabriola Island, BC Canada: New Society Publishers, 1999.

[55] Ibid.

[56] Theo Colborn, Dianne Dumanoski and John Peter Meyers, *Our Stolen Future,* New York: Plume Penquin, 1997.

[57] Patrick D. Eagan and Wayne Pferdehirt, "Expanding the Benefits of Environmental Management Systems through Design for the Environment," working paper, 1997; Agis Veroutis and Vital Aelion, "Design for Environment: An Implementation Framework," *Total Quality Environmental Management,* Summer 1996.

[58] Brian Nattrass and Mary Altomare, *The Natural Step for Business,* Gabriola Island BC, Canada: New Society Publishers, 1999.

[59] Ibid.

[60] Ibid.

[61] Brian Nattrass and Mary Altomare, *Dancing with the Tiger,* Gabriola Island, BC Canada: New Society Publishers, 2002.

[62] Karl-Henrik Robèrt, *The Natural Step Story,* Gabriola Island, BC Canada: New Society Publishers, 2002.

[63] Michael W. Toffel, "Closing the Loop: Product Take-Back Regulations and Their Strategic Implications," *International Journal of Corporate Sustainability,"* Vol. 10, Issue 9, October 2003.

[64] Ibid.

[65] OECD, "Guiding Principles Concerning International Economic Aspects of Environmental Policies," Paris: Organization for Economic Co-operation and Development, 1972.

[66] Michael W. Toffel, "Closing the Loop: Product Take-Back Regulations and Their Strategic Implications," *International Journal of Corporate Sustainability*," Vol. 10, Issue 9, October 2003.

[67] "European Union, "Electrical and Electronic Products Directives," INFORM, Inc., July 2003, www.informinc.org.

[68] Information for WEEE and RoHS Directives from "European Union (EU) Electrical and Electronic Products Directives", INFORM, Inc., July 2003, www.informinc.org; Jon Farber, "E-waste disposal a growing problem" *Business Insurance*, May 19, 2005; Jared Wade, "Easy Being Green," *Risk Management*, July 2005.

[69] Jason West, "The Afterlife of Batteries," *Onearth*, Fall 2003

[70] Michael W. Toffel, "Closing the Loop: Product Take-Back Regulations and Their Strategic Implications," *International Journal of Corporate Sustainability*," Vol. 10, Issue 9, October 2003.

[71] www.unnaturallaw.ca.

[72] Michael W. Toffel, "Closing the Loop: Product Take-Back Regulations and Their Strategic Implications," *International Journal of Corporate Sustainability*," Vol. 10, Issue 9, October 2003.

[73] Gary A. Davis, "Automotive Take Back and Recycling Programs," *Extended Product Responsibility: A New Principle for Product-Oriented Pollution Prevention*, http://eerc.ra.utk.edu/ccpct/EPR.html.

[74] Michael W. Toffel, "Closing the Loop: Product Take-Back Regulations and Their Strategic Implications," *International Journal of Corporate Sustainability*," Vol. 10, Issue 9, October 2003.

[75] Ibid.

[76] Ibid.

[77] Parts of this section based on Elizabeth Becker and Jennifer Lee, "Europe Plan on Chemicals Seen as Threat to U.S. Exports, *New York Times,* May 8, 2003; Paul Meller, "Europe Proposes Overhaul of Chemical Industry," *New York Times,* October 30, 2003; "EU Narrows Scope of Plan to Check Chemicals' Safety," *Wall Street Journal,* October 24, 2003; "U.S. Opposes EU Effort to Test Chemicals for Health Hazards," *Wall Street Journal,* September 9, 2003; Samuel Lowenberg, "Old Europe's New Ideas," *Sierra,* January/February 2004; Hannah Karp and John W. Miller, "Chemical Rules Face Possibility of Dilution in E.U.," *Wall Street Journal,* October 1, 2004; Carolyn Aldred, "E.U. Chemical Makes fight proposed rule changes," *Business Insurance,* June 13, 2005; Jared Wade, "Easy Being Green," *Risk Management,* July 2005; Sandra Steingraber, *Living Downstream,* New York; Vintage Books, 1997.

[78] www.environmentaldefense.org.

[79] www.environmentaldefense.org/alliance.

[80] Press Release, Kraft Foods, October 7, 2003.

[81] Ann Carrns, "Office Depot, 3 Conservation Groups Form Alliance," *Wall Street Journal,* March 22, 2004.

[82] Jim Carlton, "Big Businesses Oppose Logging in Alaska Forest," *Wall Street Journal,* August 25, 2003.

[83] Jim Carlton, "Saving Private Wildlands," *Wall Street Journal,* November 13, 2002; Jim Wasserman, "A Trust in the Land, Associated Press in *The Capital Times,* March 24, 2004.

[84] www.wri.org.

[85] Ibid.

[86] H. Josef Herbert, "More Corporation Turn to Green Power," *Daily Journal of Commerce,* Seattle, WA, September 18, 2003.

[87] Claudia H. Deutsch, "Green Marketing: Label with a Cause," *New York Times,* June 15, 2003.

[88] "Citigroup, Environmental Group Reach Pact," *Wall Street Journal*, January 22, 2004.

[89] "RAN Breaks the Bank," Action Alert, RAN, Spring 2004

[90] RAN Action Alert, Fall 2004; "Victory! J.P. Morgan Chase Adopts Green Policies," memo to members, RAN, May 10, 2005.

[91] www.ISO14000.com

[92] Deborah Leipziger, *The Corporate Responsibility Code Book*, Sheffield, UK: Greenleaf Publishing, 2003; www.iso.org.

[93] Ibid.

[94] Ibid.

[95] www.CERES.org.

[96] www.ICCWHO.org.

[97] www.wbcsd.ch.

[98] Roz Bulleid, "Putting principles into practice," *Environmental Finance*, June 2004; Mark Nicholls, "Push and pull at the IFC," *Environmental Finance*, June 2004; "IFC consults on new social and environmental policy," *Environmental Finance*, September 2004.

[99] www.equator-principles.com.

[100] Heather Timmons, "Shell to Avoid Oil Drilling at Sites Listed by Unesco," *New York Times*, August 31 2003.

[101] www.unepie.org.

[102] www.globalreporting.org.

[103] Deborah Leipziger, *The Corporate Responsibility Code Book*, Sheffield, UK: Greenleaf Publishing, 2003.

[104] Ibid.

[105] Deborah Leipziger, *The Corporate Responsibility Code Book*, Sheffield, UK: Greenleaf Publishing, 2003; Peter Engardio, "Global Impact, Little Impact," *BusinessWeek,* July 12, 2004.

[106] *The Materiality of Social, Environmental and Corporate Governance Issues to Equity Pricing,* New York: UNEP Finance Initiative, June 2004.

[107] Ibid.

[108] Jim Kartalia, "Reputation at Risk?" *Risk Management,* July 2000.

[109] Judy Larkin, *Strategic Reputation,* Risk Management, Houndmills Basingstroke, Hampshire, England: Palgrave MacMillan, 2003.

[110] Poul Harremoës, et.al., editors, *The Precautionary Principle in the 20th Century,* London: Earthscan Publications Ltd., 2002.

10

SUSTAINABILITY RISK FINANCE

○ ○

One can surmise that carriers who use the broad exclusionary language cited above would resist coverage for claims in which an insured failed to adequately disclose environmental liability on financial statements,.....(or)....certified falsely that appropriate internal controls were maintained for environmental risk management.

—Kenn Anderson, Managing Director of Gallagher Environmental Risk and Insurance and Donna Ferrara, Vice President of Gallagher Executive and Professional Services Division

Purchasing sufficient environmental insurance to cap newly disclosed environmental liabilities would provide some protection to the company and its directors and reduce their potential liability to shareholders and minimize or undercut shareholders' ability to complain about the disclosure.

—Attorney Jeffery Schumacher, Sachnoff and Weaver

A number of significant environmental and social justice risks have been discussed throughout this book. These risks have included increased liabilities, boycotts, shareholder actions, and reputation damages. Risks associated with newer developments like global warming/climate change and genetically modified crops have also been examined. It might be tempting for business executives to respond by claiming that new and developing risks have always been present in conducting commerce-indeed, it is a necessary characteristic and cost of doing business. Executives may further claim that the impacts of these risks should be mitigated by insurance coverages carried by the firm. That is why we have corporate risk managers and insurance companies-to make sure that unexpected risks are insured. While that may be a common belief, it is not correct. The adverse financial consequences emanating from sustainability risks, particularly in the environmental area, are largely not covered by insurance. The insurance industry has been burned by past losses in the environmental area, and has acted to exclude these risks from standard general liability insurance policies. Insurance policies do exist for at least some of these risks. While I would argue that many corporations should purchase existing insurance coverages for environmental and social justice risks, in fact most do not.

In this chapter, I will examine the reasons for the insurance industry restricting their general liability policies through exclusions for many sustainability risks. I will also look at the existing sustainability risk financing markets and products, and discuss the reasons why so few corporations have elected to protect themselves by accessing the currently available products. New risk financing mechanisms for removing troublesome risk areas like Superfund and asbestos liabilities from a company's balance sheet will be examined. Finally, arguments for strengthening sustainability risk financing programs will be offered.

Restrictions and Exclusions in General Liability Policies

The enormous losses that the insurance industry incurred and is still incurring from asbestos and Superfund liabilities (see Chapter 6) is the primary reason for the insurance industry adding restrictions and exclusions in their liability forms. Discussions of older sustainability risks, like asbestos and superfund, provide a useful perspective for the points made below.

Except for individuals like Rachel Carson, the business world, including the insurance industry, gave little thought to risks inherent in the environmental area until the 1970s. With the advent of the National Environmental Protection Act (NEPA), the Clean Air Act and the Clean Water Act, the business world was forced to deal with environmental risks. While the insurance industry was not directly impacted by the requirements of these acts, insurance officials began pondering ways in which environmental risks could impact liability insurance policies. Concern existed with systemic pollution over extended periods of time, such as a company regularly and deliberately emitting pollutants into the air and the water. Regular and deliberate polluting emissions, of course, described the common practices of the day. Insurers began to realize that considerable liabilities could be channeled through their liability policies, causing substantial losses.

The overwhelming consensus was that such losses should be excluded. The industry's attitude is captured in an excerpt from a 1970 speech by Charles K. Cox, President of the Insurance Company of North America:

> "We will no longer insure the company, which knowingly dumps its wastes. In our opinion, such repeated actions-especially in violation of specific laws-are not insurable exposures. Moreover, we are inclined to think that any attempt to provide such insurance might well be contrary to public policy. We at INA hope that our anti-pollution exclusion may help encourage many companies to take the first, crucial steps toward improving their manufacturing processes-the steps that will lead eventually to a cleaner, healthier and, we hope, happier life for all."[1]

On the other hand, a pollution spill that was caused by a sudden fracture in a holding tank or an explosion presented less risk. While liability losses may develop, these were considered to be fortuitous and controllable through proper underwriting and actuarial techniques. Consequently, the decision was made in the early 1970s to insert a pollution exclusion into general liability policies that would exclude gradual pollution risks but cover those risks associated with sudden and accidental discharges. This was typically referred to as the gradual pollution exclusion. The exact wording of this exclusion is included in Chapter 6.

The insurance industry management claimed that the gradual pollution exclusion was not so much an exclusion, but rather a clarification of their intent. Their reasoning is that by the definition of occurrence, an important term in the policies, coverage only exists when damages are unexpected and unintended by the insured. In their minds, gradual pollution would not be covered in liability policies, even without a specific exclusion, because it expected and intended.

To add a personal note here, I published my first article on environmental risks in 1972 to counter the interpretation given by the insurance industry. I argued that the insurance industry was actually restricting and not just clarifying pollution coverage by using the gradual pollution exclusion. Implicit in insurers' arguments was the notion that all gradual pollution was intended and expected. Yet, if a company were unknowingly causing gradual pollution, occurrence policies, before the exclusion, would cover this situation. The gradual pollution exclusion would act to remove such coverage, not merely clarify it, because the gradual pollution that was causing unexpected and unintended damages was not a sudden event.[2]

The gradual pollution exclusion in general liability policies created the need for a new policy to cover gradual pollution events. The new policy that emerged was called an Environmental Impairment Liability (EIL) policy. David Dybdahl, a long time participant in environmental insurance markets as a leading broker and consultant, explained that the new policy was first offered on an experimental basis in the United States in 1974, and the first policies were written the following year. Available limits in first few years were $4,000,000-$5,000,000 per claim and $8,000,000-$10,000,000 aggregate.[3] The aggregate limit represents the maximum amount an insurer will pay in any policy period, typically one year.

When the Resource Conservation and Recovery Act was passed in 1976, it included a financial responsibility requirement for hazardous waste storage, treatment and disposal facilities. Typically, such requirements are met by purchasing insurance policies. Accordingly in 1977, the insurance markets began offering gradual pollution coverage through EIL policies to meet RCRA's financial responsibility requirement. With the passage of the U.S. Superfund program in 1980, further interest in EIL insurance was generated.

From 1977 to 1984, Dybdahl estimates that over 50 insurers in both the U.S. and London markets offered EIL insurance. The largest capacity available from a single insurance company increased to $30,000,000 per claim and $60,000,000 aggregate. Over time, it became apparent that most insurers did not understand the nature of pollution risks, particularly the difficulties of underwriting and pricing the coverage. Their exposure was greatly increased by the passage of the Superfund program in 1980. Superfund made responsible parties retroactively liable for the cleanup of past hazardous waste disposal and natural resource damages. In effect, this made insurers, who were writing EIL insurance for responsible parties, also retroactively liable. Before the hard insurance market of 1985-1987 hit, many of these insurers already were incurring serious losses. The combination of these losses, and the worldwide financial disruptions due to the hard market, caused the pollution insurance market to shrink to two insuring groups, the American International Group (AIG) and the Pollution Liability Insurance Association (PLIA), a pool of insurers writing pollution liability coverage.[4]

In the period following the introduction of the gradual pollution exclusion in the early 1970s, insurers found that this exclusion did not protect them as much as they originally supposed. In many legal jurisdictions, it was held that the "sudden and accidental" wording could be construed to cover gradual pollution events. The courts held that such events need only be unexpected, without any temporal limitations, in order for coverage to exist (see Chapter 6). The combination of these decisions, the unfavorable claims experience of insurers writing gradual pollution insurance, and the overall hard insurance market of 1985-1987 prompted the insurance industry to enact a new exclusion in 1986. This so-called "absolute pollution" exclusion excluded both gradual and sudden pollution events. This exclusion was part of a total overhaul of the Comprehensive General Liability (CGL) policy form, the basic liability insurance policy carried by virtually all businesses. While some limited coverage was still provided for products and completed operations and automobile liability claims, the insurance industry was attempting to exclude all types of pollution from existing liability forms and provide this coverage under separately underwritten and priced policies.

The period following the hard market was a very lean time in the environmental risk financing markets. Initially only two insurers, AIG and PLIA, were actively involved in providing environmental coverage. In 1986, limits of $10,000,000 per occurrence and $10,000,000 aggregate were available from AIG and PLIA would provide up to $4,000,000 per occurrence and $4,000,000 aggregate. Because of stiff underwriting and high premiums, few policies were written in this period.[5]

Development of Environmental Risk Financing Markets

The period of the late1980s and into the 1990s saw a gradual loosening of the tight environmental liability insurance markets. The combination of continued overall softening of the insurance markets, increasing competition, a better understanding of the underwriting complexities of environmental risks, and increasing demand for coverage gradually attracted new insurers into the environmental insurance markets. Environmental Compliance Services (ECS), through a relationship with the Reliance Insurance Group, entered the market in 1987, with limits of $1,000,000 per occurrence and $2,000,000 aggregate. At the beginning of 1988, PLIA lost its reinsurance for EIL policies and could no longer offer coverage, although it did remain active in the underground tank insurance market for a few more years.

In 1992, Zurich Insurance Company entered the markets as the third major writer of environmental insurance coverages. United Coastal entered the markets as the prominent player of a number of providers that write specialty products for certain segments of the market. By 1996, AIG and ECS/Reliance were offering limits of $40,000,000 each occurrence and aggregate; Zurich's maximum capacity was $30,000,000 each occurrence and aggregate; and United Coastal offered up $10,000,000 per occurrence and aggregate.[6]

When the Reliance Insurance Company ran into financial difficulties, which eventually led them to being placed into insolvency, the ECS Underwriting Group was acquired by XL Capital of Bermuda. XL Capital is a major excess and D&O liability insurer that was formed in 1986 to meet the demands of Fortune 500 companies for these coverages. Kemper Insurance Company later joined the environmental insurance market as a major player, but difficulties within the Kemper organization led them to sell their environmental business to Zurich Insurance Company. Financial difficulties also led to United Coastal exiting the market. In 2001, Chubb Insurance Group entered the environmental insurance market. ACE and ARCH, two other Bermuda based insurers, and Liberty Mutual (Liberty Underwriters International) and St. Paul Travelers round out the list of major environmental underwriters going into the 21st century.[7] A number of other insurers, including Quanta, Hudson and Everest, are experimenting with involvement in more specialized environmental insurance products.[8]

The above discussion, which briefly summarizes developments in environmental insurance over the last 30 plus years, is important to understanding current market conditions. The insurance industry has had a most unpleasant experience with pollution type claims. Billions of dollars have been paid out and are still being paid out for Superfund mandated hazardous waste cleanup claims under old Comprehensive General Liability policies issued decades ago (see Chapter 6). Because of these negative experiences, most insurers are reluctant to be involved in the current market, which helps to explain the small number of actively involved insurers. At the same time, the fact that pollution risks have been excluded from the standard liability forms means that only those corporations that actively seek insurance will be covered. Many businesses may not realize that they have no pollution liability coverage under standard forms. This is not unlike many homeowners and small business persons, who only realize after they incur flood or earthquake losses that these claims are not covered under standard homeowners and property insurance forms. If environmental claims escalate, as I have predicted throughout this book, there could be a lot of surprised corporate executives.

Current Environmental Risk Financing Markets

It is estimated that current environmental insurance markets produce around $2.0 billion of annual premium income.[9] In 1990, only $100 million of premiums were written and as recently as 1995, $900 million of environmental insurance premiums were generated. As of 2005, the main environmental insurers are AIG, XL, Zurich, ACE, Chubb, St. Paul Travelers, Liberty Mutual, Quanta and ARCH. Most of these insurers are large and well capitalized. High start up costs and the general risk level suggests that only insurers with substantial capital will be successful in writing environmental insurance. Similarly, large global brokers, like Marsh, Aon, Gallagher and Willis, dominate the environmental insurance brokerage market. Dybdahl estimates that around one half of one percent of all brokers/agents control about 80 percent of the environmental insurance market, although the emerging specialized environmental wholesale insurance brokers are gaining market share by enabling independent agents to service their clients' insurance needs in this area.[10]

Alan Bressler, a major environmental broker with Marsh, notes that each of the major individual insurers typically provide limits of $100,000,000 per occurrence and in the aggregate, although amounts can go higher if facultative insurance can be placed. Higher limits may be obtained by layering the individual capacities of multiple insurers. In addition, global reinsurance capacity is in excess of $500,000,000 for any one placement.[11]

Due to the lack of published data, it is difficult to make documented statements about profitability in environmental insurance markets. According to David Dybdahl, early writings of EIL insurance in the late 1970s and early 1980s produced big losses, with loss ratios in the multiples of a hundred percent. He estimates that environmental insurance writings of the last decade and a half in the U.S. have been quite profitable as insurers have learned to better underwrite, price, reserve for and control their exposures. Still, there are individual examples of product lines with loss ratios of 500 percent in the environmental insurance business.[12]

Environmental Insurance Policy Types

Environmental insurance coverage can now be provided for nearly any industrial, commercial or institutional risk. There are currently more than 100 different environmental policies that provide insureds with a wide variety of options to insure pollution exposures. The principal coverage types are briefly described below. For an excellent discussion of these various coverage types and common features I would recommend "Environmental Insurance" Chapter 11 written by David Dybdahl and Rodney Taylor, which is included in the CPCU text, *Commercial Liability Insurance and Risk Management.*[13] I have based parts of my discussion below on this source. More specific information on these insurance forms can be obtained from the major providers of environmental insurance noted above, as well as the major insurance brokers, Marsh, Aon, Willis and Gallagher, and at the website of the Environmental Risk Resources Association (ERRA).[14]

Site-Specific EIL Policies

Site-Specific EIL insurance policies were the first type of environmental insurance written, going back to the 1970s. These policies are designed to plug the holes left by the pollution exclusions in the Commercial General Liability (CGL) (note the name changed from Comprehensive to Commercial in 1986) policy, which is the principal liability insurance policy carried by virtually all businesses. Third party bodily injury and property damage claims and associated defense costs, arising out of either sudden or gradual releases of pollutants from insured locations, are covered. Coverage for the costs of on-site cleanup, claims from releases at third party disposal sites and claims arising from preexisting pollution at the site can be added for additional premiums, or sometimes these additional coverages may be included in a more expanded coverage form.

EIL policies respond to loss situations involving "pollution conditions." A typical definition of "pollution conditions" would read as follows:

> "Pollution conditions means the discharge, dispersal, release or escape of smoke, vapors, soot, fumes, acids, alkalis, toxic chemicals, liquids or gases, waste materials or other irritants, contaminants or pollutants into or upon land, the atmosphere or any water course or body of water."

Policyholders today include waste disposal sites, factories, chemical companies, farms, municipalities, golf courses, warehouses and oil refineries. These insureds all have a fairly obvious environmental liability exposure. A large number of other businesses and industries with less obvious exposures may find themselves uninsured for environmental liabilities. A major focus of this book has been to present and document the assertion that environmental liabilities will increase substantially in the future. Many businesses may be caught unprepared and without appropriate insurance coverage. It is estimated that only about one percent of businesses carry some type of EIL coverage.[15] Risk managers, consultants and brokers should be carefully examining the exposures of their companies and clients for potential environmental liabilities. There is tremendous opportunity for insurers and brokers to market more environmental insurance as well as providing more environmental loss control expertise.

Contractors EIL Policies

Contractors that perform environmental remediation services at Superfund and other contaminated sites need to carry Contactors EIL coverage. These policies were first introduced in 1987. A contractor in carrying out remediation services may create a pollution incident, which results in third party bodily injury or property damage claims or on-site cleanup costs. Contractors EIL policies provide coverage for such claims and their related defense costs. These policies are similar to site-specific EIL policies except that coverage is designed to cover a contractor's operations and activities at project sites, and also to cover the contractor's completed operations and contractual liability exposures.

Contractors that work on waste disposal or storage sites, handle or store materials with contaminants or pollutants, or might unexpectedly in their work come into contact with materials that could cause contamination or pollution are advised to purchase this coverage. Environmental services vendors also often buy contractors EIL policies. The increasing number of mold claims has resulted in plumbers and air conditioning contractors, working with water systems in buildings, needing to purchase contractors EIL policies to cover their mold exposure. Roofers also have a mold exposure as leaking roofs may lead to mold claims.[16]

Environmental Professional E&O Liability Policies

A wide variety of consultants, engineers, and other environmental service vendors provide professional advice and services in connection with the evaluation and remediation of contaminated sites. Environmental Professional E&O Liability policies cover liabilities and defense costs arising from negligent professional errors, acts, or omissions. These policies were first introduced in 1989. Common exposures include failure to identify contaminants, errors in their characterization and in the evaluation of a site, faulty design plans for remediation of the contamination, mistakes in the analysis of samples, and the general failure to perform in accordance with the standards of their professions. Most policies are written on a blanket basis, which covers not only professional liability exposures arising out environmental work, but also traditional E&O exposures of engineers and consultants for their non-environmental work.

Remediation Stop-Loss (Cost Cap) Environmental Policies

Remediation Stop-Loss or Cost Cap Environmental policies are designed to cover remediation costs that exceed estimated costs to complete the work. These policies have proven to be very effective in facilitating the sale of contaminated property and are becoming a more widely used environmental insurance coverage. These are first party insurance policies, but third party liability coverage can be added for an extra premium.

When a contaminated property is the subject of a potential sale, there is typically a wide difference between the remediation costs estimated by the seller and those estimated by the buyer. Assuming the remediation on some sites will have to be done after the sale, the estimate of the remediation costs would decrease the value of the property. The seller naturally would look to lower estimated costs to increase the sales price. The buyer would tend to conservatively estimate higher costs to provide a margin of error since the buyer will be responsible for the remediation. These higher costs would decrease the offering price for the property. Since environmental remediation can take 20 years to complete, there can be a wide range in cost estimates to complete the work over such a long period of time. In addition, because Superfund laws impose joint and several liability for cleanup costs on all parties in the chain to title, potential purchasers are understandably cautious about taking title to the contaminated party. Stop-loss policies are used to close this gap between the seller's and the buyer's perceptions or estimates of the expected remediation costs.

Take for example, a contaminated site with an estimated value, without contamination, of $10,000,000. The best estimate of expected cleanup cost is $3,000,000, but complications could result in doubling this amount. The seller with an asking price of $7,000,000 and the buyer with an offering price of $4,000,000 result in an impasse. The transaction can be facilitated by the buyer purchasing a stop-loss policy. The insurer typically would ask for a deductible above the best estimate of remediation costs. If this deductible was $500,000, the insurer would start to pick up the tab when cleanup costs exceeded $3,500,000. The buyer could offer $7,000,000, less the policy premium and the $500,000 deductible for the property, and eliminate the risk. Since a remediation cost overrun could still be a possibility, there will probably still be negotiating to do between the buyer and the seller. But the maximum difference of $500,000, plus the premium, has certainly narrowed the $3,000,000 gap that had created the original impasse.

Secured Creditors Environmental Policies

Secured Creditors Environmental policies are designed to protect lenders. This policy is essentially a stripped down EIL policy with only on site cleanup coverage. It is designed to pay off a secured creditor for an environmental loss that threatens the collateral value of the property in the event the borrower defaults on the loan. This policy provides no coverage for the borrower and should not be confused with true EIL coverage that could insure both the borrower and lender. Secured creditor policies are often used to replace environmental due diligence for new loans by purchasing an insurance policy, instead of conducting expensive site assessments.[17]

Asbestos and Lead Abatement Contractors General Liability Policies

In the mid to late 1980s, the combined effects of legislation, increased public awareness of asbestos and lead risks, and a strong real estate market created a demand for asbestos and lead abatement services. Asbestos and Lead Abatement Contractors General Liability Policies were designed to respond to this demand to remove asbestos and lead from buildings, such as schools and apartment buildings. Contractors need this coverage to protect themselves from liabilities that may arise out of their work in removing asbestos and lead. The policy is essentially a CGL policy that contains an amendment to the pollution exclusion deleting asbestos or lead from the definition of pollutants. This is different from the contractors EIL policy, which is a separate policy that fills the gap left by the pollution exclusion. While general contractors need both a CGL policy and an EIL contractors policy, asbestos and lead abatement contractors only need a single modified CGL policy.

Underground Storage Tank Financial Responsibility Compliance Policies

Underground Storage Tank Financial Responsibility Compliance policies were developed to meet the financial responsibility regulations created by RCRA for owners and operators of underground storage tanks. RCRA was modified in 1986 to provide regulations that apply to the owners and operators of underground storage tanks. When underground tanks are used to store fuel or hazardous material, RCRA regulations require the owners and operators to demonstrate their financial ability to pay claims resulting form the release of such materials from the tank. One popular method of demonstrating financial responsibility is to purchase an underground storage tank or UST policy. The typical required limit is $1,000,000 per claim, although larger retailers of petroleum products may be required to purchase a $2,000,000 per claim limit.

The basic required policy only applies to the underground storage tanks and underground piping. If owner/operators also have aboveground storage tanks, the policy can be endorsed to include these tanks. For both underground and above ground tanks, coverage can also be extended to pumps, valves, and other equipment directly attached to the insured tank.

Closure/Post Closure Policies

Closure/Post Closure policies are designed to satisfy the closure/post closure financial responsibility requirements imposed on hazardous waste and solid waste treatment, storage and disposal facilities (TSDFs). Often highly polluted sites are partially cleaned up and then put on a long term monitoring regime. The policy is a first party policy and covers the future costs to close and monitor these regulated sites. It provides a financial guaranty that the owner/manager will close the regulated site in accordance with the closure plan and maintain the site for 30 years or more during the post closure period.

Time Element Coverage

A pollution coverage for sudden releases, called time element, has been developed and included in umbrella or excess policy forms issued by the big excess liability insurers like ACE and XL. The coverage typically requires that pollution incidents are discovered within 7 days from their commencement, and be reported to the insurer within 30-45 days of their discovery. These large excess policies require underlying insurance or self-insurance of $25 million, so only larger corporations would be expected to carry these policies.

Combination Policies

Combination policies were developed for those types of businesses that may need more than one form of environmental insurance. For instance, an environmental consulting firm, which is also involved with on-site remediation, would have both professional and contractor environmental liability exposures. For these types of businesses, a combination professional and contractor environmental liability policy has been developed. Another popular combination would be an EIL/CGL policy. Virtually all businesses need a CGL policy. For those firms with environmental exposures, this combination policy would provide both coverages under a single policy form.

A recent combination policy was introduced by ACE USA, which provides a lead umbrella policy with premises pollution liability coverage. Limits are available up to $25 million, and applied separately for the two coverages. Since the minimum premium is $100,000, this policy is aimed at large risks. ACE reported that its target markets are energy, utility and chemical companies. AIG, with its Environmental and General Liability Exposures (Eagle) product, wraps up to $10 million of pollution coverage with a general liability policy.[18]

Combination policies offer the convenience of providing all the required environmental coverages under a single policy, which typically results in premium cost savings. In addition, disputes arising from risks that may come within a gray area of possible coverage under both policies would be eliminated. Under combination policies, insureds must be careful that adequate limits are selected as often a single limit applies to losses that may develop under both coverages.

Mold Exposures

Beginning in 2000, mold claims began to be a concern for property owners, builders and insurers. As mold claims developed, questions were raised as to whether coverage would exist in either property or liability policies or both. In property policies, mold resulting from water damage would probably be covered, but claims arising from defective construction would not. Under liability policies for builders, mold may or may not be impacted by the pollution exclusion and the definition of pollutants, depending on the specific jurisdiction of the incident. Insurance companies, remembering and fearing a repeat of an asbestos type situation, moved quickly to exclude mold exposures from property and liability policies. Some insurers offer a coverage buyback at extra premiums. Ironically, mold claims have been exasperated by efficient construction techniques to conserve energy, which is a positive environmental development. If the building is insulated but not allowed to breath, then the lack of air circulation can promote the growth of mold. In those parts of the country with high humidity where air conditioning is widely used, excessive water condensation also helps to generate the growth of mold. Property owners, builders and professionals like engineers and architects and even insurance brokers/agents need to be alert to the fact that their respective policies probably now include some type of mold exclusion. Separate insurance coverage to cover mold risks should be investigated, and risk control methods should be emphasized to mitigate mold losses.[19]

Other Common Coverage Situations

Bressler of Marsh notes some other risk situations where environmental insurance can be employed. In mergers and acquisitions, environmental insurance protects the acquiring company from unanticipated cost overruns associated with known cleanup obligations, as well as the discovery of unknown, pre-merger pollution conditions. In Brownfield redevelopments, developers employ environmental insurance to guarantee that a project's financial success will not be hampered by known or unknown environmental conditions, including those that cause delays in project completion.[20]

Common Features of Environmental Insurance Policies

Certain common features are included in most environmental insurance policies. The most important feature, which is characteristic of all environmental insurance products, with the exception of asbestos and lead abatement contractors general liability policies, is that coverage is on a **claims-made basis**. The reader might recall the problems that occurrence-based policies caused the insurance industry in the asbestos and Superfund areas (see Chapter 6). The problem with occurrence-based liability policies is that older policies written in the past can be triggered, i.e., made to respond to current claims, if it can be established that the injuries or damages were incurred during the policy periods of these older policies.

With a claims-made policy, the policy can only be triggered if a claim is made within the policy period. Once a policy period has been closed out, insurers do not have to worry about future claims being applied to these closed out policies. Coverage can be extended into the future for a limited period of time, like one to five years, by purchasing extended reporting period or tail coverage for an additional per year premium. But going back decades, as characterized the asbestos and Superfund situations, is not possible under claim-made coverage. Obviously, it is still important to properly underwrite and price policies. A number of sizeable claims, within the policy period of a claims-made policy, can still create major losses for an insurer.

Environmental insurance policies are usually written **without a retroactive date**, which often is used in other claims-made policies like the CGL. When a retroactive date is in place, it is set as the beginning date of the policy. No coverage exists under a claims-made policy for injuries or damages that occurred before the retroactive date. Removing the retroactive date restriction expands available coverage to all injuries and damages that occurred from prior acts, which result in claims being made within the policy period. The only excluded claims are those that result from **known pre-existing conditions**. This exclusion is most reasonable in that coverage is not provided when the insured knows of an impending claim that would be covered under the policy.

Another problem with occurrence-based policies is that the policies could be interpreted as providing full limit coverage for each of several claims arising out of a single pollution event. An insurer, who had written, say a $1,000,000 occurrence limit might find that payouts could be many times this amount if the limit is applied in full to each of the claims. Of course, the insurer would be somewhat protected by the annual aggregate limit, but these claims could still be made over several policy years. Environmental insurance policies protect against this extension of coverage by including clear language that states that **all claims arising from a pollution incident are treated as a single loss with one per loss limit.**

Defense cost coverage, with environmental liability policies, typically provides that **defense costs are within the limit** of the policy. The one major exception would be underground storage tank policies that provide a separate limit of liability for defense costs. Under the standard CGL policy, defense costs are in addition to the limit or outside the limit. When defense costs are within the limit, this means that both third party injuries and property damages, for which the insured is liable, as well as the associated defense costs are combined to determine whether the limit has been reached. Let us say that a policy has a $1,000,000 per claim limit. If $100,000 has been spent on costs defending the policyholder, then only $900,000 is available to cover injury and property damage claims. If this were a claim under the CGL policy and $100,000 had been spent for defense, the entire $1,000,000 limit would be available to pay for injury and property damage claims.

The main impact of having defense costs within the limit is that coverage amounts for injury and damage claims are eroded. Defending environmental claims can be costly because technical experts and expensive testing procedures are often required as part of the defense strategy. The erosion of monies available to pay for injury and damage claims can be particularly acute in environmental claims. This adverse impact can be countered by purchasing additional limits.

In addition to per claim or loss limits of liability, environmental insurance policies typically have **aggregate limits.** An aggregate limit specifies the total amount of funds that the insurance contract will pay for the policy period, which is usually one year. Aggregate limits protect the insurance company when the insured incurs a series of claims. If only a per claim limit was in place, the insurer could end up paying out many times the per claim limit. Aggregate limits keep this from happening. Sometimes the aggregate limit is the same as the per claim (loss) limit and sometimes it is a multiple, like two to three times. As with defense costs, the policyholder needs to purchase higher limits in order to guard against the aggregate limit being exceeded, which would cease coverage for further injury and property damage claims as well as defense costs.

Environmental insurance policies usually **exclude coverage for punitive damages,** as well as environmental fines and penalties. In those states where insuring punitive damages is permitted, coverage for punitive damages could be added for an additional premium. Environmental policies also exclude losses that are caused by the insured's intentional, willful, or deliberate non-compliance with any current environmental statute or regulation.

Environmental insurance policies are **non-standardized forms**. This means that there is flexibility for both the insurer and insureds to make changes in a basic policy form and set the policy up to best meet their needs. Sometimes a new risk situation may require the construction of a **manuscript policy**, which means that an entirely new policy is put together from scratch. For insurance buyers this is both good news and bad news. The good news is that insureds have the opportunity to negotiate with the insurer to arrive at an environmental policy that best meets their needs. The bad news is that with this opportunity comes the responsibility to closely check the policy form to make sure it meets their needs. With standardized forms, the insured can be guaranteed that various terms, conditions, and coverages are in the policy. With non-standardized forms, no particular guarantees are present so it is incumbent on the prospective policyholder, with the assistance of the their insurer and broker, to make sure that the terms, conditions, coverages and other parts of the policy meet their needs and expectations.[21]

Loss Portfolio Transfers to Cap Liability

Corporations often carry substantial environmental liabilities on their balance sheets. These liabilities can create uncertainties for the corporations and their investors. Such liabilities impede the efforts of companies that may be interested in merger and acquisitions activities. To remove these uncertainties, one of the more exciting risk financing techniques in the environmental area involves the transfer or capping of liabilities via innovative risk financing contracts. A major broker, Sedgwick (now part of Marsh) put together two substantial contracts, which illustrate this trend.

T&N, a former British asbestos manufacturer now in auto parts, effectively capped its asbestos liabilities through a finite risk reinsurance arrangement. Under the arrangement, T&N retains up to approximately $1.14 billion (690 million pounds) of outstanding asbestos liability claims. In the unlikely event that future asbestos claims exceed this retention, Sedgwick placed coverage with a group of three reinsurers, Munich Re, Swiss Re, and Centre Re, who reinsure the next $825 million (500 million pounds) of claims. The reinsurers received a $151 million (92 million pounds) premium (18 percent rate on line) for the coverage, some of which may be returned to T&N in the future, based on favorable loss experience. On the day the deal was completed, T&N stock rose 22 percent.[22]

In the second deal, Sedgwick assembled $800 million in environmental remediation coverage for Hanson P.L.C., a British building materials company. The policy, the largest of its type ever written at that time, provides coverage to pay for any cost overruns associated with the cleanup of some 200 sites nationwide, including several state and federal Superfund sites. The premium is $275 million (34 percent rate on line). It is reinsured by Centre Solutions, a member of the Zurich group, and European Re, a member of Swiss Re Group. The policy is a 50-50 combination of pure risk transfer and finite risk insurance.[23]

These two risk financing arrangements illustrate the flexibility and creativity that insurers can exhibit. Alternative financing techniques using finite risk methods, self insurance retentions, full risk transfer and attractive tax advantages can be used to provide innovative environmental risk financing schemes, as these two cases illustrate.

Restricted Coverage in D&O Policies

The exposure of directors and officers in the environmental area was discussed in Chapter 5. Since directors and officers are typically covered by Directors and Officers (D&O) liability insurance policies, they may have complacent attitudes regarding their exposure. If risks develop, they are covered by D&O insurance. Actually, the D&O liability insurance policies do not provide that much protection as is explained below.

D&O liability insurance policies are nonstandard policies, so the coverage provided may vary from insurer to insurer. Directors and officers are covered for liabilities resulting from their wrongful acts. An example of a definition of a wrongful act is included below:

> "Any error, misstatement, misleading statement, act, omission, neglect, or breach of duty committed, attempted, or allegedly committed or attempted, by an insured person when they are in their capacity as a director or officer for the corporation."[24]

D&O liability damages are typically for financial harm suffered by stockholders, employees, customers, or competitors. Liabilities for bodily injuries, property damages, personal injury, or advertising injury are not covered as these would be covered under the firms CGL (Commercial General Liability) and Umbrella/Excess Liability Policies. Coverage under the CGL would be limited by the pollution exclusion if some type of pollution spill is involved.

When directors and officers are sued, any losses incurred are typically reimbursed or indemnified by the corporation. D&O insurance policies provide reimbursement to the corporation for these indemnification amounts paid to directors and officers. In circumstances where the corporation does not indemnify the directors and officers, say if the company goes bankrupt, D&O policies provide coverage directly to the directors and officers. D&O policies may also contain a third insuring agreement to provide coverage to the corporate entity itself in those situations where claims are made against the corporation.

Directors and officers could be sued by shareholders, whose stock values were diminished by mismanagement of a sustainability risk event. For instance, sales could go down because of a NGO boycott that causes the stock price to fall. Recall that the corporation has no insurance coverage for the loss of sales and reputation damage that results from a boycott. But if the directors and officers and or the corporation are sued by shareholders for mismanaging their boycott strategy, the directors and officers, and possibly the entity, could be covered for their actions. Thus indirectly, coverage may be provided to the stockholders if their suit was successful.

If directors and officers are sued for financial harm to shareholders resulting from a pollution spill, coverage will almost surely be restricted by a pollution exclusion in D&O policies. Kenn Anderson, Managing Director of Gallagher Environmental Risk and Insurance and Donna Ferrara, Vice President of Gallagher Executive and Professional Services Division, discuss these exclusions in a recent paper. They offer a typical pollution exclusion that is used by the Chubb Insurance Group, a leading writer of D&O policies:

> "The company shall not be liable for loss on account of any claim made against any insured person: based upon, arising from, or in consequence of:
> (1) the actual, alleged or threatened discharge, release, escape or disposal of

pollutants into or on real or personal property, water or the atmosphere; or (2) any direction or request that the insured test for, monitor, cleanup, remove, contain, treat, detoxify or neutralize pollutants, or any voluntary decision to do so; including but not limited to any claim for financial loss to the insured organization, its security holders or its creditors based upon, arising from, or in consequence of the matters described in this exclusion." Chubb 14-0209-43 (1/92) (For-Profit Companies)[25]

If the corporation in the above example did not carry environmental insurance to cover bodily injury, property damage, defense costs and cleanup costs, directors and officers may be sued for losses resulting from their failure to carry such coverage. Directors and officers may again find themselves vulnerable in this situation as virtually all D&O policies exclude claims arising out of the failure to obtain or maintain insurance. Of course, losses resulting from failure to carry environmental insurance can be eliminated by purchasing such coverage.

These exclusions emphasize the importance of carrying appropriate environmental insurance. The risk of directors and officers being sued in a pollution event would be reduced by having environmental insurance available to cover resulting injuries and damages. In addition, suits brought for failure to obtain or maintain environmental insurance would obviously be eliminated by purchasing such coverage.

When the Sarbanes-Oxley bill passed, requiring top company officials to certify their financial statements and internal controls, many D&O policies excluded claims involving environmental liability disclosures arising out of certification under Sarbanes-Oxley. As pointed out by Anderson and Ferrera in their article:

> "One can surmise that carriers who use the broad exclusionary language cited above would resist coverage for claims in which an insured failed to adequately disclose environmental liability on financial statements,....(or)....certified falsely that appropriate internal controls were maintained for environmental risk management...."[26]

CEOs and CFOs are particularly vulnerable, as they are required to certify and sign off on financial statements. They, along with other directors and officers, may still be protected financially by indemnification provisions in the company by-laws. But if there is no coverage under D&O policies, then the corporation is not reimbursed by the insurance carrier, and must retain the loss. The financial condition of the firm could be hurt, which could further aggravate shareholders. D&O policies are designed to mitigate adverse financial effects of claims brought against the directors and the corporation, but if exclusions are in place that relate to the claim in question, there is no financial mitigation and the corporation itself and its directors and officers must absorb these losses. In a worse case risk situation, where the corporation was forced into bankruptcy, no indemnification would be provided to the directors and officers-they would be forced to personally carry the burden of the financial losses.

Risk Control Services of Insurers

When the decision is made to pursue the risk financing option of purchasing environmental insurance, policyholders receive the loss mitigation and engineering services of insurers, which can provide substantial benefits. If coverage is written through a broker with in house engineering capabilities, then the broker's risk control services are also available. In the underwriting process, when the insurer is deciding whether to accept the risk, the insured often receives advice for adopting measures to reduce the risk. In many cases, the insured's willingness to accept and implement the advice becomes a condition for the insurer accepting the risk. The underwriting process may also require that certain tests are performed on the property to be insured.

The actuarial process of setting the premium also facilitates loss mitigation. Insurance companies are willing to reduce the premium for insureds that present less risk. By adopting risk control measures that reduce losses, the insured receives a reduction in their premium. For instance, one of the major insurance brokers, Willis, established a risk and premium reduction program with The Responsible Care Program, established by the Chemical Manufacturers Association, to promote improved environmental performance. Participating firms can receive up to a 30 percent reduction in EIL premiums through a premium modification factor process that rewards good loss experience.[27]

Once the insurance is in place, both the policyholder and the insurer have financial incentives to control environmental risks. When my first article in the environmental risk area was published in 1972,[28] one of my major concerns when insurers adopted the gradual pollution exclusion was that their incentive to reduce losses would be lessen by the fact that coverage was restricted.

Environmental insurance, particularly if combined with RCRA type regulations, would follow the model of an older type of insurance, Boiler and Machinery (B&M). With B&M insurance, monies spent on risk control typically exceeds the losses paid out for claims. Most of the premiums are spent on expenses for boiler inspections to prevent explosions from occurring. Prior to

B&M insurance, such explosions were a common occurrence. The strong emphasis on loss prevention keeps losses and overall premiums low. Other examples include elevator insurance and HPRs (Highly Protected Risks). When one rides in an elevator it is hard to not notice the listing of frequent inspections. These inspections keep elevators in good working conditions, with the result being that elevator accidents are rare. Properties, which meet HPR standards set by insurers, have an extremely low risk of fire due to the substantial required loss control measures like sprinklers. In the environmental area, another example would be the Real Estate Environmental Liability (REEL) HPR. This program provides mold coverage through Zurich for real estate risks, coupled with substantial engineering to reduce the mold exposure.[29]

If more environmental insurance were in force, the substantial loss mitigation services provided by insurers and brokers would be more frequently employed by insureds. The presence of insurance can actually act like a regulatory system, as insureds are required to meet certain minimum underwriting standards and their premium costs are reduced in the process. Martin Katzman, is his book, *Chemical Catastrophes: Regulating Environmental Risk Through Pollution Liability Insurance*,[30] and Paul Freeman and Howard Kunreuther, in their book, *Managing Environmental Risk Through Insurance*,[31] make strong cases for the importance of environmental insurance in managing and regulating environmental risks.

All the major writers of environmental insurance offer substantial engineering, inspection, and control services. The major environmental insurance brokers provide similar services. Services can also be obtained from environmental risk management consultants.

Risk control is particularly important and cost-effective in the environmental area because once a harmful substance gets into the air, waterways, and/or aquifers, it becomes extremely difficult, costly and oftentimes impossible to remove. Linda Bagneschi, an environmental consultant, emphasizes that "from a risk management standpoint, source reduction is preferred to recycling and treatment options because it is likely to pose the lowest environment risk."[32] Industries are developing new technologies to reduce the generation of hazardous waste, and more industries are treating hazardous wastes on site, rather than shipping wastes to disposal sites.[33] Writers of environmental insurance can be instrumental in assisting businesses and industries in creating effective loss mitigation methods. Insurers can also use their premium setting techniques to reward insureds that adopt their methods and produce favorable loss experience.

Claims Management

When environmental insurance is procured, insurance companies and brokers provide claims services. Claims services are also available through consulting groups or loss adjustment firms for additional fees. While risk control is emphasized with environmental risks, environmental accidents will occur and require claims management services of insurers, loss adjustment firms and consultants. Managing environmental claims often requires innovative approaches. Alberto Gutierrez, President of Geoscience Conscience Consultants Ltd. GCL, an environmental consulting firm, states that "an aggressive claims management approach to controlling those costs is essential for insurers." He further states "The complex technical and regulatory issues associated with environmental cleanups are forcing insurers to bring in a whole range of consultants to develop innovative remedial strategies to oversee the process of remediation and establish procedures within which the insurer can monitor the remediation process and protect its own interests."[34] Randall Hobbs, an environmental claims consultant, echoes Gutierrez's views:

> "The extraordinary complexity of an environmental claim can cripple a company without the proper resources. Unlike traditional contract or tort claims, environmental losses do not always offer clearly defined areas of liability and damages. Resolving them can require tremendous amounts of technical support."[35]

Companies that choose to purchase insurance to provide environmental risk financing also acquire the specialized risk control and claims management services of environmental insurers and brokers. Because of the complexity of environmental risks and claims, these services can be an enormous advantage to policyholders.

European Environmental Insurance Markets

I conducted a study in 1998 on the status of European environmental insurance markets and published the results in the *1998 Proceedings of the International Insurance Society*.[36] The discussion below is based on the results of that study, with updates as appropriate.

The environmental insurance markets in Europe have been slower to develop than the markets in the United States. Probably the most significant reason is that European insurers were reluctant to exclude pollution coverage in general liability policies. As noted earlier in this chapter, U.S. insurers have been excluding gradual pollution from general liability policies since the early 1970s and all pollution since 1986. Insurers in most European countries would eventually exclude gradual pollution, but it took many years and did not occur simultaneously across various countries.

W. Pfennigstorf stated at a 1985 conference that, "In most countries the commercial liability policy usually covers sudden and unexpected events. By implication it excludes events that are neither sudden nor unexpected."[37] Baruch Berliner and Juerg Spuehler reported in 1988 that insurers in a vast majority of European countries cover pollution on a sudden and accidental basis in general liability policies.[38] Thus by the mid to late 1980s, insurers in most European countries had followed the U.S. example in the early 1970s of removing gradual pollution coverage from general liability policies, but they had not followed the U.S. in excluding sudden and accidental pollution.

Carolyn Aldred of *Business Insurance* reported that a notable exception was Germany, which as late as 1990, still provided pollution coverage for both sudden and accidental, and gradual, pollution on an occurrence basis in general liability policies. It should be pointed out that in German policies, only bodily injury claims were covered for sudden and accidental, and gradual, pollution; property damage claims were only covered for sudden and accidental events. Another notable exception was the United Kingdom, where many general liability policies did not mention (exclude) pollution damages, in any form, thus presumably pollution claims would be covered. Some countries excluded all pollution under general liability policies. These included Italy, Denmark (required a special endorsement at extra cost for sudden and accidental pollution coverage), and Greece (sudden and accidental coverage on request in certain situations).[39]

Markets

As environmental laws stiffen, and gradual pollution was largely removed from general liability policies, distinct environmental liability insurance markets and products developed throughout Europe. A 1996 report by the Swiss Reinsurance Company indicated that in some countries, insurers have excluded all pollution, meaning that a separate policy is needed to cover gradual as well as sudden and accidental pollution. Specifically mentioned in the report are Germany, Italy and to a large extent France. On the other hand, the Swiss Re report also indicated that with these few exceptions, other European insurers offer insurance protection against liability for sudden and accidental environmental impairment in their traditional policies covering general third-party liability and product liability.[40]

Interviews with leading environmental underwriters from AIG, Zurich American, and ECS Underwriting in 1998 indicated that the presence of sudden and accidental coverage in general liability policies was an impediment to writing environmental policies in Europe. Questions over the ability to write claims-made forms in some countries, like France and Spain, also had a dampening effect on environmental insurance writings. In contrast, as previously mentioned, the United States has excluded all pollution, including sudden and accidental from general liability policies, since 1986. By taking all pollution coverage out of general liability policies, there was more pressure and demand to develop separate environmental liability insurance products and markets. Claims-made forms were common on professional liability policies and available for general liability policies in the United States, so there was little hesitancy to use these forms for environmental insurance.

Pools

Environmental liability insurance pools have been formed in five countries, The Netherlands, France, Italy, Denmark and Spain. The pools are comprised of a number of insurers, banding together and sharing premiums and losses to provide environmental liability coverage. While individual insurers can write policies in these countries, most of the environmental liability coverage is placed with the pools. Table 10-1 provides basic information on the five pools.

Table 10-1
Environmental Liability Insurance Pools

Country	Name	Year Started	# Insurers Involved
France	Assurpol (originally GARPOL)	1977	50 insurers, 14 reinsurers
Italy	Pool Inquinamento	1979	76 insurers
Netherlands	MAS–Pool	1985	80 insurers
Denmark	Danpool	1992	15 insurers
Spain	PEC	1994	16 insurers

Sources:
Carolyn Aldred, "Pollution Crackdown in Europe," *Business Insurance,* October 8, 1990;
Baruch Berliner and Juerg Spuehler, "Insurability Issues Associated with Managing
Existing Hazardous Waste Sites," *Integrating Insurance and Risk Management for
Hazardous Wastes,* Howard Kunreuther and M.V. Rajeev Gowda, editors, Boston:
Kluwer Academic Publishers, 1990; William Kronenberg, III, "The Environmental
Insurance Markets in the U.S. and Western Europe: A U.S. Underwriter's Observations,"
The Geneva Papers on Risk and Insurance, No. 76, July 1995, 336-347; Eduardo
Pavelek, "The Spanish Environmental Risks Pool," Proceedings of the MORE 10 –
Seminar "Environment and Insurability," Geneva Switzerland: Geneva Association,
March 1995; Eric B. Rothenberg and Dean Jeffery Telego, editors, *Environmental Risk
Management,* Alexandria, Virginia: RTM Communications, Inc., 1991; Swiss
Reinsurance Company, *Insuring Environmental Impairment Liability,* Zurich: Swiss
Reinsurance Company, 1996; Edwin Unsworth, French Pool Addresses Pollution
Liability," *Business Insurance,* October 21, 1996.

In the Netherlands, the Dutch have established a unique approach in dealing
with environmental insurance. When the MAS—Pool was set up in 1985, it
mainly provided liability coverage for gradual pollution events. A liability policy,
AVB (Asnsprakeliijkheidsverzekering bedrijven), provided coverage for sudden
environment risks. In 1998, the Dutch introduced a new product, the environmental damage insurance policy, MSV (Milieuschadeverzekering). MSV is a first
party coverage for clean-up costs, both on site and on third party sites. While
environmental liability still exists, it is expected that the coverage provided in
MSV will act to mitigate environmental liability claims.[41]

Leading Insurers

William Kronenberg III, President and CEO of Environmental Compliances Services (ECS), one of the major environmental writers in the mid 1990s, in a 1995 paper, observed that "with two exceptions, no significant multi-line EIL insurance market had yet developed in the countries of the EU." He noted that the first exception was in the U.K., where ECS and AIG offered a wide range of environmental insurance products. Some other U.K. insurers, notably Lloyds and Sun Alliance, also offered third party pollution liability coverage. The second exception was Germany, where a number of private insurers offered third party pollution liability coverage. The remainder of the European environmental market at that time was comprised of the five national pools.[42]

The Swiss Re report discusses environmental regulations and insurance in fourteen countries—the 5 pool countries, plus Germany, Luxembourg, Belgium, U.K., Sweden Switzerland, Finland, Norway and Austria. While no figures are available on written premiums or market shares, Royal Belge, Assurances Générales, Winterthur, Skandia, and Royal Sun Alliance are mentioned as having taken initiatives to introduce stand-alone environmental impairment liability policies in countries without pools.[43]

Telego, in an earlier paper, mentioned AIU (AIG), Zurich Insurance, ECS (Reliance), Swiss Re (first policy was actually developed in 1975), Commercial Union, Sun Alliance, and Lloyds Syndicates as being actively involved in European insurance markets.[44] Interviews with leading environmental underwriters from AIG, Zurich American and ECS Underwriting in 1998 confirm the presence of many of the above mentioned insurers at that time, as well as the Allianz and some other reinsurers including Munich Re, Gerling Re and Cologne Re.

Germany

The situation in Germany is particularly noteworthy. When Germany's Environmental Liability Act (ELA) took effect in 1991, it caused major repercussions in the liability insurance markets. The ELA imposes strict liability for injury or damages caused by an environmental impact on soil, air or water on an estimated 20,000 facilities in the former West Germany alone, which are deemed to be particularly hazardous to the environment.[45]

Liability also includes damage arising out of normal operations. This means that no defense exists for an operator to claim that the authorities had granted him a license for the emission in question.[46] That is, even if the operations were in compliance with existing laws and regulations at the time, the operator can still be held liable.[47] No defense based on state of the art concepts can be used. This means that operators can be held responsible for environmental impacts in the past, which are later discovered as being dangerous.[48] The Act calls for joint and several liability and has a limit on liability for both bodily injury and property damage of DM $160 million that may result from one environmental impact.[49]

The ELA also required compulsory environmental liability insurance for the facilities subject to the Act. This became the impetus for the HUK-Verband (Association of Casualty Insurers) in Germany, together with all those involved in the market, to devise a new insurance model. Pollution coverage for both sudden and accidental and gradual events was removed from general liability policies, at least for the facilities affected by the act. In effect, this was an absolute pollution exclusion. A new separate environmental liability policy was developed for all pollution related events.[50] At that time, a separate environmental insurance policy covered all liabilities on a prospective basis, but the policy limit was below the DM $160 million limit called for in the Act.[51] Other insurance availability problems have resulted in the compulsory insurance requirements not being fully implemented. While a compulsory insurance requirement was put in force, the insurance market in Germany has had problems providing the full coverage needed.[52]

The situation in Germany is an excellent example of one of the central features of environmental insurance—namely that environmental insurance development is critically impacted by government regulations. Absent the ELA, environmental insurance markets would have seen little development as adequate coverage was produced under general liability policies. Passage of the ELA not only increased the environmental risks and exposures of the regulated facilities, it also was the catalyst of the development of a new separate environmental liability policy and market. Possibly the most important consequence of Germany's ELA is the influence it has had on the development on a EU directive on environmental insurance to be discussed below.

Summary Points on European Environmental Insurance Markets

Based on available published information and interviews, along with the author's judgment, the following observations can be made on the European environmental insurance markets as we enter the 21st Century:

- While a great deal of activity exists in the European insurance markets, they are not nearly as developed as the U.S.

- To the extent that they have developed, insurance organizations include several European insurers, insurers participating in the five pools, and the major environmental insurers in the U.S. Principally because of the insurance pools, a larger number of insurers are involved in Europe than in the United States.

- Like the U.S., insurers in virtually all European countries have removed coverage for gradual pollution events from their general liability policies.

- Unlike the U.S., insurers in many European countries still include sudden and accidental pollution coverage in their general liability policies.

- The presence of sudden and accidental pollution coverage inside the general liability policies dampens to a considerable extent the demand by policyholders for separate environmental liability coverage. Since many gradual pollution events may not be insured even with gradual pollution coverage (e.g., pollution from normal operations, intended pollution), an insured may feel that most insured pollution risks would arise from sudden and accidental pollution events, which are typically included in their general liability policies.

- If more laws like Germany's Environmental Liability Act were passed, it would be expected to bolster environmental insurance markets as has been the case in Germany.

- To date, little evidence exists that insurance coverage litigation involving pollution claims is a problem in Europe. With the exception of the U.K., other European countries have chosen to not access liability retroactively.

Recent articles confirm that my findings in 1998 accurately describe European environmental insurance markets up to the present.[53] These articles also point out that European markets are on the verge of potential expansion. Jim Cox, managing director of Aon Environmental states that, "A lot of people believe that in the next five years it will become a pretty dominant speciality product line in Europe,"[54] Karl Russek, Senior V.P. of ACE Environmental Risk, notes that environmental insurance markets are expected to expand, "as companies in EU member states work to incorporate the risk management effects of the new EU legislation and seek to add an element of retrospective cover."[55] The new EU legislation, to which Russek refers, is the EU's Environmental Liability Directive, to be discussed in the next section.

His comment on retrospective cover refers to the issue that the EU does not have a Superfund system, like in the U.S. But the EU still has hazardous waste sites, and questions arise as to who should be responsible for their cleanup. Along with Russek, Peter Brietstone, President of Brietstone & Company, a brokerage specializing in construction and pollution liability, and Quanta's Jim Finnamore and Bill Hazelton, all agree that more pressure will be put on polluters in the EU to finance cleanups. This pressure will create demand for environmental insurance products.[56] Russek also foresees an upswing in demand in Australia, New Zealand, Japan, and many countries in Latin America.[57]

European Union's Environmental Liability Directive

The European Union's Environmental Liability Directive could have a major impact on the development of environmental insurance markets. The directive is a good example of how a new regulation can dramatically increase the potential liability of the corporate world. The final draft of the directive, which has been discussed since the 1980s, was agreed to in spring 2004 by the European Parliament and the Council of the European Union.

The directive will increase corporate environmental liability exposures. Companies that cause or threaten to cause environmental damages i.e., those firms involved in dangerous or hazardous activities, will be required to bear the costs of remediation or prevention measures. Environmental damages include water and land damage, and also damage to protected species and natural habitats. The land and water damage section merely harmonizes the E.U. member states' existing regulations and minimum standards. The damage to species and natural habitats creates a new liability exposure. These damages are similar to natural resources damages in U.S. environmental regulations. Strict liability is imposed for dangerous activities and fault based (negligence) liability will apply to non-dangerous activities.

At present, this new biodiversity liability exposure for European companies would not be expected to be covered under existing policies. As mentioned in the previous section, most businesses have coverage for sudden and accidental pollution events under their general liability policies. Others have purchased EIL policies that provide coverage for gradual pollution events. EIL policies cover third party bodily injury and property damage claims, plus defense costs, and often times cleanup costs. Even if natural resource damage is included, it may not conform with the liabilities created by the EU Directive. If natural resource damage is not included, present policy definitions of these damages and costs would not be expected to include species and natural habitat damages. I would imagine that if there is any question on this issue, insurers will move to put in a clearly worded exclusion into their policies, and then offer buy back coverage on a selected basis for an additional premium.

The concern level of both corporations and insurers was lessened by the removal of a rule in earlier drafts that would have mandated that corporations purchase insurance for the new liabilities under the directive. Both corporations and insurers opposed compulsory insurance, as corporations worried that coverage may not be available and too costly, and insurers wondered if they were prepared to provide the necessary capacity to write and actuarially price the volume of these new environmental liability exposures. Clearly, many companies will seek coverage as their environmental liability risks have been increased by the directive and will need to be financed by some means. It is expected that insurers will write such coverages deliberately as they will need to learn how to properly underwrite and price this new risk.

The final draft of the directive also eliminated the requirement that liability be on a joint and several basis. This requirement was also opposed by both corporations and insurers, and they were successful in their efforts. In discussing the difficulties of writing insurance polices to cover the Directive's liabilities, Tony Lennon, European manager of Chubb Environmental Solutions, notes the uncertainties involved with the likely magnitude of the environmental damages, "This is where the problem comes: What cost will courts assign to companies? That is perhaps the scariest bit both for operators and insurers."[58] Corporate risk managers and underwriters might become even more concerned if they review the issues I raised in Chapter 1 on the damages being done to ecosystems.

The issue of compulsory environmental insurance will not go away. Upon implementation of the directive, member states will have three years to incorporate the provisions into national laws. Three years following, the European Commission will consider whether to establish some form of mandatory financial responsibility, including insurance, to cover the environmental liabilities under the directive. The six year period would seem to give the insurance industry adequate time to develop the capability to provide the necessary coverage capacity if it becomes mandated.[59]

Social Justice Risks

Risk financing for social justice risks raises a number of issues. Some social justice risks are covered under standard business liability insurance policies. For instance, injured workers would be compensated for their medical expenses and loss wages through mandatory workers compensation insurance or self-insurance schemes.

Under workers compensation laws, businesses have a financial incentive to make working environments safe for workers, since employers are responsible for paying all of the workers compensations costs. Federal laws like the Occupational Safety and Health Act (OSHA) in the United States and similar legislations in other countries strengthen these financial incentives. Insurance coverage for workers injuries are backed up by unions, which bargain for adequate wages and benefits for workers, and by legislation like the minimum wage laws.

Businesses that discriminate against or wrongfully discharge workers, or do not have procedures in place to protect workers from sexual harassment, are subject to employment practice liabilities. Coverage for these liabilities is available through employment practice liability insurance policies. Unlike workers compensation insurance, employment practice liability (EPL) insurance is not mandatory, and EPL coverage is often not carried by corporations. In Chapter 1, several cases of sizeable EPL judgments/settlements against major corporations, such as Texaco, Morgan Stanley, Boeing and Merrill Lynch were discussed. Wal-Mart, the world's largest corporation, is involved in the largest class action suit involving 1.6 million female workers over their compensation and promotion policies. EPL risks are well established and may be expected to increase. Sound EPL risk control and financing strategies remain an important component of a firm's sustainability risk management program.

While certainly there are exceptions, in general full time regular workers in developed countries present relatively low social justice risks from a risk financing standpoint. When losses develop, insurance protection to compensate for these losses is available through numerous insurance and financing schemes. But when temporary workers are used, when work is outsourced to independent contractors or to businesses in other countries, or when corporations set up operations in countries with lax regulation, corporations have less responsibility over these workers and less financial incentive to see that they are treated adequately and fairly.

A good example is provided by a new and important book, *The Silicon Valley of Dreams*, by David Naguib Pellow and Lisa Sun-Hee Park.[60] The authors performed an extensive study of the computer industry. While semiconductors or integrated circuits (chips) and capacitors may be manufactured under highly controlled systems in modern facilities, the assembly of the chips on printed circuit boards and the attachment of cables and other tasks are typically outsourced. They may be outsourced to single independent contractor individuals and their families, or they may be outsourced to businesses in other countries. Pellow and Park document a wide variety of social justice risks associated with this outsourcing. Work related injuries essentially end up being absorbed by the effected workers. Generally, no liability or risk costs comes back to the parent corporation.

As explained earlier, no risk financing exists for loss of sales and profits from reputation damages caused by boycotts, which are related to the poor treatment of workers. It is possible that some type of claims may reach D&O insurance policies. New legal developments may bring more direct responsibility to corporations when workers of outsourced business or workers in other countries are not treated fairly and equitably. Recent developments under the Alien Torts Claims Act (ATCA) provide an excellent example.

As noted in several cases in Chapter 5, the ATCA has recently been used to litigate against U.S. corporations and make them accountable for their poor treatment of workers in foreign countries. In June 2004, the U.S. Supreme Court affirmed that non-U.S. citizens may sue U.S. corporations for human rights abuses in U.S. federal courts under the Alien Tort Claims Act. In *Sosa v. Alvarez-Machain* in June 2004, the Supreme Court concluded, on a 9-0 vote, that the arbitrary detention of a Mexican national by a DEA agent was not actionable under the Federal Tort Claims Act or the Alien Tort Claims Act. However, the court also made clear, on a 6-3 vote, that perpetrators of other offenses, if widely accepted as violations of international law, could be held liable. The Court's opinion allows victims to continue to sue for violations such as torture and genocide, and appears to apply both to government officials, such as police or army officers, and private entities, such as multinational corporations.[61]

While significant liabilities have yet to develop, new ground is being pursued to charge international corporations for their behavior in these countries-traditionally an area where little if any risk exposure previously existed. Of particularly importance under ATCA, actions may be initiated in U.S. courts, awards in foreign courts can be enforced in U.S. courts, and U.S. standards may be applied for worker treatment and environmental performance in developing countries. The negative publicity and potential boycotts associated with this litigation, even if not successful, can be damaging. Shareholder resolutions associated with ATCA claims may cause further disruption for boards of directors.

Need to Strengthen Sustainability Risk Financing

Most corporations do not have adequate financing for sustainability risks. Dave Dybdahl, who has been referenced above, estimates that around one percent of businesses carry some form of environmental insurance. Many may not realize that environmental risks have been excluded from standard liability policies.

Others may not feel that they have a meaningful exposure. A good chance exists that their insurance agents/brokers have never raised the issue with them. It is estimated that one half of one percent of all insurance agents/brokers control 80 percent of the environmental insurance market. So many policyholders and risk managers have agents/brokers that are not involved and familiar with these insurance markets and the risks they cover.[62]

While I would not recommend that all businesses carry environmental insurance, I clearly feel that there are a large number of corporations that would benefit from the purchase of these policies. For the record, I have no affiliation with any insurance organizations and in no way would benefit from more corporations buying environmental insurance. A central theme of this book is that environmental liabilities will increase substantially in the future. Without appropriate risk financing, many firms could incur debilitating financial losses. Recall the 67 bankruptcies of companies in the asbestos business and most of them had insurance, just not enough. At a minimum, I would advise risk managers to consider making an appointment with a broker that specializes in the environmental insurance markets. Typically, these brokers are going to be found with the major brokerage firms like Marsh, Aon, Gallagher and Willis. Risk managers have no obligation to purchase coverage, but the broker, as part of the proposal process, will be able to provide an indication of the nature of the firm's exposure to environmental liabilities. Some brokers may provide risk managers with a detailed risk assessment of their environmental exposures.

The broker has an incentive to sell an insurance policy. To ease any doubts about objectivity, risk managers can arrange to just purchase environmental risk assessment consulting services from the brokers or from independent consultants that are not involved in the insurance markets. Risk managers should be conducting environmental risk assessments of their own firms, but often a broker or consultant can provide a "second set of eyes" to make the assessment more thorough. Risk managers can also seek information from environmental risk organizations like Environmental Risk Resources Association, whose web site provides considerable information on environmental risks.

When an environmental insurance policy is purchased, the firm is provided with more than just a financial guaranty of performance if a loss arises. The firm is also provided with the extensive loss control and engineering services of the insurer. As mentioned above, environmental insurance closely resembles B&M and HPR insurance systems. Strong emphasis is on the prevention and the control of the loss. A good part of the premium goes towards providing these risk control services. Ideally, no losses will ever develop. With almost any type of insured risk, it is always better if the loss does not occur. While one may collect for damages and expenses from insurance, the disruption and inconvenience of incurring the loss produces more burdens than if the loss never occurred in the first place.

Environmental insurance helps to mitigate litigation against directors and officers. This will become particularly important as more pressure is brought on corporations to adequately disclose their environmental liabilities. Shareholders may get angry over disclosures of environmental liabilities and file suits against directors and officers for failing to disclose those liabilities sooner. Having coverage in place for those liabilities would tend to ameliorate the shareholders anger. As noted by policyholder attorney, Jeffery Schumacher of Sachnoff and Weaver:

> "Purchasing sufficient environmental insurance to cap newly disclosed environmental liabilities would provide some protection to the company and its directors and reduce their potential liability to shareholders and minimize or undercut shareholders' ability to complain about the disclosure."[63]

In addition, as noted by John O'Brien, Executive Vice President for AIG Environmental, "many D&O carriers have eliminated coverage for officers and directors if they get into an environmental action, broadly, because of failure to properly disclose."[64] Anderson and Ferrera of Gallagher also noted this restriction (see earlier section in this chapter).

Social justice risks have more adequate risk financing than environmental risks. Workers' injuries are covered by workers compensation insurance, which is compulsory. Employment practice liability insurance is available to cover firms for claims resulting from discrimination (sex, age, race), sexual harassment, and wrongful discharge claims. While not all firms purchase this coverage, increasingly it is part of a business' risk financing portfolio. Even though social justice risks may be adequately financed, the negative publicity and reputation damage that accompany high worker injury rates, or claims for discrimination or sexual harassment, can still cause substantial disruption to the firm. While insurance coverage may be in place for workers in developed countries, workers in developing countries are usually not covered.

While insurance is extremely important in risk financing, I always tell my students that you hope never to use your insurance. By that I mean emphasis should be put on risk control and loss prevention to avoid insurance claims in the first place. With environmental and social justice risks, this advice is particularly important because of the complicated nature of these claims and the fact that they are often accompanied by negative publicity and reputation damage. Financial losses caused by the negative publicity and reputation damage, typically loss of revenues and profits, are not covered by any type of risk financing scheme. In addition, sustainability risks, particularly in the environmental arena, often have no risk financing in place. This means that a company with poor risk control will end up retaining or paying for the adverse financial consequences of a claim including defense costs, bodily injury and property damage claims, in addition to any resulting loss of revenues and profits. Mitigating such situations requires sound sustainability risk management strategies and practices, including sustainability risk finance.

CHAPTER 10—ENDNOTES

[1] Charles K. Cox, "Liability Insurance in the Era of the Consumer," a speech before The Annual Conference of the American Society of Insurance Management, Bal Harbour, Florida, April 9, 1970.

[2] Dan R. Anderson, What Role Will the Insurance Industry Play in the Fight Against Pollution?" *CPCU Annuls*, Vol. 25, No. 1, March 1972.

[3] David Dybdahl, Founder and Senior Consultant, American Risk Management Resources, LLC and Founder, Environmental Risk Resources Association, Interviews, 2005.

[4] David Dybdahl, Founder and Senior Consultant, American Risk Management Resources, LLC and Founder, Environmental Risk Resources Association, Interviews, 2004; David J. Dybdahl, "EIL Coverage: Action and Reaction," *Risk Management*, September 1985; Robert S. Faron, "The Pollution Liability Dilemma," *Risk Management*, May 1985; Peter Huber, "The Environmental Liability Dilemma," *CPCU Journal*, December 1987; Donald V. Jernberg and Mark C. Furse, "Environmental Risk Insurance: Don't Count on It," *Risk Management*, July 1987; Bradford W. Rich, "Environmental Litigation and the Insurance Dilemma," *Risk Management*, December 1985; David A. Tweedy and Daniel G. Tracy, "Surviving the Pollution Liability Crisis," *Risk Management*, October 1985.

[5] David Dybdahl, Founder and Senior Consultant, American Risk Management Resources, LLC and Founder, Environmental Risk Resources Association, Interviews, 2005.

[6] Ibid.

[7] Ibid.

[8] David Dybdahl, Founder and Senior Consultant, American Risk Management Resources, LLC and Founder, Environmental Risk Resources Association, Interviews, 2005; Wallace L. Clapp, "Environmental Liability Markets Expand," *Rough Notes*, July, 1997; *Ctittenden's Environmental Liability News*, Oct 20, 1997; November 3, 1997.

[9] David Dybdahl, Founder and Senior Consultant, American Risk Management Resources, LLC and Founder, Environmental Risk Resources Association, Interviews, 2005; Karl Russek, "Emerging International Issues for Environmental Liability," *Risk Management,* July 2005; "Sarbanes-Oxley, Exposures Drive Growth of Environmental Insurance Market, Advisen FPN, January 7, 2005.

[10] David Dybdahl, Founder and Senior Consultant, American Risk Management Resources, LLC and Founder, Environmental Risk Resources Association, Interviews, 2005; Report by ECS in 1997 cited in "Sarbanes-Oxley, Exposures Drive Growth of Environmental Insurance Market," Advisen FPN, January 7, 2005.

[11] Alan Bressler, "Navigating the U.S. Environmental Liability Market" (Part 1), March 2002 at www.irmi.com.

[12] David Dybdahl, Founder and Senior Consultant, American Risk Management Resources, LLC and Founder, Environmental Risk Resources Association, Interviews, 2005.

[13] David Dybdahl and Rodney Taylor, "Environmental Insurance," Chapter 11 in Donald S. Malecki and Arthur L. Flitner, *Commercial Liability Risk Management and Insurance,* 5th Ed., Malvern, PA: American Institute, 2001.

[14] Environmental Risk Resources Association, www.erraonline.org.

[15] David Dybdahl, Founder and Senior Consultant, American Risk Management Resources, LLC and Founder, Environmental Risk Resources Association, Interviews, 2005.

[16] Ibid.

[17] Ibid.

[18] "ACE Offers Lead Umbrella," Zurich RiskWire Headlines, April 19, 2004; "Sarbanes-Oxley, Exposures Drive Growth of Environmental Insurance Market," Advisen FPN, January 7, 2005.

[19] David Dybdahl, Founder and Senior Consultant, American Risk Management Resources, LLC and Founder, Environmental Risk Resources Association, Interviews, 2005.

[20] Alan Bressler, "Navigating the U.S. Environmental Liability Market" (Part 1), March 2002 at www.irmi.com.

[21] Parts of the above section taken from Dan R. Anderson, "Development of Environmental Liability Risk Management and Insurance in the United States: Lessons and Opportunities," *Risk Management and Insurance Review*, Vol 2, No 1, Summer 1998.

[22] "Asbestos Package on Its Way," *The Journal of Commerce*, June 20, 1996; Edwin Unsworth, "T&N Aiming to Cap Asbestos Liabilities," *Business Insurance*, December 9, 1996.

[23] "$800 Million Placement Marks Largest Ever Pollution Program," *Business Insurance*, August 10, 1998.

[24] Donald S. Malecki and Arthur L. Flitner, "Professional Liability Insurance, Part II," Chapter 10, *Commercial Liability Insurance and Risk Management*, 5th edition, Malvern PA: American Institute for CPCU, 2001.

[25] Kenn E. Anderson and Donna Ferrara, "Disclosing Environmental Liabilities: Director, Officer and Insurance Issues," Arthur J. Gallagher & Co., August 2003.

[26] Ibid.

[27] Willis Corroon, *Environment Impairment Liability Insurance Responsible Care Premium Modification Factor.*

[28] Dan R. Anderson, What Role Will the Insurance Industry Play in the Fight Against Pollution?" *CPCU Annuls*, Vol. 25, No. 1, March 1972.

[29] Real Estate Environmental Liability with Mold Insurance, American Risk Management Resources, LLC, webmaster@ARMR.net.

[30] Martin T. Katzman, *Chemical Catastrophes: Regulating Environmental Risk through Pollution Liability Insurance,* Philadelphia, PA: University of Pennsylvania, Huebner Foundation Series, Wharton School, 1985.

[31] Paul K. Freeman and Howard Kunreuther, *Managing Environmental Risk through Insurance,* Boston/Dordrecht/London: Kluwer Academic Publishers, 1997.

[32] Linda Bagneschi, "Pollution Prevention, The Best-Kept Secret in Loss Control," *Risk Management,* July 1998.

[33] Thomas M. Yuill, Director, Institute for Environmental Studies, University of Wisconsin-Madison, interview, 1997.

[34] Alberto A. Gutierrez, "Claims Management Cuts Environmental Loss Costs," *Best's Review,* P/C Edition, April 2, 1996.

[35] Randall E. Hobbs, "Don't Be Caught Off Guard: New Options in Managing Environmental Incidents," *Risk Management,* August 1996.

[36] Dan R. Anderson, "Environmental Insurance Markets: Development and Strategies For Growth," *Proceedings of the International Insurance Society,* New York: International Insurance Society, 1998.

[37] W. Pfennigstorf, "The Role of Insurance in Risk Spreading and Risk Bearing," *Insuring and Managing Hazardous Risks: From Seveso to Bhopal and Beyond,* Paul R. Kleindorfer and Howard C. Kunreuther, editors, New York: Springer-Verlag, 1987.

[38] Baruch Berliner and Juerg Spuehler, "Insurability Issues Associated with Managing Existing Hazardous Waste Sites," *Integrating Insurance and Risk Management for Hazardous Wastes,* Howard Kunreuther and M.V. Rajeev Gowda, editors, Boston: Kluwer Academic Publishers, 1990.

[39] Carolyn Aldred, "Pollution Crackdown in Europe," *Business Insurance,* October 8, 1990; Carolyn Aldred, "U.K. Pollution Coverage to Shrink," *Business Insurance,* October 8, 1990.

[40] Swiss Reinsurance Company, *Insuring Environmental Impairment Liability*, Zurich: Swiss Reinsurance Company, 1996.

[41] Michael Faure, ed., *Detterence, Insurability and Compensation in Environmental Liability: Future Developments in the European Union*, Tort and Insurance Law Vol. 5, European Centre of Tort and Insurance Law, Wien, New York: Springer-Verlag, 2003.

[42] William Kronenberg, III, "The Environmental Insurance Markets in the U.S. and Western Europe: A U.S. Underwriter's Observations," *The Geneva Papers on Risk and Insurance*, 20, No. 76, July 1995.

[43] Swiss Reinsurance Company, *Insuring Environmental Impairment Liability*, Zurich: Swiss Reinsurance Company, 1996.

[44] Dean Jeffery Telego, "Risk Financing: Insuring Potential Pollution Exposures," *Environmental Risk Management*, Eric B. Rothenberg and Dean Jeffery Telego, editors, Alexandria, Virginia: RTM Communications, Inc., 1991.

[45] Patrick Peugeot, "Evolving Environmental Impairment Liability: Is the EC Heading Toward a United States-Style Liability Crisis? How Will These Risks Be Written?" *Journal of Reinsurance*, Vol. 1, No. 1, Fall 1993.

[46] Reiner Bellenbaum, "Reinsurance of Environmental Risk Pricing and Risk Assessment," *The Geneva Papers on Risk and Insurance*, 20, No. 76, July 1995.

[47] Patrick Peugeot, "Evolving Environmental Impairment Liability: Is the EC Heading Toward a United States-Style Liability Crisis? How Will These Risks Be Written?" *Journal of Reinsurance*, Vol. 1, No. 1, Fall 1993.

[48] Reiner Bellenbaum, "Reinsurance of Environmental Risk Pricing and Risk Assessment," *The Geneva Papers on Risk and Insurance*, 20, No. 76, July 1995.

[49] Willis Corroon, *FAACT Country Information*, 1998.

[50] Reiner Bellenbaum, "Reinsurance of Environmental Risk Pricing and Risk Assessment," *The Geneva Papers on Risk and Insurance*, 20, No. 76, July 1995.

[51] Willis Corroon, *FAACT Country Information,* 1998.

[52] Michael Faure, ed., *Detterence, Insurability and Compensation in Environmental Liability: Future Developments in the European Union,* Tort and Insurance Law Vol. 5, European Centre of Tort and Insurance Law, Wien, New York: Springer-Verlag, 2003.

[53] Roberto Ceniceros, "EU cleanup laws may spur demand for stand-along pollution coverage," *Business Insurance,* June 13, 2005; Karl Russek, "Emerging International Issues for Environmental Liability," *Risk Management,* July 2005; "Environmental Insurance Comes of age in Europe," *IQ-Insider Quarterly,* Summer 2005.

[54] Roberto Ceniceros, "EU cleanup laws may spur demand for stand-along pollution coverage," *Business Insurance,* June 13, 2005.

[55] Karl Russek, "Emerging International Issues for Environmental Liability," *Risk Management,* July 2005.

[56] Roberto Ceniceros, "EU cleanup laws may spur demand for stand-along pollution coverage," *Business Insurance,* June 13, 2005; Karl Russek, "Emerging International Issues for Environmental Liability," *Risk Management,* July 2005; "Environmental Insurance Comes of age in Europe," *IQ-Insider Quarterly,* Summer 2005.

[57] Karl Russek, "Emerging International Issues for Environmental Liability," *Risk Management,* July 2005.

[58] Peta Miller, "Pollution Directive Adds Uncertainty," *Business Insurance,* March 8, 2004.

[59] Ibid.

[60] David Naguib Pellow and Lisa Sun-Hee Park, *The Silicon Valley of Dreams,* New York: New York University Press, 2002.

[61] www.earthrights.org; Linda Greenhouse, "Human Rights Abuses Worldwide Are Held to Fall Under U.S. Courts," *New York Times,* June 30, 2004.

[62] David Dybdahl, Founder and Senior Consultant, American Risk Management Resources, LLC and Founder, Environmental Risk Resources Association, Interviews, 2005.

[63] Dave Lenckus, "Governance law hasn't fueled big EIL interest," *Business Insurance*, June 16, 2003.

[64] "Sarbanes-Oxley, Exposures Drive Growth of Environmental Insurance Market," Advisen FPN, January 7, 2005.

11

HOPE AND OPPORTUNITIES

○ ○

A phenomenal expansion of economic activity is projected for the decades immediately ahead. Down one path, this growth can protect, regenerate, and restore the environment. It can provide sustainable livelihoods for the world's poor and lead to large improvements in quality of life for all. There is still world enough and time to realize this future. But it will not be won without a profound commitment to urgent action.

> —Gus Speth, Yale University, author of **Red Sky at Morning**

We're at a tipping point where energy efficiency and emissions reduction also equal profitability.

> —Jeff Immelt, CEO, General Electric

Paying your employees well is not only the right thing to do but makes good business sense.

> —James Sinegal, CEO, Costco

When one discusses issues like the deteriorating state of environmental and social justice conditions, there is a tendency to become overwhelmed and give up hope. The purpose of my book is to give people and businesses hope. I do believe it is critical to appreciate and understand these deteriorating conditions, which can then act as a catalyst for taking action. Time exists to make these changes. Focus should be placed on the hope that necessary changes are possible and on the business opportunities that accompany these changes.

In the Chinese language, the character for "crisis" is comprised of two characteristics meaning "danger" and "opportunity." Clearly, the current state of environmental and social conditions has a component of danger. But the opportunities presented by the crisis may be of greater importance. Sustainability risk management acts to reduce environmental harm and improve social justice conditions. In the process, new business opportunities are created. In general business opportunities can provide a competitive edge, increase market share, differentiate products and services, reduce costs, and bolster profits.

Business Opportunities

Throughout the book, I have given examples of corporations, individuals and organizations offering new strategies to counter deteriorating environmental and social conditions. In the following section, I will discuss several more examples, while emphasizing the substantial business opportunities each presents. These examples provide a positive influence and serve as role models for other businesses wrestling with sustainability issues. In order to survive, we will have to do things differently. Innovation is the key. As noted in that famous quote by Einstein:

"You can't solve a problem using the thinking that created the problem."

General Electric

General Electric, one of the largest and most venerable corporations, announced in May 2005, a major commitment to environmental investments. Jeff Immelt, CEO, in a speech at the George Washington University Business School, said that:

> "He would double G.E.'s investments in energy and environmental technologies to prepare it for what he sees as a huge global market for products that help other companies—and countries like China and India—reduce emissions of greenhouse gases."[1]

In launching this new initiative, called "ecomagination," Immelt stated that both GE's research and development in new technologies and the marketing of more environmentally friendly products would double over the period 2005-2010. New technologies include wind power generation, solar panels, coal gasification power plants, diesel-electric hybrid locomotives, more efficient aircraft engines and appliances, advanced water treatment and conservation systems, and agricultural silicon that cuts the amount of water and pesticides used in spraying fields. GE has around 15 percent of the global wind energy market, which is expected to grow 10-15 percent a year. James Lyons, a chief engineer at GE's Global Research Center, states:

> "There are a lot of wild and crazy ideas in the wind industry, but there is an incredible amount of pent-up demand as well."[2]

Immelt expects that more then half of GE's product revenues will come from environmentally approved products by 2015. Immelt pledged that by 2012, GE's energy efficiency would improve by 30 percent and its worldwide greenhouse gas emissions would decrease by one percent, as opposed to a 40 percent increase if no action was taken. GE will release its first ever "Citizenship Report," which will lay out their plans on this new initiative and other related issues.[3]

GE's strategic initiative will reduce the negative impacts of their operations on the environment. The probability of future liability and boycott risks are also reduced, and their company's image and reputation is improved. GE expects its more environmentally oriented business strategy will result in increased revenues, profits, and competitive advantage. Immelt may have summed it up best:

> "We're at a tipping point where energy efficiency and emissions reduction also equal profitability."[4]

Chicago Climate Exchange

The Chicago Climate Exchange was discussed in Chapter 7. It is a voluntary program to trade carbon emission credits with the expectation that at some point in time the U.S. will enact mandatory carbon caps and emission trading schemes. As a requirement of being on the Exchange, member companies and organizations have pledged four percent reductions in their greenhouse gas emissions through 2006. Member corporations include Ford, DuPont, Motorola, IBM and Baxter. This is a new business opportunity that will help to slow global warming. It will also reduce global warming risks of the participating companies.

Gretchen Daily

Gretchen Daily, Director of Stanford's tropical research program at the Center for Conservation Biology, feels that such market based systems could be employed to help protect biodiversity and ecosystems. Daily thinks that ecosystems should not be viewed as vacant land for development, but as a:

> "Capital asset that must be not squandered, even if that means compensating landowners for keeping forests green."[5]

She gives Costa Rica's pioneering system as an example. The Costa Rican government pays landowners to not cut down their forests. Forest can be considered a capital asset. The government payments can be thought of going towards maintaining services provided by the forests including clean water, flood control, habitat and biodiversity preservation and promoting ecotourism. Since this program was enacted, Costa Rica has gone from having one of the highest deforestation rates to one of the lowest.

Another example she notes is the ecosystem marketplace that was launched in March 2005. It is the world's first clearing house for ecosystem assets, where buyers and sellers can get together. She gives the example of a developer paying $100,000, to buy a pair of woodpeckers. The buyer was developing an area where woodpeckers live. The seller owns land where the pair of woodpeckers habit, and will conserve the habitat. While this marketplace is in its infancy, recall that 50 years ago there were no markets for stock options.[6]

In an article in *Science* with several collaborators, Daily sums up the essence of her thinking:

> "The world's ecosystems are capital assets. If properly managed, they yield a flow of vital services, including the production of goods (such as seafood and timber), life support processes (such as pollination and water purification), and life-fulfilling conditions (such as beauty and serenity). Moreover, ecosystems have value in terms of the conservation of options (such as genetic diversity for future use)."[7]

Developing economic and market systems for valuing ecosystems and their services offer enormous business opportunities. Typically, the value of these ecosystems and their services has been ignored by economic markets. This is starting to change and will escalate as ecosystems come under more pressure and their values rise.

Toyota

Toyota is one of the most successful corporations in the world today. Anticipating reductions in greenhouse gas emissions and potential oil shortages, it introduced the first mass produced automobile, the Prius, in Japan in 1997. While well known for its Prius, Toyota has introduced several other environmental initiatives. For instance, it reduced the average energy consumption per vehicle produced by over 17 percent from 2000 to 2004. Toyota's 5Rs program to refine, reduce, reuse, recycle and retrieve energy, is aimed at reducing waste. Toyota has reduced their land disposal of waste by 68 percent and has a goal of an 80 percent reduction. For six consecutive years, Toyota has been in 100 percent compliance with hazardous waste regulations, which should eliminate future Superfund liabilities. While subject to take back or end of life regulations in the EU and Japan, Toyota is voluntarily employing these practices at their U.S. operations.

Toyota has also introduced several social justice initiatives. Toyota has incorporated programs to reduced employee injuries including one whose goal is to reduce to zero six types of accidents that may cause disability or death. Toyota promotes campaigns for traffic safety education for children and for the proper use of seatbelts and child safety seats. They also contribute to several NGOs and charitable groups.

As the world leader of hybrid technology, Toyota was particularly well positioned in the market when gas prices reached high levels in 2005. While Ford and General Motors, with their continued emphasis on large SUVs and trucks, are struggling with weak financial performance, sizeable layoffs and bonds rated near or at junk bond status, Toyota is producing record financial results. If current trends continue, Toyota will overtake General Motors and Ford as the world's leading automobile manufacturer. While GM and Ford face unusually high and persistent health and pension costs relative to Toyota, it seems reasonable that Toyota's efforts in reducing sustainability risk costs have contributed to their record financial performance. Indeed, in January 2005, at the World Economic Forum held in Davos, Switzerland, the *Corporate Knights* unveiled its list of the 100 most sustainable corporations in the world. Toyota was ranked number one.[8]

Integrated Gasification

Business opportunities associated with renewable energy sources like solar and wind, have been discussed in previous portions of the book (see Chapter 7). While there is a great deal of emphasis on the development of renewable energy sources, it is generally conceded that coal will need to be used as a significant source of electrical power plants. A new technology, called integrated gasification combined cycle, can turn coal into a relatively clean gas, and operate more efficiently (about 10-15 percent) and use less water (about 40 percent). In addition, the technology has the potential ability to eventually all but eliminate greenhouse gases.

Integrated gasification is a terrific example of looking upstream to remove pollutants from the process so they do not have to be removed downstream. Pollutants can be chemically stripped from gasified coal before it is burned more efficiently and at less expense than scrubbing it out of exhaust gases. Half of sulfur dioxide and nitrogen oxides and 95 percent of mercury can be stripped out before combustion. Of greater significance in terms of curbing global warming, integrated gasification technology has the ability to capture carbon before combustion. The captured carbon would then need to be sequestered, most likely in some type of geologic formation.

Surprisingly, this technology was incorporated in the Tampa Electric plant a decade ago, but this is the only commercial plant operating today. The main reason this technology has not been used in other plants is that the Tampa plant cost about 20 percent more to build than a conventional plant that burns pulverized coal. A federal grant helped to cover the extra cost. Sequestering carbon would increase the cost even more and without the financial incentives of Kyoto Protocol like requirements, simple economics do not make the plant attractive to utilities, ratepayers or regulators.

Strong arguments can be made that long term sustainability risks will be reduced through integrated gasification technology by curtailing mercury, sulfur dioxide, nitrogen oxides and GHG emissions. Assuming the United States adopts mandatory GHG emissions limits, more integrated gasification plants will in all likelihood be built. Companies like General Electric and Bechtel are currently working on strategies to build integrated gasification plants. Business opportunities exist now, and at some point in time, such opportunities will almost certainly grow.[9]

Citiraya Industries

Ng Teck, a high school dropout, was a truck driver until 1989. He quit his job thinking he could make more money sifting through Singapore garbage dumps for valuable metals from discarded electronic components. Ng decided to set up a business to reprocess electronic waste. Today his company, Citiraya Industries, is the world's largest processor of corporate electronic waste. It has captured 70 percent of the corporate market for recycling electronic waste. Corporate customers include Intel, Nokia and Hewlett-Packard.

With its location in Singapore, Citiraya Industries is subject to extremely strict environmental regulations. Electronic waste has typically been sent to poor countries in Asia where workers, often without any protective wear, comb through the dangerous waste. Toxic materials like lead, cadmium and mercury often contaminate water systems. Having such waste handled in a high tech fashion under strict environmental and worker safety controls reduces sustainability risk costs.

Deutsche Bank predicts that Citiraya's revenues will double and profits triple from 2004 to 2006. And Citiraya is only dealing with discarded computers. In the United States alone, an incredible 100 million cell phones were taken out of service in 2004. The replacement cycle for cell phones in North America has dropped from three years to 18-24 months in just the last three years, and the cycle continues to drop. With the European Union's WEEE and RoHS requirements coming on board (see Chapter 9), along with similar laws in Taiwan, Japan and South Korea, plus a handful of state laws (California, Massachusetts, Minnesota and Maine), the potential market for recycling all forms of electronic waste is enormous. These new regulations, plus voluntary efforts, will result in the transformation of environmentally destructive and dangerous working practices into modern high tech operations. These efforts to reduce and eliminate sustainability risks will result in business opportunities, as exemplified Citiraya Industries.[10]

Costco

Wal-Mart has come under heavy criticisms for the low wages and benefits paid to its workers. The class action discrimination suit brought against Wal-Mart by 1.6 million female workers represents one of the largest social justice risks discussed in this book. Wal-Mart, the largest company in the world in terms of revenues, argues that it needs to keep wages and benefits down to keep its prices low.

Costco is a competitor of Wal-Mart and is the 11th largest retailer in the world and number 29 of Fortune 500 companies. Costco remains competitive with Wal-Mart and does not attract the negative criticism aimed at Wal-Mart. Costco's positive image is explained by *Business Week* data shown in Table 11-1.

Table 11-1

	COSTCO	WAL-MART'S SAM'S CLUB
Average hourly wage	$15.97	$11.52
Annual health costs per worker	$5,735	$3,500
Covered by health plan	82%	47%
Annual retirement costs per worker	$1,330	$747
Covered by retirement plans	91%	64%
Employee turnover	6% a year	21% a year
Labor and overhead costs	9.8% of sales	17% of sales
Sales per square foot	$795	$516
Profits per employee	$13,647	$11,039
Yearly operating-income growth	10.1%	9.8%

Source: Stanley Holmes and Wendy Zellner, "The Costco Way," *Business Week,* April 12, 2004.

Costco's wages and benefits are substantially higher than those that Wal-Mart provides to its workers, but clearly Costco is still competitive. How is this accomplished? Costco workers have fewer turnovers and are more productive, and Costco's profits are comparable to Wal-Mart as shown in Table 11-1. Costco's strategy not only reduces sustainability risk costs, like Wal-Mart's class action discrimination suit, it almost provides a competitive and profitable model with more satisfied and productive workers. In the words of Costco CEO, James Sinegal:

> "Paying your employees well is not only the right thing to do but it makes good business sense."[11]

FedEx

FedEx diesel trucks present both economic and environmental risks for their shipping business. If the price of oil increased or supplies became limited, financial performance could suffer. Pollutants and greenhouse gas emissions from burning diesel could present liability, boycott or reputation risks. In 2000, Environmental Defense approached FedEx with the idea of producing a hybrid truck to replace FedEx's old diesel trucks. A partnership was formed. After careful thought, FedEx made a commitment to replace its entire 30,000 express van fleet with hybrid gas-electric models in 10 years. In March of 2004, the first two hybrid trucks were introduced in California.

While the hybrid models are more expensive initially, fuel costs are cut in half, which saves money and reduces FedEx's reliance on oil markets. Since a regenerative braking system is used, there is less wear and tear on the brakes, which is particularly important given the stop-and-go nature of the delivery business. Between fuel savings and lower maintenance costs, FedEx expects to break even on the hybrid vans in about a decade.

Burning less fuel reduces environmental costs of smog, pollutants and greenhouse gases. Particulate emissions are cut by 90 percent. This is obviously good public relations for a historically dirty industry. FedEx's strategy alleviates potential liability and boycott risks as well as future regulatory risks, say if mandatory GHG emissions limits become law.

FedEx's actions impacted a number of other parties. Its main competitor, UPS, had started even earlier using alternative technologies. UPS has around 2000 vans running on natural gas and other fuel sources, and is testing a zero emission, hydrogen powered fuel cell. Still, FedEx's decision to replace its entire fleet with hybrids must be getting attention from UPS. The Eaton Corporation, which was chosen to manufacture the electro-mechanical power systems for FedEx hybrids, received an obvious financial boost. The U.S. Postal Service, a consortium of utilities and even the Departments of Defense and Energy are all making plans to incorporate hybrid models. Consumer consultant J.D. Power and Associates estimates that by 2008, 500,000 hybrid vehicles will be on the roads, with 40 percent of them trucks.[12]

Green Building

Green building presents tremendous opportunities for innovation and developing new methods of design and construction. While Europe has been active in green building for decades, the United States has only been actively involved since around 2000. A critical juncture came in 2000 with the development of LEED (Leadership in Energy and Environment Design) certification. LEED certification was established by the U.S. Green Building Council, a nonprofit organization founded in 1993 and comprised of designers, developers, government institutions, builders, environmentalists and manufacturers. Prior to LEED certification, no standards for green building existed. Someone could say they built a green building but no one knew exactly what that meant.

LEED certification and green building in general involves minimizing the use of energy and water, the use of sustainability produced, nontoxic and recycled materials, emphasis on access to public transportation or carpools, green roofs and maximization of the advantages of nature like fresh air, natural sunlight, views and outdoor access. Initial additional investment costs range from 1 to 16 percent, with an average of 6 to 7 percent of total building costs. LEED status can be at four levels (platinum, gold, silver, standard), with the higher rankings typically costing more.

Additional green investments pay for themselves overtime with energy savings, less water use, less extensive mechanical systems, lower workers compensation costs, more pleasant working environments, more productive employees, and less turnover and absenteeism. A State of California commissioned study of its 33 LEED certified buildings found that they cost an average of $4 more per square foot, but over a 20 year period, they generate savings of $48.87 (standard and silver) to $67.31 (gold and platinum) per square foot. In April 2004, Genzyme Corporation opened its new LEED certified headquarters in Cambridge, Massachusetts. Henri Termeer in explaining his rationale stated:

> "The business case is that our return comes from the productivity of our people, and the building helps us hire and retain those who can make the right decisions."[13]

Favorable publicity/advertising, an improved public image and an augmented reputation produce further value.

As of June 2005, 216 buildings have been LEED certified and 1,936 are going through the process. Of greater significance is the potential market. Green building experts estimate that 20 percent of government and institutional buildings are being built to LEED standards, but only five percent for commercial construction. In addition, new LEED certification programs are being developed for tenants renting property, existing building residential homes, and communities.[14]

William McDonough, whose work has been highlighted in this book, is exporting his ideas on green building and other sustainability strategies to China. He is working with the China Housing Industry Association, which has the responsibility for building housing for 400 million people in the next 12 years. McDonough's firm is working with the Housing Association to design seven new cities. He is using new nontoxic polystyrene that is strong, lightweight, with excellent insulating properties. New toilets minimize water use, bamboo-wetlands purify the waste, and farm fields are built on rooftops. He is suggesting that square miles of marginal land be covered with solar panels.[15]

Sustainability experts have been worried that with China's growing economy, it could become a country of American type consumers with disastrous environmental consequences. One method of mitigating environmental damages is to have China incorporate state of the art sustainability technologies with help from other countries. William McDonough's work is an excellent example of employing such a strategy.

Others

While space does not allow discussion of more examples, I might suggest a couple other sources that have not yet been referenced in this book. An article "Here comes the new gold rush," in *FSB: Fortune Small Business,* presented plans of 14 entrepreneurs to profit from the coming green revolution.[16] The entrepreneurs, companies, and business concepts are listed below.

Kimberly Jordan, CEO, New Belgium Brewing Co., Fort Collins, CO: Create award-winning beer, with environmental passion.

Simon Hodsoim, CEO, Earthshell Corp., Lutherville, MD: Biodegradable packaging to ease the fast-food garbage pileup.

John Young, CEO and Kang P. Lee, Founder, Aspen Aerogel, Marlborough, MA: Ultrathin insulation to save timber and energy.

Mitch Rofsky and Todd Silberman, Founders, Better World Club, Portland, OR: Auto club without all the pro-pavement lobbying.

Bruce Ferguson, Founder and CEO, Edenspace, Dulles, VA: Use common plants to clean up polluted land.

Tom Dinwoodie, CEO, Powerlight, Berkeley, CA: More competitive solar power.

Dan Juhl, Founder, Danmar & Associates, Woodstock, MN: Wind power—helping farmers profit.

John Mackey, CEO and Founder, Whole Foods Market, Austin, TX: Specialty supermarket emphasizing healthy food.

Weil Peterson, CEO, Flexcar, Seattle, WA: Car-sharing company.

Judy Wicks, Owner, Whitedog Café, Philadelphia, PA: Being good to the earth can be good for the wallet too.

Roger Wittenberg, Co-Founder, Trex Company, Winchester, VA: Reducing the plastic in landfills.

Rich Marino, President and Scott Reisfield, COO, Active Life Pet Products, Boulder, CO: Organic food for the house cat.

Leroy Ohlsen, Founder, Neah Power Systems, Bothell, WA: Silicon-powered fuel cell to power laptops.

Oliver Peoples, Founder, Metabolix Inc., Cambridge, MA: Making plastics by harnessing the inner life of plants.

Pamela Gordon authored a book entitled, *Lean and Green*.[17] In her book, she featured the success stories of 20 organizations listed below.

Agilent Technologies	Kyocera Corporation
Apple Computer Corporation	Louisiana-Pacific Corporation
British Aerospace	LSI Logic Corporation
Celestica Inc.	NEC Corporation
Compaq Computer Corporation	Philips Electronics N.V.
Horizon Organic Dairy, Inc.	Polaroid Corporation
IBM Corporation	Santa Monica California
Intel Corporation	Sony Corporation
ITT Cannon, a division of ITT Industries	Texas Instruments Inc.
ITT Gilfillan	Thomson Multimedia

In my sustainability risk management classes, I had the students select a corporation and analyze its environmental and social justice records. Based on their work, I placed companies in various categories. Established companies with strong environmental and/or social records included:

S C Johnson	Cinergy	Johnson Controls
UPS	Anheuser Busch	3M
Xerox	Veolia	General Mills
Toyota	Timberland	Costco
Canon	Baxter	Dell Computers

Several companies initially ignored their environmental and social justice problems, faced boycotts, but made positive changes to rectify their problems. Many have gone beyond rectifying their problems and created exemplary sustainability systems. They are included below with the main problem that was subject of boycott.

Denny's (racial discrimination)	Home Depot (old growth forests)
IKEA (formaldehyde in products)	Citigroup (financing destructive projects)
Chiquita (poor labor and environment record)	Boise Cascade (old growth forests)
Nike (sweatshops)	Adidas/Solomon (sweatshops)
Shell Oil (Brent Spar and Nigeria)	

Three companies, Aveda (Estee Lauder), Ben and Jerry's (Unilever), and Patagonia were categorized as being committed to environmental and social responsibility from Day 1. There were several companies with poor environmental and social justice records. They will go unnamed as I am emphasizing positive examples and business opportunities in this chapter.

Survive and Prosper

Corporate survival will require change and innovation. But with change comes opportunity and potential prosperity. All the examples of business opportunities discussed above are characterized by efforts to improve environmental quality or social justice conditions or both. They represent creative, forward thinking businesses, which care about future generations. Virtually all the opportunities have or will produce positive financial results. By cutting sustainability risk costs, improvements are registered across the triple bottom line. For those companies not willing to innovate, there will be considerable, "creative destruction" in the words of Joseph Schumpeter. Doing things differently will take an enormous amount of effort and change in basic attitudes. As noted by Jared Diamond, author of *Guns, Germs and Steel* and *Collapse*.

"The most difficult values to jettison are those that have helped you in the past."[18]

Change Inevitable

I have argued that the forces of liability suits, boycotts, shareholders, competitors and regulators will result in making change inevitable. Corporations have the option of leading change or they can wait until forced to change. I feel that the advantages gained by capturing competitive leverage, maintaining productive employees, reducing long term sustainability risk costs, achieving immediate savings by cutting waste and energy use, and augmenting corporate reputation overwhelmingly support making changes now. All these advantages are lost by waiting and in a worst case scenario may result in the corporation not surviving.

The best efforts at corporate change are clearly those that are CEO led. Numerous examples have been given of CEOs like Jeff Immelt, GE, Ray Anderson, Interface, and Sir John Brown, BP, assuming leadership positions in building more sustainable companies. For those companies beginning the process, such actions as becoming ISO 14001 certified, encouraging (requiring) suppliers to become ISO 14001 certified, joining CERES or related groups, partnering with an NGO, participating in United Nations programs, and publishing a corporate sustainability report will all contribute to getting movement started. The details of these actions and numerous other strategies have been discussed in Chapter 9.

Education

I see my book as an educational tool. As I stated in the Introduction, strong moral and ethical arguments can be and should be made for managing sustainability risks. Emphasis in this book has been on educating and providing the business case for sustainability risk management. As noted by Katherine Reed, 3M's chief environmental officer, "Refining business as usual requires education more than changing hearts and minds."[19]

In writing this book I enjoyed reading a number of other books. For the interested reader I have listed (alphabetically) my top 10 recommended books on risks and issues concerning the environment, social justice, sustainability, and sustainable business management. While my personal and professional attitudes are consistent with the views expressed in these books, even if one disagrees with their philosophies or aspects of their arguments, a great deal can be learned from these texts.

Cannibals with Forks by John Elkington

Climate Change 2001 by the Intergovernmental Panel on Climate Change

Cradle to Cradle by William McDonough and Michael Braungart

Ecology of Commerce by Paul Hawken

Living Downstream by Sandra Steingraber

Natural Capitalism by Paul Hawken, Amory Lovins and L. Hunter Lovins

Our Stolen Future by Theo Colburn, Dianne Dumanoski and John Peterson Myers

Red Sky at Morning by James Gustave Speth

Silent Spring by Rachel Carson

Strategic Reputation Risk Management by Judy Larkin

Ultimate Risk Management Objectives

The basic objectives of risk management are to protect the assets of the corporation and to preserve corporate earnings (profits). I would suggest that the ultimate objectives of risk management are to protect ecosystems as capital assets, to preserve their continuing services; and to maintain fair and equitable social systems. This is the essence of sustainability risk management as examined in this book. Corporations that fail to accomplish the ultimate objectives of risk management will incur increasing sustainability risk costs.

I have argued in this book that the risk management and insurance industry should be a leader in developing sustainability risk management systems. Risk managers, insurers, brokers, consultants and academics are the experts in risk management. A central purpose of this book is to help them develop an expertise in sustainability risk management. Dave Lenckus, senior editor of *Business Insurance* poses the question:

> "Do many risk managers have a potentially career-enhancing opportunity to help guide their organizations toward a well-reasoned approach in handling their environmental liabilities?"[20]

I would answer yes. And the answer is yes not just for risk managers, but for all involved parties in the risk management process. Insurers will provide more risk financing, brokers will negotiate more contracts, consultants will solve more problems and professors will conduct more innovative research and transfer new knowledge to students. I feel that risk experts have an obligation to become more involved in sustainability risk management. Those in risk management are charged with the duty to anticipate current and future risks facing the firm. Risk managers may not have direct responsibilities for environmental quality and corporate social responsibility, but they still need to systematically access sustainability risks across their firms.

Final Thoughts

This book is about risks, survival, hope, opportunities and innovation. I have tried to demonstrate how sustainability risk management, by reducing environmental and social justice risks, can augment a firm's financial performance. Liability suits, boycotts and shareholder actions are reduced or eliminated, workers are happier, more motivated and more productive, community image is improved, reputation is enhanced and competitive advantages are gained. Environmental quality and social justice conditions are enhanced. The triple bottom line, financial, environmental, social, trends upward.

I decided to close with the words of Gus Speth of Yale, my alma mater. Gus Speth is dean and professor in the practice of environmental policy and sustainable development at Yale's School of Forestry and Environmental Studies. In his path breaking book, *Red Sky at Morning*, he concludes his chapter entitled, "The Most Fundamental Transition of All," with a section that reflects the spirit of my book:

> "A phenomenal expansion of economic activity is projected for the decades immediately ahead. Down one path, this growth can protect, regenerate, and restore the environment. It can provide sustainable livelihoods for the world's poor and lead to large improvements in quality of life for all. There is still world enough and time to realize this future. But it will not be won without a profound commitment to urgent action. President John F. Kennedy often told the story of the aged Marshal Lyautey of France debating with his gardener the wisdom of planting a certain tree.

> "It will not bloom," the gardener argued, "for decades."

> "Then," said the marshal, "plant it this afternoon."[21]

CHAPTER 11—ENDNOTES

[1] *New York Times*, May 19, 2005

[2] Diane Brade, "Reaping The Wind, *Business Week*, October 11, 2004

[3] This section based on, Kathryn Kranhold and Jeffrey Ball, "GE to Spend More On Projects Tied To Climate Changes," *Wall Street Journal*, May 9, 2005; Alan Murray, "Will 'Social Responsibility' Harm Business?" *Wall Street Journal*, May 18, 2005; Greg Schneider, "GE wants to be seen as green," *Washington Post* in *The Capital Times*, May 10, 2005; Felicity Barringer and Matthew C. Wald, "G.E. Chief Urges U.S. to Adopt Clearer Energy Policy, *New York Times*, May 10, 2005.

[4] Kathryn Kranhold and Jeffrey Ball, "GE to Spend More on Projects Ties to Climate Change," *Wall Street Journal*, May 9, 2005

[5] Investing in Green," *Newsweek*, June 6, 2005

[6] Ibid.

[7] Gretchen C. Daily, et.al., "The Value of Nature and the Nature of Value," *Science*, Vol. 289, No. 5478, July 21, 2000.

[8] This section on Toyota was partly based on a paper by Suchitra Karthikeyan, a graduate student in my class who is majoring in environmental engineering.

[9] Parts of this section from Kenneth J. Stier, "Dirty Secret: Coal Plants Could Be Much Cleaner," *New York Times*, May 22, 2005.

[10] Parts of this section from Cris Prystay, "Recycling 'E-Waste,'" *Wall Street Journal*, September 23, 2004; Jesse Drucker, "Old Cell Phones Pile Up by the Millions," *Wall Street Journal*, September 23, 2004.

[11] Stanley Holmes and Wendy Zellner, "The Costco Way," *Business Week*, April 12, 2004.

[12] Parts of this section based on Charles Haddad and Christine Tierney, "FedEx and Brown Are Going Green," *Business Week,* August 11, 2003; "Corporate Innovation: Delivering Clean Air to NYC and Tampa, "www. Environmentaldefense.org/partnership.

[13] Susan Diesenhouse, "Innovative Boston-Area Buildings at a Green Standard," *New York Times,* April 28, 2004.

[14] Parts of the above section from Barnaby J. Feder, "Environmentally Conscious Developers Try to Turn Green Into Platinum," *New York Times,* August 25, 2004; Susan Diesenhouse, "Innovative Boston-Area Buildings at a Green Standard," *New York Times,* April 28, 2004; Ted Smalley Bowen, "A Boston Federal Building Is Going Green at age 72," *New York Times,* December 8, 2004; www.usgbc.org.

[15] This section based on "Designing the Future," *Newsweek,* May 16, 2005.

[16] "Here comes the new gold rush," in *FSB: Fortune Small Business,* June 2003, Vol. 13, Iss.5.

[17] Pamela J. Gordon, *Lean and Green,* San Francisco: Berrett-Koehler, 2001.

[18] Pat Joseph, "Societies Choose to Fail or Succeed," *Sierra,* May/June 2005

[19] Katherine Ellison, "the bottom line redefined," *Nature Conservancy,* Winter 2002.

[20] Dave Lenckus, "New Environment for Risk Managers," *Business Insurance,* June 16, 2003.

[21] James Gustave Speth, *Red Sky at Morning,* New Haven, CT: Yale University Press, 2004.

APPENDIX A

Area	Organization	Website	Description
Ocean and Water	World Water Forum	www.worldwaterforum.net www.world.water-forum3.com	Provides the information and report of World Water Forum
Ocean and Water	World Water Council	www.worldwatercouncil.org	It is the International Water Policy Think Tank, and covers almost all the issues associated with water.
Ocean and Water	World Water Assessment Programme	www.unesco.org/water/wwap	Give access to UN World Water Development Report.
Ocean and Water	Water Supply & Sanitation Collaborative Council	www.wsscc.org	Provides information about the activities supported by WSSCC.
Ocean and Water	2003 International Year of Fresh Water	www.wateryear2003.org	The official site of the International Year of Freshwater 2003.
Ocean and Water	March22, 2003-World Day for Water	www.waterday2003.org	World Water Day 2003 website held by United Nations Environment Programme (UNEP).
Ocean and Water	World Water Day	www.worldwaterday.org	Offers information about World Water Day from 1994 to now.
Ocean and Water	Western Water Alliance	www.westernwateralliance.org	An US western water resource protection website.
Ocean and Water	The Ocean Conservancy	www.oceanconservancy.org	The Ocean Conservancy is an organization to protect ocean ecosystems and conserve the global abundance and diversity of marine wildlife.
Ocean and Water	Ocean Futures Society	www.oceanfutures.org	An organization to explore our global ocean, inspiring and educating people to act responsibly for its protection, documenting the critical connection between humanity and nature, and celebrating the ocean's vital importance to the survival of all life on the planet.
Ocean and Water	Shifting Baselines	shiftingbaselines.org	Shifting Baselines is a "media project" -- a partnership between ocean conservation and Hollywood to help bring attention to the severity of ocean decline.
Ocean and Water	Global Coral Reef Monitoring Network	www.gcrmn.org	Works to improve management and conservation of coral reefs by providing manuals, databases, training, problem solving and fund raising efforts.
Forest	Rainforest Action Network	www.ran.org	Provides up-to-the-minute information RAN's campaigns, and offer fact sheet about rainforest.
Forest	Rainforest Alliance	www.rainforest-alliance.org	Sponsors Smart Wood program which certified forests under FSC accreditation. Gives information about tropic forest and rainforest.
Forest	Forest Ethics	www.forestethics.org	The website for world's endangered forest protection.
Forest	American Forests	www.americanforests.org	An organization to encourage people to plant trees, to improve understanding of the relationship between trees and greenhouse gases, and to protects wildlife living in American forests.

Area	Organization	Website	Description
Forest	Forest Stewardship Council	www.fsc.org	An organization provides standard setting, trademark assurance and accreditation services for companies and organizations interested in responsible forestry. Its mission is to promote environmentally appropriate, socially beneficial, and economically viable management of the world's forests.
Environmental Issues and/or Social Justice	National Environmental Trust	www.environet.org	Offers information about National Environmental Trust Campaigns on environmental issues.
Environmental Issues and/or Social Justice	Co-op America	www.coopamerica.org	Provides the economic strategies, organizing power and practical tools to address today's social and environmental problems.
Environmental Issues and/or Social Justice	Corporate Accountability International (formerly Infact)	www.stopcorporateabuse.org	A membership organization that protects people by waging and winning campaigns that challenge irresponsible and dangerous corporate actions around the world
Environmental Issues and/or Social Justice	Organic Consumers Association/Fund	www.organicconsumers.org	A boycott website focused on food safety, organic agriculture, fair trade and sustainability.
Environmental Issues and/or Social Justice	Ecopledge	www.ecopledge.com	Centers around university student participation and provides information about the campaigns and boycotts held by ecopledge.com
Environmental Issues and/or Social Justice	Union of Concerned Scientists	www.ucsusa.org	UCS augment rigorous scientific analysis with innovative thinking and committed citizen advocacy to build a cleaner, healthier environment and a safer world.
Environmental Issues and/or Social Justice	Generation Green	www.generationgreen.org	A website focused on keeping toxins out of food, homes and world for the health of the next generation.
Environmental Issues and/or Social Justice	Earth Policy Institute	www.earth-policy.org	A website dedicated to building an environmentally sustainable economy: an "eco-economy".
Environmental Issues and/or Social Justice	Natural Resources Defense Council	www.nrdc.org	The website of the nation's most effective environmental action organization, using law, science, and the support of 1 million members and online activists to protect the planet's wildlife and wild places.
Environmental Issues and/or Social Justice	World Resource Institute	www.wri.org	A website to protect Earth's environment and its capacity to provide for the needs of current and future generations, offering information about 50 projects carried out by WRI
Environmental Issues and/or Social Justice	Sierra Club	www.sierraclub.org	A website using all lawful means to protect the wild places of the earth.
Environmental Issues and/or Social Justice	Sierra Student Coalition	www.ssc.org	The website of the student run arm of Sierra Club, working for wilderness, sustainability and peace.
Environmental Issues and/or Social Justice	Friends of the Earth	www.foe.org	Friends of the Earth defends the environment and champions a healthy and just world, providing information about Index of Sustainable Economic Welfare (ISEW).

Area	Organization	Website	Description
Environmental Issues and/or Social Justice	Greenpeace	www.greenpeace.org	Website of Greenpeace. Greenpeace's goal is to ensure the ability of the Earth to nurture life in all its diversity.
Environmental Issues and/or Social Justice	Earthjustice	www.earthjustice.org	Earthjustice is a non-profit public interest law firm dedicated to protecting the magnificent places, natural resources, and wildlife of this earth and to defending the right of all people to a healthy environment.
Environmental Issues and/or Social Justice	World Wildlife Fund	www.wwf.org	The website of WWF whose mission is the conservation of nature and the protection of the world's wildlife and wildlands.
Environmental Issues and/or Social Justice	League of Conservation Voters	www.lcv.org	The League of Conservation Voters (LCV) is the political voice of the national environmental movement and the only organization devoted full-time to shaping a pro-environment Congress and White House.
Environmental Issues and/or Social Justice	CFACT	www.cfactcampus.org	The website of Collegians For A Constructive Tomorrow, dedicated to promoting a smarter future for people and nature and addressing a variety of important environmental and public-interest issues.
Environmental Issues and/or Social Justice	Responsible Shopper	responsibleshopper.org	Provides lists of irresponsible companies and offers shopping information from socially responsible view.
Environmental Issues and/or Social Justice	Working Assets	www.workingassets.com	Working Assets is a long distance, wireless, credit card and broadcasting company that was created to build a world that is more just, humane and environmentally sustainable.
Environmental Issues and/or Social Justice	Eco-Labels	eco-labels.org	The website of the Consumer Union Guide to Environmental Labels, providing about 114 eco-labels' report card.
Environmental Issues and/or Social Justice	World Conservation Union	www.iucn.org	A comprehensive environmental protection website to influence, encourage and assist societies throughout the world to conserve the integrity and diversity of nature and to ensure that any use of natural resources is equitable and ecologically sustainable.
Environmental Issues and/or Social Justice	Corpwatch	www.corpwatch.org	Provides information about the campaigns, boycotts and actions held by Corpwatch, against environmental and humanrights abuses by large corporations and corporate-led globalization
Environmental Issues and/or Social Justice	Environmental Defense	www.environmentaldefense.org	An organization to protect human health, safeguard oceans, stabilize the earth's climate and defend biodiversity.
Environmental Issues and/or Social Justice	US Green Building Council (USGBC)	www.usgbc.org	The U.S. Green Building Council is the nation's foremost coalition of leaders from across the building industry working to promote buildings that are environmentally responsible, profitable and healthy places to live and work.
Environmental Issues and/or Social Justice	Leadership in Energy and Environmental Design (LEED)	www.usgbc.org/LEED	The LEED (Leadership in Energy and Environmental Design) Green Building Rating System is a voluntary, consensus-based national standard for developing high-performance, sustainable buildings. Members of the U.S. Green Building Council representing all segments of the building industry developed LEED and continue to contribute to its evolution.

Area	Organization	Website	Description
Environmental Issues and/or Social Justice	Inform, Inc	www.informinc.org	INFORM, Inc. is an independent research organization that examines the effects of business practices on the environment and on human health. Our goal is to identify ways of doing business that ensure environmentally sustainable economic growth. Our reports are used by government, industry, and environmental leaders around the world.
Environmental Issues and/or Social Justice	Resources For The Future	www.rff.org	Resources for the Future improves environmental and natural resource policymaking worldwide through objective social science research of the highest caliber. As the premier independent institute dedicated exclusively to analyzing environmental, energy, and natural resource topics, RFF gathers under one roof a unique community of scholars conducting impartial research to enable policymakers to make sound choices.
Environmental Issues and/or Social Justice	The Pew Charitable Trusts	www.pewtrusts.com	The Pew Charitable Trusts serves the public interest by providing information, policy solutions and support for civic life.
Labor or Human Rights	International Labor Rights Fund	www.laborrights.org	ILRF is an advocacy organization dedicated to achieving just and humane treatment for workers worldwide.
Labor or Human Rights	Center for Constitutional Rights	www.ccr-ny.org	CCR is a non-profit legal and educational organization dedicated to protecting and advancing the rights guaranteed by the U.S. Constitution and the Universal Declaration of Human Rights.
Labor or Human Rights	Center for Economic and Social Rights	www.cesr.org	The website of CESR to promote social justice through human rights, the universal right of every human being to housing, education, health and a healthy environment, food, work, and social security.
Labor or Human Rights	International Labor Organization	www.ilo.org	A UN website providing comprehensive information about global labor issues.
Labor or Human Rights	Fair Labor Association	www.fairlabor.org	The website to promote adherence to international labor standards and improve working conditions worldwide.
Labor or Human Rights	Oxfam	oxfam.org	Oxfam International is an international group of independent non-governmental organizations dedicated to fighting poverty and related injustice around the world.
Labor or Human Rights	Human Development Indicator (HDI)	www.undp.org/hdr2003/indicator	UN Data base of Human Development Indicator.
Labor or Human Rights	Global Exchange	www.globalexchange.org	Global Exchange is an international human rights organization dedicated to promoting political, social and environmental justice globally.
Labor or Human Rights	National Labor Committee (NLC)	www.nlcnet.org	The National Labor Committee (NLC) is a human rights advocacy group, dedicated to promoting and defending the rights of workers.
Labor or Human Rights	Amnesty International (AI)	www.amnesty.org	An organization to promotes human rights enshrined in the Universal Declaration of Human Rights.
Labor or Human Rights	Grassroots International	www.grassrootsonline.org	Grassroots International is a human rights and development campaign organization, providing cash grants and material aid to partners in Africa, the Middle East, Latin America and the Caribbean.
Labor or Human Rights	United Students Against Sweatshops	www.studentsagainstsweatshops.org	An international student movement of campuses and individual students fighting for sweatshop free labor conditions and workers' rights.

Area	Organization	Website	Description
Labor or Human Rights	Sweatshop Watch	www.sweatshopwatch.org	An organization aiming to eliminate sweatshops in the garment industry and raise awareness of sweatshops across the world and the companies that use them.
Labor or Human Rights	Worker Rights Consortium	www.workersrights.org	The WRC's purpose is to assist in the enforcement of manufacturing Codes of Conduct adopted by colleges and universities; these Codes are designed to ensure that factories producing clothing and other goods bearing college and university names respect the basic rights of workers.
Labor or Human Rights	Global Alliance for Workers and Communities	www.theglobalalliance.org	An organizations to improve the workplace experience and future prospects of workers involved in global production and service supply chains in developing countries.
Socially Responsible Corporate Governance	The Global Sullivan Principles	globalsullivanprinciples.org	Offers the information about the Global Sullivan Principles of social responsibility of the companies.
Socially Responsible Corporate Governance	Social Accountability International	www.cepaa.org	Provides information of the SA8000 standard and verification system to maintain just and decent working conditions throughout the supply chain.
Socially Responsible Corporate Governance	The Global Reporting Initiative (GRI)	www.globalreporting.org	Offers information about the GRI guidelines, which 323 companies in 31 countries are using as sustainability reporting guidelines.
Socially Responsible Corporate Governance	OECD Guidelines for Multinational Enterprises	www.oecd.org	Provides information about OECD (Organization for Economic Cooperation and Development) Guidelines for Multinational Enterprises, a set of nonlegally binding standards to multinational enterprises business operations.
Socially Responsible Corporate Governance	Coalition for Environmentally Responsible Economies	www.ceres.org	Provides the CERES annual report, CERES endorsing company performance reviews, and corporate environmental or sustainability reports released by CERES endorsing companies, also provides information about the CERES Principles for environmentally sound business practices.
Socially Responsible Corporate Governance	Institute of Social and Ethical Accountability	www.accountability.org.uk/	A website dedicated to the promotion of social, ethical and overall organizational accountability, a precondition for achieving sustainable development, provides information about AccountAbility 1000 framework and series.
Socially Responsible Corporate Governance	New Economics Foundation (NEF)	www.neweconomics.org/	Provides information about social auditing and accounting.
Socially Responsible Corporate Governance	International Center for Corporate Accountability	www.mattel.com/about_us/Corp_ Responsibility/cr_mattel.asp	Website about corporate responsibility. Provides information about Global Manufacturing Principle (GMP) and Audit Report of ICCA.

Area	Organization	Website	Description
Socially Responsible Corporate Governance	Global Business Network	www.gbn.org	Global Business Network was founded in 1987 as a unique learning community based on ruthless curiosity, collaboration, and powerful new tools for thinking about and shaping the future.
Socially Responsible Corporate Governance	UN Global Compact	www.unglobalcompact.org	Provides information about UN Global Compact, a program seeking to advance responsible corporate citizenship so that business can be part of the solution to the challenges of globalization.
Socially Responsible Corporate Governance	International Organization for Standardization (ISO)	www.iso14000.org	Governs ISO 14001, international standard for environmental management systems, developed by International Organization for Standardization (ISO).
Socially Responsible Corporate Governance	Ethical Trading Initiative (ETI)	www.ethicaltrade.org	The ETI is an alliance of companies, non-governmental organizations (NGOs), and trade union organizations committed to working together to identify and promote ethical trade - good practice in the implementation of a code of conduct for good labor standards (labor standards), including the monitoring and independent verification of the observance of ethics code provisions, as standards for ethical sourcing.
Socially Responsible Corporate Governance	Association of British Insurers	www.abi.org.uk	The Association of British Insurers is the trade association for the UK's insurance industry, providing guidelines on investing in social responsibility.
Socially Responsible Corporate Governance	Business for Social Responsibility	www.bsr.org	A global organization that helps member companies achieve success in ways that respect ethical values, people, communities and the environment.
Socially Responsible Corporate Governance	Corporateregister	www.corporateregister.com	Lists corporations that issue socially responsible and environmental "sustainability" reports.
Socially Responsible Corporate Governance	The Corporate Social Responsibility Newswire Service	www.csrwire.com	Gives access to sustainability reports issued by some 100 companies, plus dozens of corporate press releases tied to socially responsible subjects.
Socially Responsible Corporate Governance	Global Environmental Management Initiative (GEMI)	www.gemi.org	GEMI was formed in 1990 in the USA in response to heightened awareness about the changing demands of conscientious consumers. Its core mission is to help businesses achieve environmental, health and safety excellence.
Socially Responsible Corporate Governance	Business Charter for Sustainable Development	http://www.iccwbo.org/home/envi ronment_and_energy/charter.asp	The International Chamber of Commerce (ICC) created the Business Charter for Sustainable Development in 1991 in Rotterdam, Netherlands. Sixteen principles for environmental management are set forth by the charter, which has been published in over twenty languages, including all official languages of the United Nations.

Area	Organization	Website	Description
Socially Responsible Corporate Governance	The Natural Step	www.naturalstep.org	The Natural Step is a principle-based program founded in 1989 by Swedish cancer scientist Karl-henrick Robert. Its purpose is to encourage and support environmental development strategies in corporations, cities, governments, unions and academic institutions.
Socially Responsible Corporate Governance	World Business Council for Sustainable Development (WBCSD)	www.wbcsd.org	A coalition of over 120 international companies united by a commitment to the environment and to the principles of economic growth and sustainable development. Its members are drawn from thirty-five countries and more than twenty major industrial sectors.
Socially Responsible Corporate Governance	United Nations Environmental Program	www.unep.org	The United Nations Environmental Program (UNEP) created the Industry and Environment Centre to work with business and industry, national and local governments, international groups and nongovernmental organizations.
Socially Responsible Corporate Governance	The Equator Principles	www.equator-principles.com	The Equator Principles were initiated by 10 of the world's largest banks to address in 2003 to address the social and environmental impacts of large projects, which they finance. As of September 2004, a total of 27 of the world's banks have joined the group, which account for around 80 percent of all project financing in the world.
Fair Trade	Just Coffee	www.justcoffee.net	A website that offers several Fair Trade coffees and advocates people to committed to fair trade and to real relationships with our grower-partners.
Fair Trade	Equal Exchange	www.equalexchange.org	A fair trade website.
Fair Trade	Transfair	www.transfair.org	A fair trade website. Certifies fair traded coffee.
Fair Trade	International Coffee Organization	www.ico.org	Provides comprehensive information and historical statistics of international coffee trade.
Fair Trade	Fairtrade Labeling Organization International (FLO)	www.fairtrade.net	German federation. Certifies producers of fair-trade products.
Comprehensive Environment Protection	US Public Interest Research Group (USPIRG)	www.uspirg.org	The website of USPIRG to deliver persistent, result-oriented public interest activism that protects our environment, encourages a fair, sustainable economy, and fosters responsive, democratic government; provides the annual Congressional Scorecard from 1994 to now
Comprehensive Environment Protection	International Union for Conservation of Nature and Natural Resource	www.iucn.org	A world organization to conserve the integrity and diversity of nature and to ensure that any use of natural resources is equitable and ecologically sustainable.
Comprehensive Environment Protection	Save our environment Action Center	www.saveourenvironment.org	A collaborative effort of the nation's most influential environmental advocacy organizations harnessing the power of the internet to increase public awareness and activism on today's most important environmental issues.
Comprehensive Environment Protection	BUND	www.bund.net	The German Federation for Environmental and Nature conservation.
Comprehensive Environment Protection	Conservation International	www.conservation.org	An environmental conservation website. Conservation International is an organization whose mission is to conserve living natural heritage, global biodiversity, and to demonstrate that human are able to live harmoniously with nature.

Area	Organization	Website	Description
Comprehensive Environment Protection	National Wildlife Federation	www.nwf.org	An organization to protect wildlife, wild places and the environment.
Comprehensive Environment Protection	Public Citizen	www.citizen.org	An organization to fight for openness and democratic accountability in government; for the right of consumers to seek redress in the courts; for clean, safe and sustainable energy sources; for social and economic justice in trade policies; for strong health, safety and environmental protections; and for safe, effective and affordable prescription drugs and health care.
Comprehensive Environment Protection	Transparency International (TI)	www.transparency.org	The only international non-governmental organization devoted to combating corruption, brings civil society, business, and governments together in a powerful global coalition.
Animal Rights	Animal Concerns Community	www.animalconcerns.org	This community serves as a clearinghouse for information on the Internet related to animal rights and welfare.
Animal Rights	Animal Rights	www.animalrights.net	Animal rights advocates regularly mislead the public and misrepresent the facts about the use of animals in our society. This web site provides a critical analysis of the animal rights movement and debunks many of their claims.
Animal Rights	Mercy for Animals	www.mercyforanimals.org	MFA takes much needed action to end factory farming, the abuse of animals in entertainment, the bloody fur trade, animal testing and many other injustices that animals suffer.
Animal Rights	Animal Legal Defense Fund	www.aldf.org	The Animal Legal Defense Fund takes direct legal action to protect animals from exploitation and abuse. Works to establish legal rights for animals.
Animal Rights	People for the Ethical Treatment of Animals (PETA)	www.peta-online.org	An organization to promote an understanding of the right of animals to be treated with respect, and be against animals being used for entertainment purposes and animal testing.

APPENDIX B

Area	Organization	Website	Description
Socially Responsible Investment	Shareholder Action Network	www.shareholderaction.org	The SAN serves as a clearinghouse of information and analysis to the socially responsible investing community on shareholder advocacy.
Socially Responsible Investment	Shareholder Activism Center	asp.sriworld.com/domini/sa/index.cgi	Provides shareholder resolutions database on a wide range of social and environmental issues.
Socially Responsible Investment	Interfaith Center on Corporate Responsibility	www.iccr.org	A socially responsible investment website.
Socially Responsible Investment	Social Investment Forum	www.socialinvest.org	A comprehensive socially responsible investment website, providing SRI trends reports.
Socially Responsible Investment	Investor Responsibility Research Center	www.irrc.org	IRRC is an independent research firm that has been the leading source of high quality, impartial information on corporate governance and social responsibility issues affecting investors and corporations.
Socially Responsible Investment	Innovest Strategic Value Advisors	www.innovestgroup.com	Innovest Strategic Value Advisors is an internationally recognized investment research and advisory firm specializing in analyzing companies' performance on environmental, social, and strategic governance issues, with a particular focus on their impact on competitiveness, profitability, and share price performance.
Socially Responsible Investment	Crosswalk	www.crosswalk.com	Offers "value reports," based on fundamentalist Christian beliefs, that criticize companies for producing anti-family entertainment and other activities. Click on Tools, then Investigator.
Socially Responsible Investment	FOLIOfn	www.foliofn.com	Investing service that offers six preselected baskets of socially responsible stocks based on different screening criteria; these folios can be customized.
Socially Responsible Investment	The Motley Fool	www.themotleyfool.com	Offers a socially responsible investing discussion board.
Socially Responsible Corporate Governance	Institutional Shareholder Services	www.issproxy.com	Provides solutions for institutional investors and corporate issuers of proxy voting and corporate governance services.
Socially Responsible Corporate Governance	FTSE4Good Index	www.ftse.com	FTSE4Good Index series, a family of benchmark and tradable financial indices, which assesses members of the FTSE All-Share Index (excluding tobacco, nuclear and weapons systems) against a range of social, environmental and management criteria.
Socially Responsible Investment	Social Funds	www.socialfunds.com	The largest personal finance website devoted to socially responsible investing. Provides social and ethical information on more than 1,800 companies
Socially Responsible Investment	Dow Jones Sustainability Indexes	www.sustainability-indexes.com	Dow Jones Sustainability Indexes are the first global indexes tracking the financial performance of the leading sustainability-driven companies worldwide.
Socially Responsible Investment	Social Responsible Investing	www.socialinvest.org	A membership organization to promote the concept, practice and growth of socially responsible investing.

Index